MW00785095

G.I. JOE

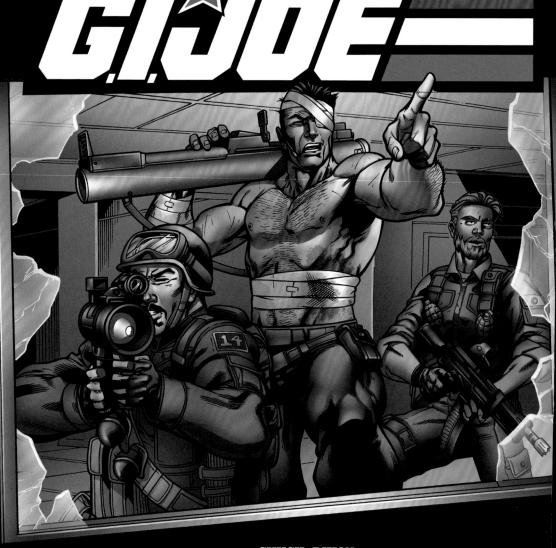

Written by CHUCK DIXON
Art by ROBERT ATKINS
Inks by CLAYTON BROWN & JOHN WYCOUGH
Colors by ANDREW CROSSLEY
Letters by CHRIS MOWRY, ROBBIE ROBBINS, and NEIL UYETAKE

Original Series Edits by ANDY SCHMIDT
Collection Edits by JUSTIN EISINGER
Collection Design by NEIL UYETAKE
Cover by GABRIELE DELL'OTTO

IDW Publis
Operati
Ted Adams, Chief Executive Of
Greg Goldstein, Chief Operating Of
Matthew Ruzicka, CPA, Chief Financial Of
Alan Payne, VP of S
Lorelei Bunjes, Dir. of Digital Ser
AnnaMaria White, Marketing & PR Man
Marci Hubbard, Executive Assis
Alonzo Simon, Shipping Man

Edit
Chris Ryall, Publisher/Editor-in-
Scott Dunbier, Editor, Special Pro
Andy Schmidt, Senior E
Justin Eisinger, E
Kris Oprisko, Editor/Foreign
Denton J. Tipton, E
Tom Waltz, E
Mariah Huehner, Assistant E

De
Robbie Robbins, EVP/Sr. Graphic
Ben Templesmith, Artist/Des
Neil Uyetake, Art Dir
Chris Mowry, Graphic
Amauri Osorio, Graphic
Gilberto Lazcano, Production Ass

Licensed by:

www.IDWPUBLISHING.com
ISBN: 978-1-60010-467-1   12 11 10 09   1 2 3 4

Special thanks to Hasbro's Aaron Archer, Michael Kelly, Amie Lozanski, Ed Lane, Michael Provost, Joe Furfaro, Sarah Baskin, Jos Huxley, Michael Richie, Samantha Lomow, and Michael Verrechia for their invaluable assistance.

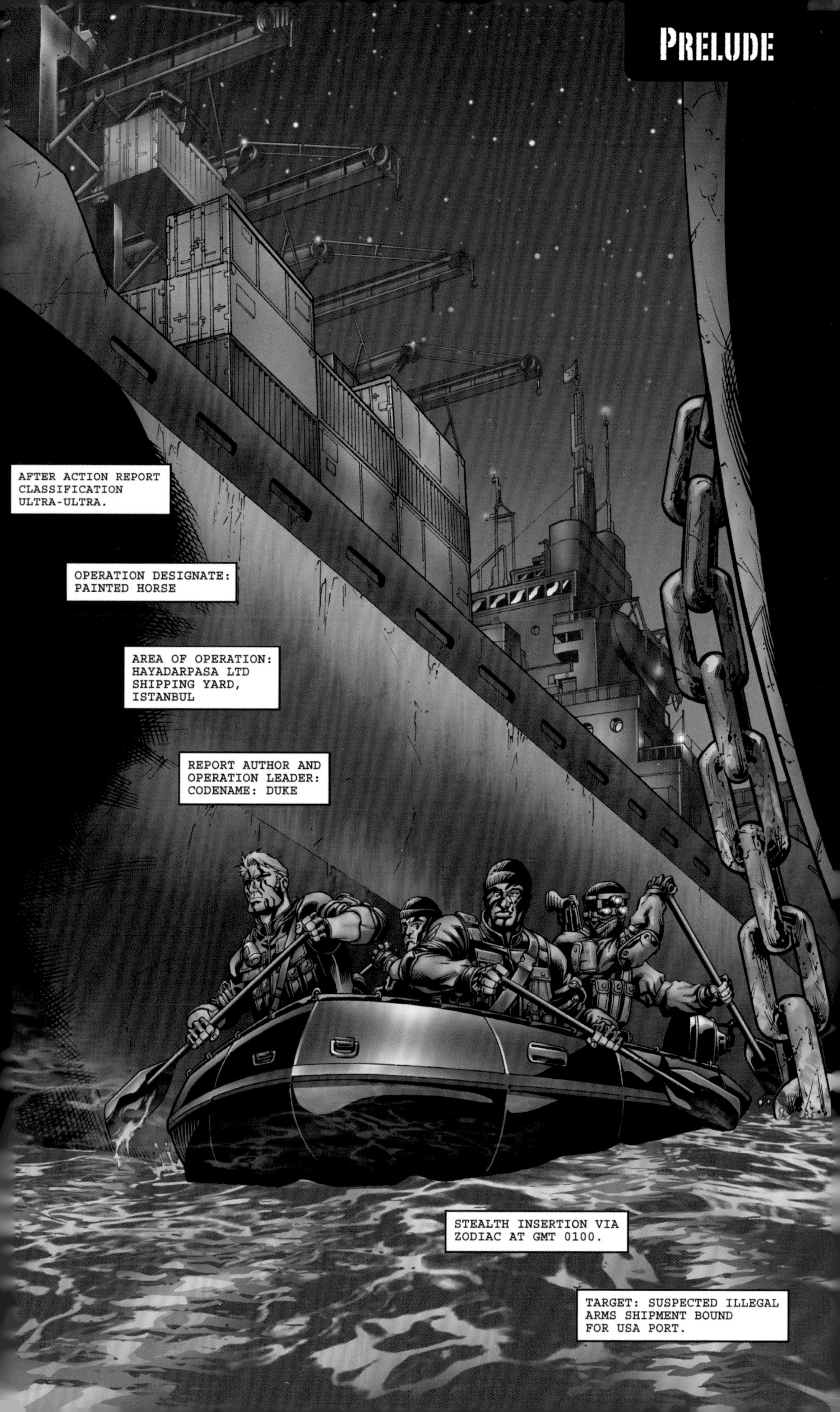
PRELUDE
AFTER ACTION REPORT CLASSIFICATION ULTRA-ULTRA.
OPERATION DESIGNATE: PAINTED HORSE
AREA OF OPERATION: HAYADARPASA LTD SHIPPING YARD, ISTANBUL
REPORT AUTHOR AND OPERATION LEADER: CODENAME: DUKE
STEALTH INSERTION VIA ZODIAC AT GMT 0100.
TARGET: SUSPECTED ILLEGAL ARMS SHIPMENT BOUND FOR USA PORT.

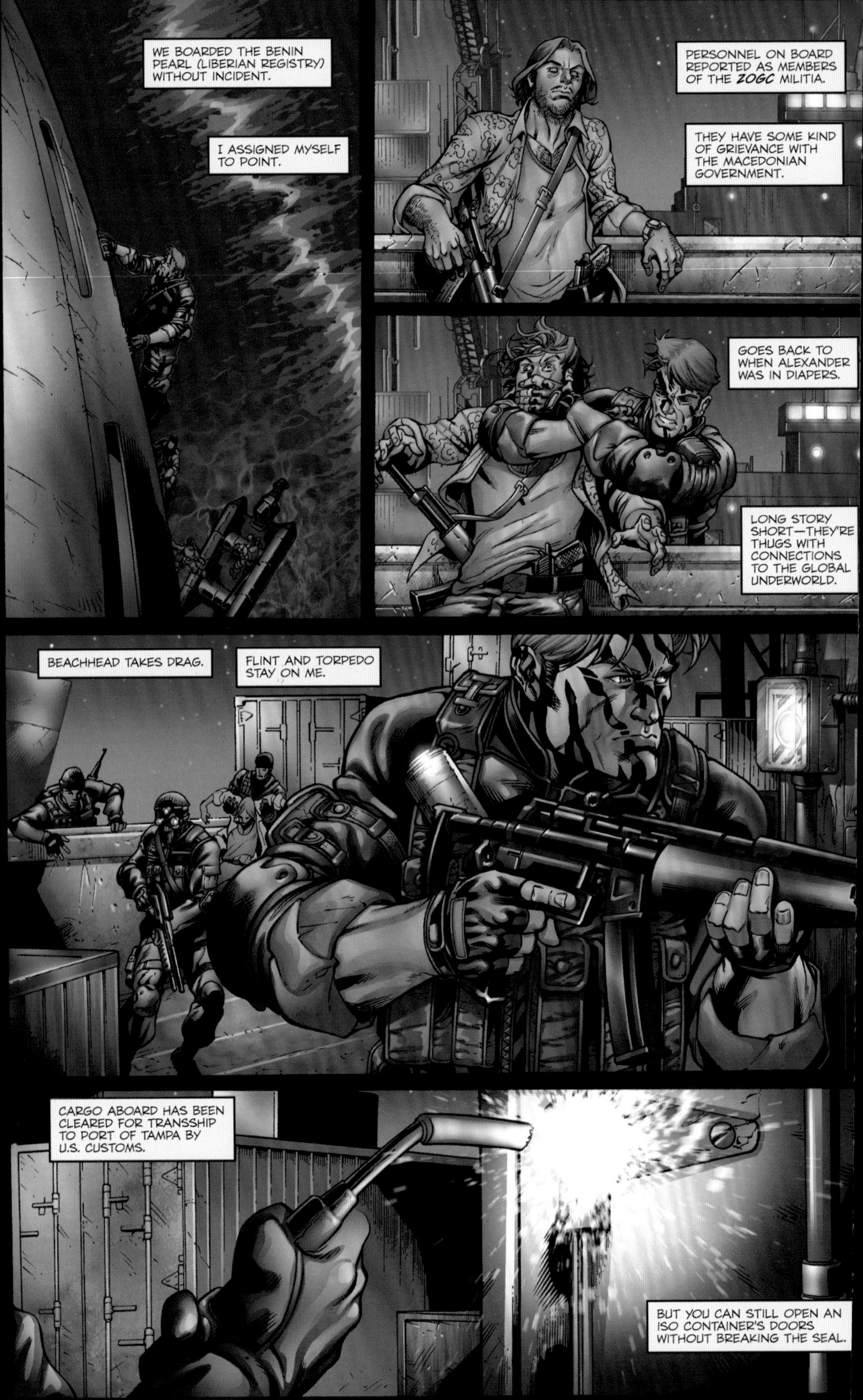
WE BOARDED THE BENIN PEARL (LIBERIAN REGISTRY) WITHOUT INCIDENT.
I ASSIGNED MYSELF TO POINT.
PERSONNEL ON BOARD REPORTED AS MEMBERS OF THE ZOGC MILITIA.
THEY HAVE SOME KIND OF GRIEVANCE WITH THE MACEDONIAN GOVERNMENT.
GOES BACK TO WHEN ALEXANDER WAS IN DIAPERS.
LONG STORY SHORT—THEY'RE THUGS WITH CONNECTIONS TO THE GLOBAL UNDERWORLD.
BEACHHEAD TAKES DRAG.
FLINT AND TORPEDO STAY ON ME.
CARGO ABOARD HAS BEEN CLEARED FOR TRANSSHIP TO PORT OF TAMPA BY U.S. CUSTOMS.
BUT YOU CAN STILL OPEN AN ISO CONTAINER'S DOORS WITHOUT BREAKING THE SEAL.

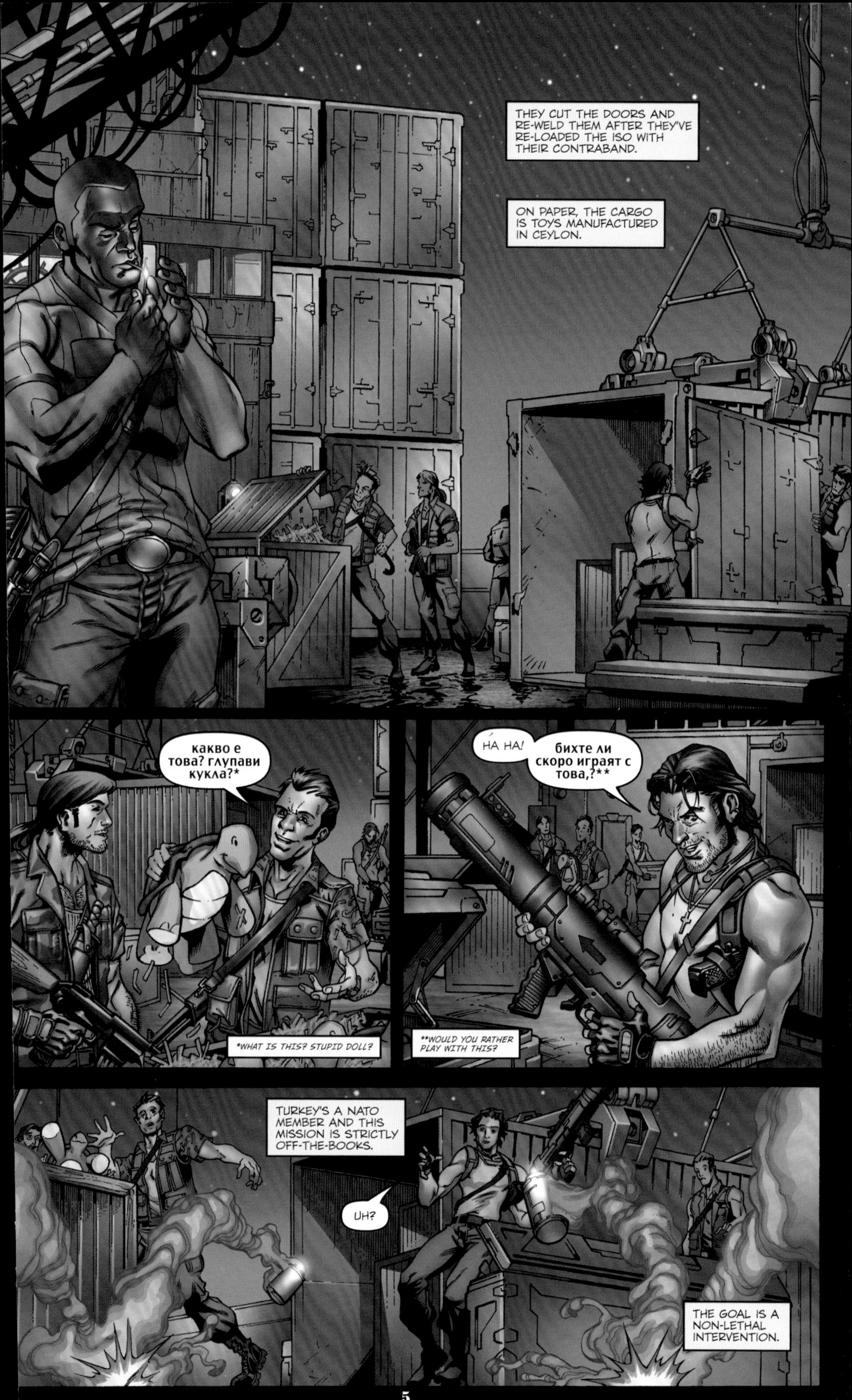
THEY CUT THE DOORS AND RE-WELD THEM AFTER THEY'VE RE-LOADED THE ISO WITH THEIR CONTRABAND.
ON PAPER, THE CARGO IS TOYS MANUFACTURED IN CEYLON.
какво е това? глупави кукла?*
*WHAT IS THIS? STUPID DOLL?
НА НА!
бихте ли скоро играят с това,?**
**WOULD YOU RATHER PLAY WITH THIS?
TURKEY'S A NATO MEMBER AND THIS MISSION IS STRICTLY OFF-THE-BOOKS.
UH?
THE GOAL IS A NON-LETHAL INTERVENTION.

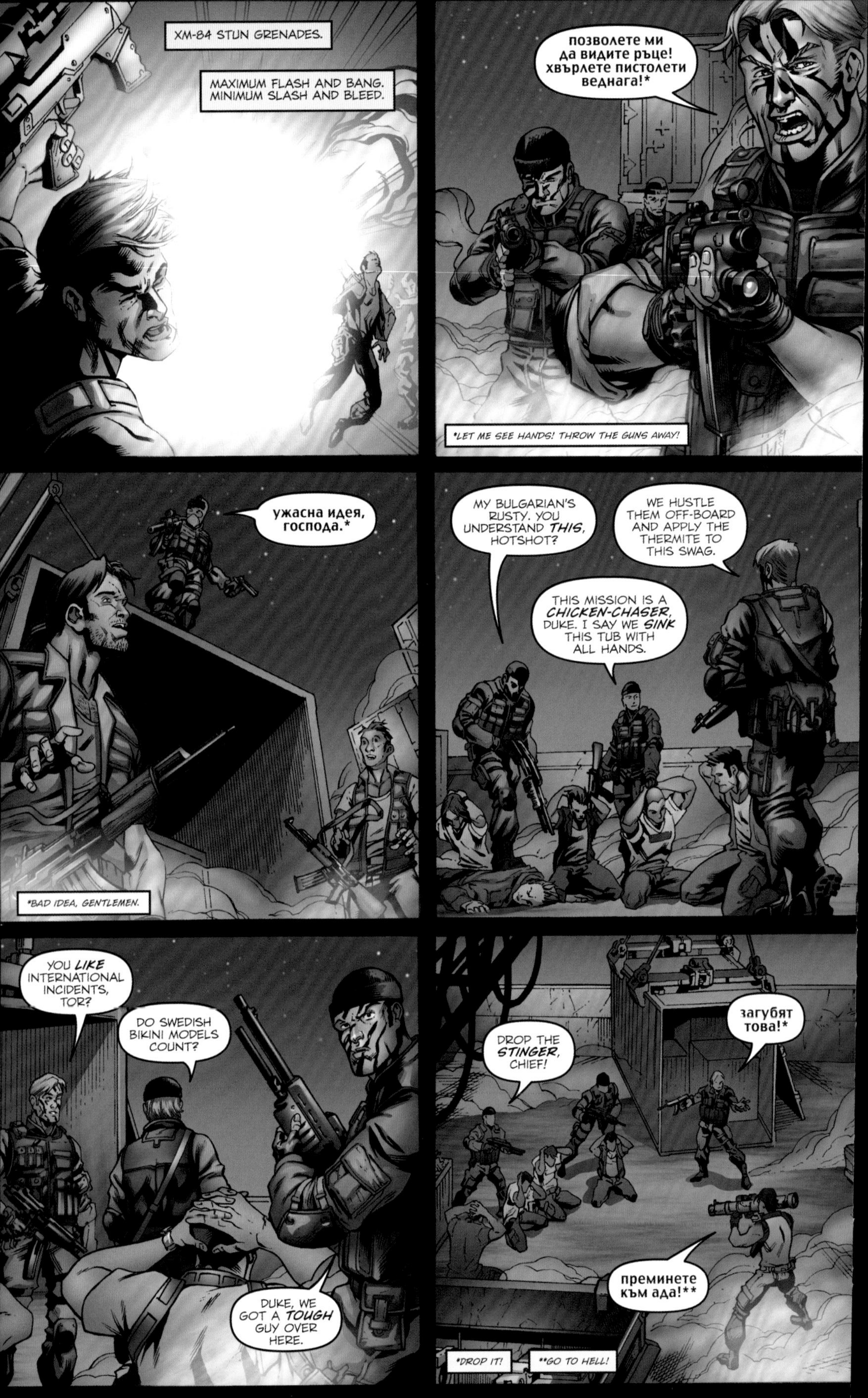
XM-84 STUN GRENADES.
MAXIMUM FLASH AND BANG. MINIMUM SLASH AND BLEED.
позволете ми да видите ръце! хвърлете пистолети веднага!*
*LET ME SEE HANDS! THROW THE GUNS AWAY!
ужасна идея, господа.*
*BAD IDEA, GENTLEMEN.
MY BULGARIAN'S RUSTY. YOU UNDERSTAND THIS, HOTSHOT?
WE HUSTLE THEM OFF-BOARD AND APPLY THE THERMITE TO THIS SWAG.
THIS MISSION IS A CHICKEN-CHASER, DUKE. I SAY WE SINK THIS TUB WITH ALL HANDS.
YOU LIKE INTERNATIONAL INCIDENTS, TOR?
DO SWEDISH BIKINI MODELS COUNT?
DUKE, WE GOT A TOUGH GUY OVER HERE.
DROP THE STINGER, CHIEF!
загубят това!*
преминете към ада!**
*DROP IT!
**GO TO HELL!

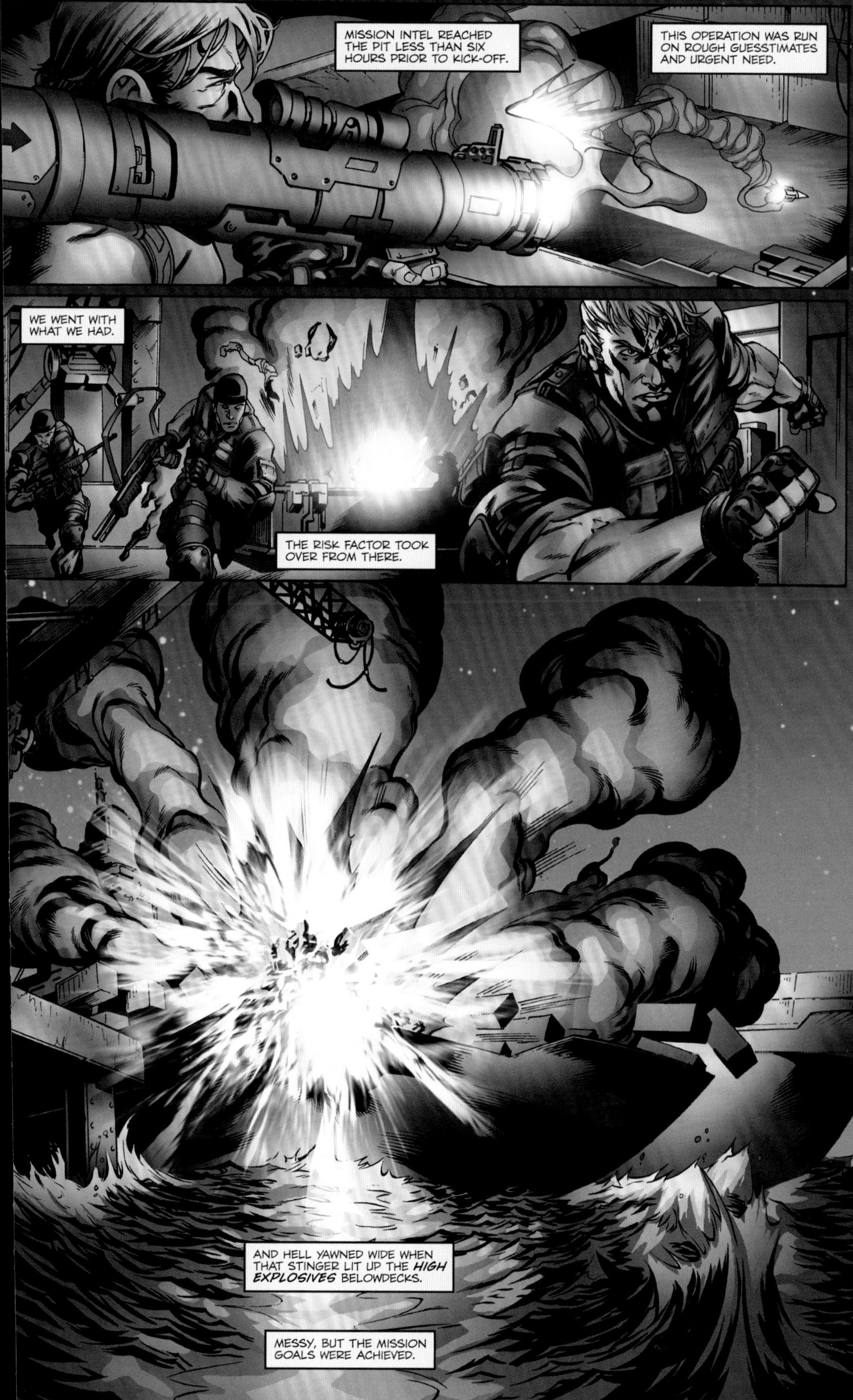
MISSION INTEL REACHED THE PIT LESS THAN SIX HOURS PRIOR TO KICK-OFF.
THIS OPERATION WAS RUN ON ROUGH GUESSTIMATES AND URGENT NEED.
WE WENT WITH WHAT WE HAD.
THE RISK FACTOR TOOK OVER FROM THERE.
AND HELL YAWNED WIDE WHEN THAT STINGER LIT UP THE *HIGH EXPLOSIVES* BELOWDECKS.
MESSY, BUT THE MISSION GOALS WERE ACHIEVED.

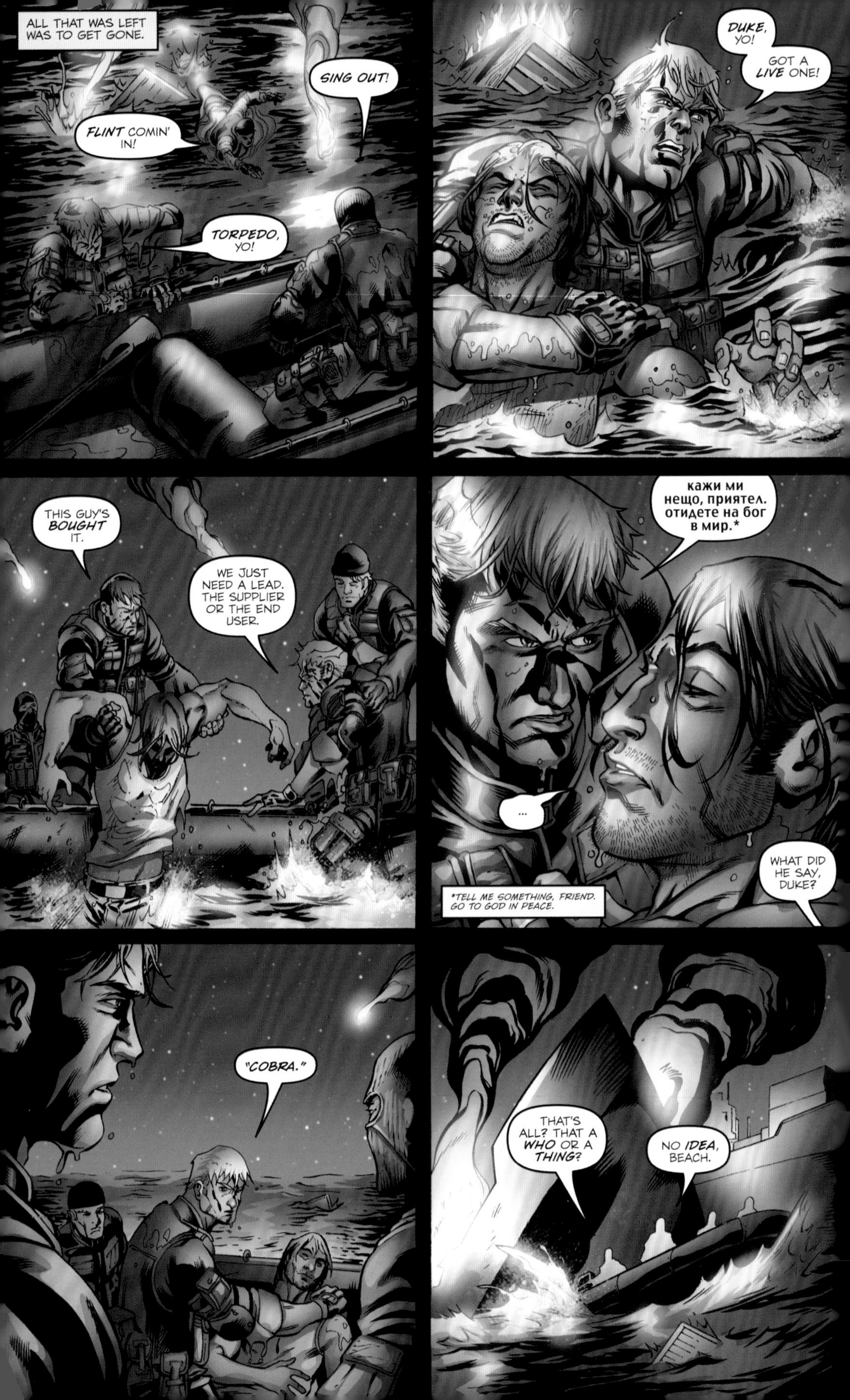
ALL THAT WAS LEFT WAS TO GET GONE.
SING OUT!
FLINT COMIN' IN!
TORPEDO, YO!
DUKE, YO!
GOT A LIVE ONE!
THIS GUY'S BOUGHT IT.
WE JUST NEED A LEAD. THE SUPPLIER OR THE END USER.
кажи ми нещо, приятел. отидете на бог в мир.*
...
*TELL ME SOMETHING, FRIEND. GO TO GOD IN PEACE.
WHAT DID HE SAY, DUKE?
"COBRA."
THAT'S ALL? THAT A WHO OR A THING?
NO IDEA, BEACH.

CHAPTER 1

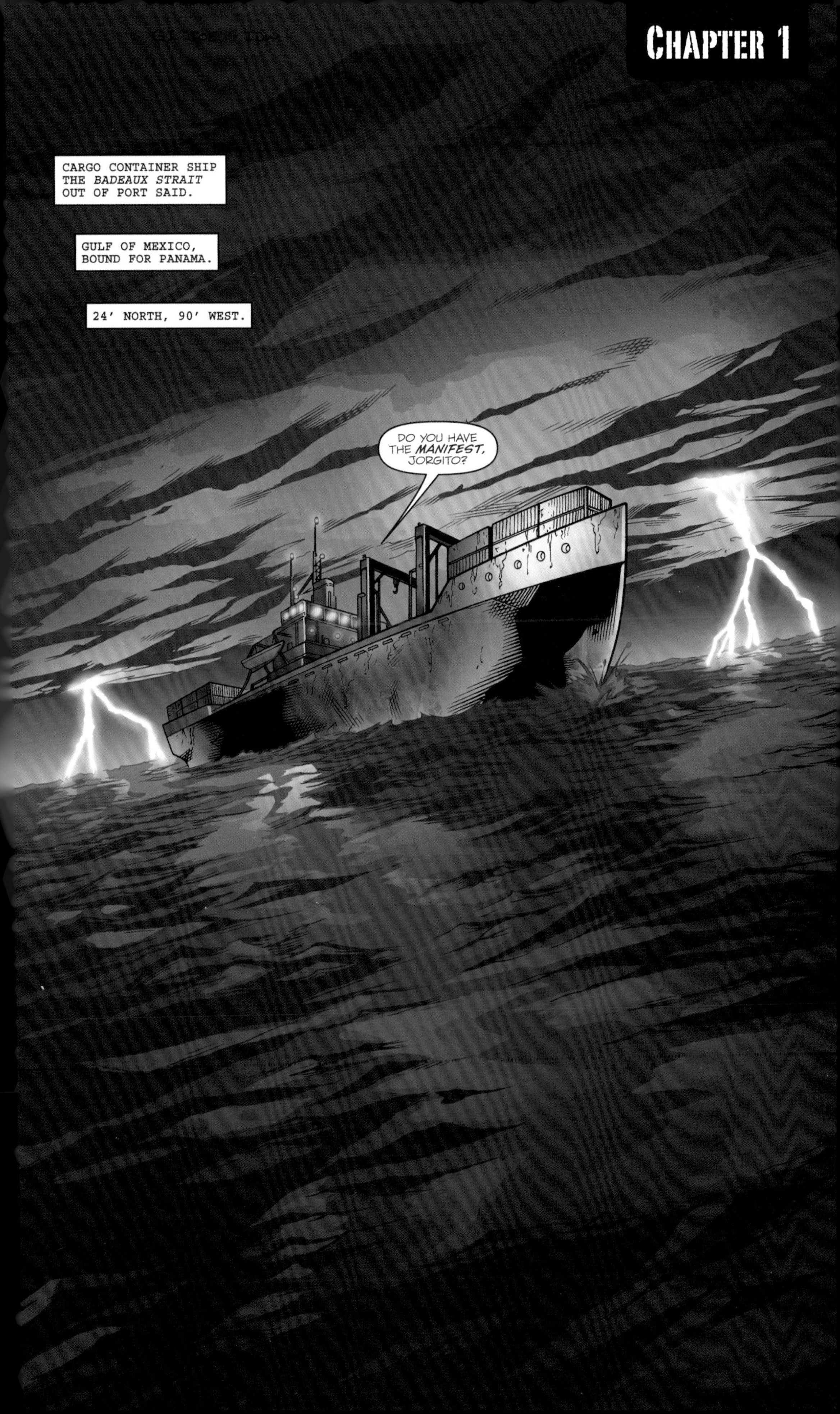
CARGO CONTAINER SHIP THE *BADEAUX STRAIT* OUT OF PORT SAID.
GULF OF MEXICO, BOUND FOR PANAMA.
24' NORTH, 90' WEST.
DO YOU HAVE THE ***MANIFEST,*** JORGITO?

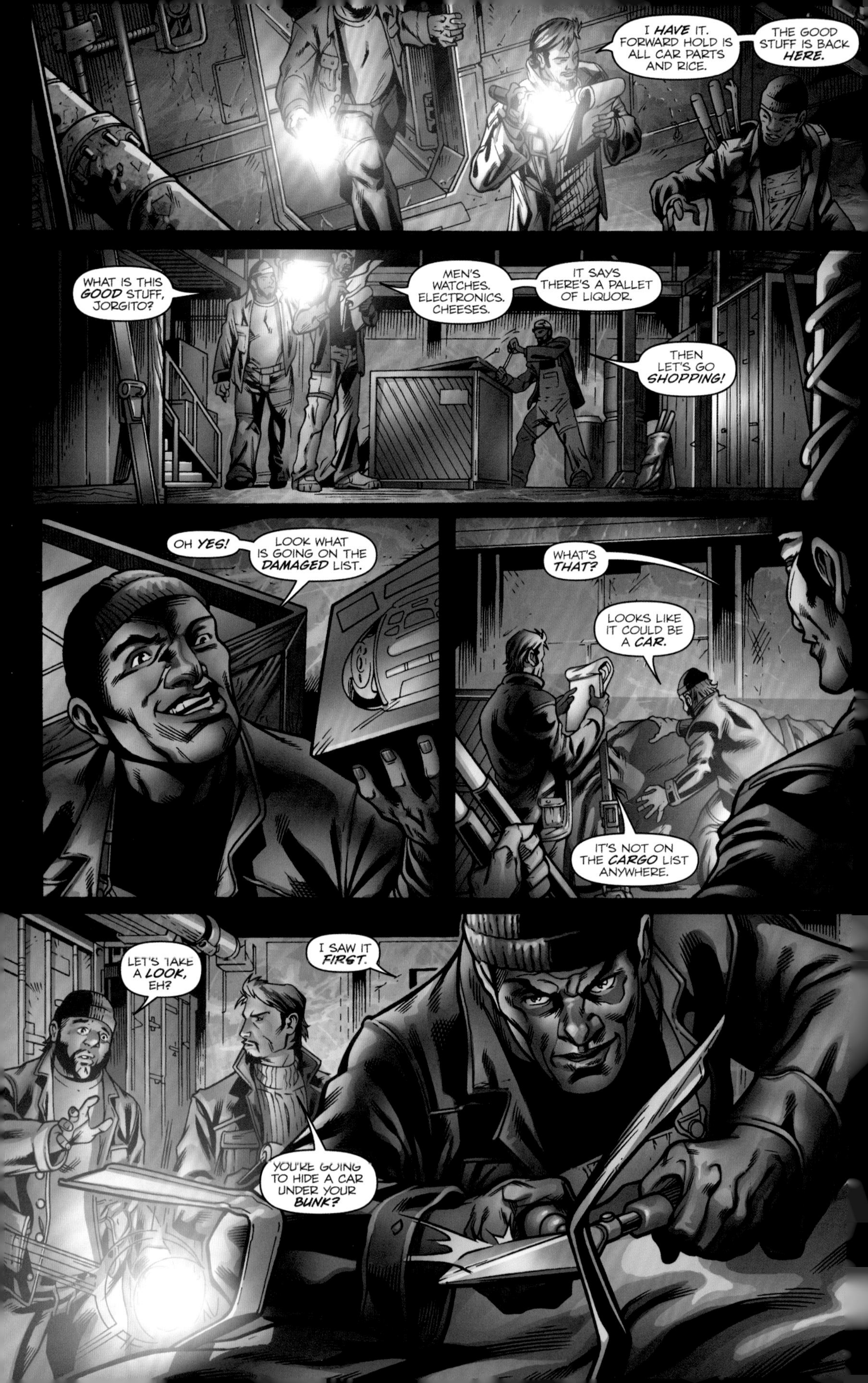
I HAVE IT. FORWARD HOLD IS ALL CAR PARTS AND RICE.
THE GOOD STUFF IS BACK HERE.
WHAT IS THIS GOOD STUFF, JORGITO?
MEN'S WATCHES. ELECTRONICS. CHEESES.
IT SAYS THERE'S A PALLET OF LIQUOR.
THEN LET'S GO SHOPPING!
OH YES!
LOOK WHAT IS GOING ON THE DAMAGED LIST.
WHAT'S THAT?
LOOKS LIKE IT COULD BE A CAR.
IT'S NOT ON THE CARGO LIST ANYWHERE.
LET'S TAKE A LOOK, EH?
I SAW IT FIRST.
YOU'RE GOING TO HIDE A CAR UNDER YOUR BUNK?

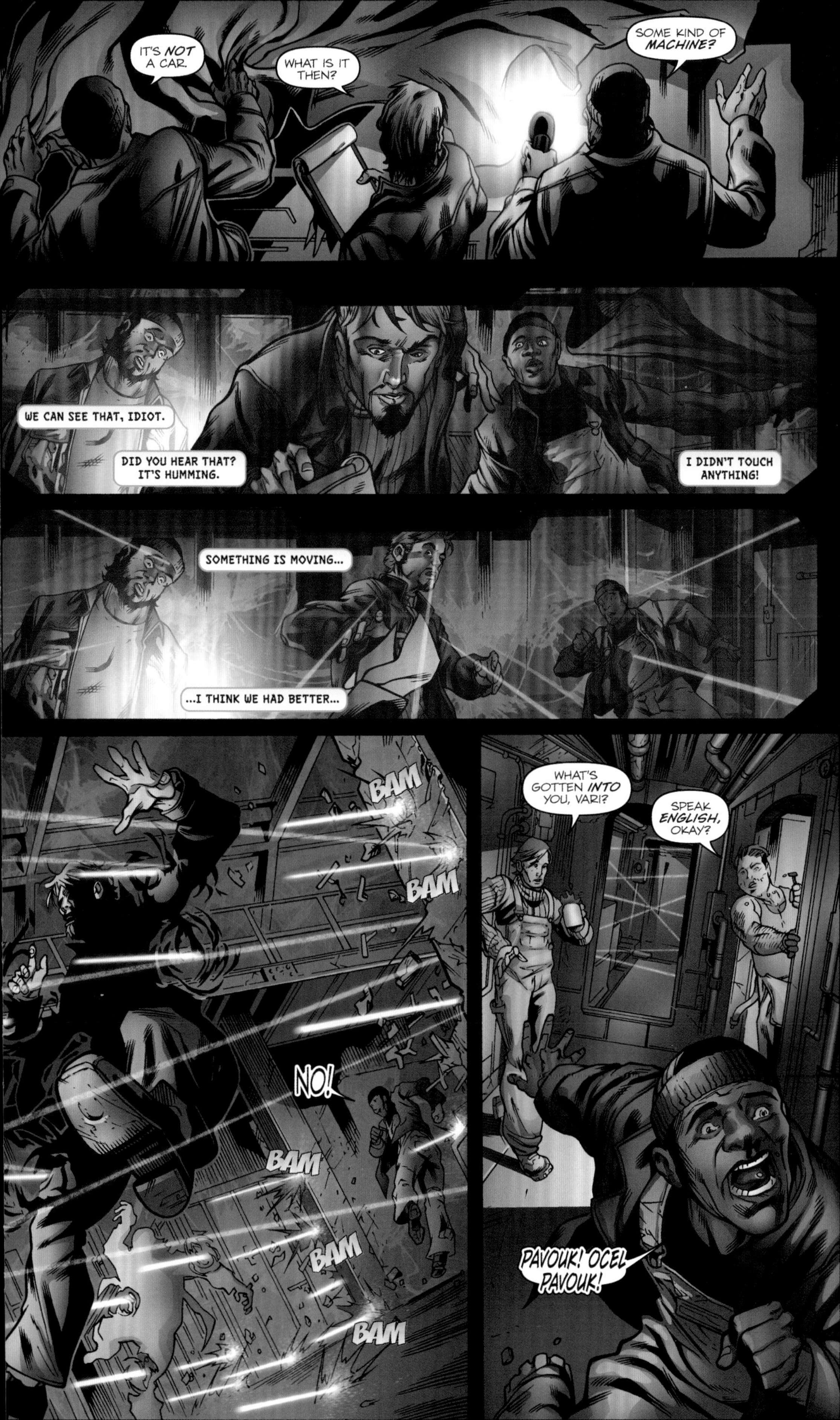
IT'S NOT A CAR.
WHAT IS IT THEN?
SOME KIND OF MACHINE?
WE CAN SEE THAT, IDIOT.
DID YOU HEAR THAT? IT'S HUMMING.
I DIDN'T TOUCH ANYTHING!
SOMETHING IS MOVING...
...I THINK WE HAD BETTER...
BAM
BAM
NO!
BAM
BAM
BAM
WHAT'S GOTTEN INTO YOU, VARI?
SPEAK ENGLISH, OKAY?
PAVOUK! OCEL PAVOUK!

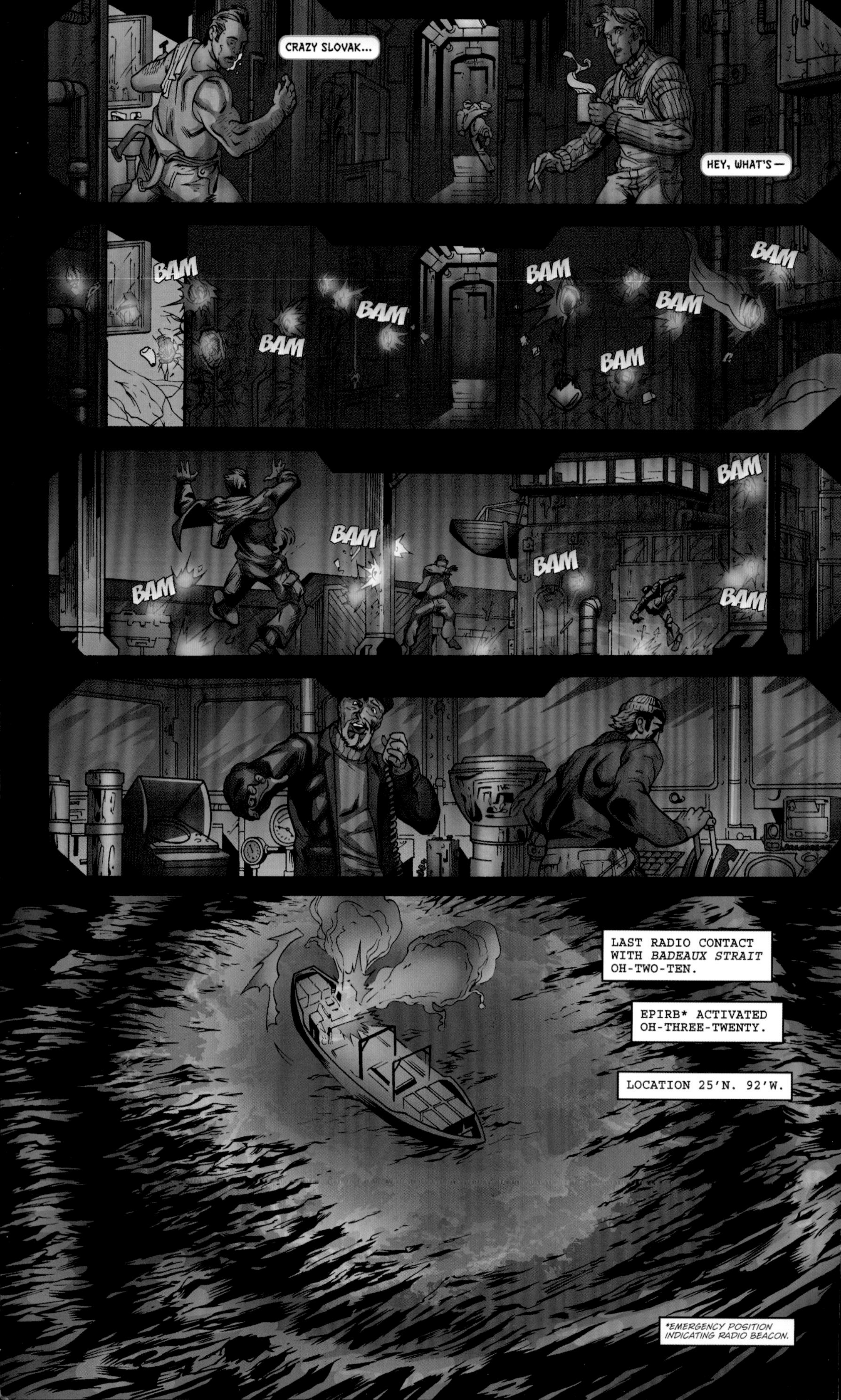
CRAZY SLOVAK...
HEY, WHAT'S—
BAM
BAM
BAM
BAM
BAM
BAM
BAM
BAM
BAM
BAM
BAM
BAM
LAST RADIO CONTACT WITH *BADEAUX STRAIT* OH-TWO-TEN.
EPIRB* ACTIVATED OH-THREE-TWENTY.
LOCATION 25'N. 92'W.
*EMERGENCY POSITION INDICATING RADIO BEACON.

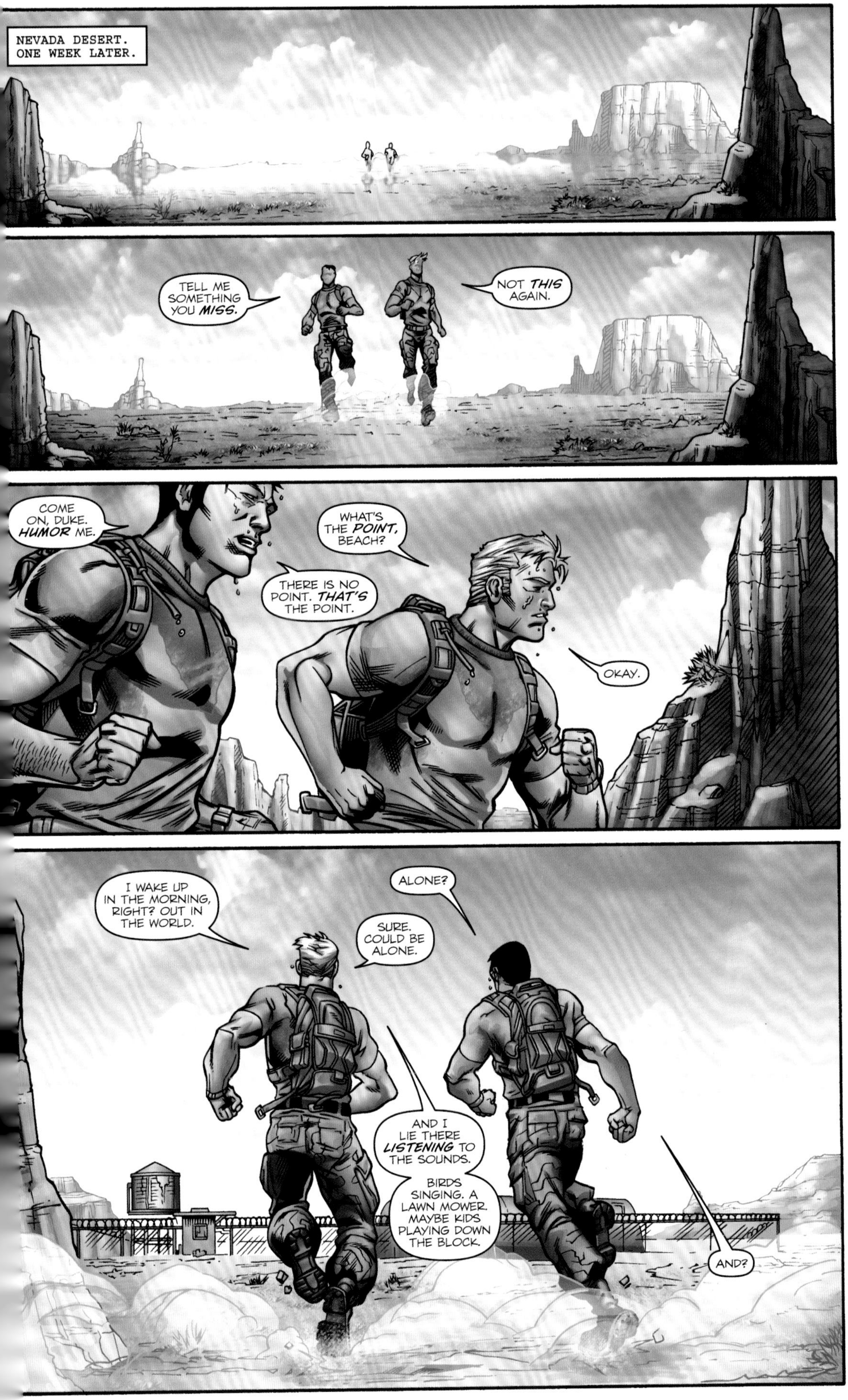
NEVADA DESERT. ONE WEEK LATER.
TELL ME SOMETHING YOU MISS.
NOT THIS AGAIN.
COME ON, DUKE. HUMOR ME.
WHAT'S THE POINT, BEACH?
THERE IS NO POINT. THAT'S THE POINT.
OKAY.
I WAKE UP IN THE MORNING, RIGHT? OUT IN THE WORLD.
ALONE?
SURE. COULD BE ALONE.
AND I LIE THERE LISTENING TO THE SOUNDS.
BIRDS SINGING. A LAWN MOWER. MAYBE KIDS PLAYING DOWN THE BLOCK.
AND?

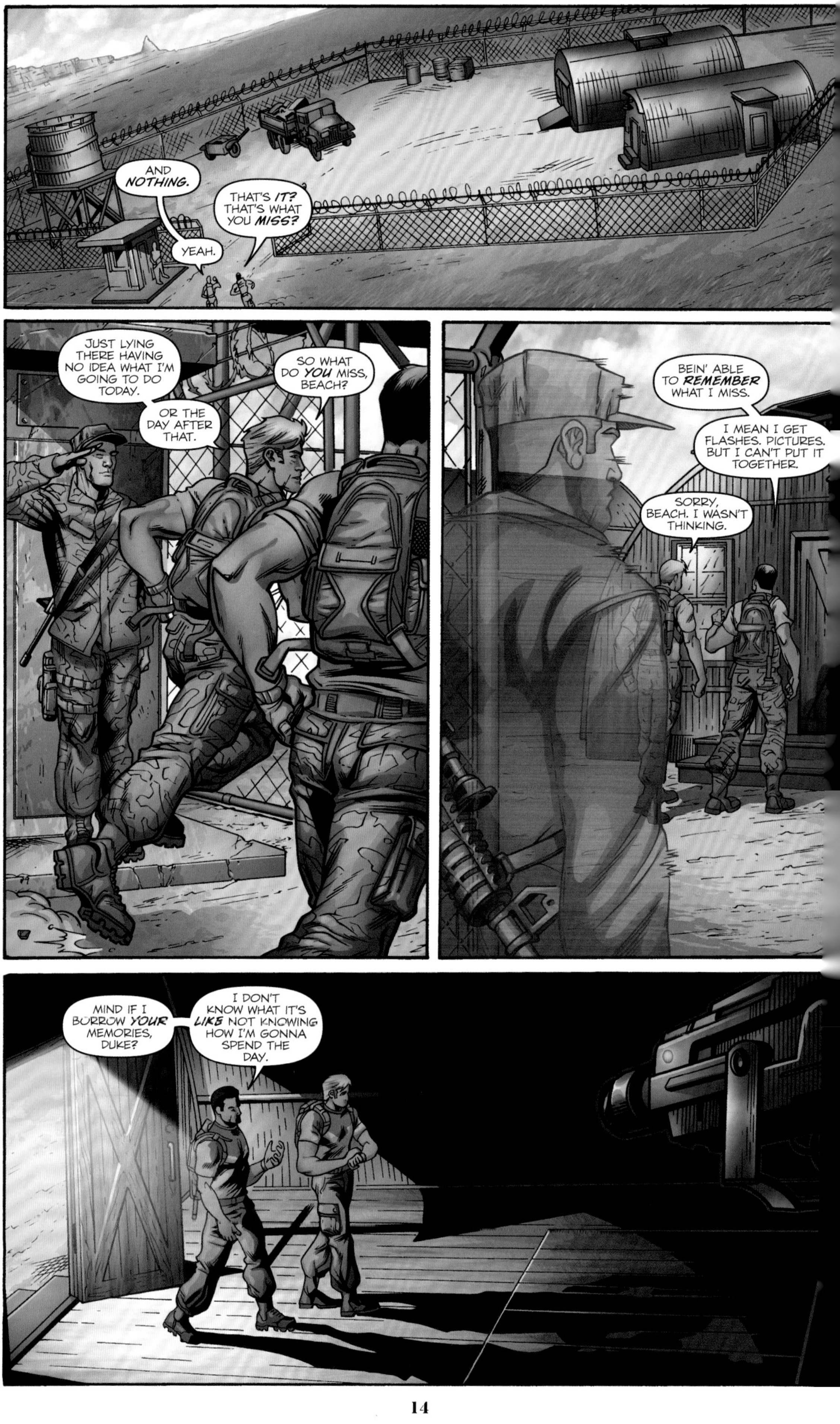
AND NOTHING.
THAT'S IT? THAT'S WHAT YOU MISS?
YEAH.
JUST LYING THERE HAVING NO IDEA WHAT I'M GOING TO DO TODAY.
OR THE DAY AFTER THAT.
SO WHAT DO YOU MISS, BEACH?
BEIN' ABLE TO REMEMBER WHAT I MISS.
I MEAN I GET FLASHES. PICTURES. BUT I CAN'T PUT IT TOGETHER.
SORRY, BEACH. I WASN'T THINKING.
MIND IF I BORROW YOUR MEMORIES, DUKE?
I DON'T KNOW WHAT IT'S LIKE NOT KNOWING HOW I'M GONNA SPEND THE DAY.

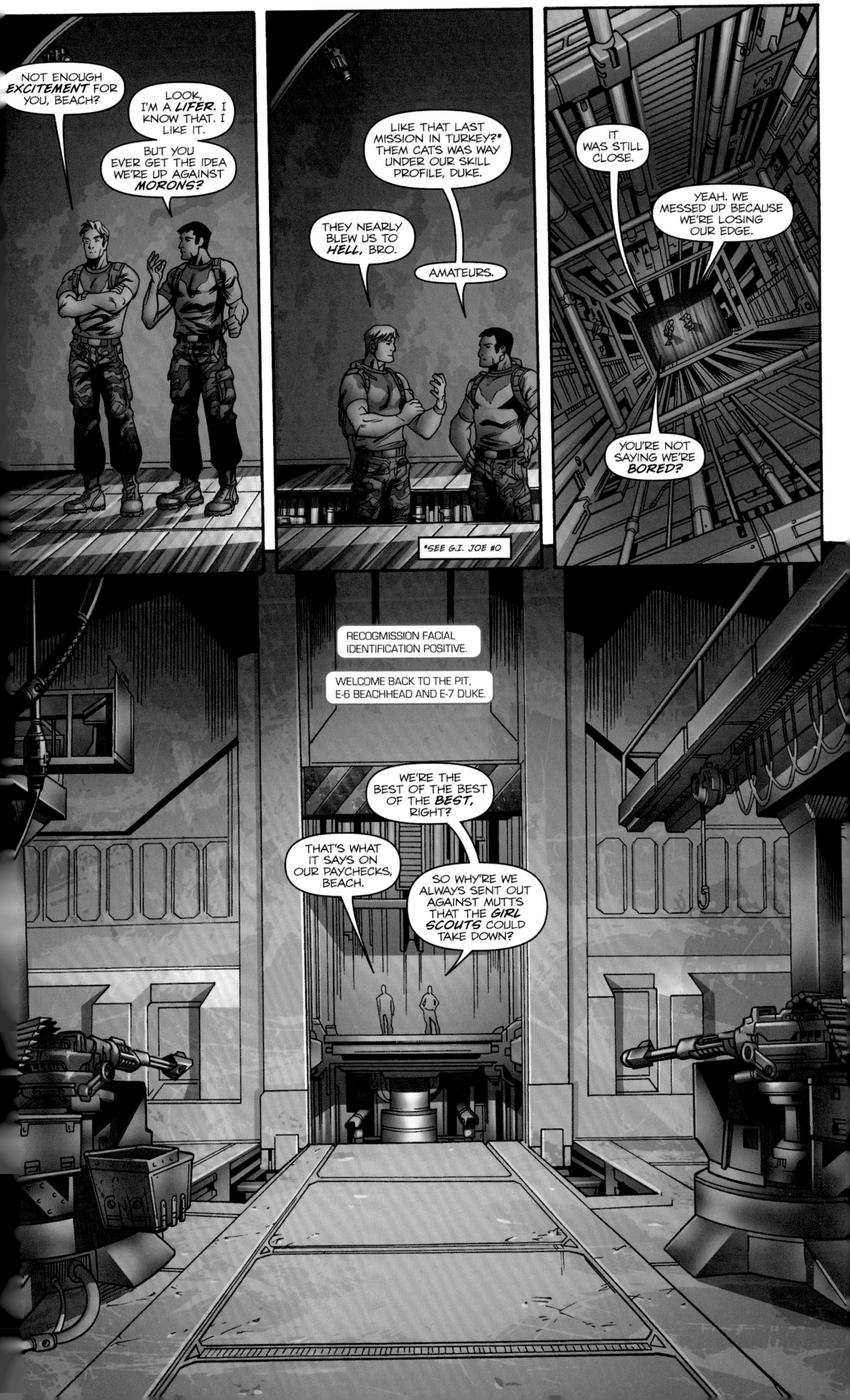
NOT ENOUGH EXCITEMENT FOR YOU, BEACH?
LOOK, I'M A LIFER. I KNOW THAT. I LIKE IT.
BUT YOU EVER GET THE IDEA WE'RE UP AGAINST MORONS?
LIKE THAT LAST MISSION IN TURKEY?* THEM CATS WAS WAY UNDER OUR SKILL PROFILE, DUKE.
THEY NEARLY BLEW US TO HELL, BRO.
AMATEURS.
*SEE G.I. JOE #0
IT WAS STILL CLOSE.
YEAH. WE MESSED UP BECAUSE WE'RE LOSING OUR EDGE.
YOU'RE NOT SAYING WE'RE BORED?
RECOGMISSION FACIAL IDENTIFICATION POSITIVE.
WELCOME BACK TO THE PIT, E-6 BEACHHEAD AND E-7 DUKE.
WE'RE THE BEST OF THE BEST OF THE BEST, RIGHT?
THAT'S WHAT IT SAYS ON OUR PAYCHECKS, BEACH.
SO WHY'RE WE ALWAYS SENT OUT AGAINST MUTTS THAT THE GIRL SCOUTS COULD TAKE DOWN?

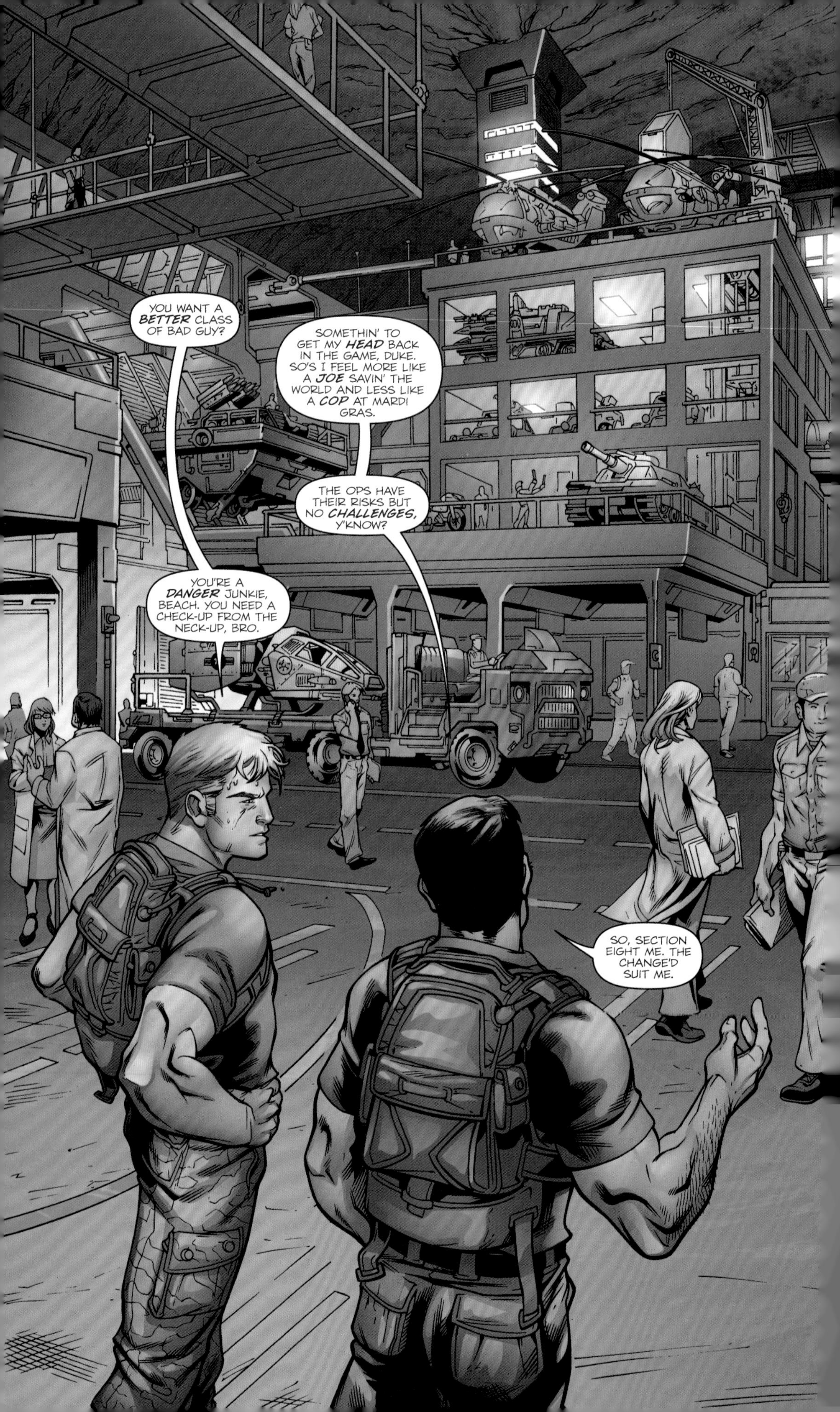
YOU WANT A BETTER CLASS OF BAD GUY?
SOMETHIN' TO GET MY HEAD BACK IN THE GAME, DUKE. SO'S I FEEL MORE LIKE A JOE SAVIN' THE WORLD AND LESS LIKE A COP AT MARDI GRAS.
THE OPS HAVE THEIR RISKS BUT NO CHALLENGES, Y'KNOW?
YOU'RE A DANGER JUNKIE, BEACH. YOU NEED A CHECK-UP FROM THE NECK-UP, BRO.
SO, SECTION EIGHT ME. THE CHANGE'D SUIT ME.

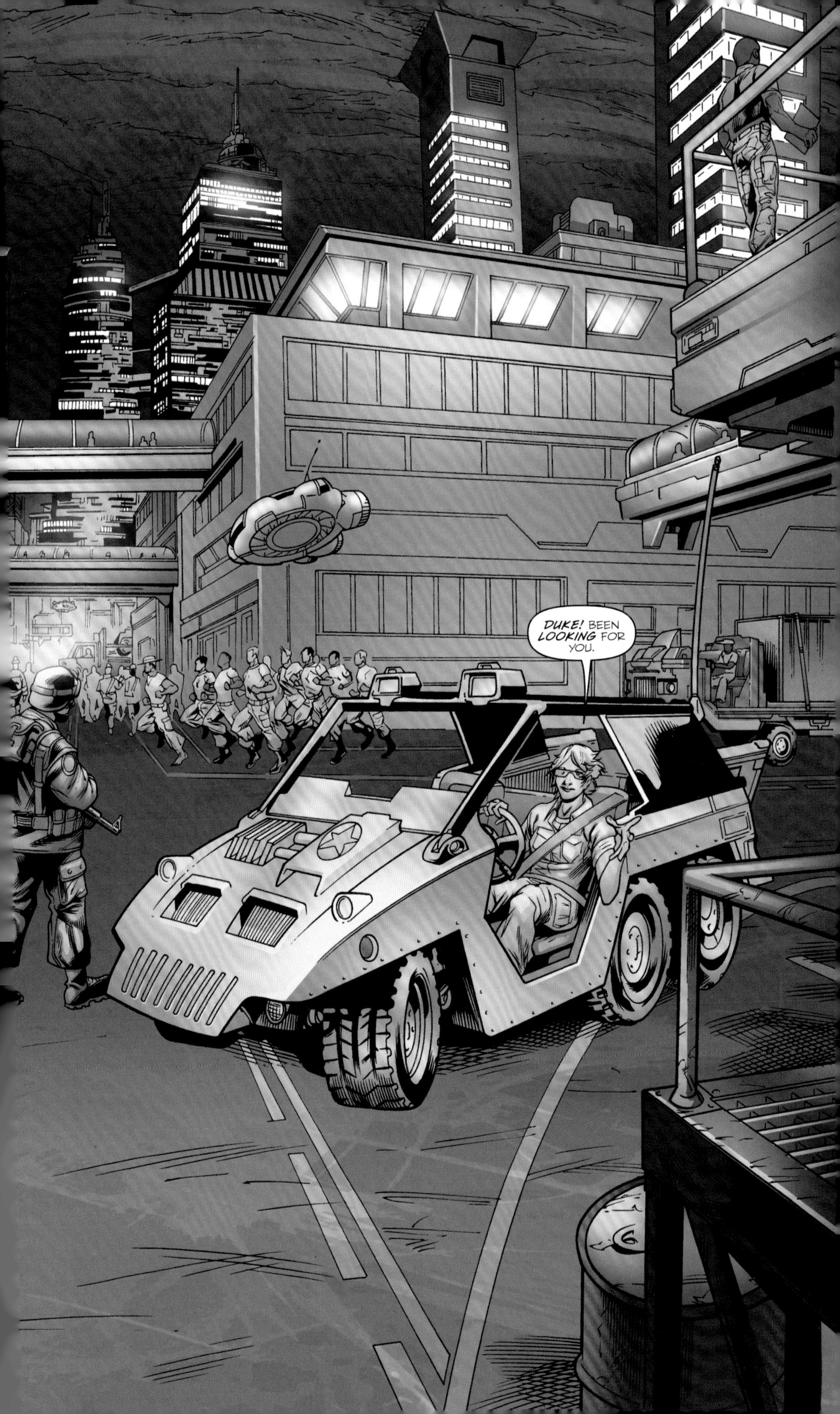
DUKE! BEEN LOOKING FOR YOU.

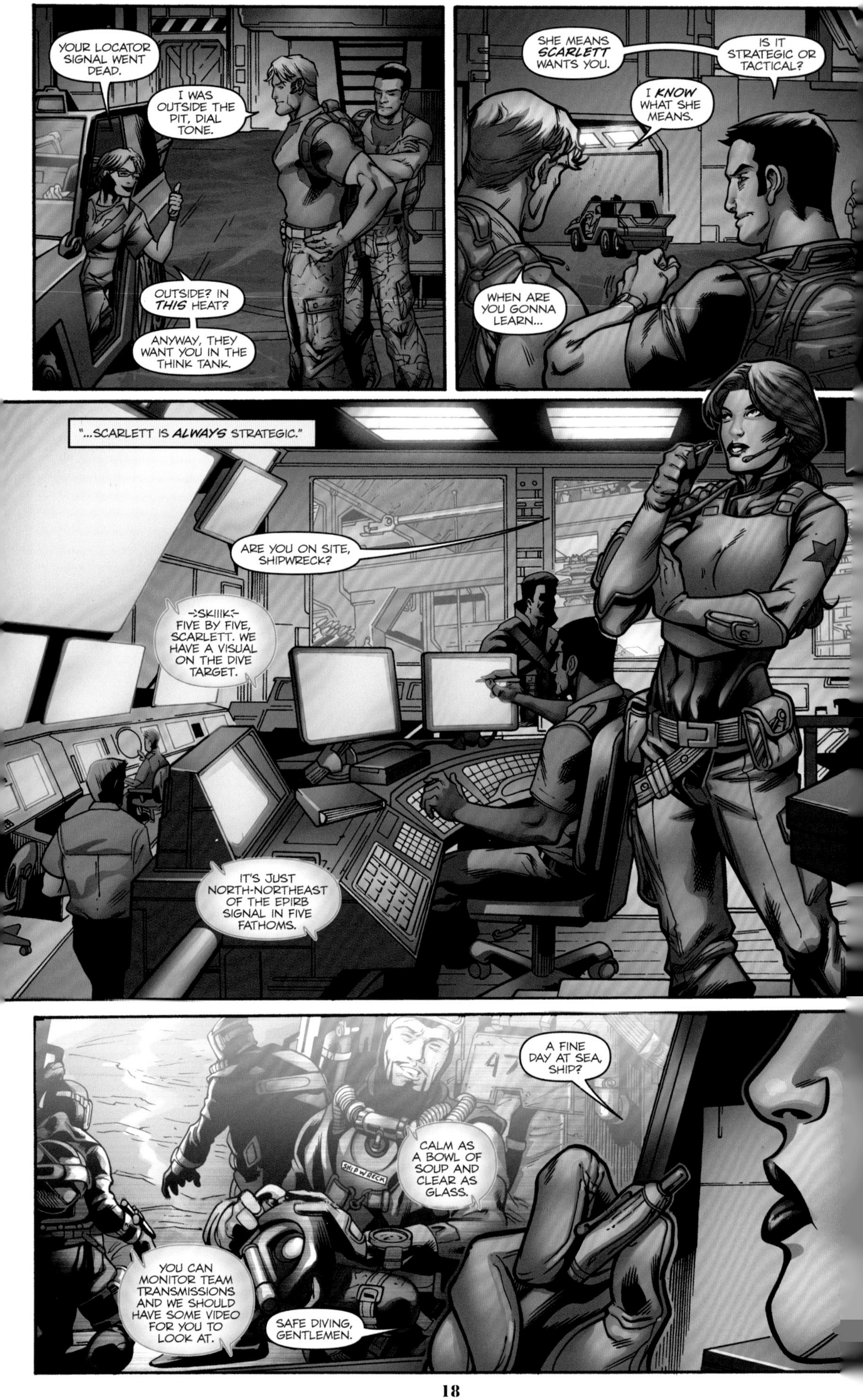
YOUR LOCATOR SIGNAL WENT DEAD.
I WAS OUTSIDE THE PIT, DIAL TONE.
OUTSIDE? IN THIS HEAT?
ANYWAY, THEY WANT YOU IN THE THINK TANK.
SHE MEANS SCARLETT WANTS YOU.
IS IT STRATEGIC OR TACTICAL?
I KNOW WHAT SHE MEANS.
WHEN ARE YOU GONNA LEARN...
"...SCARLETT IS ALWAYS STRATEGIC."
ARE YOU ON SITE, SHIPWRECK?
-SKIIIK- FIVE BY FIVE, SCARLETT. WE HAVE A VISUAL ON THE DIVE TARGET.
IT'S JUST NORTH-NORTHEAST OF THE EPIRB SIGNAL IN FIVE FATHOMS.
A FINE DAY AT SEA, SHIP?
CALM AS A BOWL OF SOUP AND CLEAR AS GLASS.
YOU CAN MONITOR TEAM TRANSMISSIONS AND WE SHOULD HAVE SOME VIDEO FOR YOU TO LOOK AT.
SAFE DIVING, GENTLEMEN.

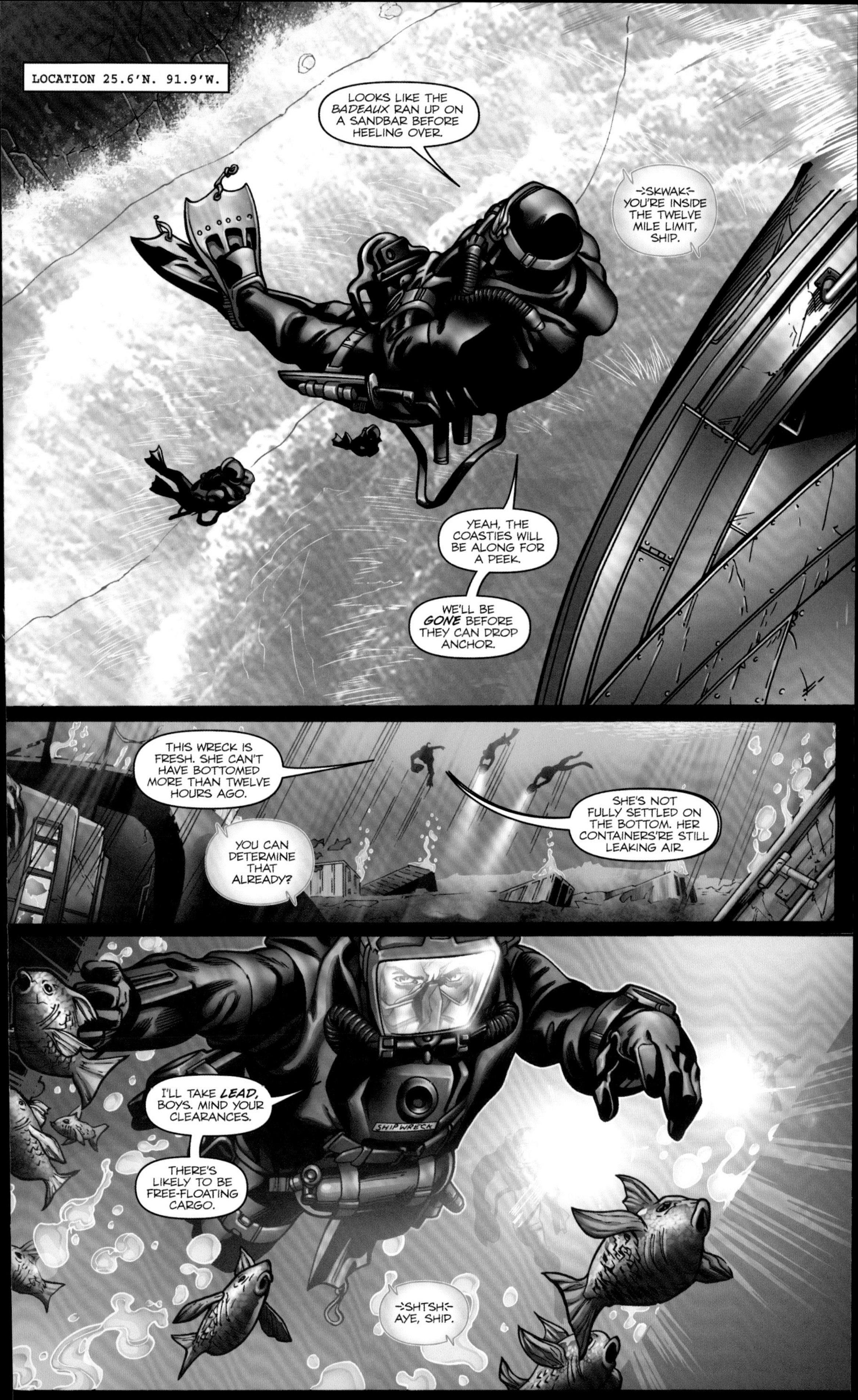
LOCATION 25.6'N. 91.9'W.
LOOKS LIKE THE BADEAUX RAN UP ON A SANDBAR BEFORE HEELING OVER.
-SKWAK- YOU'RE INSIDE THE TWELVE MILE LIMIT, SHIP.
YEAH, THE COASTIES WILL BE ALONG FOR A PEEK.
WE'LL BE GONE BEFORE THEY CAN DROP ANCHOR.
THIS WRECK IS FRESH. SHE CAN'T HAVE BOTTOMED MORE THAN TWELVE HOURS AGO.
YOU CAN DETERMINE THAT ALREADY?
SHE'S NOT FULLY SETTLED ON THE BOTTOM. HER CONTAINERS'RE STILL LEAKING AIR.
SHIPWRECK
I'LL TAKE LEAD, BOYS. MIND YOUR CLEARANCES.
THERE'S LIKELY TO BE FREE-FLOATING CARGO.
-SHTSH- AYE, SHIP.

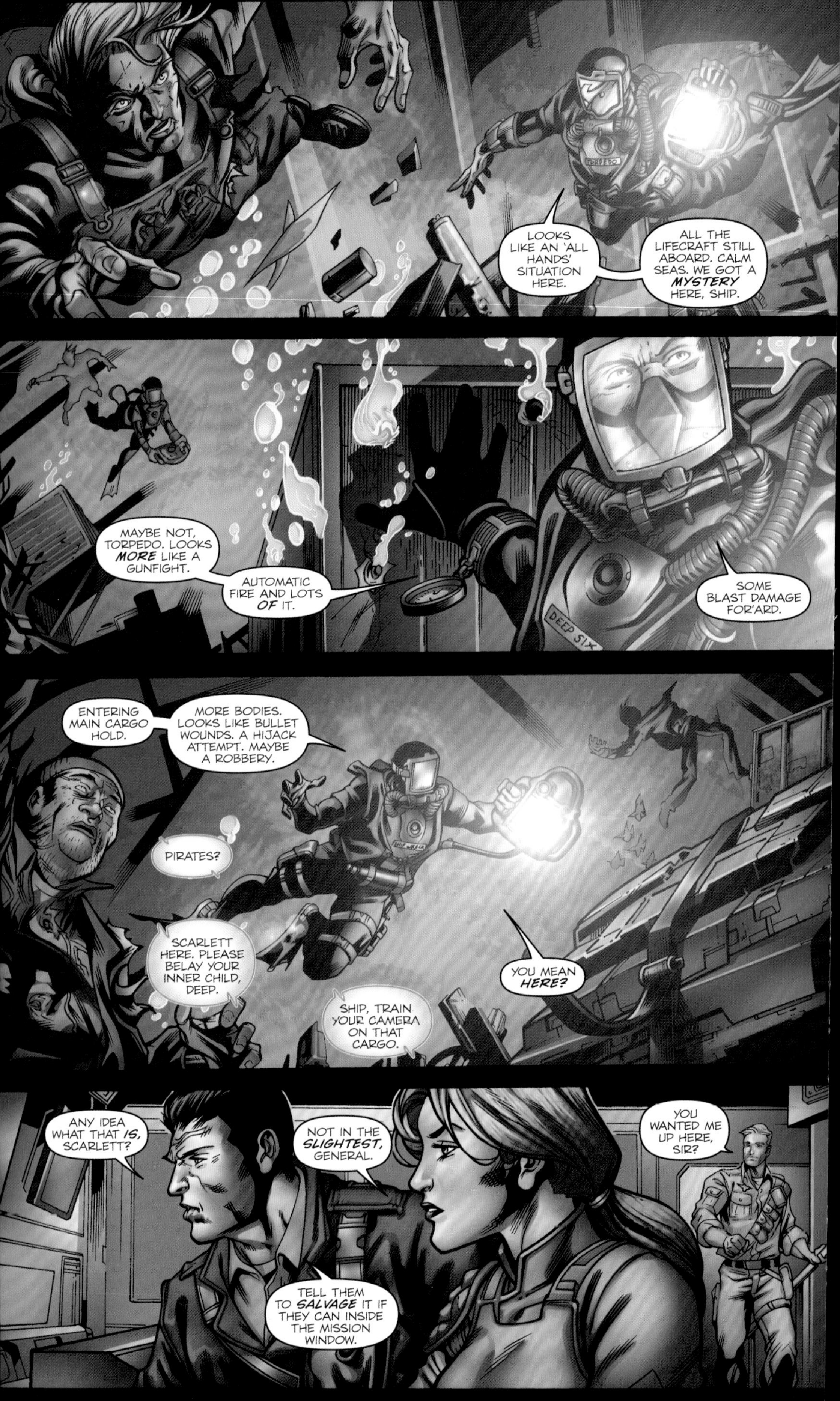

LOOKS LIKE AN 'ALL HANDS' SITUATION HERE.
ALL THE LIFECRAFT STILL ABOARD. CALM SEAS. WE GOT A MYSTERY HERE, SHIP.
TORPEDO
MAYBE NOT, TORPEDO. LOOKS MORE LIKE A GUNFIGHT.
AUTOMATIC FIRE AND LOTS OF IT.
SOME BLAST DAMAGE FOR'ARD.
DEEP SIX
ENTERING MAIN CARGO HOLD.
MORE BODIES. LOOKS LIKE BULLET WOUNDS. A HIJACK ATTEMPT. MAYBE A ROBBERY.
PIRATES?
SCARLETT HERE. PLEASE BELAY YOUR INNER CHILD, DEEP.
YOU MEAN HERE?
SHIP, TRAIN YOUR CAMERA ON THAT CARGO.
ANY IDEA WHAT THAT IS, SCARLETT?
NOT IN THE SLIGHTEST, GENERAL.
YOU WANTED ME UP HERE, SIR?
TELL THEM TO SALVAGE IT IF THEY CAN INSIDE THE MISSION WINDOW.

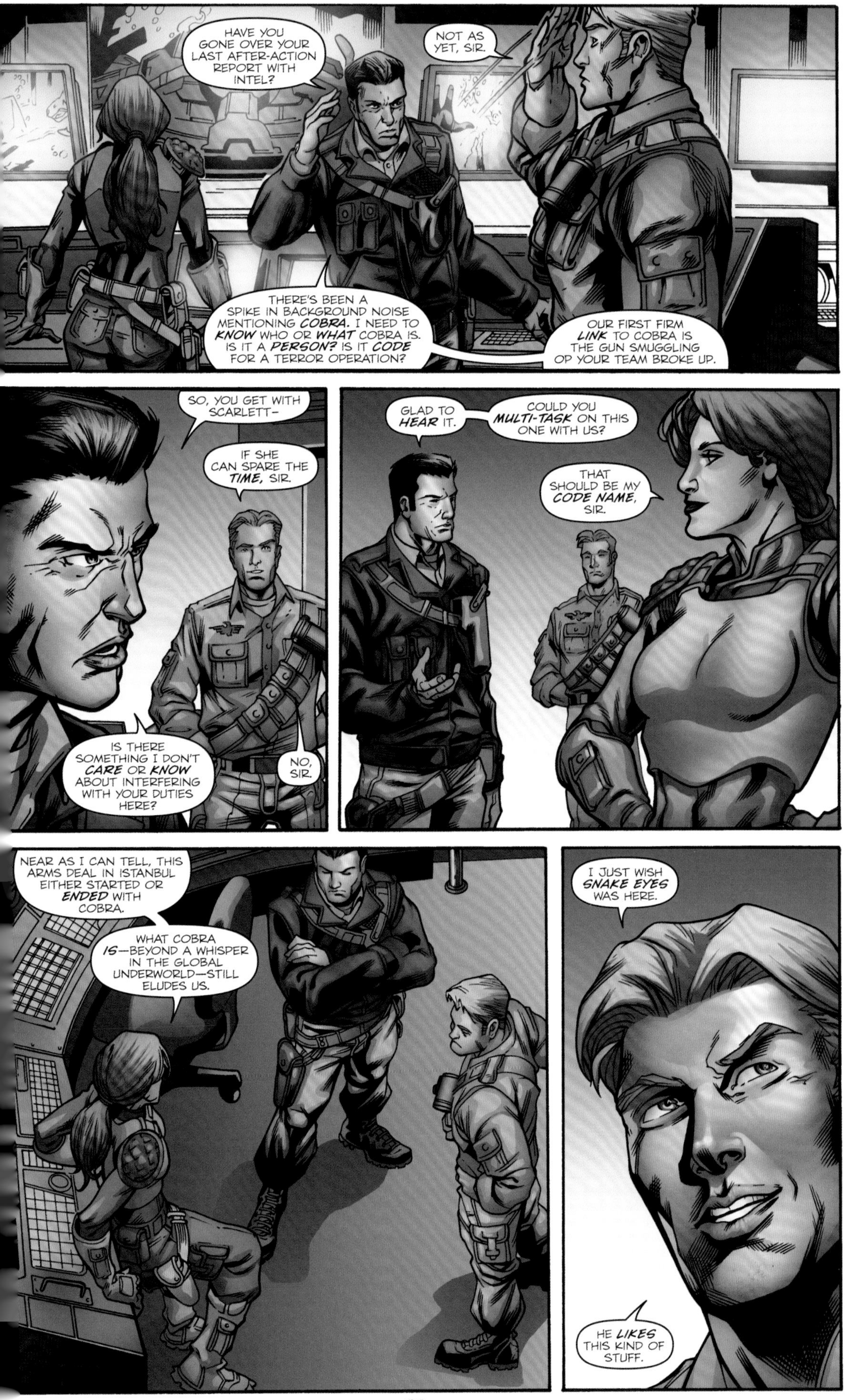
HAVE YOU GONE OVER YOUR LAST AFTER-ACTION REPORT WITH INTEL?
NOT AS YET, SIR.
THERE'S BEEN A SPIKE IN BACKGROUND NOISE MENTIONING COBRA. I NEED TO KNOW WHO OR WHAT COBRA IS. IS IT A PERSON? IS IT CODE FOR A TERROR OPERATION?
OUR FIRST FIRM LINK TO COBRA IS THE GUN SMUGGLING OP YOUR TEAM BROKE UP.
SO, YOU GET WITH SCARLETT--
IF SHE CAN SPARE THE TIME, SIR.
IS THERE SOMETHING I DON'T CARE OR KNOW ABOUT INTERFERING WITH YOUR DUTIES HERE?
NO, SIR.
GLAD TO HEAR IT.
COULD YOU MULTI-TASK ON THIS ONE WITH US?
THAT SHOULD BE MY CODE NAME, SIR.
NEAR AS I CAN TELL, THIS ARMS DEAL IN ISTANBUL EITHER STARTED OR ENDED WITH COBRA.
WHAT COBRA IS--BEYOND A WHISPER IN THE GLOBAL UNDERWORLD--STILL ELUDES US.
I JUST WISH SNAKE EYES WAS HERE.
HE LIKES THIS KIND OF STUFF.

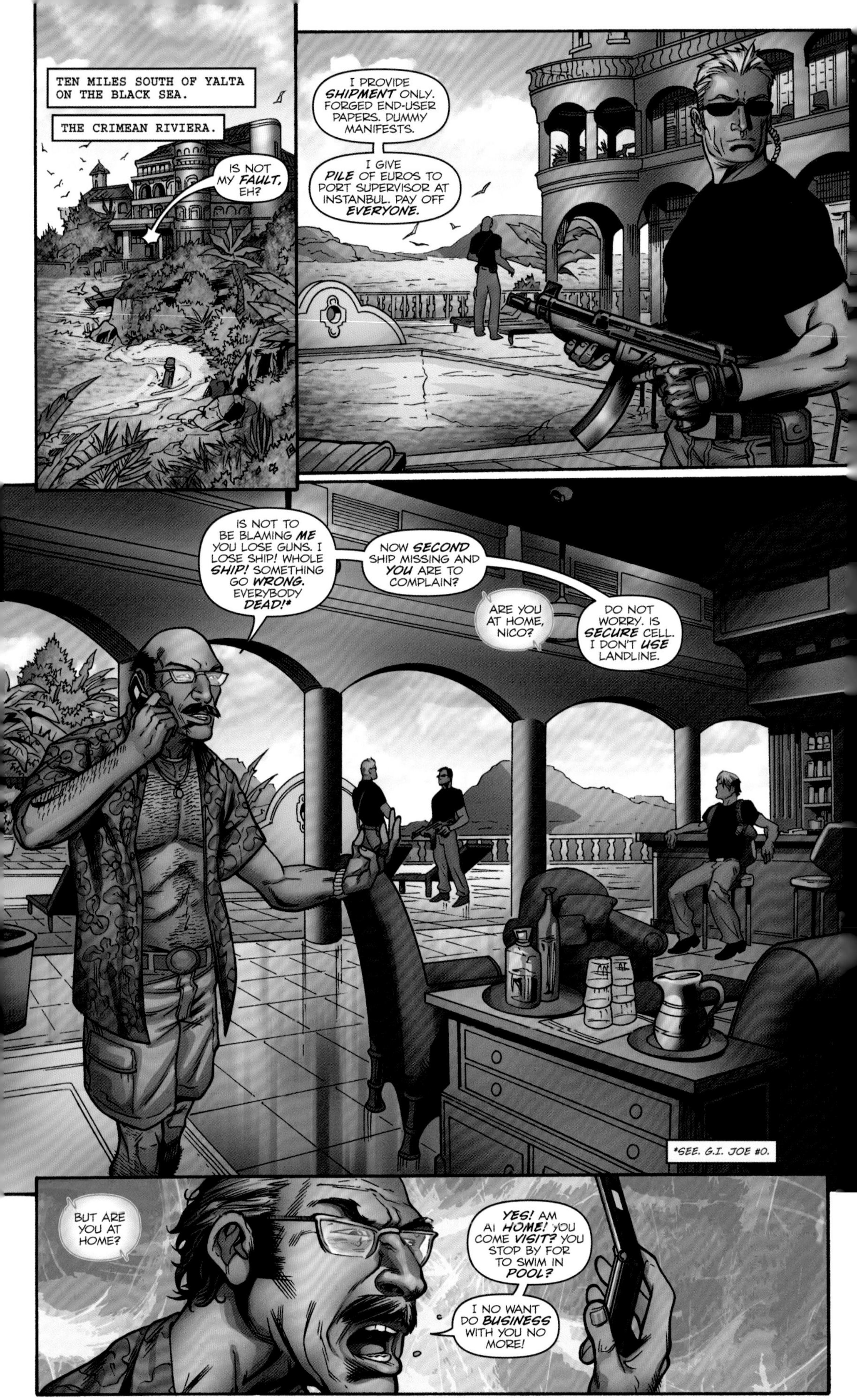
TEN MILES SOUTH OF YALTA ON THE BLACK SEA.
THE CRIMEAN RIVIERA.
IS NOT MY FAULT, EH?
I PROVIDE SHIPMENT ONLY. FORGED END-USER PAPERS. DUMMY MANIFESTS.
I GIVE PILE OF EUROS TO PORT SUPERVISOR AT INSTANBUL. PAY OFF EVERYONE.
IS NOT TO BE BLAMING ME YOU LOSE GUNS. I LOSE SHIP! WHOLE SHIP! SOMETHING GO WRONG. EVERYBODY DEAD!*
NOW SECOND SHIP MISSING AND YOU ARE TO COMPLAIN?
ARE YOU AT HOME, NICO?
DO NOT WORRY. IS SECURE CELL. I DON'T USE LANDLINE.
*SEE. G.I. JOE #0.
BUT ARE YOU AT HOME?
YES! AM AI HOME! YOU COME VISIT? YOU STOP BY FOR TO SWIM IN POOL?
I NO WANT DO BUSINESS WITH YOU NO MORE!

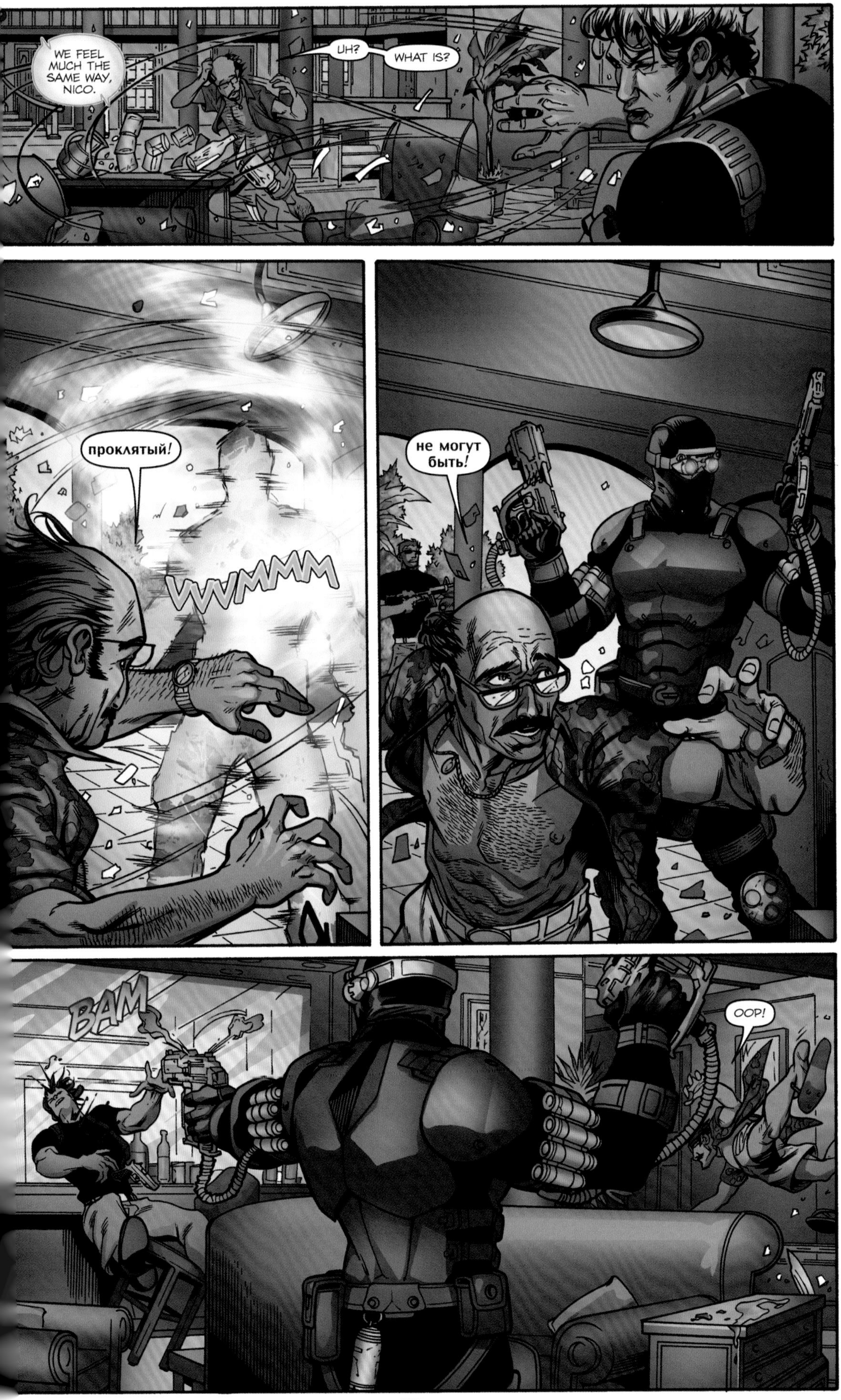

WE FEEL MUCH THE SAME WAY, NICO.
UH?
WHAT IS?
проклятый!
VVVMMM
не могут быть!
BAM
OOP!

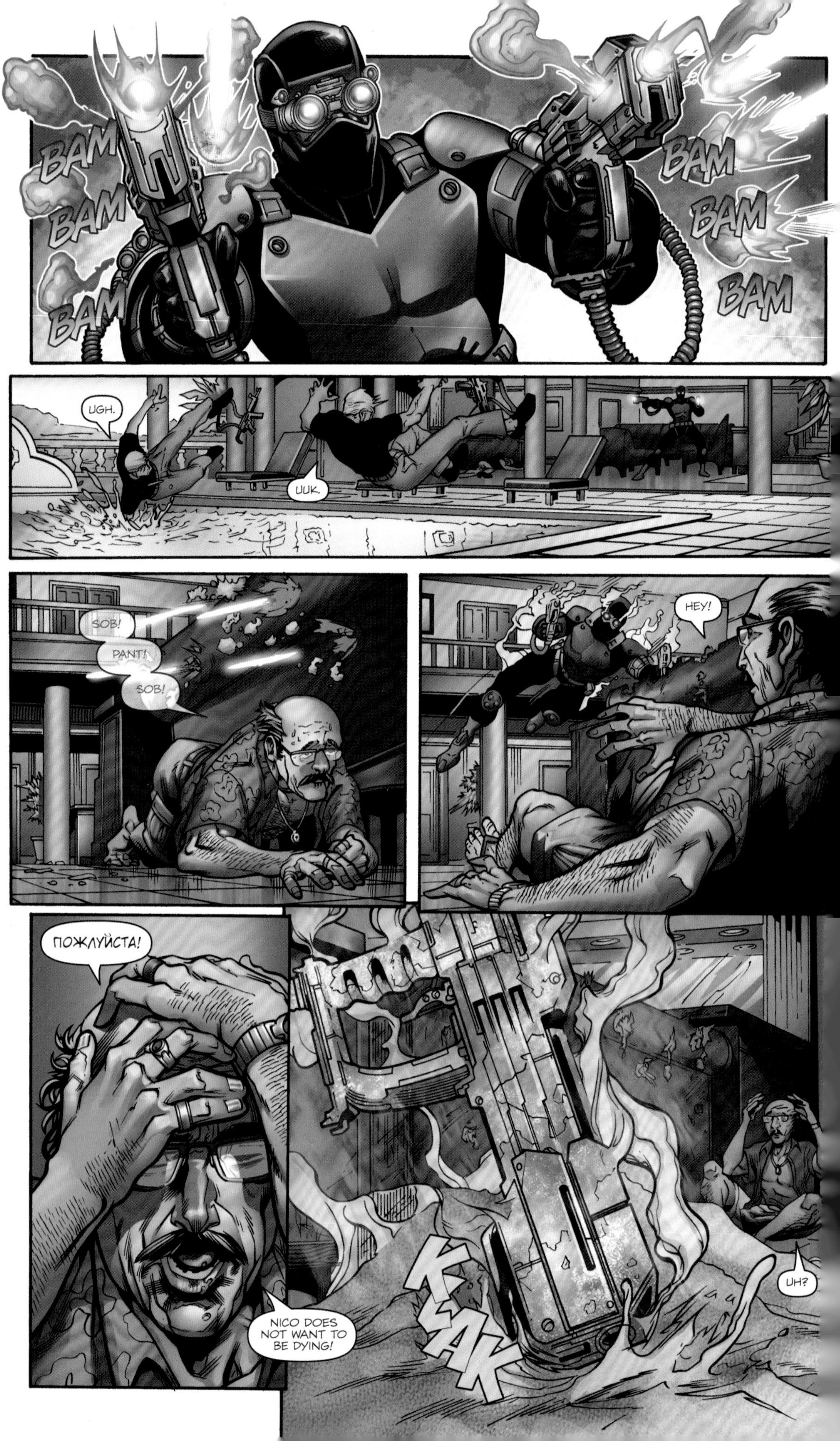
BAM
BAM
BAM
BAM
BAM
BAM
UGH.
UUK.
SOB!
PANT!
SOB!
HEY!
ПОЖЛУЙСТА!
NICO DOES NOT WANT TO BE DYING!
KAK
UH?

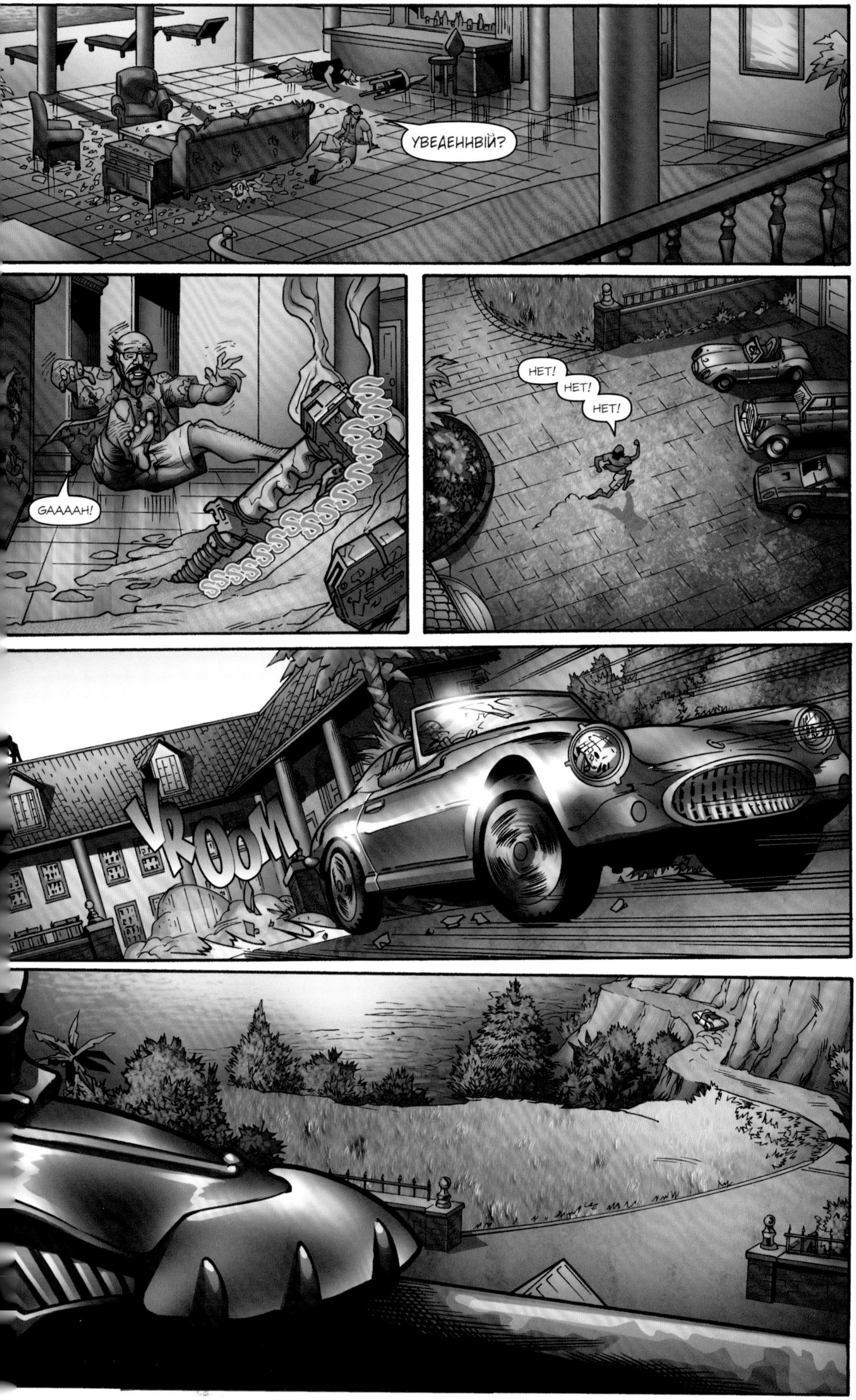
УВЕДЕННВІЙ?
GAAAAH!
НЕТ!
НЕТ!
НЕТ!
VROOM!

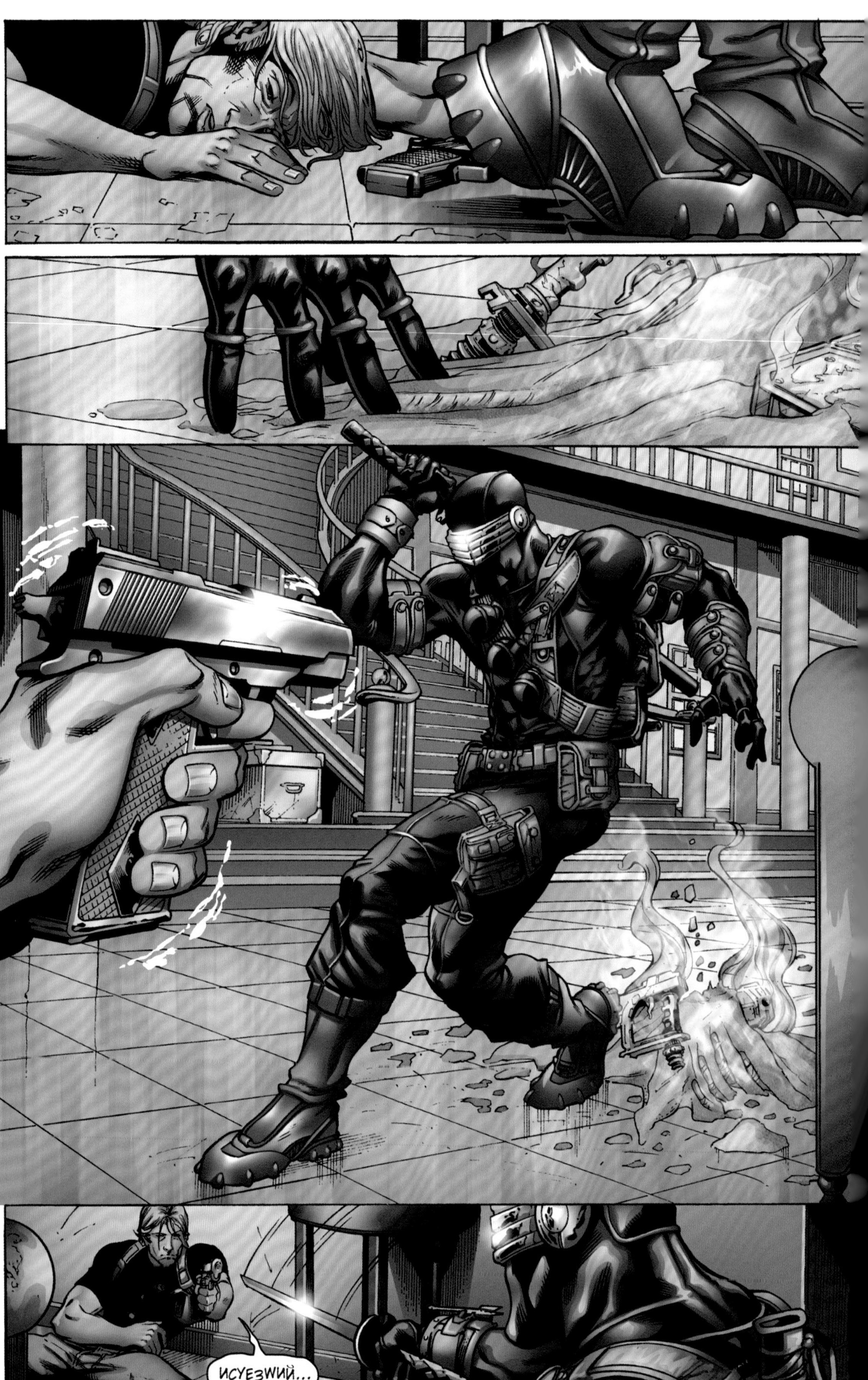
ИСЧЕЗШИЙ...

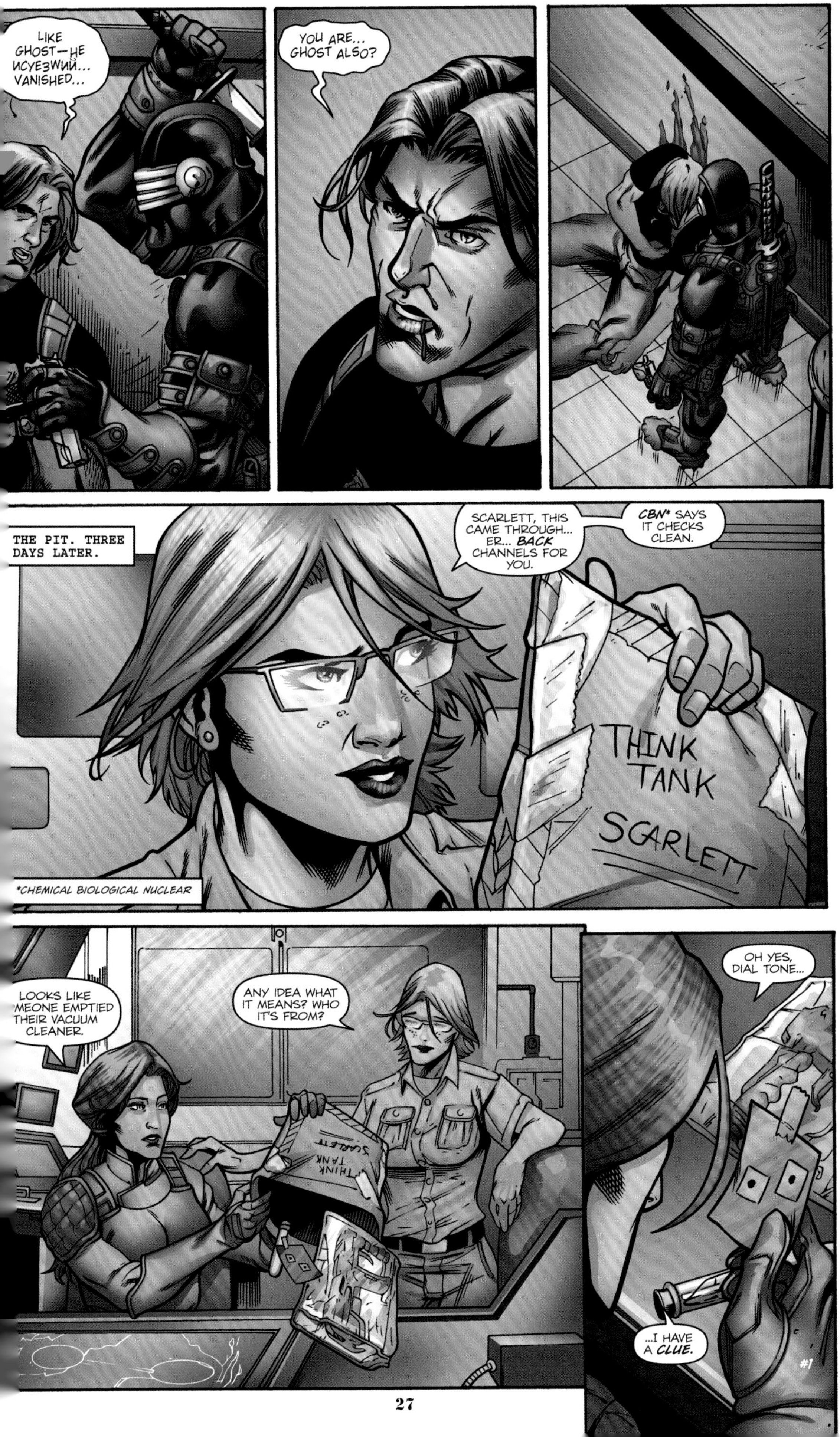
LIKE GHOST—НЕ ИСУЕЗНИЙ... VANISHED...
YOU ARE... GHOST ALSO?
THE PIT. THREE DAYS LATER.
SCARLETT, THIS CAME THROUGH... ER... BACK CHANNELS FOR YOU.
CBN* SAYS IT CHECKS CLEAN.
THINK TANK
SCARLETT
*CHEMICAL BIOLOGICAL NUCLEAR
LOOKS LIKE MEONE EMPTIED THEIR VACUUM CLEANER.
ANY IDEA WHAT IT MEANS? WHO IT'S FROM?
OH YES, DIAL TONE...
...I HAVE A CLUE.
#1

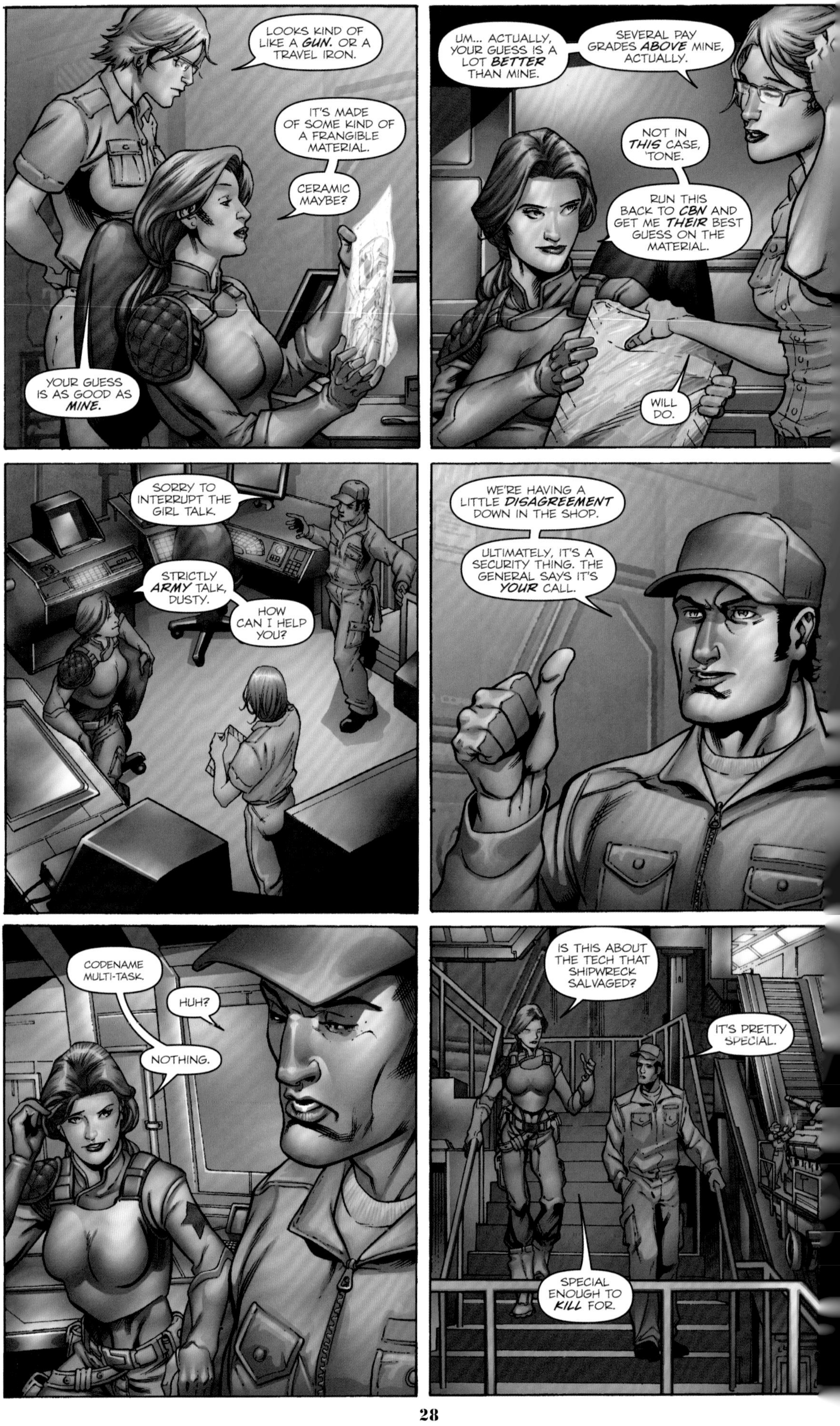
LOOKS KIND OF LIKE A GUN. OR A TRAVEL IRON.
IT'S MADE OF SOME KIND OF A FRANGIBLE MATERIAL.
CERAMIC MAYBE?
YOUR GUESS IS AS GOOD AS MINE.
UM... ACTUALLY, YOUR GUESS IS A LOT BETTER THAN MINE.
SEVERAL PAY GRADES ABOVE MINE, ACTUALLY.
NOT IN THIS CASE, 'TONE.
RUN THIS BACK TO CBN AND GET ME THEIR BEST GUESS ON THE MATERIAL.
WILL DO.
SORRY TO INTERRUPT THE GIRL TALK.
STRICTLY ARMY TALK, DUSTY.
HOW CAN I HELP YOU?
WE'RE HAVING A LITTLE DISAGREEMENT DOWN IN THE SHOP.
ULTIMATELY, IT'S A SECURITY THING. THE GENERAL SAYS IT'S YOUR CALL.
CODENAME MULTI-TASK.
HUH?
NOTHING.
IS THIS ABOUT THE TECH THAT SHIPWRECK SALVAGED?
IT'S PRETTY SPECIAL.
SPECIAL ENOUGH TO KILL FOR.

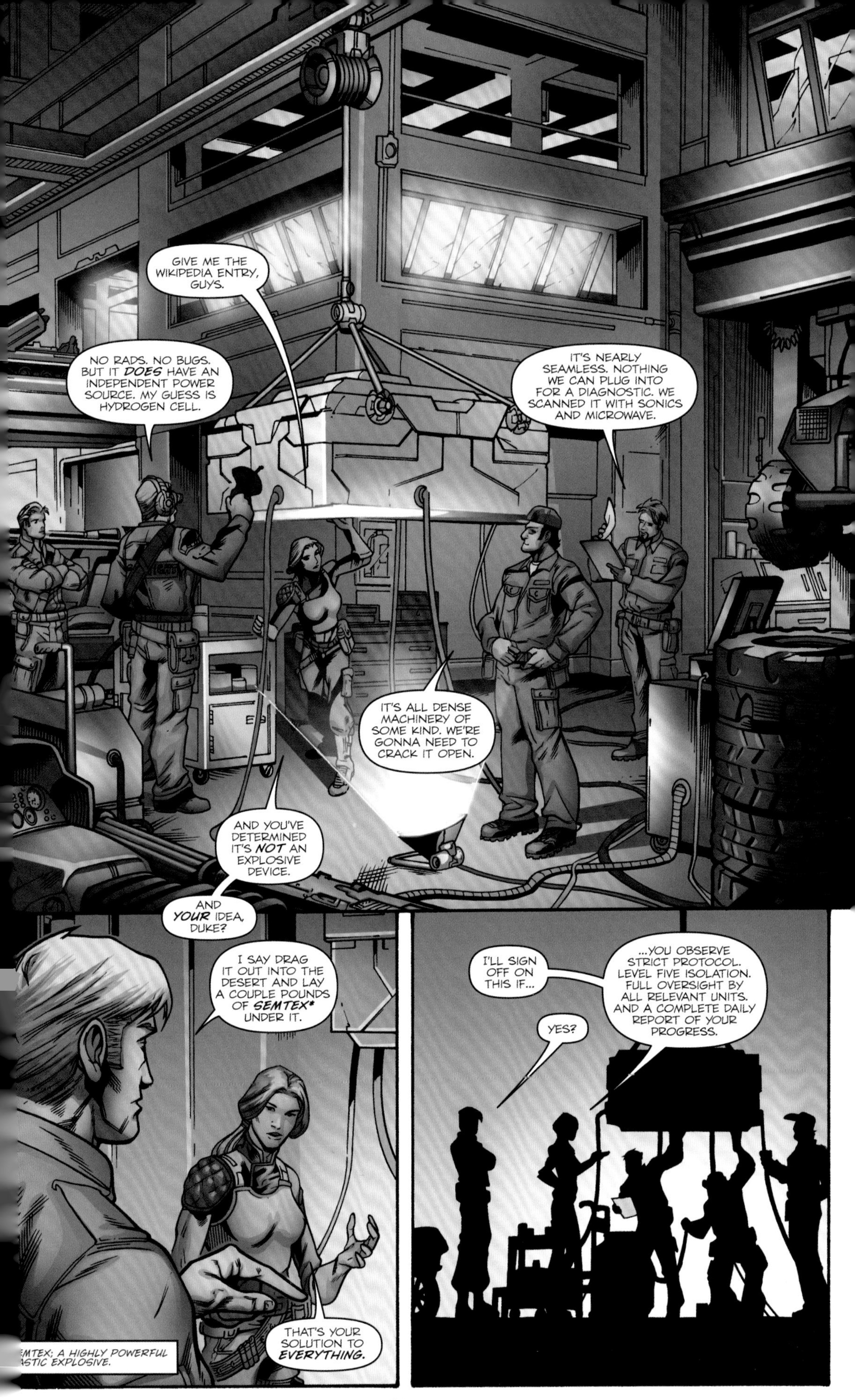

GIVE ME THE WIKIPEDIA ENTRY, GUYS.
NO RADS. NO BUGS. BUT IT DOES HAVE AN INDEPENDENT POWER SOURCE. MY GUESS IS HYDROGEN CELL.
IT'S NEARLY SEAMLESS. NOTHING WE CAN PLUG INTO FOR A DIAGNOSTIC. WE SCANNED IT WITH SONICS AND MICROWAVE.
IT'S ALL DENSE MACHINERY OF SOME KIND. WE'RE GONNA NEED TO CRACK IT OPEN.
AND YOU'VE DETERMINED IT'S NOT AN EXPLOSIVE DEVICE.
AND YOUR IDEA, DUKE?
I SAY DRAG IT OUT INTO THE DESERT AND LAY A COUPLE POUNDS OF SEMTEX* UNDER IT.
THAT'S YOUR SOLUTION TO EVERYTHING.
EMTEX; A HIGHLY POWERFUL
ASTIC EXPLOSIVE.
I'LL SIGN OFF ON THIS IF...
YES?
...YOU OBSERVE STRICT PROTOCOL. LEVEL FIVE ISOLATION. FULL OVERSIGHT BY ALL RELEVANT UNITS. AND A COMPLETE DAILY REPORT OF YOUR PROGRESS.

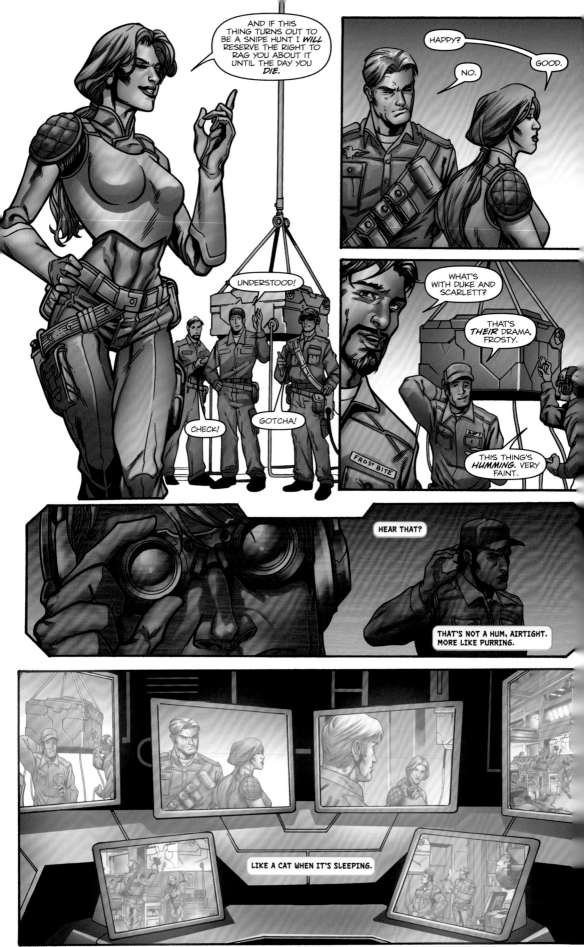

AND IF THIS THING TURNS OUT TO BE A SNIPE HUNT I *WILL* RESERVE THE RIGHT TO RAG YOU ABOUT IT UNTIL THE DAY YOU *DIE.*

HAPPY?

NO.

GOOD.

UNDERSTOOD!

CHECK!

GOTCHA!

WHAT'S WITH DUKE AND SCARLETT?

THAT'S *THEIR* DRAMA, FROSTY.

THIS THING'S *HUMMING.* VERY FAINT.

FROST BITE

HEAR THAT?

THAT'S NOT A HUM, AIRTIGHT. MORE LIKE PURRING.

LIKE A CAT WHEN IT'S SLEEPING.

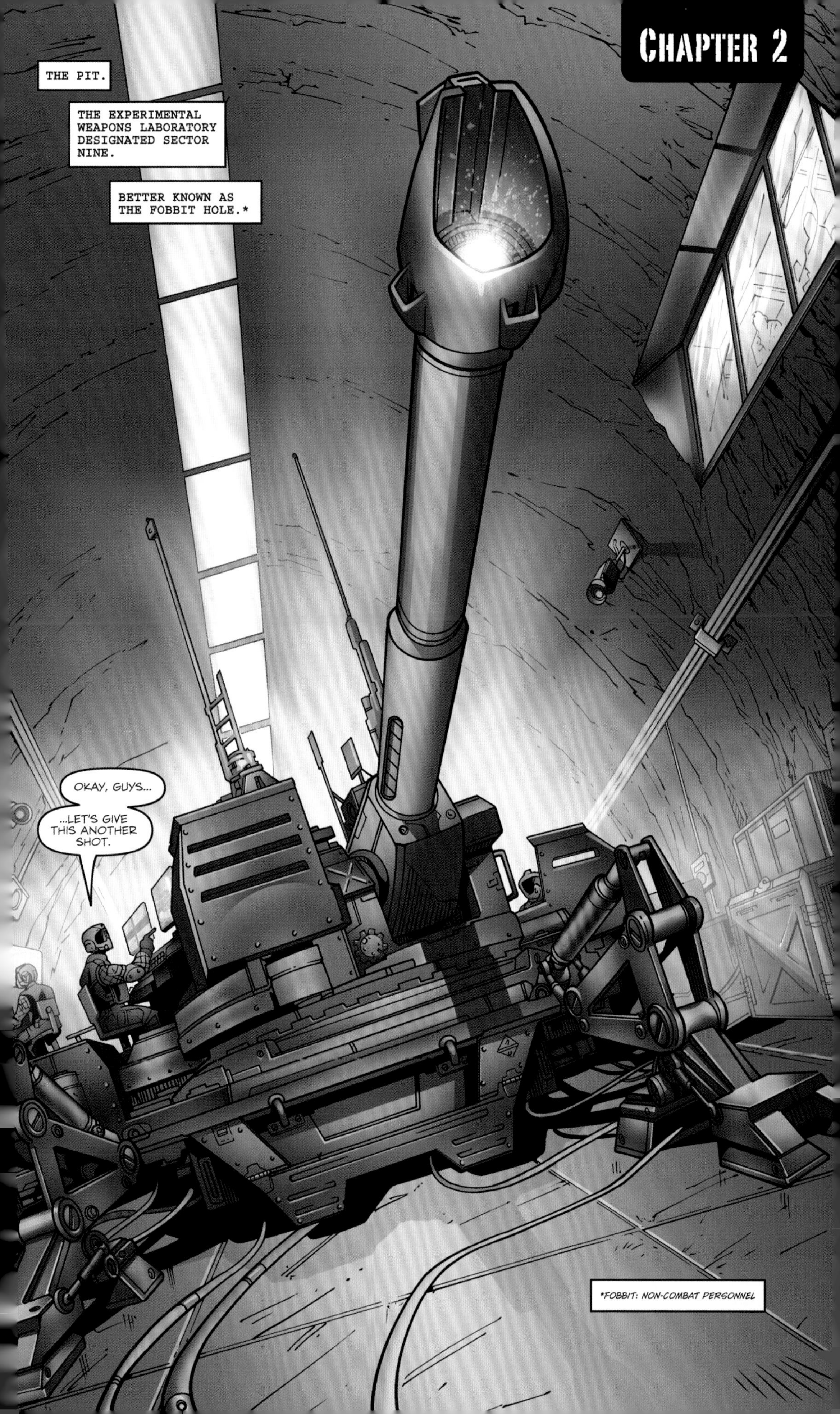
CHAPTER 2
THE PIT.
THE EXPERIMENTAL WEAPONS LABORATORY DESIGNATED SECTOR NINE.
BETTER KNOWN AS THE FOBBIT HOLE.*
OKAY, GUYS...
...LET'S GIVE THIS ANOTHER SHOT.
*FOBBIT: NON-COMBAT PERSONNEL

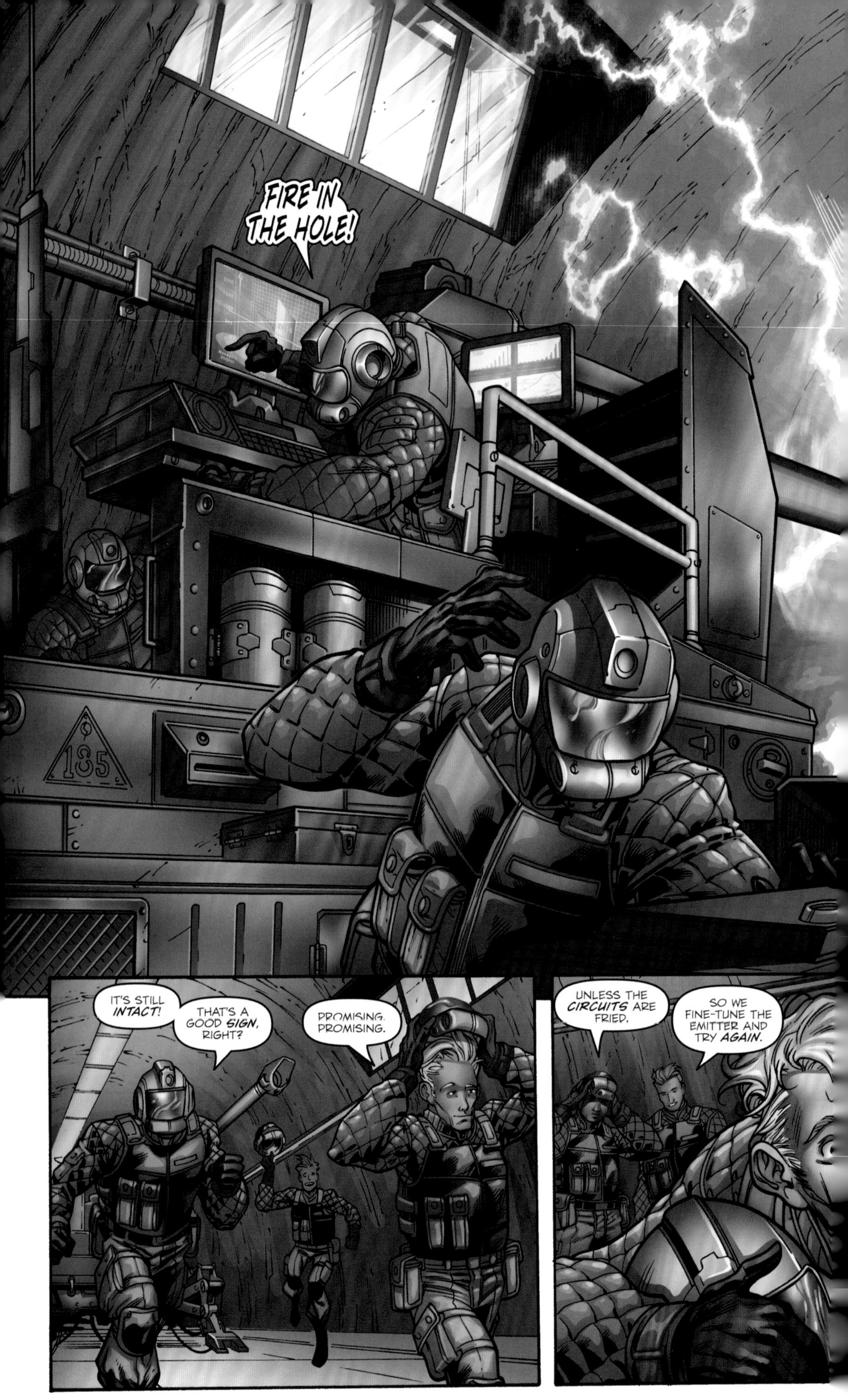
FIRE IN THE HOLE!
IT'S STILL *INTACT*!
THAT'S A GOOD *SIGN*, RIGHT?
PROMISING. PROMISING.
UNLESS THE *CIRCUITS* ARE FRIED.
SO WE FINE-TUNE THE EMITTER AND TRY *AGAIN*.

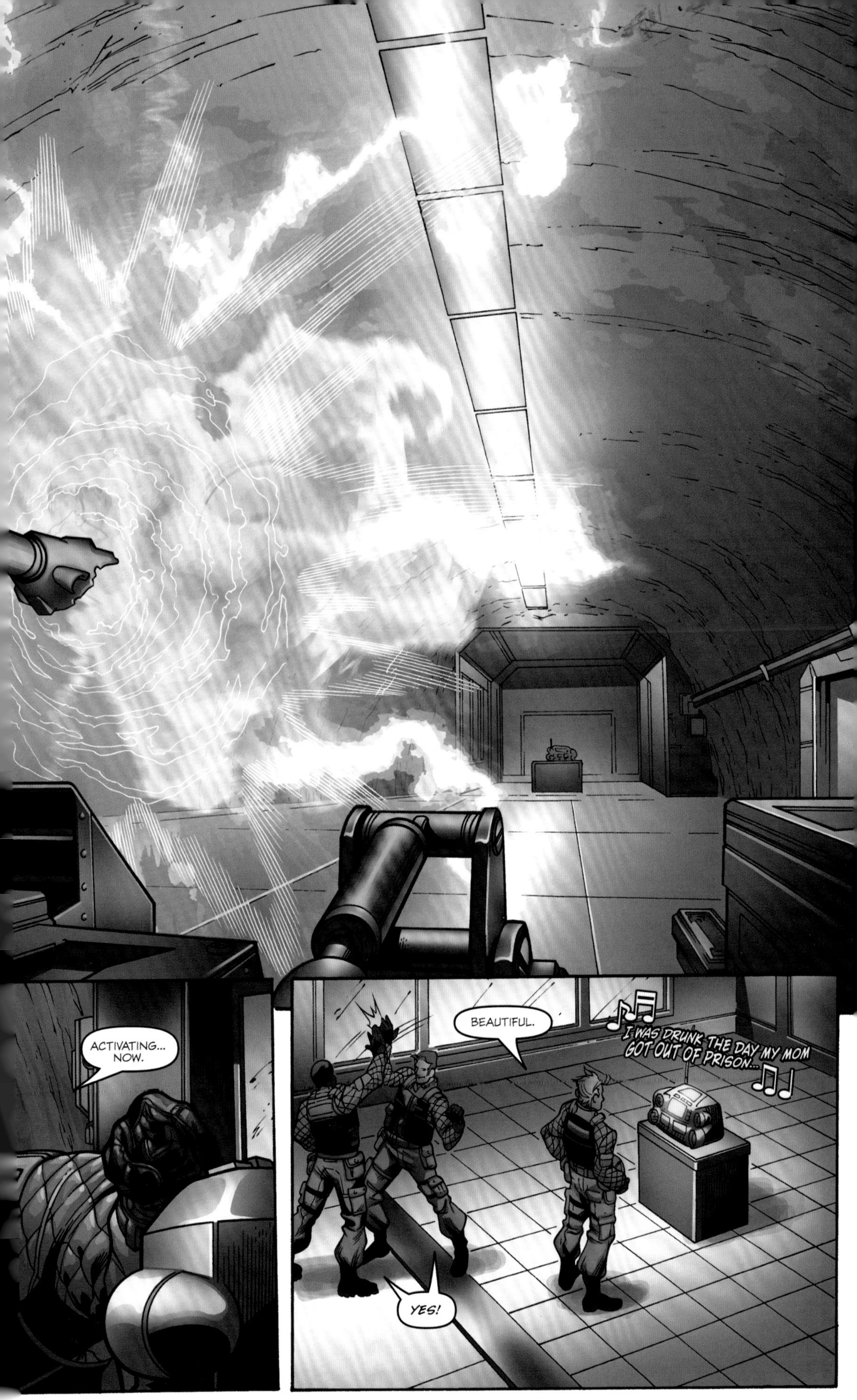
ACTIVATING... NOW.
BEAUTIFUL.
I WAS DRUNK THE DAY MY MOM GOT OUT OF PRISON...
YES!

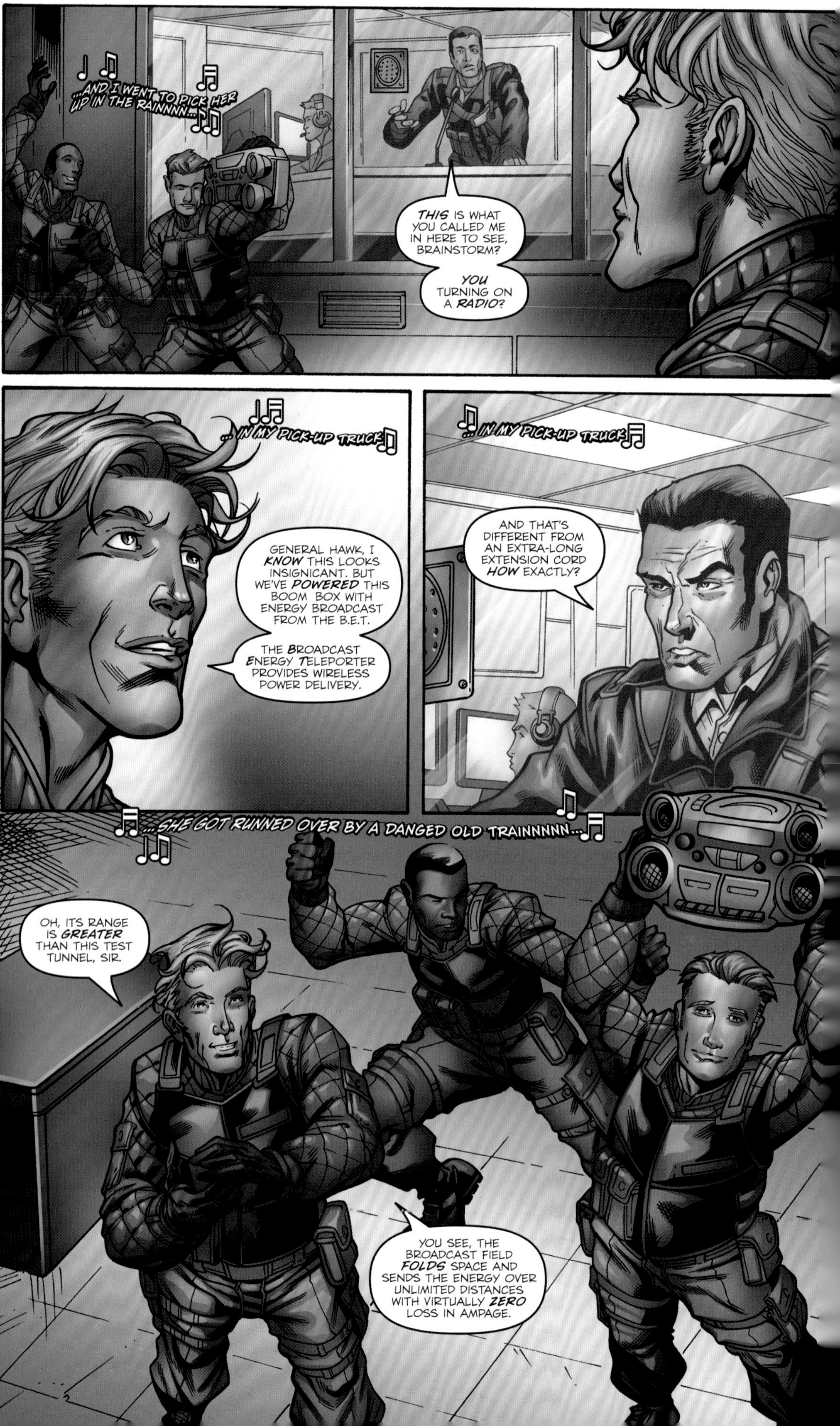

...AND I WENT TO PICK HER UP IN THE RAINNNN...
THIS IS WHAT YOU CALLED ME IN HERE TO SEE, BRAINSTORM?
YOU TURNING ON A RADIO?
...IN MY PICK-UP TRUCK
GENERAL HAWK, I KNOW THIS LOOKS INSIGNICANT. BUT WE'VE POWERED THIS BOOM BOX WITH ENERGY BROADCAST FROM THE B.E.T.
THE BROADCAST ENERGY TELEPORTER PROVIDES WIRELESS POWER DELIVERY.
...IN MY PICK-UP TRUCK
AND THAT'S DIFFERENT FROM AN EXTRA-LONG EXTENSION CORD HOW EXACTLY?
...SHE GOT RUNNED OVER BY A DANGED OLD TRAINNNNN...
OH, ITS RANGE IS GREATER THAN THIS TEST TUNNEL, SIR.
YOU SEE, THE BROADCAST FIELD FOLDS SPACE AND SENDS THE ENERGY OVER UNLIMITED DISTANCES WITH VIRTUALLY ZERO LOSS IN AMPAGE.

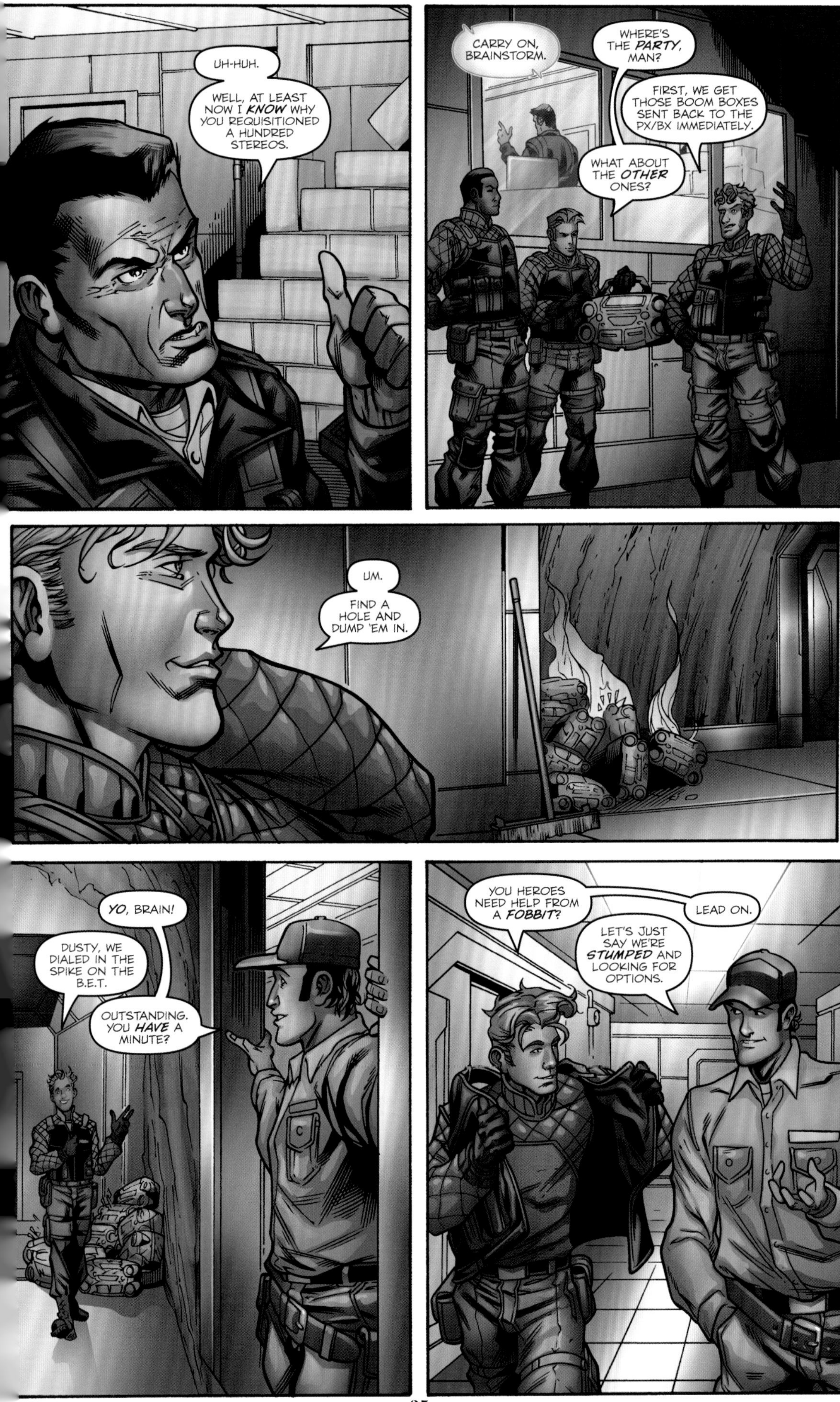
UH-HUH.
WELL, AT LEAST NOW I KNOW WHY YOU REQUISITIONED A HUNDRED STEREOS.
CARRY ON, BRAINSTORM.
WHERE'S THE PARTY, MAN?
FIRST, WE GET THOSE BOOM BOXES SENT BACK TO THE PX/BX IMMEDIATELY.
WHAT ABOUT THE OTHER ONES?
UM.
FIND A HOLE AND DUMP 'EM IN.
YO, BRAIN!
DUSTY, WE DIALED IN THE SPIKE ON THE B.E.T.
OUTSTANDING. YOU HAVE A MINUTE?
YOU HEROES NEED HELP FROM A FOBBIT?
LEAD ON.
LET'S JUST SAY WE'RE STUMPED AND LOOKING FOR OPTIONS.

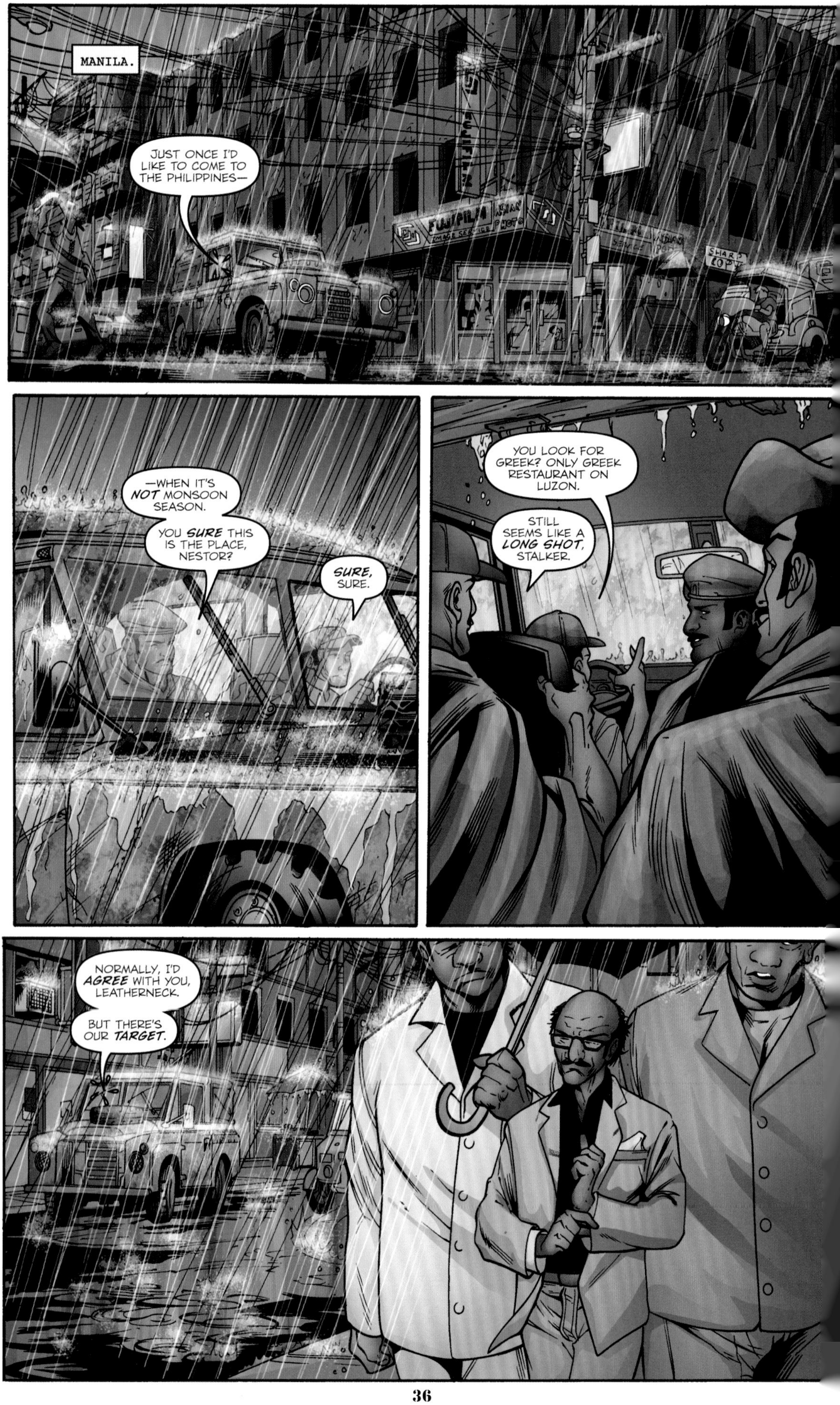
MANILA.
JUST ONCE I'D LIKE TO COME TO THE PHILIPPINES—
—WHEN IT'S NOT MONSOON SEASON.
YOU SURE THIS IS THE PLACE, NESTOR?
SURE, SURE.
YOU LOOK FOR GREEK? ONLY GREEK RESTAURANT ON LUZON.
STILL SEEMS LIKE A LONG SHOT, STALKER.
NORMALLY, I'D AGREE WITH YOU, LEATHERNECK.
BUT THERE'S OUR TARGET.

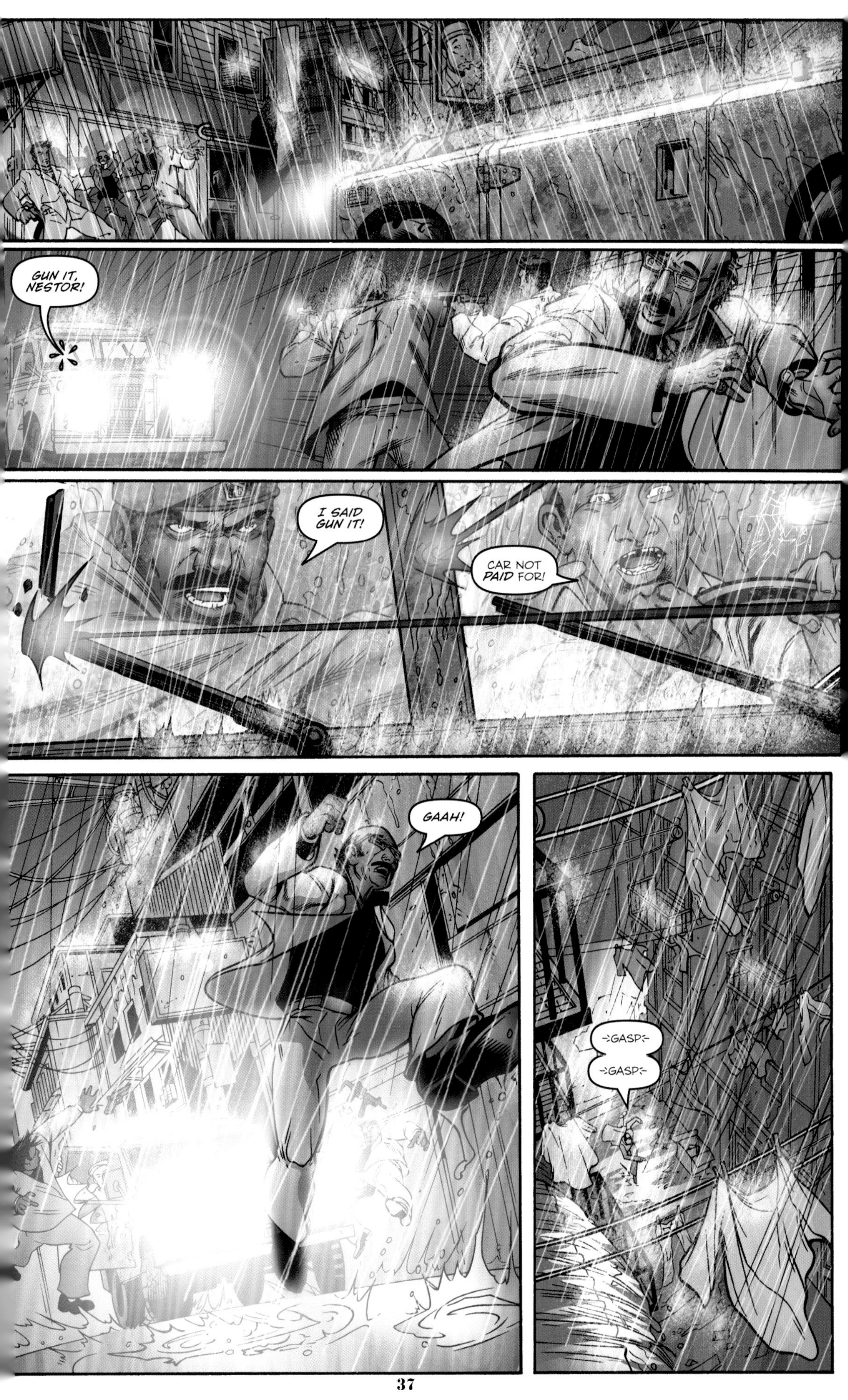
GUN IT, NESTOR!
I SAID GUN IT!
CAR NOT PAID FOR!
GAAH!
-GASP-
-GASP-

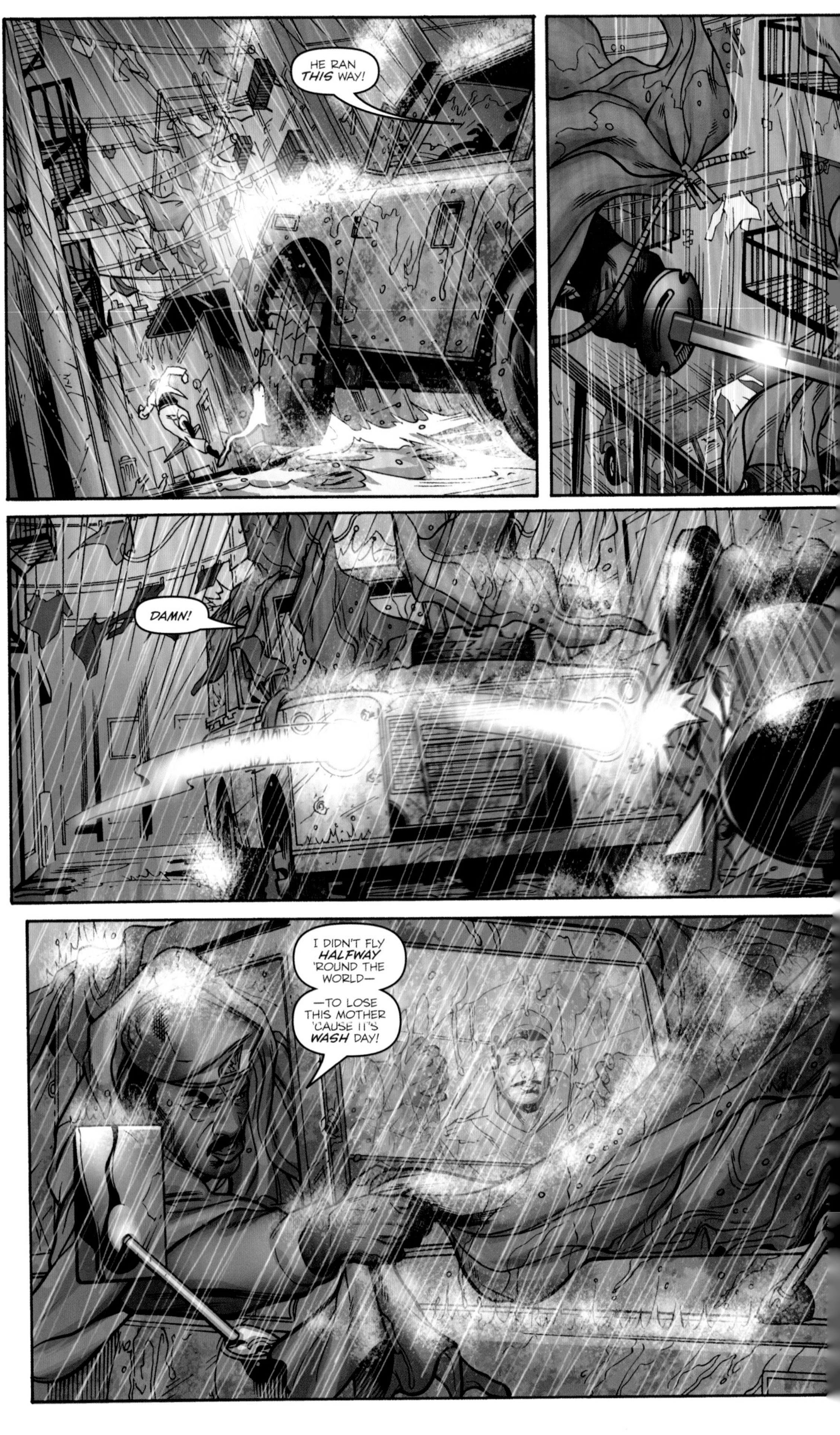
HE RAN THIS WAY!
DAMN!
I DIDN'T FLY HALFWAY 'ROUND THE WORLD—
—TO LOSE THIS MOTHER 'CAUSE IT'S WASH DAY!

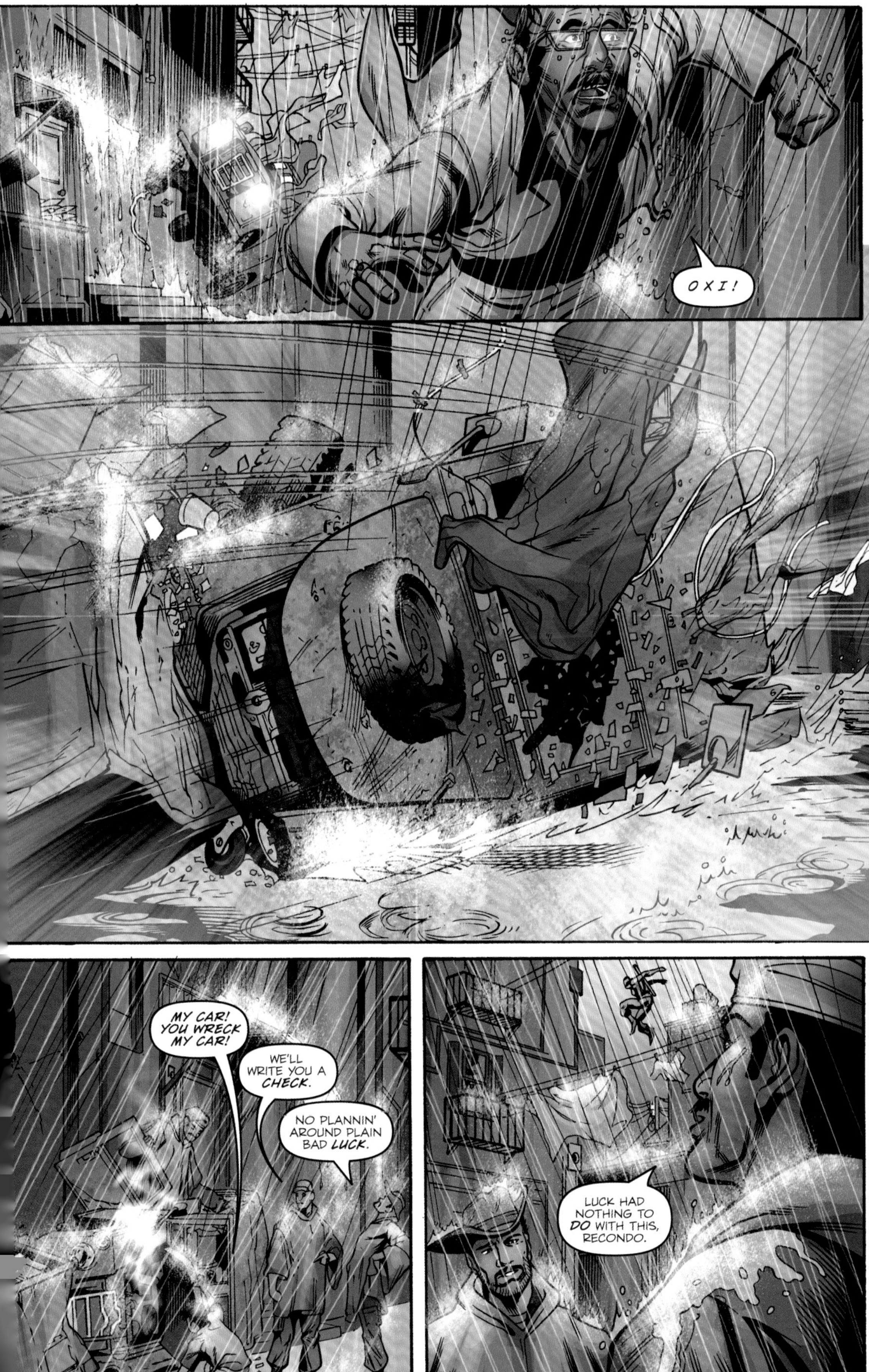
OXI!
MY CAR! YOU WRECK MY CAR!
WE'LL WRITE YOU A CHECK.
NO PLANNIN' AROUND PLAIN BAD LUCK.
LUCK HAD NOTHING TO DO WITH THIS, RECONDO.

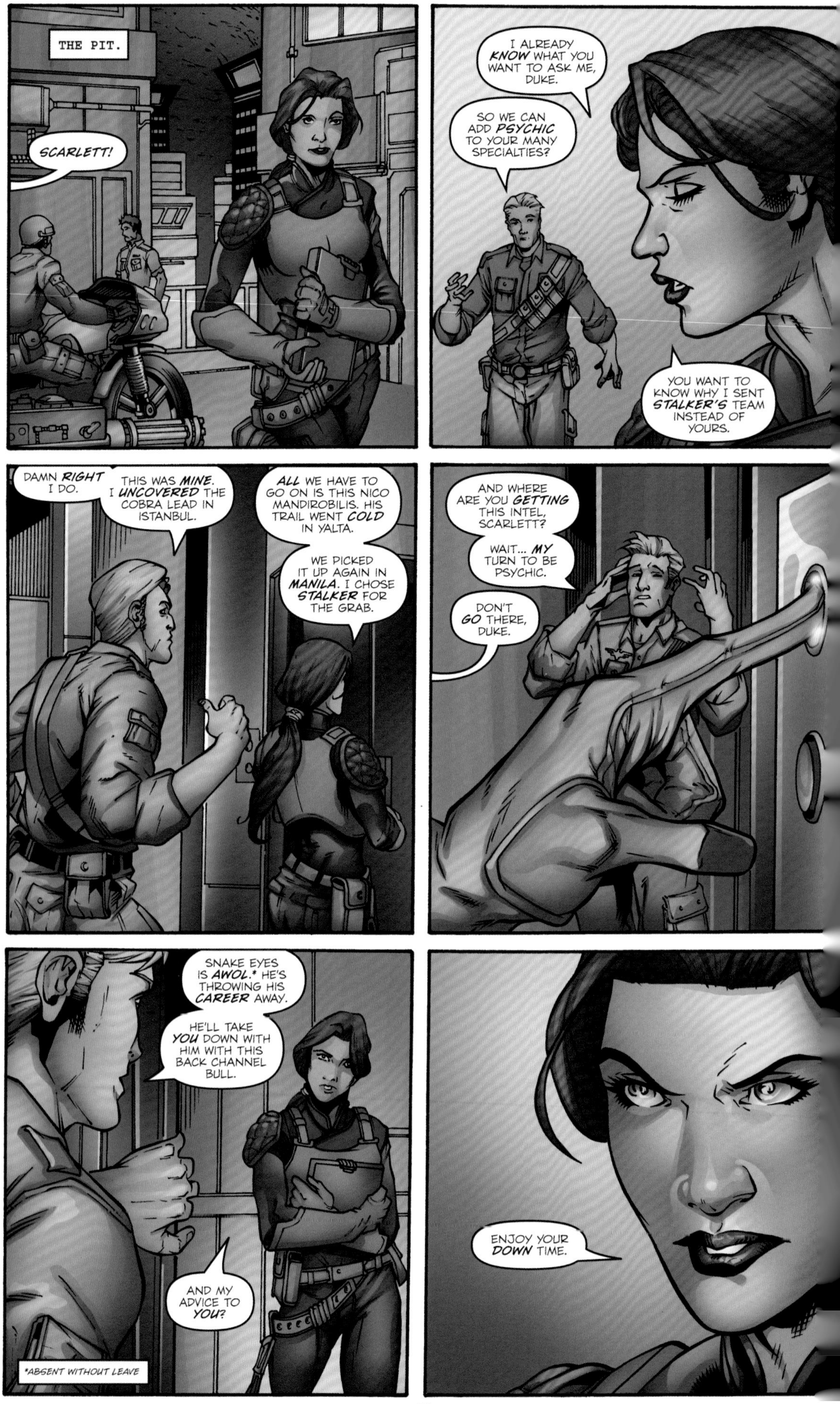
THE PIT.
SCARLETT!
I ALREADY KNOW WHAT YOU WANT TO ASK ME, DUKE.
SO WE CAN ADD PSYCHIC TO YOUR MANY SPECIALTIES?
YOU WANT TO KNOW WHY I SENT STALKER'S TEAM INSTEAD OF YOURS.
DAMN RIGHT I DO.
THIS WAS MINE. I UNCOVERED THE COBRA LEAD IN ISTANBUL.
ALL WE HAVE TO GO ON IS THIS NICO MANDIROBILIS. HIS TRAIL WENT COLD IN YALTA.
WE PICKED IT UP AGAIN IN MANILA. I CHOSE STALKER FOR THE GRAB.
AND WHERE ARE YOU GETTING THIS INTEL, SCARLETT?
WAIT... MY TURN TO BE PSYCHIC.
DON'T GO THERE, DUKE.
SNAKE EYES IS AWOL.* HE'S THROWING HIS CAREER AWAY.
HE'LL TAKE YOU DOWN WITH HIM WITH THIS BACK CHANNEL BULL.
AND MY ADVICE TO YOU?
*ABSENT WITHOUT LEAVE
ENJOY YOUR DOWN TIME.

I WAS COMING TO GET *YOU*.

SAVED YOU THE *TROUBLE*, LAB RAT. WHAT DO YOU *HAVE* FOR ME?

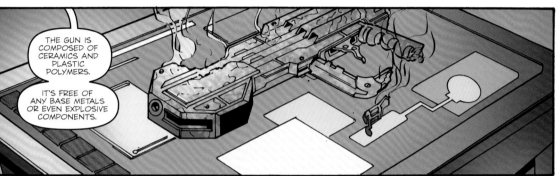

THE GUN IS COMPOSED OF CERAMICS AND PLASTIC POLYMERS.

IT'S FREE OF ANY BASE METALS OR EVEN EXPLOSIVE COMPONENTS.

OUR SCANS REVEAL THAT IT FIRED THIN, POLYMER NEEDLES ON A STREAM OF HIGHLY COMPRESSED AIR.

IT'S *DEADLY?*

SURE. *ENOUGH* NEEDLES FIRED AT SUB-BALLISTIC SPEED WOULD RUIN YOUR DAY. IT HAD THE CAPACITY FOR NEARLY A *HUNDRED* SHOTS.

WHAT'S THE *PURPOSE* OF A GUN LIKE THIS?

TOO MUCH *TROUBLE* JUST TO SLIP THROUGH AIRPORT SECURITY. PLENTY OF *EASIER* WAYS TO SMUGGLE A GUN ONTO A PLANE.

IF THERE'S ANOTHER REASON FOR MAKING A METAL-FREE PIECE—I DON'T KNOW IT.

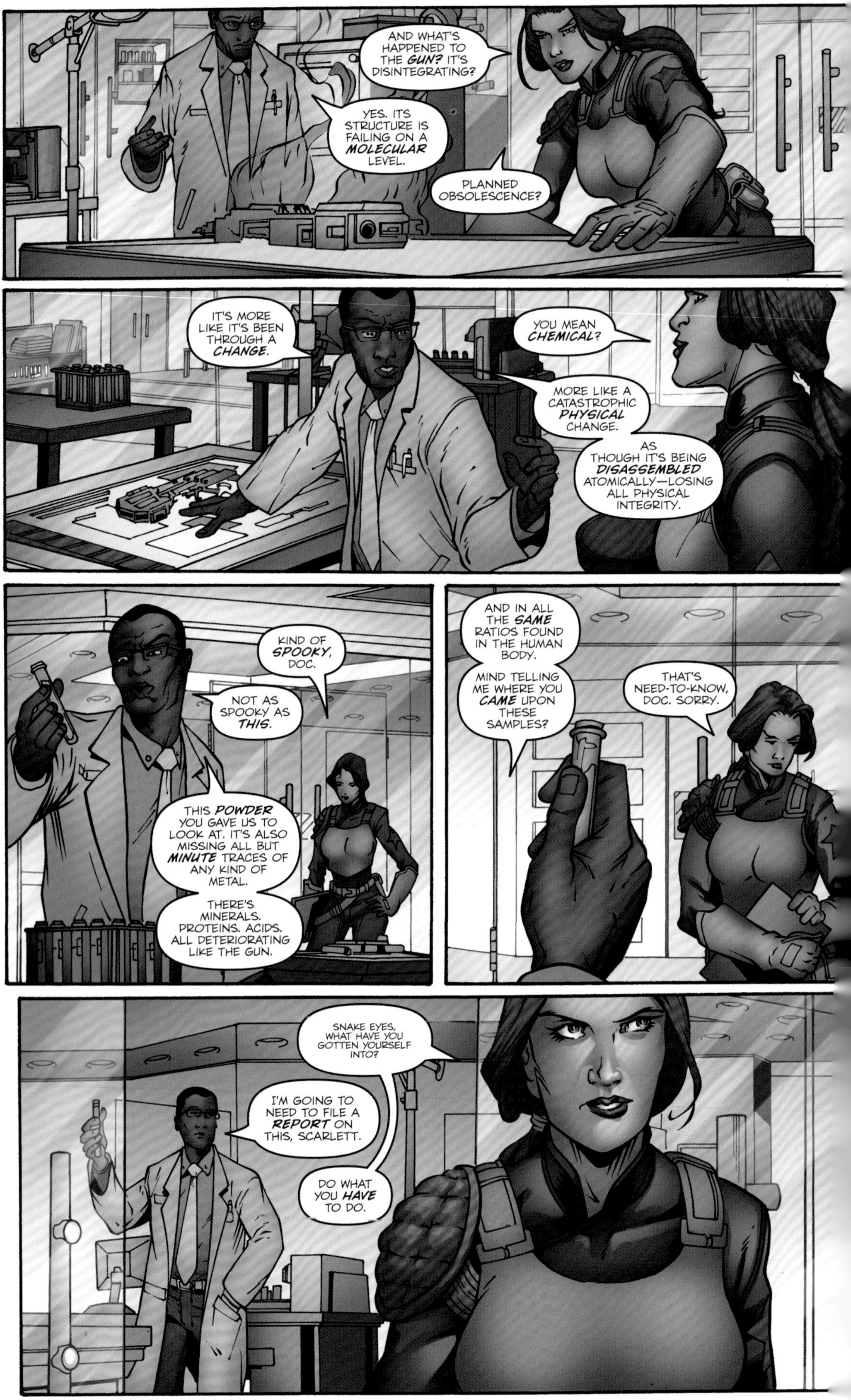
AND WHAT'S HAPPENED TO THE GUN? IT'S DISINTEGRATING?
YES. ITS STRUCTURE IS FAILING ON A MOLECULAR LEVEL.
PLANNED OBSOLESCENCE?
IT'S MORE LIKE IT'S BEEN THROUGH A CHANGE.
YOU MEAN CHEMICAL?
MORE LIKE A CATASTROPHIC PHYSICAL CHANGE.
AS THOUGH IT'S BEING DISASSEMBLED ATOMICALLY—LOSING ALL PHYSICAL INTEGRITY.
KIND OF SPOOKY, DOC.
NOT AS SPOOKY AS THIS.
THIS POWDER YOU GAVE US TO LOOK AT. IT'S ALSO MISSING ALL BUT MINUTE TRACES OF ANY KIND OF METAL.
THERE'S MINERALS. PROTEINS. ACIDS. ALL DETERIORATING LIKE THE GUN.
AND IN ALL THE SAME RATIOS FOUND IN THE HUMAN BODY.
MIND TELLING ME WHERE YOU CAME UPON THESE SAMPLES?
THAT'S NEED-TO-KNOW, DOC. SORRY.
SNAKE EYES, WHAT HAVE YOU GOTTEN YOURSELF INTO?
I'M GOING TO NEED TO FILE A REPORT ON THIS, SCARLETT.
DO WHAT YOU HAVE TO DO.

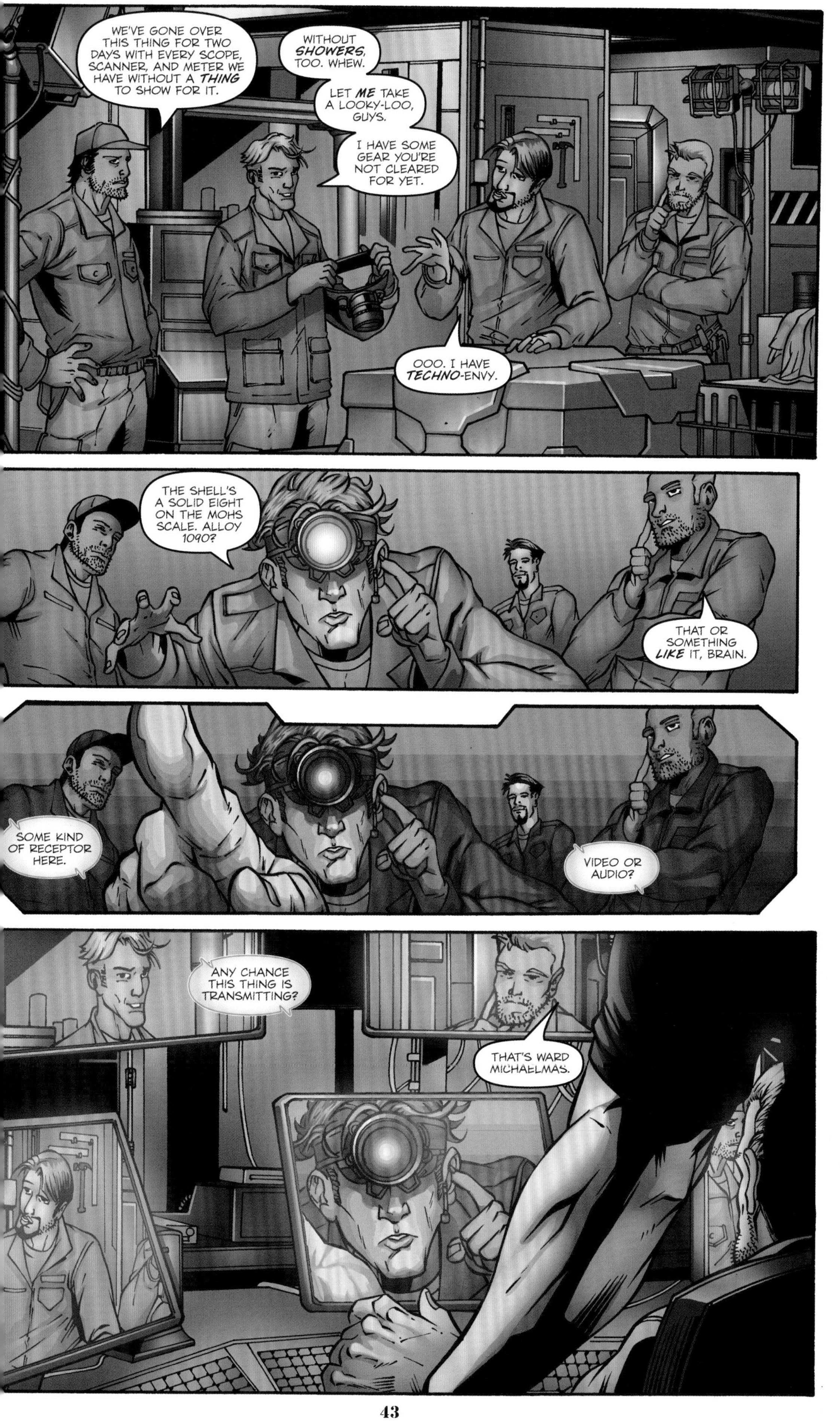
WE'VE GONE OVER THIS THING FOR TWO DAYS WITH EVERY SCOPE, SCANNER, AND METER WE HAVE WITHOUT A THING TO SHOW FOR IT.
WITHOUT SHOWERS, TOO. WHEW.
LET ME TAKE A LOOKY-LOO, GUYS.
I HAVE SOME GEAR YOU'RE NOT CLEARED FOR YET.
OOO. I HAVE TECHNO-ENVY.
THE SHELL'S A SOLID EIGHT ON THE MOHS SCALE. ALLOY 1090?
THAT OR SOMETHING LIKE IT, BRAIN.
SOME KIND OF RECEPTOR HERE.
VIDEO OR AUDIO?
ANY CHANCE THIS THING IS TRANSMITTING?
THAT'S WARD MICHAELMAS.

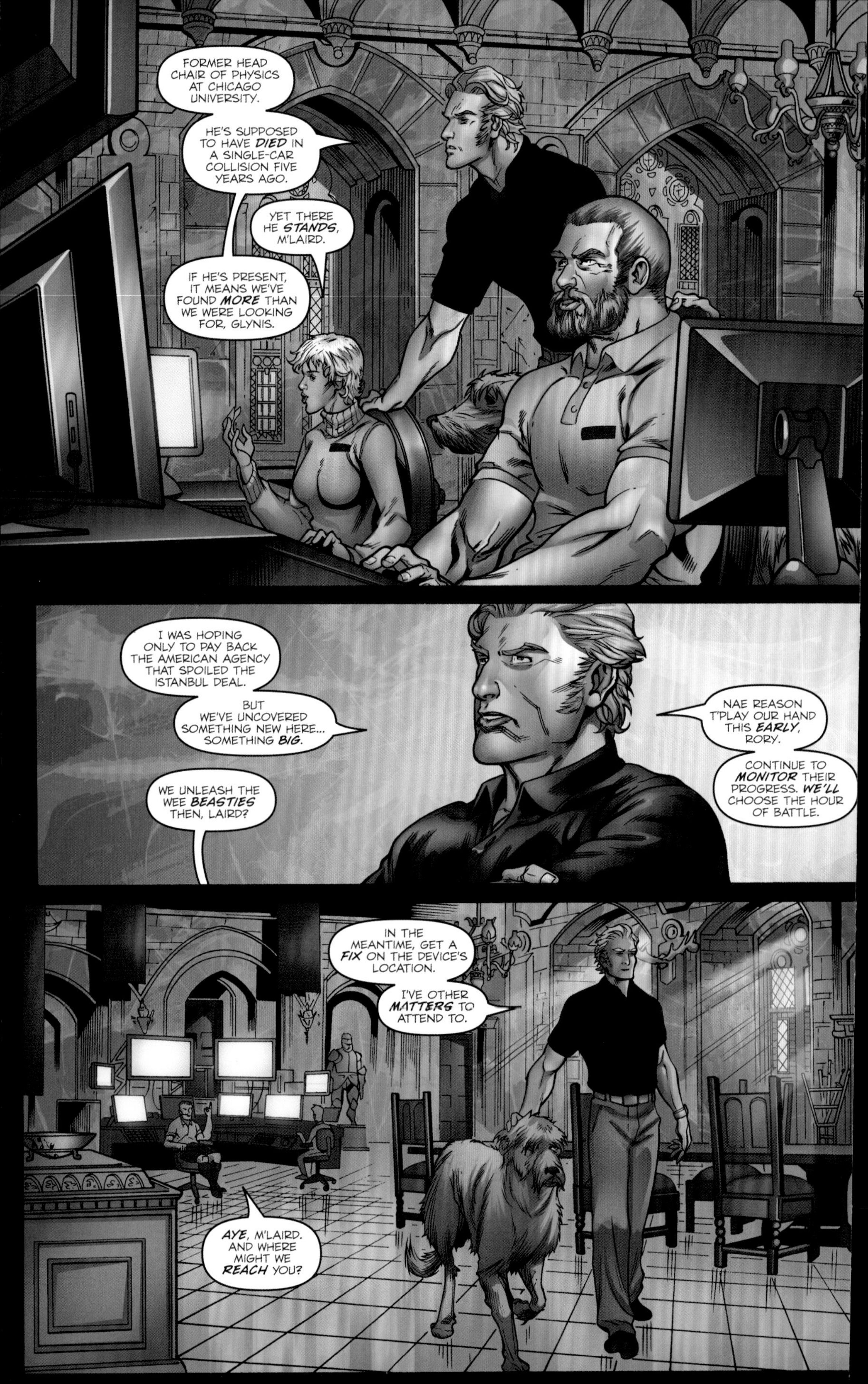
FORMER HEAD CHAIR OF PHYSICS AT CHICAGO UNIVERSITY.
HE'S SUPPOSED TO HAVE DIED IN A SINGLE-CAR COLLISION FIVE YEARS AGO.
YET THERE HE STANDS, M'LAIRD.
IF HE'S PRESENT, IT MEANS WE'VE FOUND MORE THAN WE WERE LOOKING FOR, GLYNIS.
I WAS HOPING ONLY TO PAY BACK THE AMERICAN AGENCY THAT SPOILED THE ISTANBUL DEAL.
BUT WE'VE UNCOVERED SOMETHING NEW HERE... SOMETHING BIG.
WE UNLEASH THE WEE BEASTIES THEN, LAIRD?
NAE REASON T'PLAY OUR HAND THIS EARLY, RORY.
CONTINUE TO MONITOR THEIR PROGRESS. WE'LL CHOOSE THE HOUR OF BATTLE.
IN THE MEANTIME, GET A FIX ON THE DEVICE'S LOCATION.
I'VE OTHER MATTERS TO ATTEND TO.
AYE, M'LAIRD. AND WHERE MIGHT WE REACH YOU?

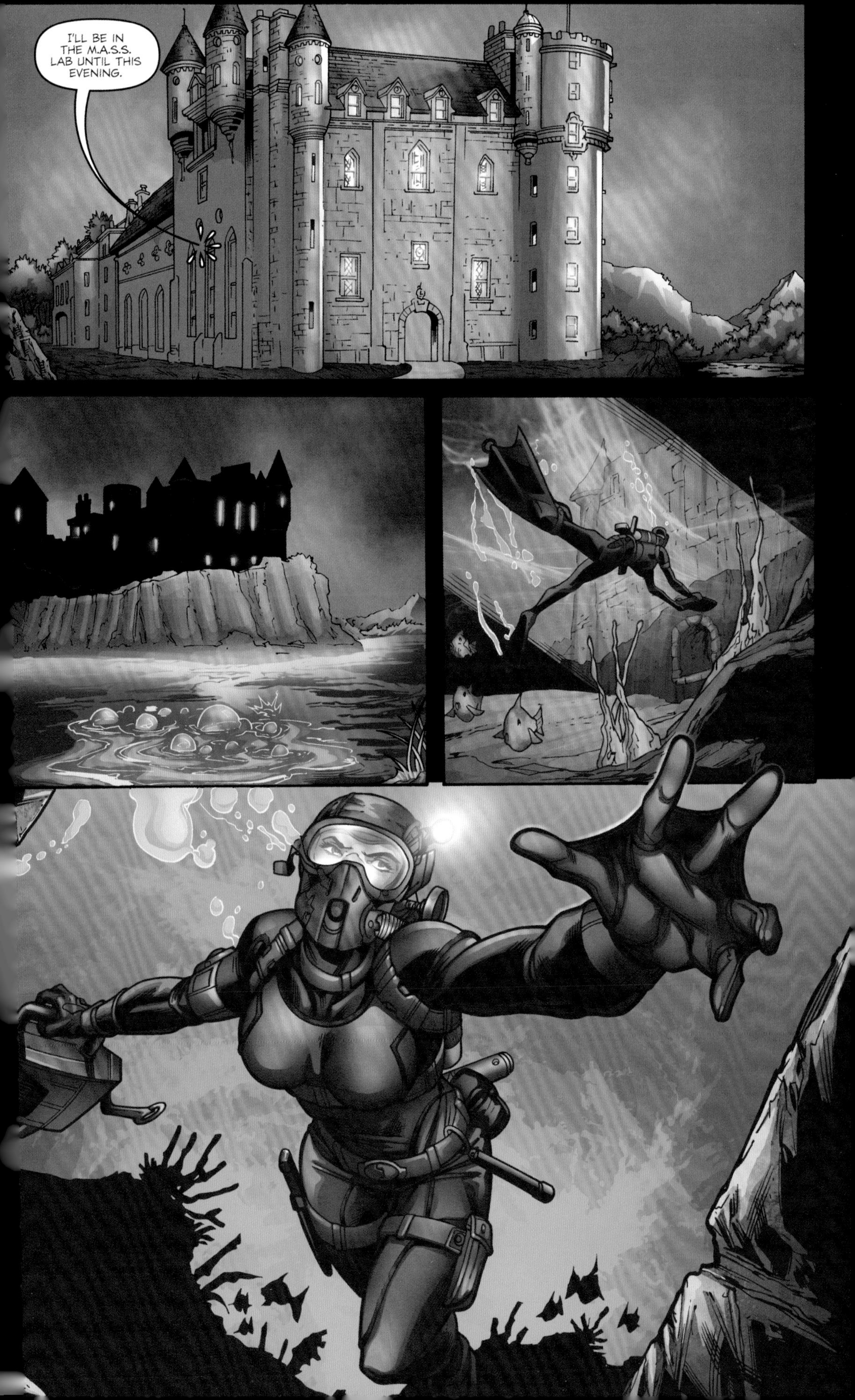
I'LL BE IN THE M.A.S.S. LAB UNTIL THIS EVENING.

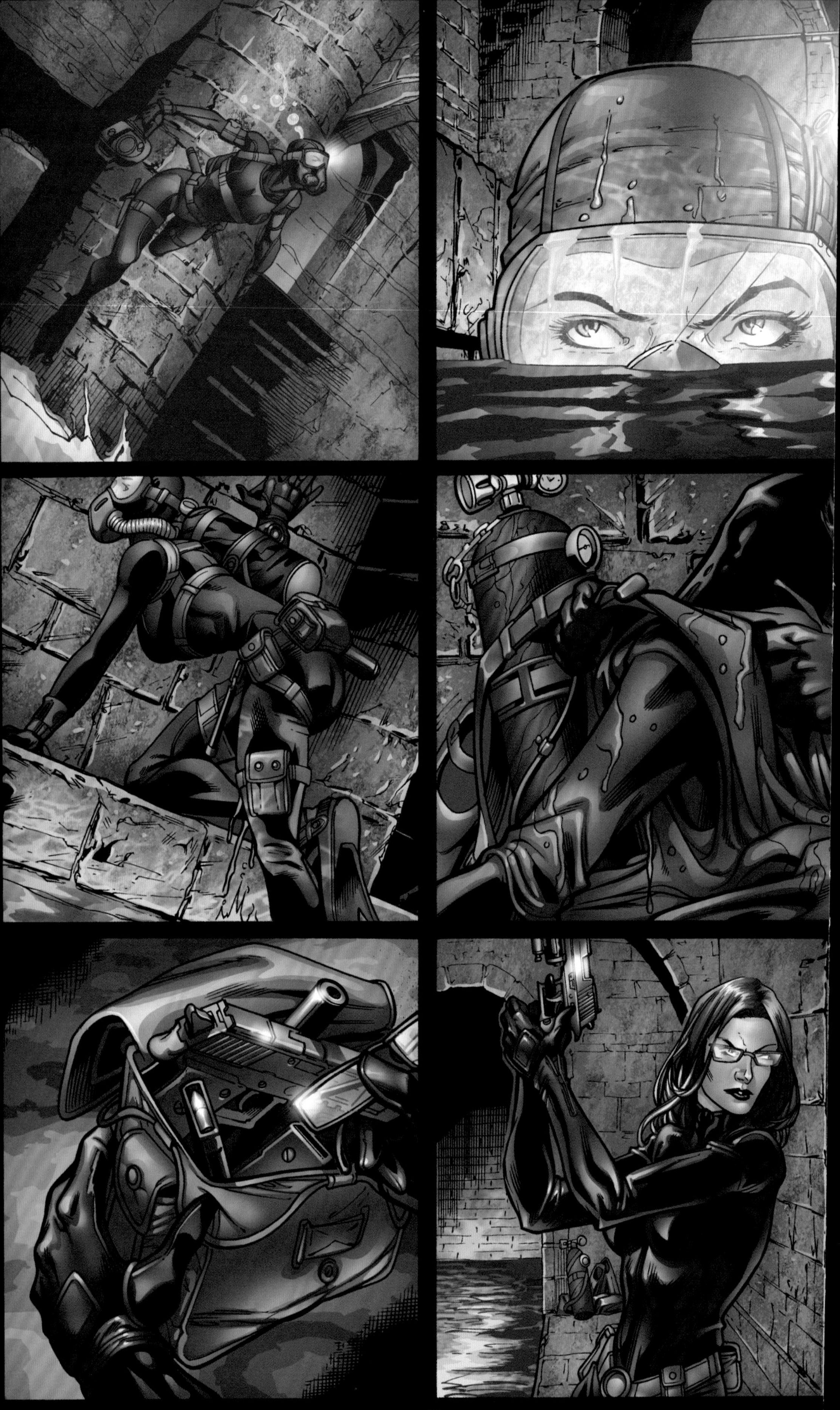

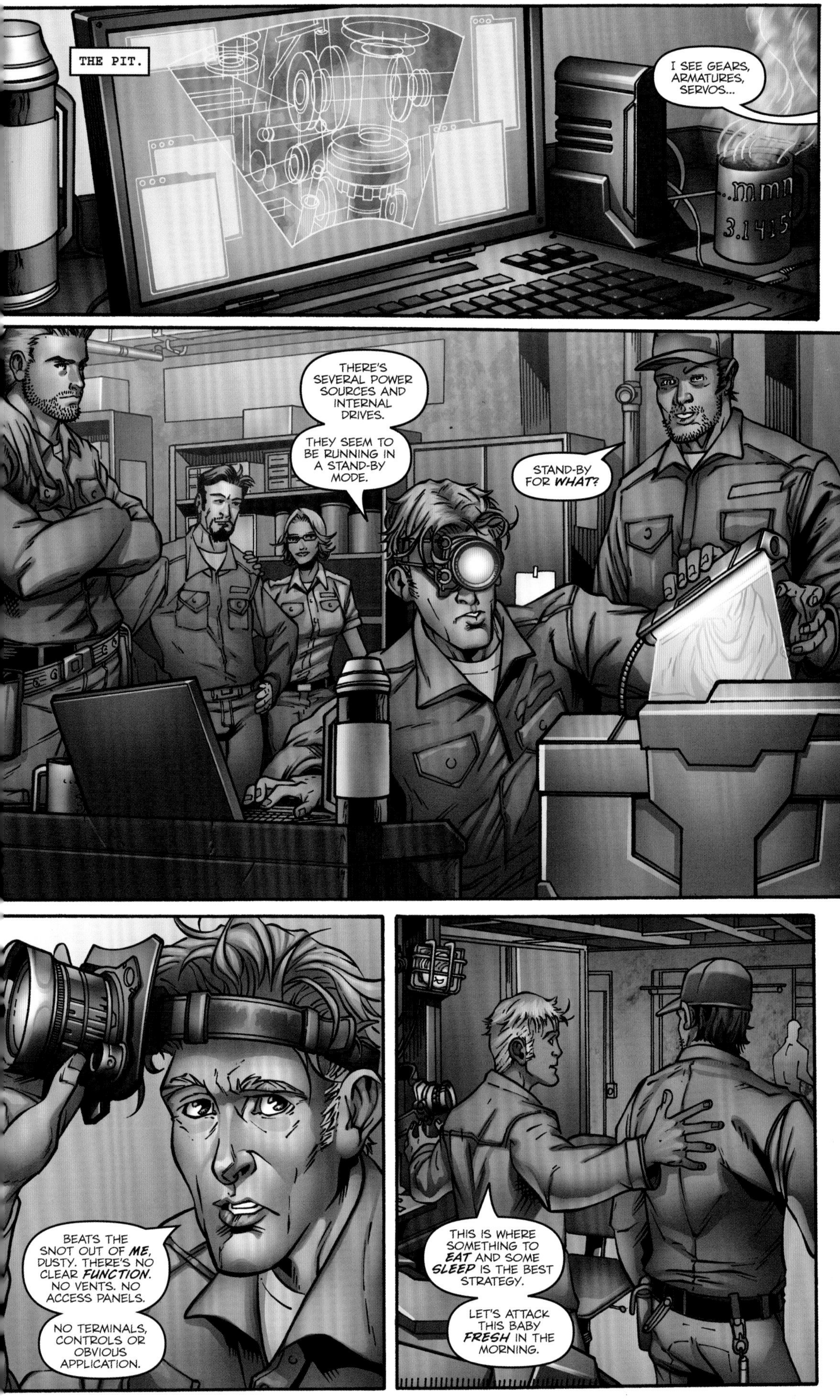
THE PIT.
I SEE GEARS, ARMATURES, SERVOS...
...mmn
3.1415
THERE'S SEVERAL POWER SOURCES AND INTERNAL DRIVES.
THEY SEEM TO BE RUNNING IN A STAND-BY MODE.
STAND-BY FOR *WHAT*?
BEATS THE SNOT OUT OF *ME*, DUSTY. THERE'S NO CLEAR *FUNCTION*. NO VENTS. NO ACCESS PANELS.
NO TERMINALS, CONTROLS OR OBVIOUS APPLICATION.
THIS IS WHERE SOMETHING TO *EAT* AND SOME *SLEEP* IS THE BEST STRATEGY.
LET'S ATTACK THIS BABY *FRESH* IN THE MORNING.

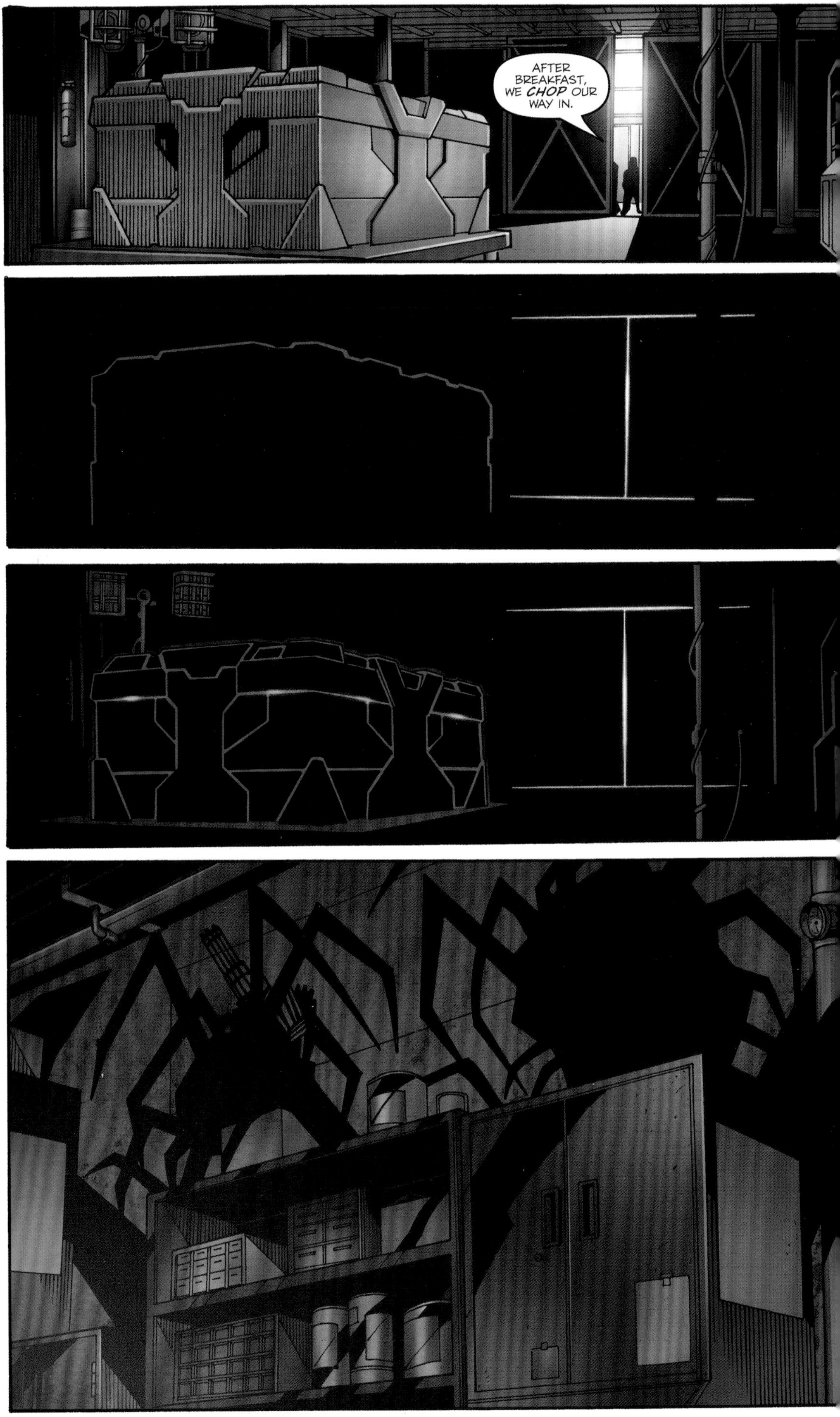
AFTER BREAKFAST, WE CHOP OUR WAY IN.

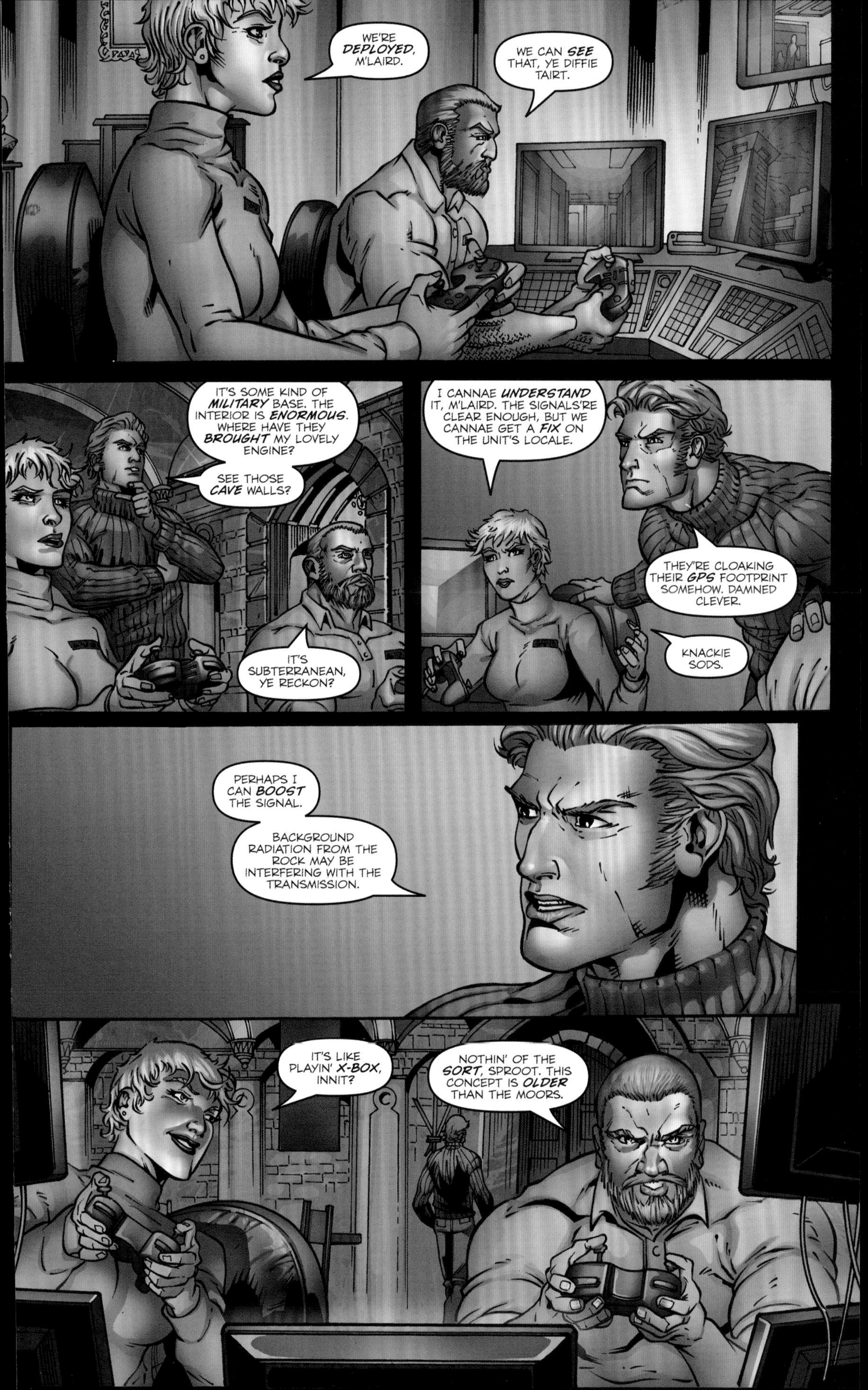
WE'RE DEPLOYED, M'LAIRD.
WE CAN SEE THAT, YE DIFFIE TAIRT.
IT'S SOME KIND OF MILITARY BASE. THE INTERIOR IS ENORMOUS. WHERE HAVE THEY BROUGHT MY LOVELY ENGINE?
SEE THOSE CAVE WALLS?
IT'S SUBTERRANEAN, YE RECKON?
I CANNAE UNDERSTAND IT, M'LAIRD. THE SIGNALS'RE CLEAR ENOUGH, BUT WE CANNAE GET A FIX ON THE UNIT'S LOCALE.
THEY'RE CLOAKING THEIR GPS FOOTPRINT SOMEHOW. DAMNED CLEVER.
KNACKIE SODS.
PERHAPS I CAN BOOST THE SIGNAL.
BACKGROUND RADIATION FROM THE ROCK MAY BE INTERFERING WITH THE TRANSMISSION.
IT'S LIKE PLAYIN' X-BOX, INNIT?
NOTHIN' OF THE SORT, SPROOT. THIS CONCEPT IS OLDER THAN THE MOORS.

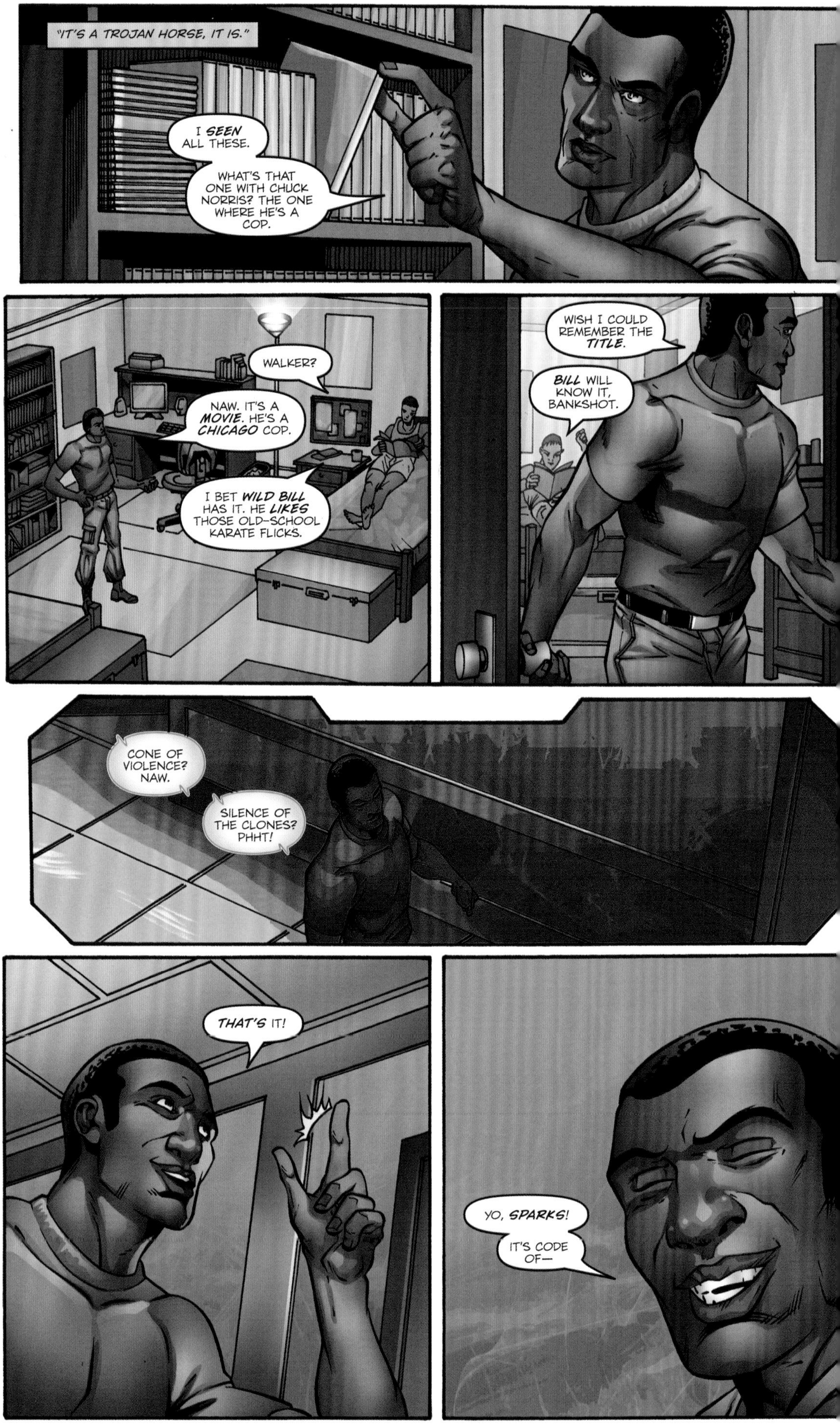
"IT'S A TROJAN HORSE, IT IS."
I SEEN ALL THESE.
WHAT'S THAT ONE WITH CHUCK NORRIS? THE ONE WHERE HE'S A COP.
WALKER?
NAW. IT'S A MOVIE. HE'S A CHICAGO COP.
I BET WILD BILL HAS IT. HE LIKES THOSE OLD-SCHOOL KARATE FLICKS.
WISH I COULD REMEMBER THE TITLE.
BILL WILL KNOW IT, BANKSHOT.
CONE OF VIOLENCE? NAW.
SILENCE OF THE CLONES? PHHT!
THAT'S IT!
YO, SPARKS!
IT'S CODE OF—

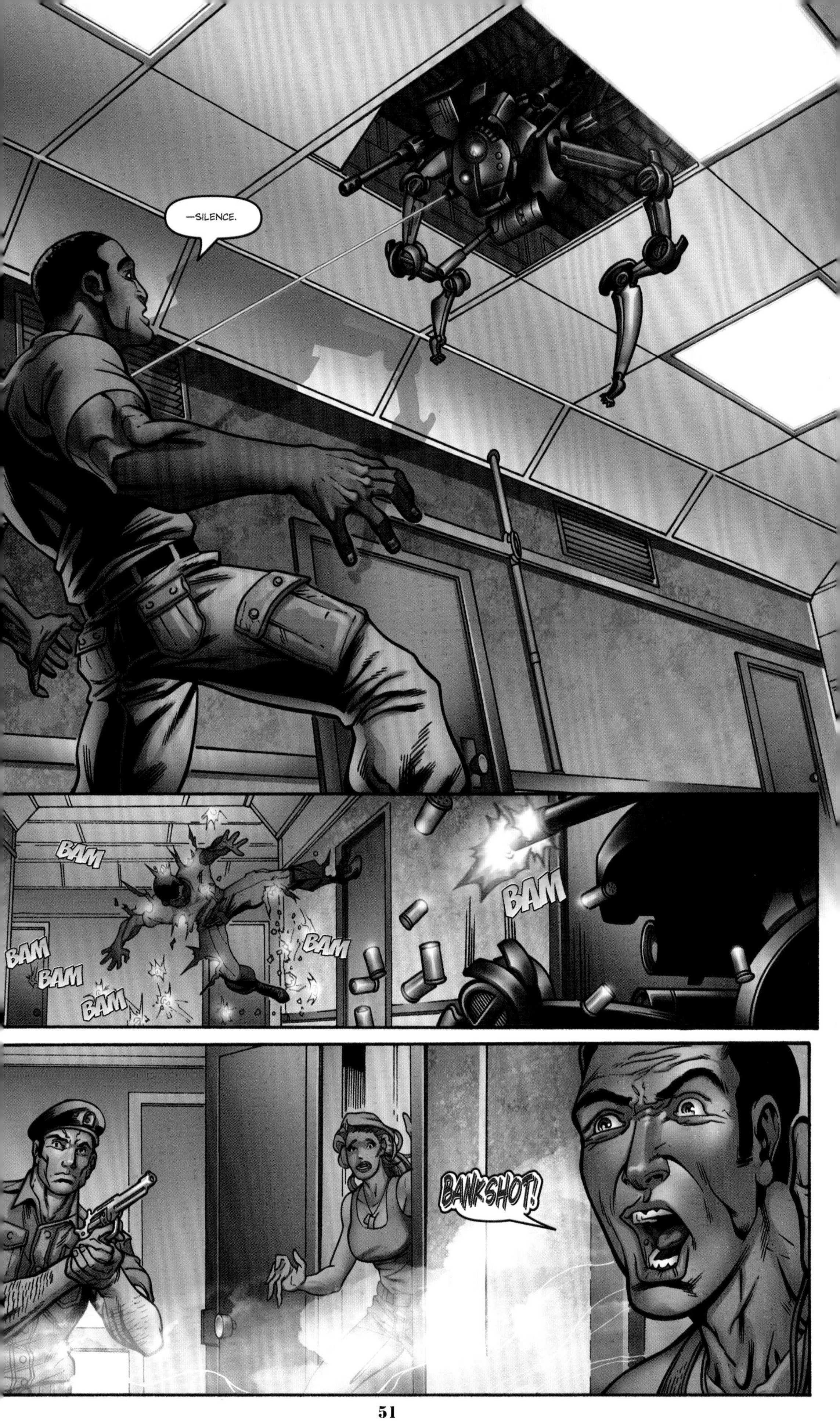
—SILENCE.
BAM
BAM
BAM
BAM
BAM
BAM
BANKSHOT!

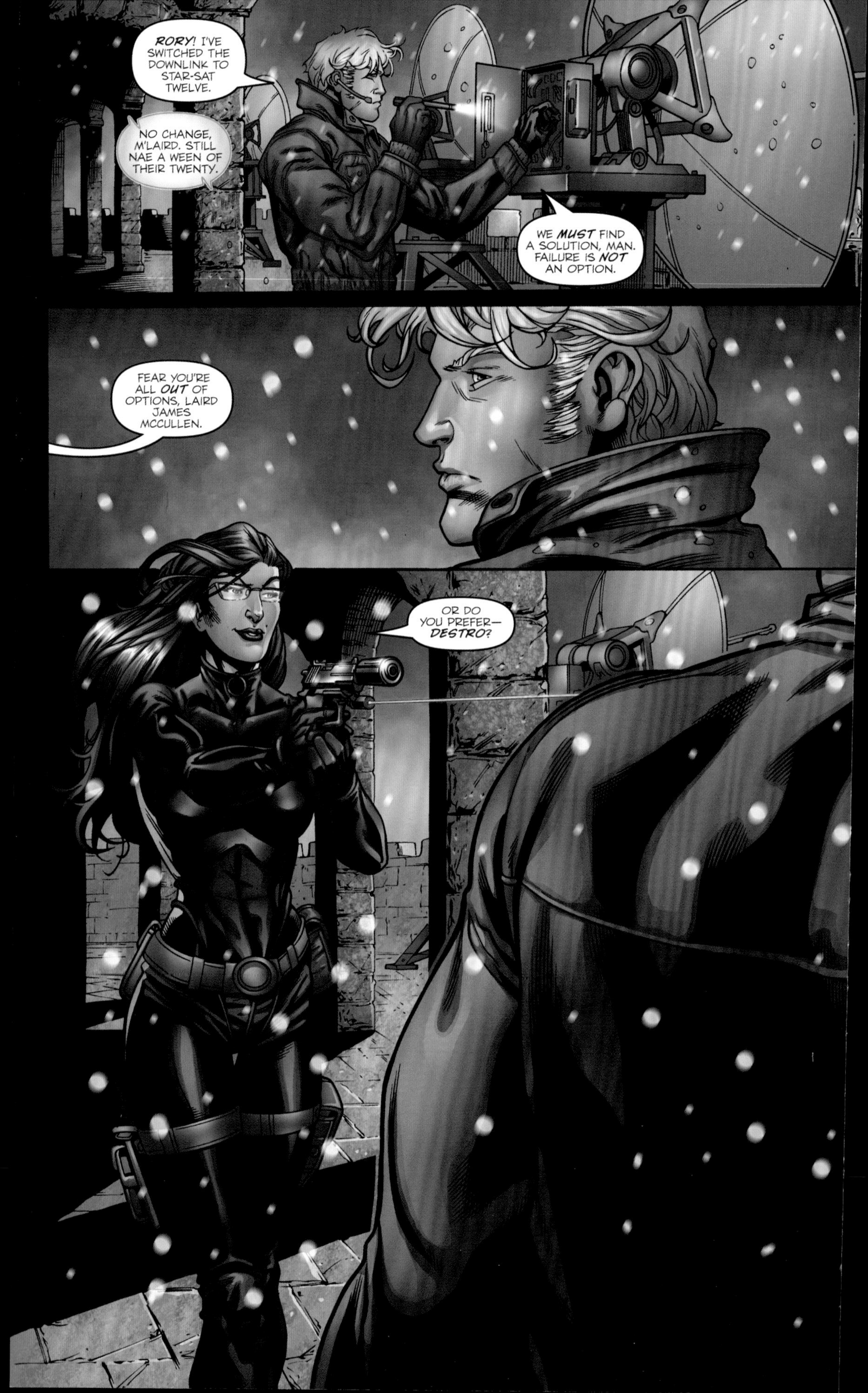
RORY! I'VE SWITCHED THE DOWNLINK TO STAR-SAT TWELVE.
NO CHANGE, M'LAIRD. STILL NAE A WEEN OF THEIR TWENTY.
WE MUST FIND A SOLUTION, MAN. FAILURE IS NOT AN OPTION.
FEAR YOU'RE ALL OUT OF OPTIONS, LAIRD JAMES MCCULLEN.
OR DO YOU PREFER— DESTRO?

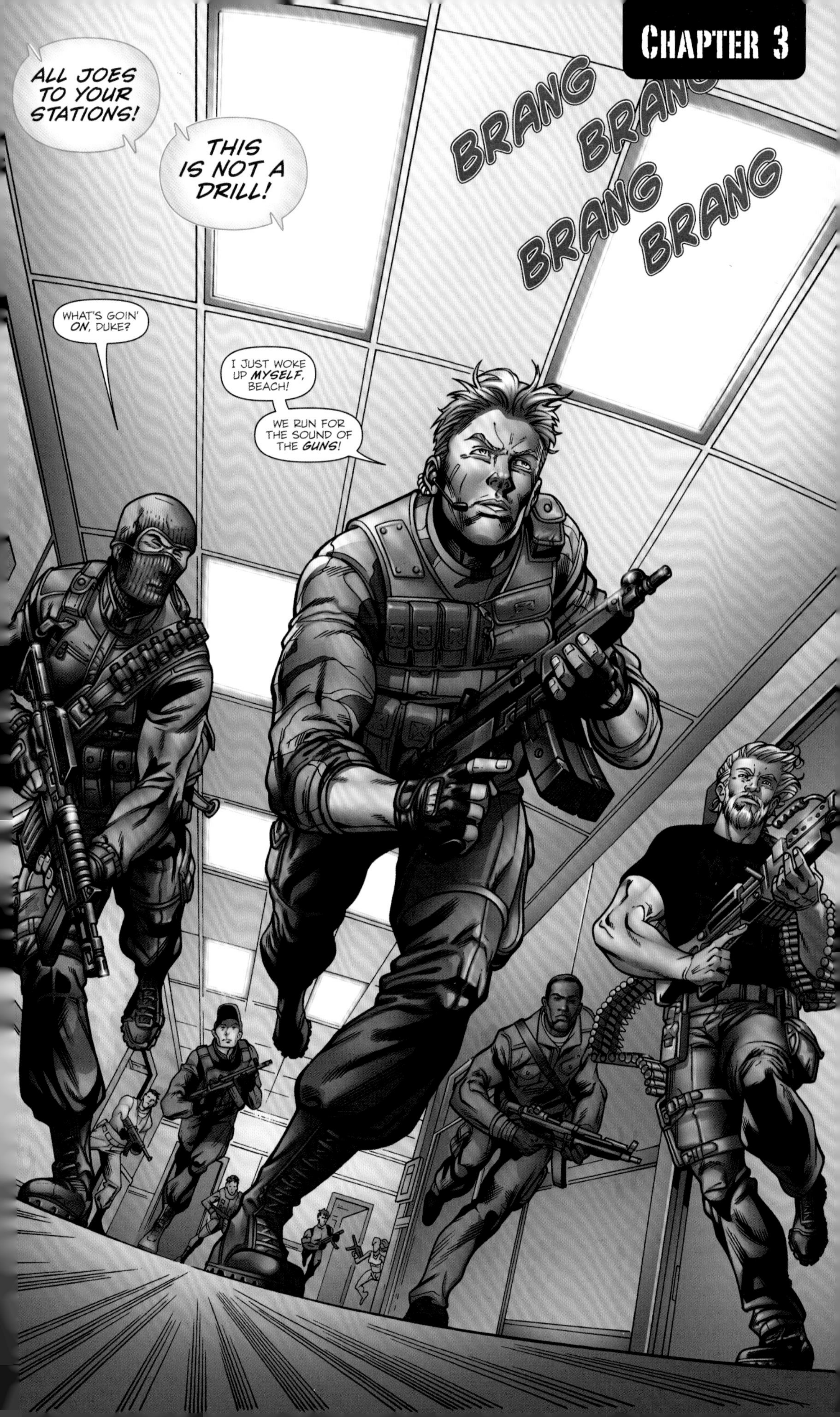
CHAPTER 3
ALL JOES TO YOUR STATIONS!
THIS IS NOT A DRILL!
BRANG BRANG BRANG BRANG
WHAT'S GOIN' ON, DUKE?
I JUST WOKE UP MYSELF, BEACH!
WE RUN FOR THE SOUND OF THE GUNS!

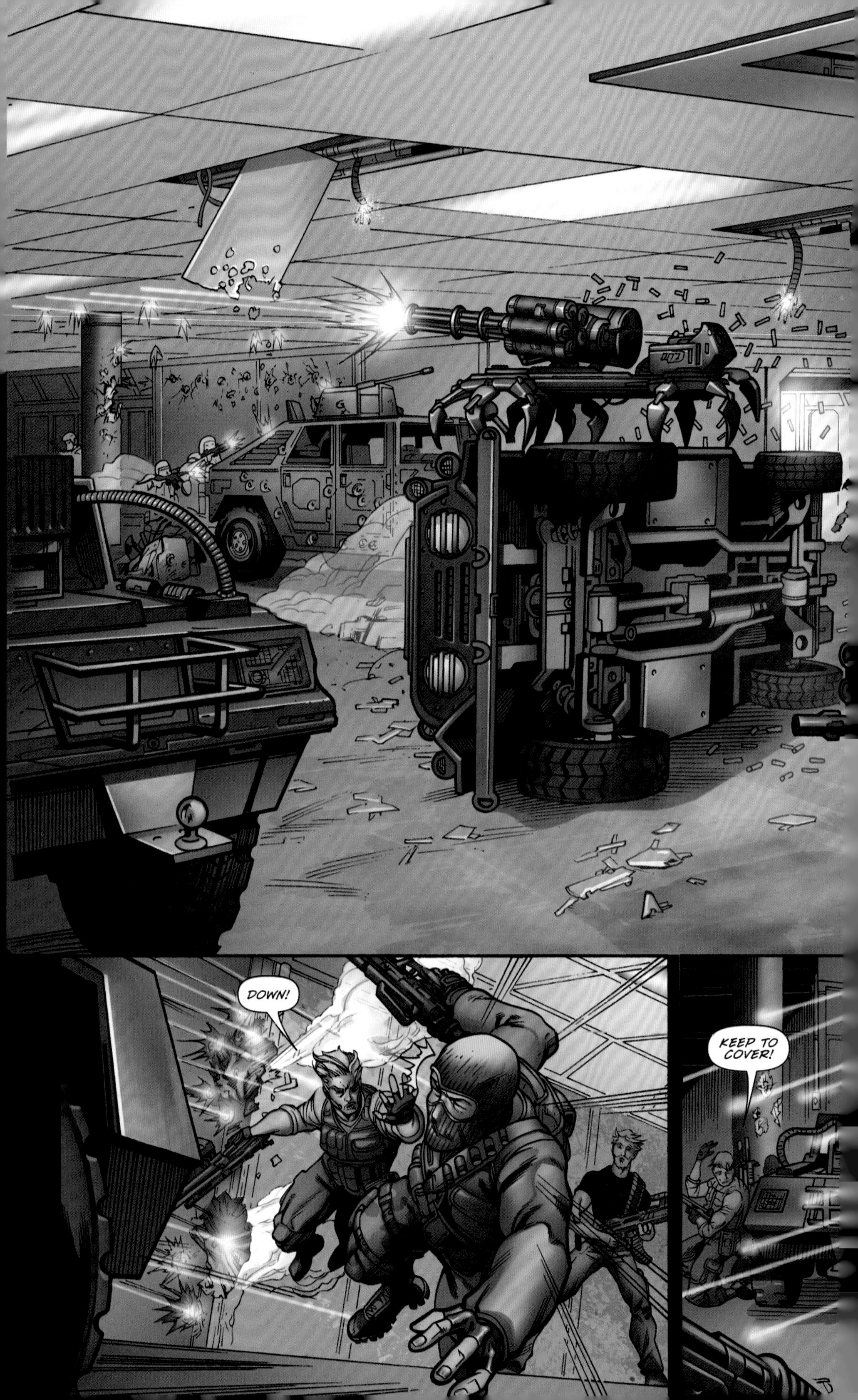
DOWN!
KEEP TO COVER!

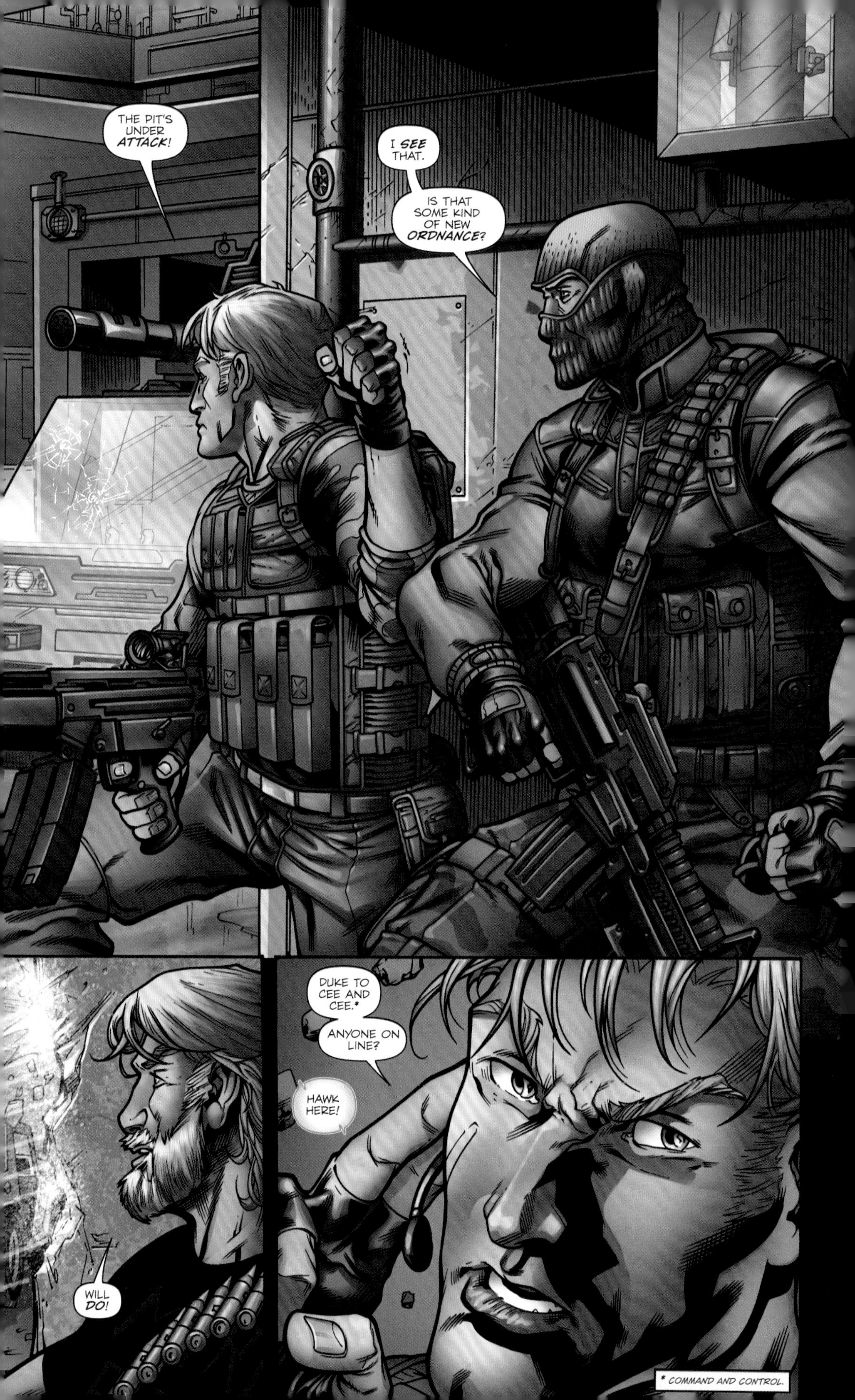
THE PIT'S UNDER ATTACK!
I SEE THAT.
IS THAT SOME KIND OF NEW ORDNANCE?
DUKE TO CEE AND CEE.*
ANYONE ON LINE?
HAWK HERE!
WILL DO!
* COMMAND AND CONTROL.

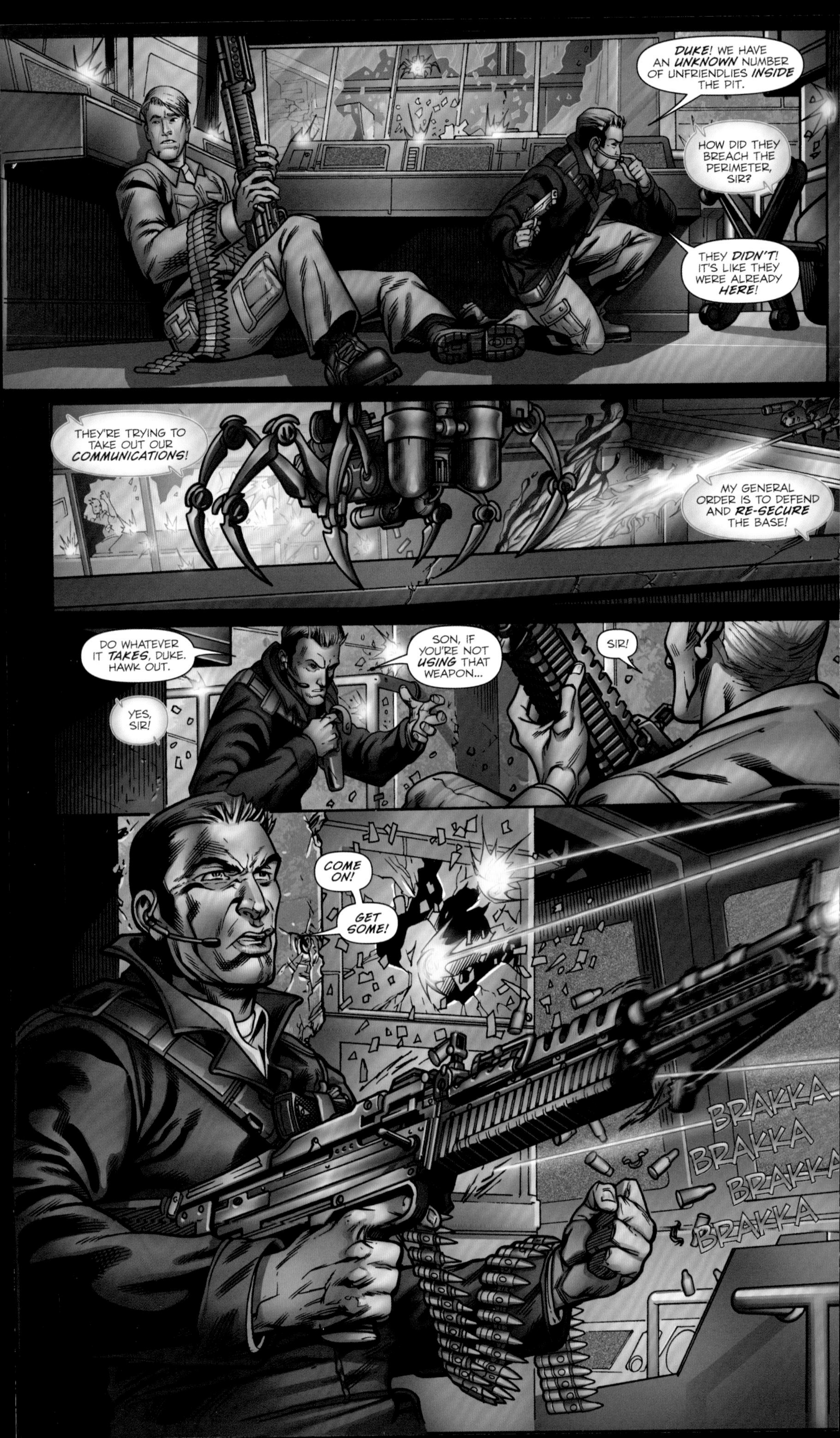
DUKE! WE HAVE AN UNKNOWN NUMBER OF UNFRIENDLIES INSIDE THE PIT.
HOW DID THEY BREACH THE PERIMETER, SIR?
THEY DIDN'T! IT'S LIKE THEY WERE ALREADY HERE!
THEY'RE TRYING TO TAKE OUT OUR COMMUNICATIONS!
MY GENERAL ORDER IS TO DEFEND AND RE-SECURE THE BASE!
DO WHATEVER IT TAKES, DUKE. HAWK OUT.
YES, SIR!
SON, IF YOU'RE NOT USING THAT WEAPON...
SIR!
COME ON!
GET SOME!
BRAKKA BRAKKA BRAKKA BRAKKA

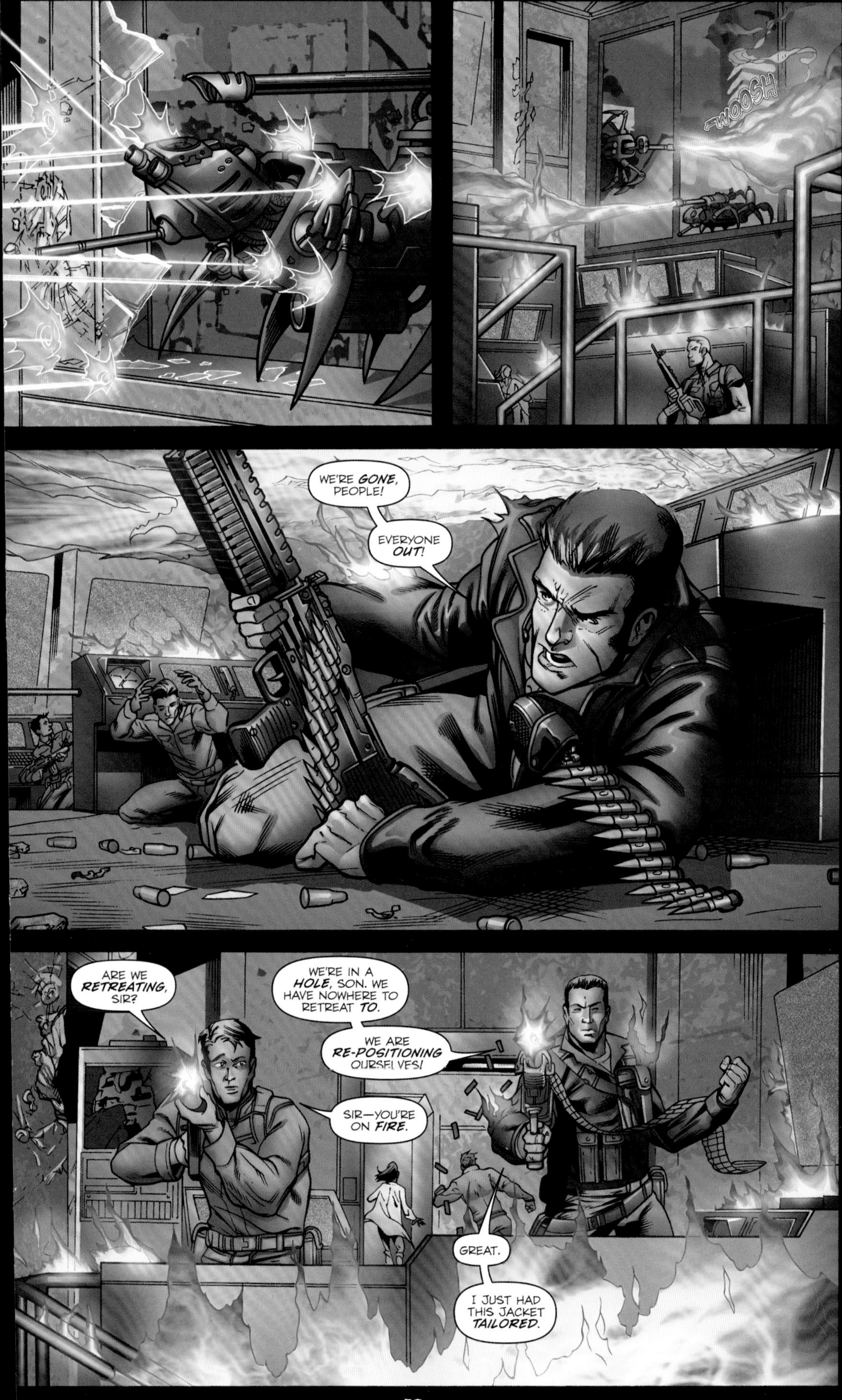
WOOSH
WE'RE GONE, PEOPLE!
EVERYONE OUT!
ARE WE RETREATING, SIR?
WE'RE IN A HOLE, SON. WE HAVE NOWHERE TO RETREAT TO.
WE ARE RE-POSITIONING OURSELVES!
SIR—YOU'RE ON FIRE.
GREAT.
I JUST HAD THIS JACKET TAILORED.

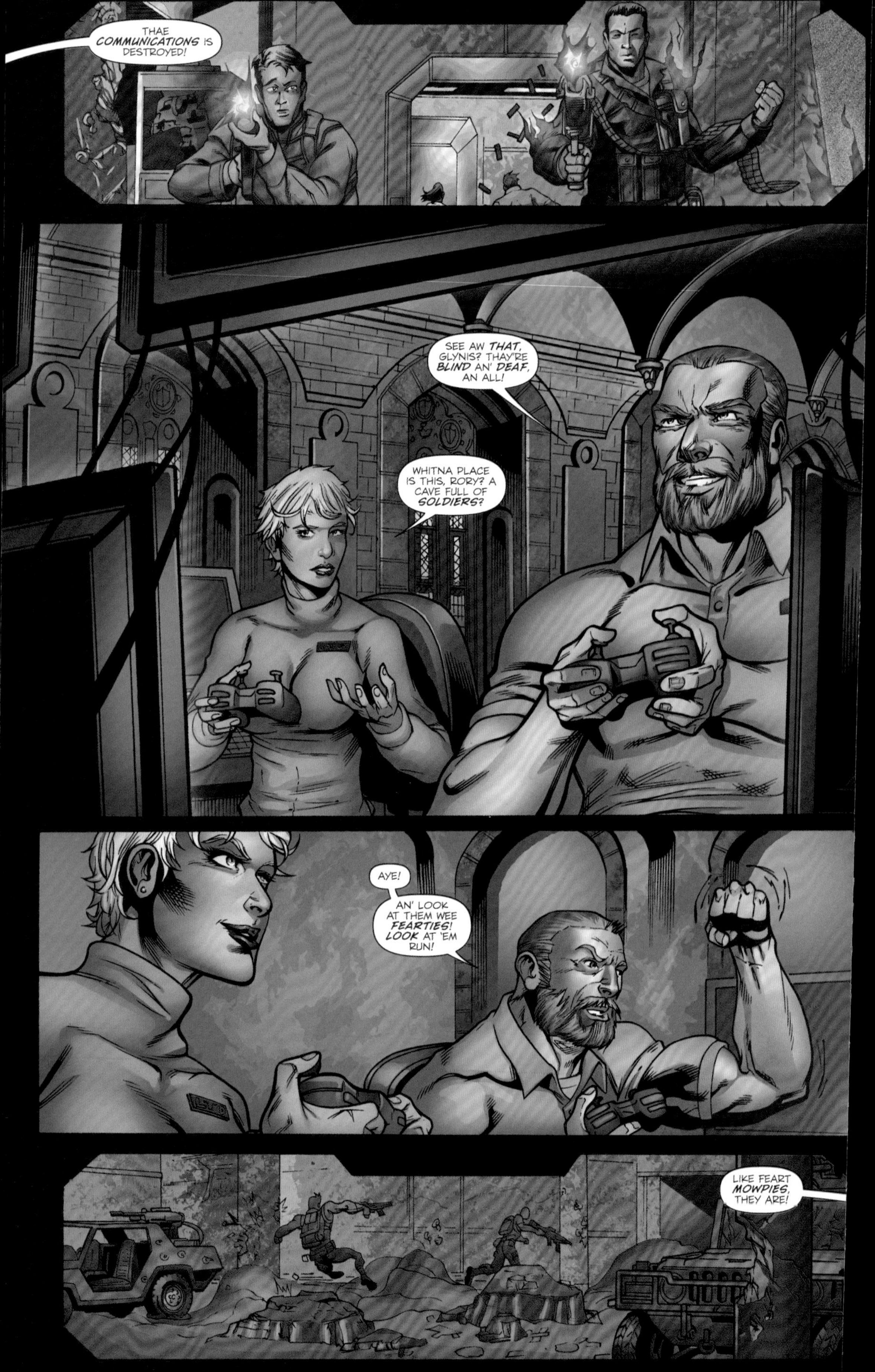
THAE COMMUNICATIONS IS DESTROYED!
SEE AW THAT, GLYNIS? THAY'RE BLIND AN' DEAF, AN ALL!
WHITNA PLACE IS THIS, RORY? A CAVE FULL OF SOLDIERS?
AYE!
AN' LOOK AT THEM WEE FEARTIES! LOOK AT 'EM RUN!
LIKE FEART MOWPIES, THEY ARE!

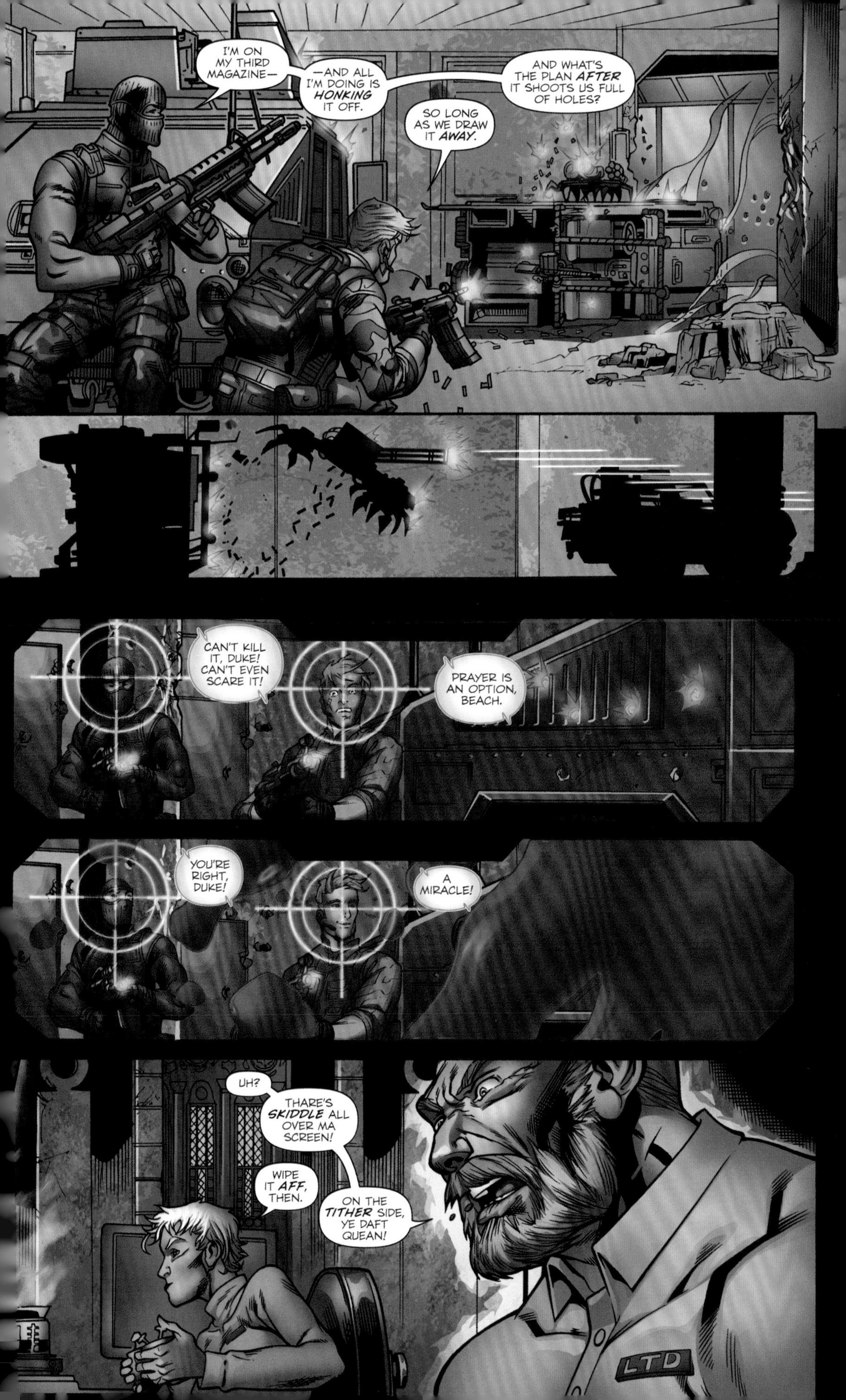
I'M ON MY THIRD MAGAZINE—
—AND ALL I'M DOING IS HONKING IT OFF.
AND WHAT'S THE PLAN AFTER IT SHOOTS US FULL OF HOLES?
SO LONG AS WE DRAW IT AWAY.
CAN'T KILL IT, DUKE! CAN'T EVEN SCARE IT!
PRAYER IS AN OPTION, BEACH.
YOU'RE RIGHT, DUKE!
A MIRACLE!
UH?
THARE'S SKIDDLE ALL OVER MA SCREEN!
WIPE IT AFF, THEN.
ON THE TITHER SIDE, YE DAFT QUEAN!
LTD

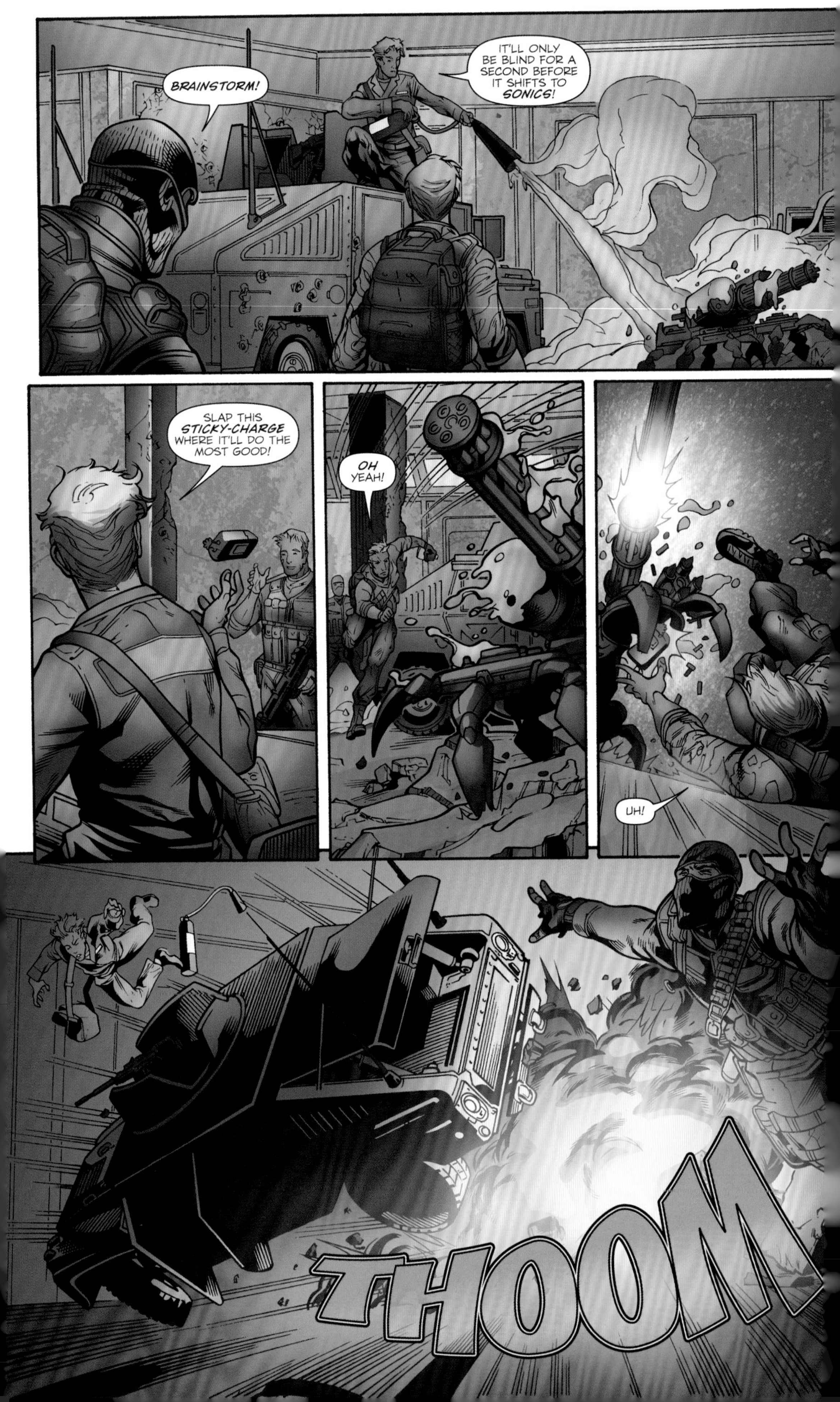
BRAINSTORM!
IT'LL ONLY BE BLIND FOR A SECOND BEFORE IT SHIFTS TO SONICS!
SLAP THIS STICKY-CHARGE WHERE IT'LL DO THE MOST GOOD!
OH YEAH!
UH!
THOOM

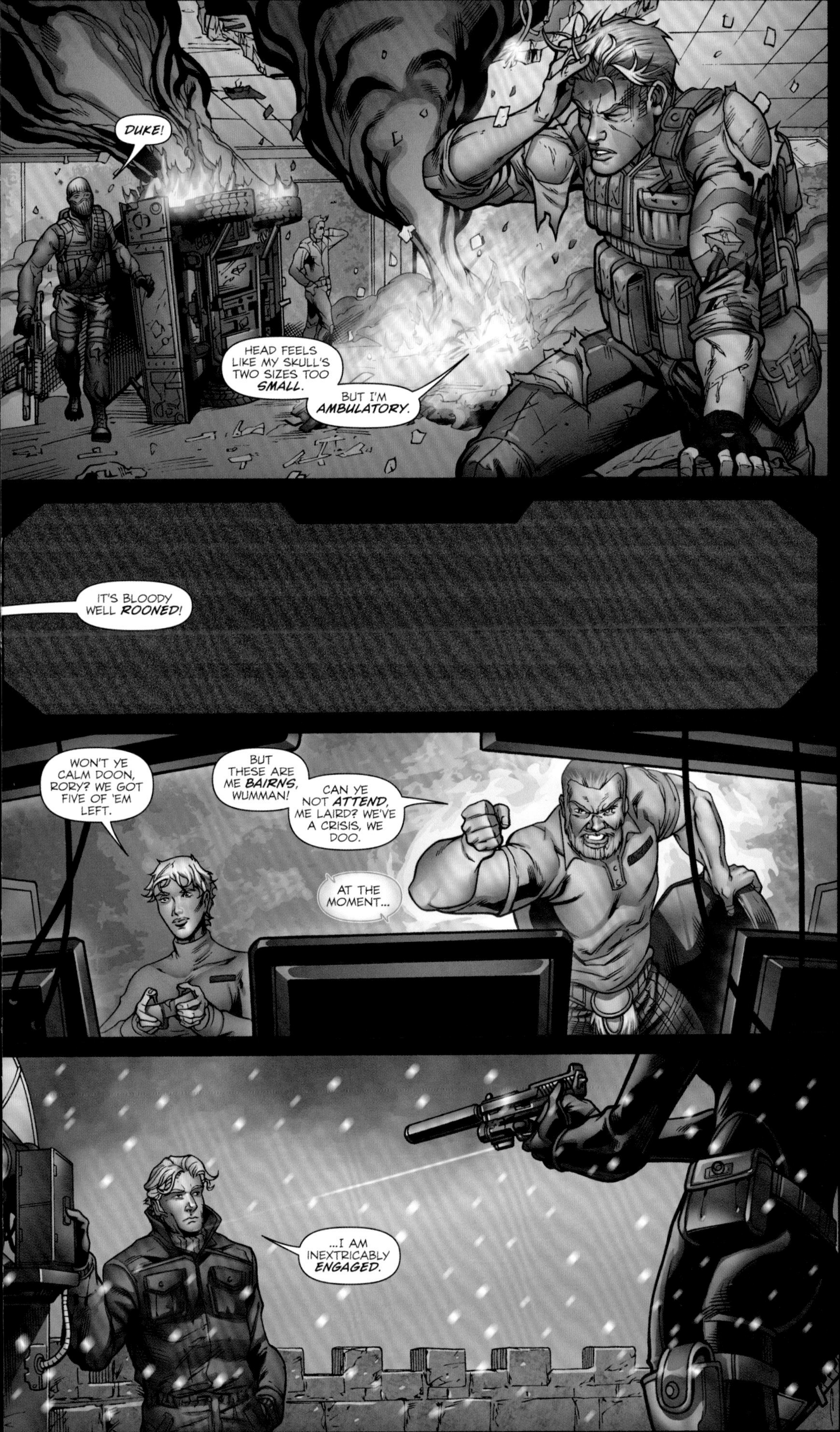
DUKE!
HEAD FEELS LIKE MY SKULL'S TWO SIZES TOO SMALL.
BUT I'M AMBULATORY.
IT'S BLOODY WELL ROONED!
WON'T YE CALM DOON, RORY? WE GOT FIVE OF 'EM LEFT.
BUT THESE ARE ME BAIRNS, WUMMAN!
CAN YE NOT ATTEND, ME LAIRD? WE'VE A CRISIS, WE DOO.
AT THE MOMENT...
...I AM INEXTRICABLY ENGAGED.

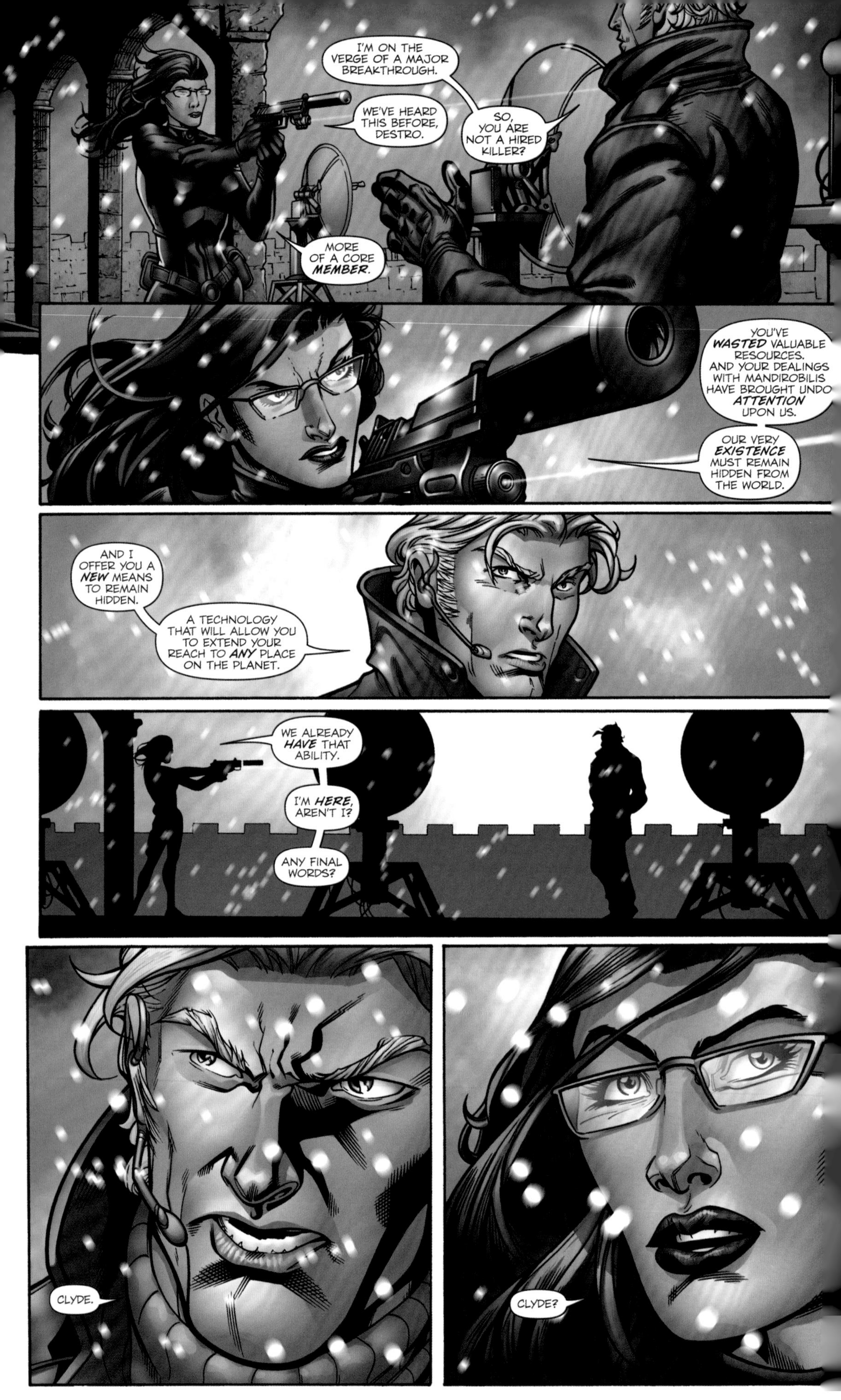
I'M ON THE VERGE OF A MAJOR BREAKTHROUGH.
WE'VE HEARD THIS BEFORE, DESTRO.
SO, YOU ARE NOT A HIRED KILLER?
MORE OF A CORE MEMBER.
YOU'VE WASTED VALUABLE RESOURCES. AND YOUR DEALINGS WITH MANDIROBILIS HAVE BROUGHT UNDO ATTENTION UPON US.
OUR VERY EXISTENCE MUST REMAIN HIDDEN FROM THE WORLD.
AND I OFFER YOU A NEW MEANS TO REMAIN HIDDEN.
A TECHNOLOGY THAT WILL ALLOW YOU TO EXTEND YOUR REACH TO ANY PLACE ON THE PLANET.
WE ALREADY HAVE THAT ABILITY.
I'M HERE, AREN'T I?
ANY FINAL WORDS?
CLYDE.
CLYDE?

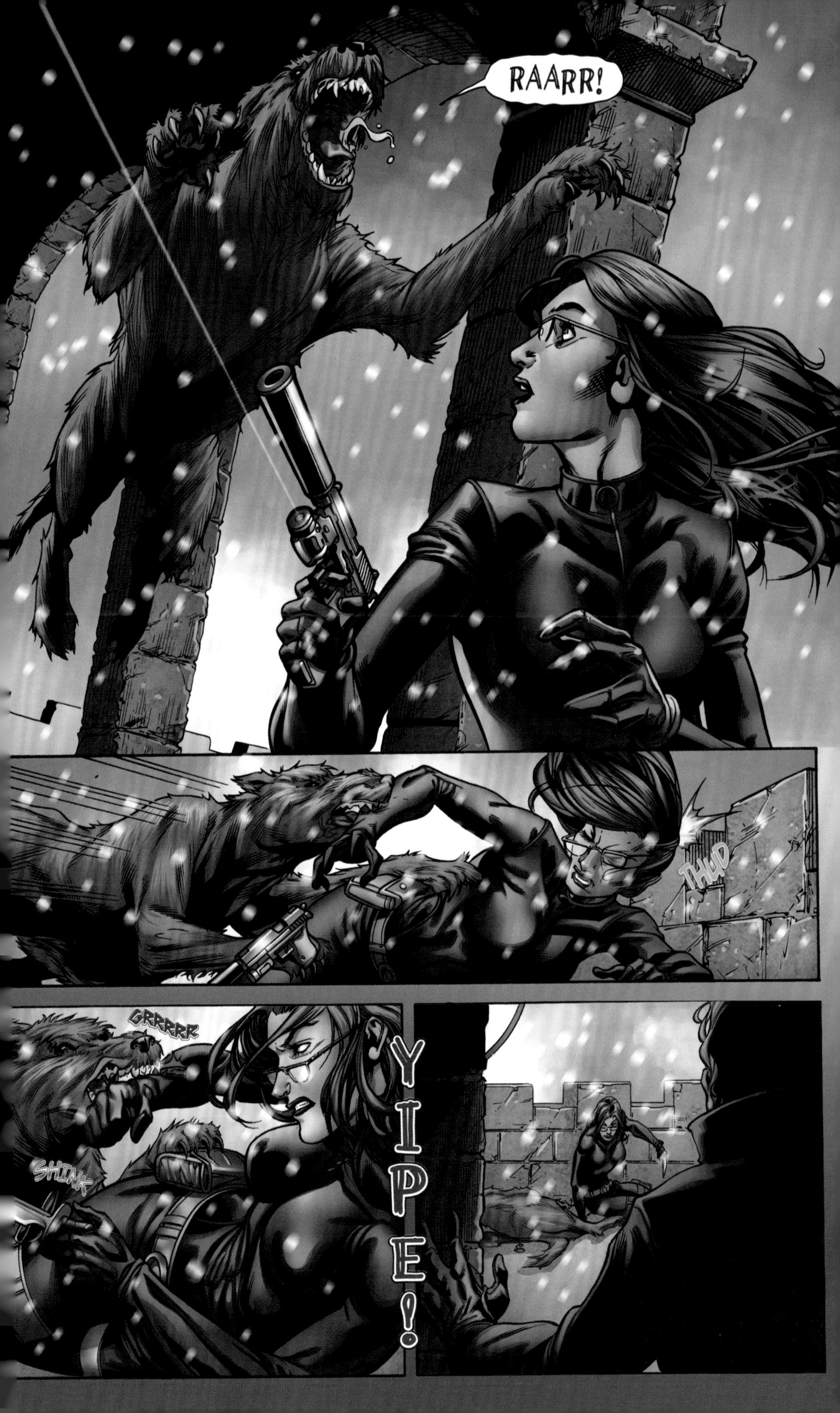
RAARR!
THUD
GRRRRR
SHINK
YIPE!

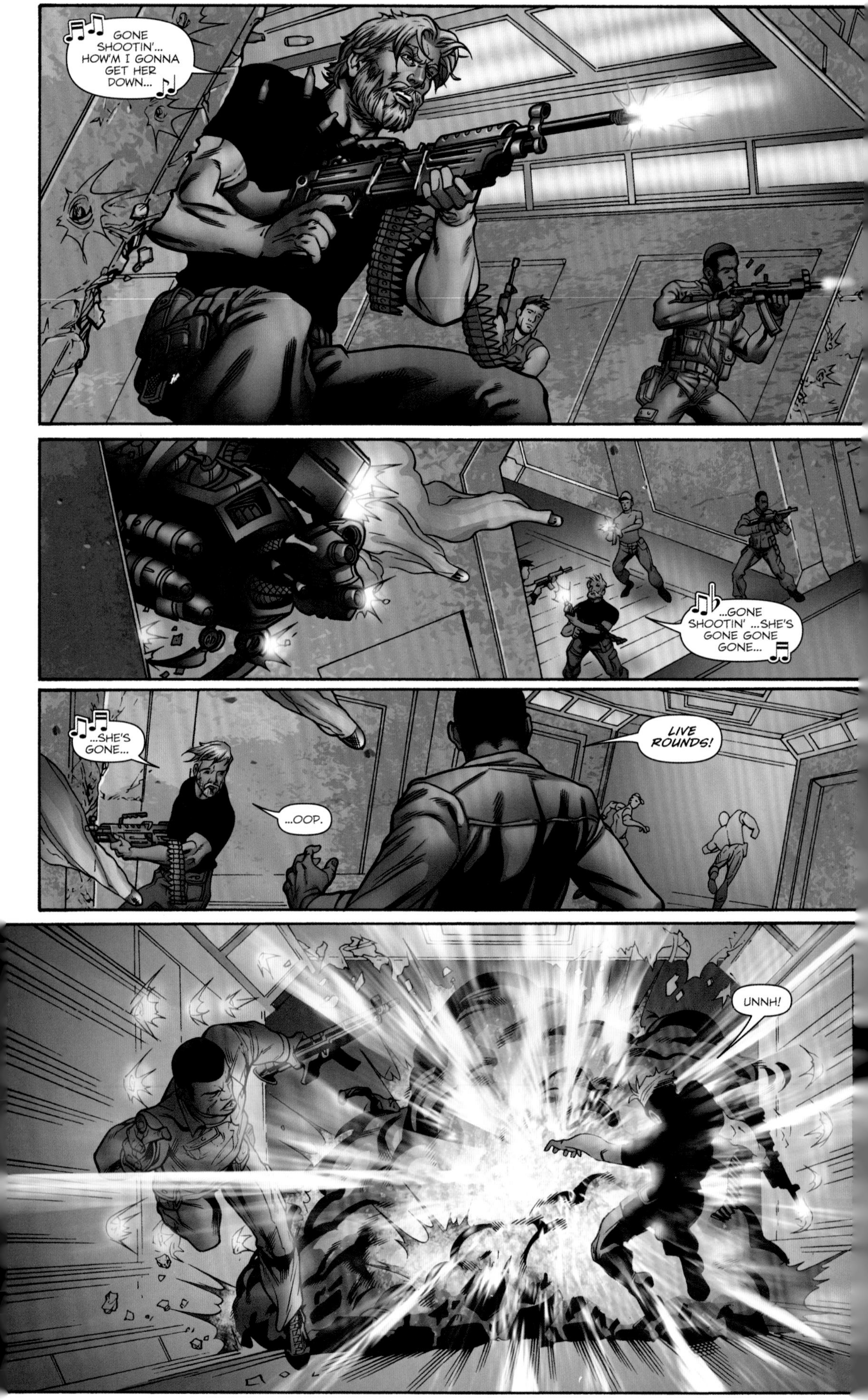
GONE SHOOTIN'... HOW'M I GONNA GET HER DOWN...
...GONE SHOOTIN' ...SHE'S GONE GONE GONE...
...SHE'S GONE...
LIVE ROUNDS!
...OOP.
UNNH!

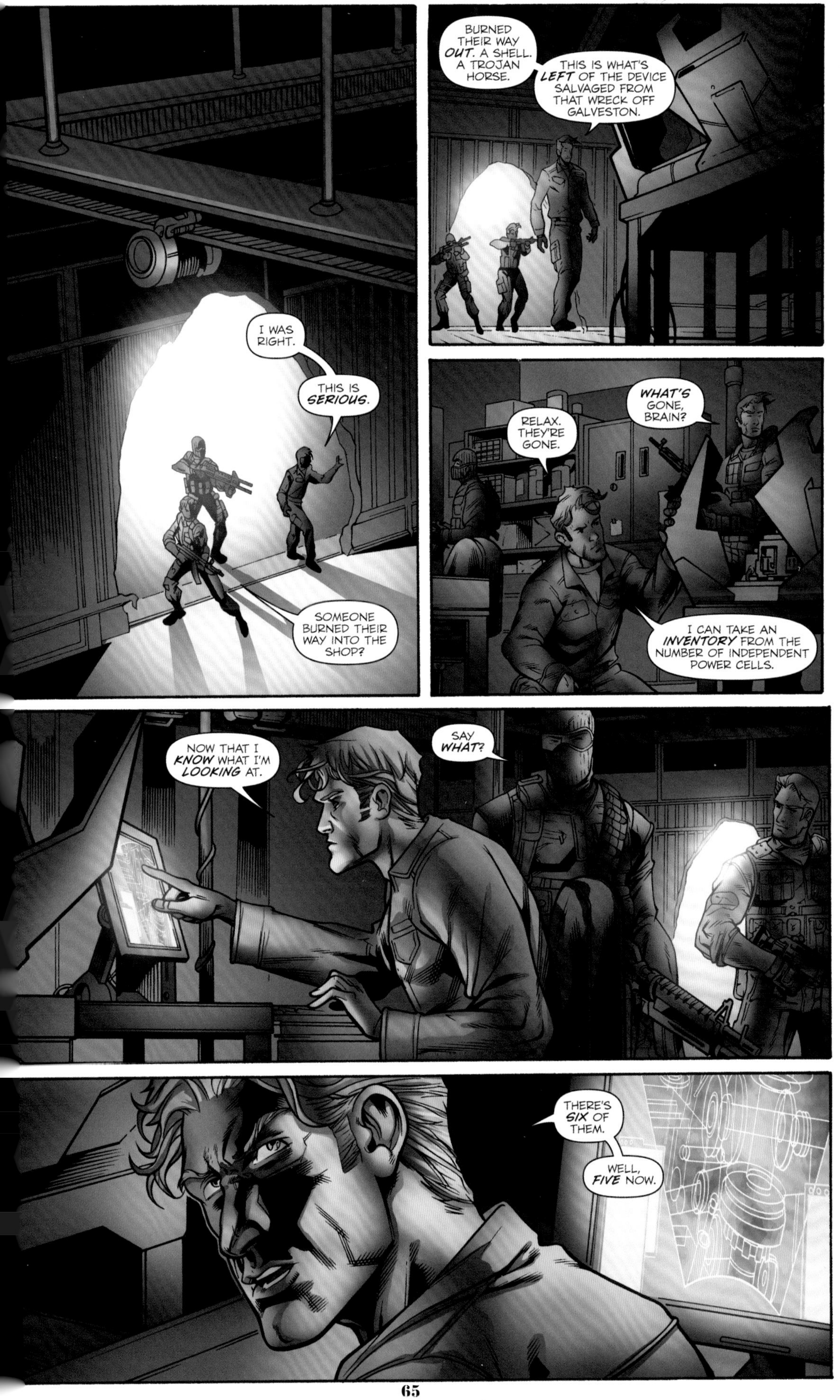
I WAS RIGHT.
THIS IS *SERIOUS*.
SOMEONE BURNED THEIR WAY INTO THE SHOP?
BURNED THEIR WAY *OUT*. A SHELL. A TROJAN HORSE.
THIS IS WHAT'S *LEFT* OF THE DEVICE SALVAGED FROM THAT WRECK OFF GALVESTON.
RELAX. THEY'RE GONE.
WHAT'S GONE, BRAIN?
I CAN TAKE AN *INVENTORY* FROM THE NUMBER OF INDEPENDENT POWER CELLS.
NOW THAT I *KNOW* WHAT I'M *LOOKING* AT.
SAY *WHAT*?
THERE'S *SIX* OF THEM.
WELL, *FIVE* NOW.

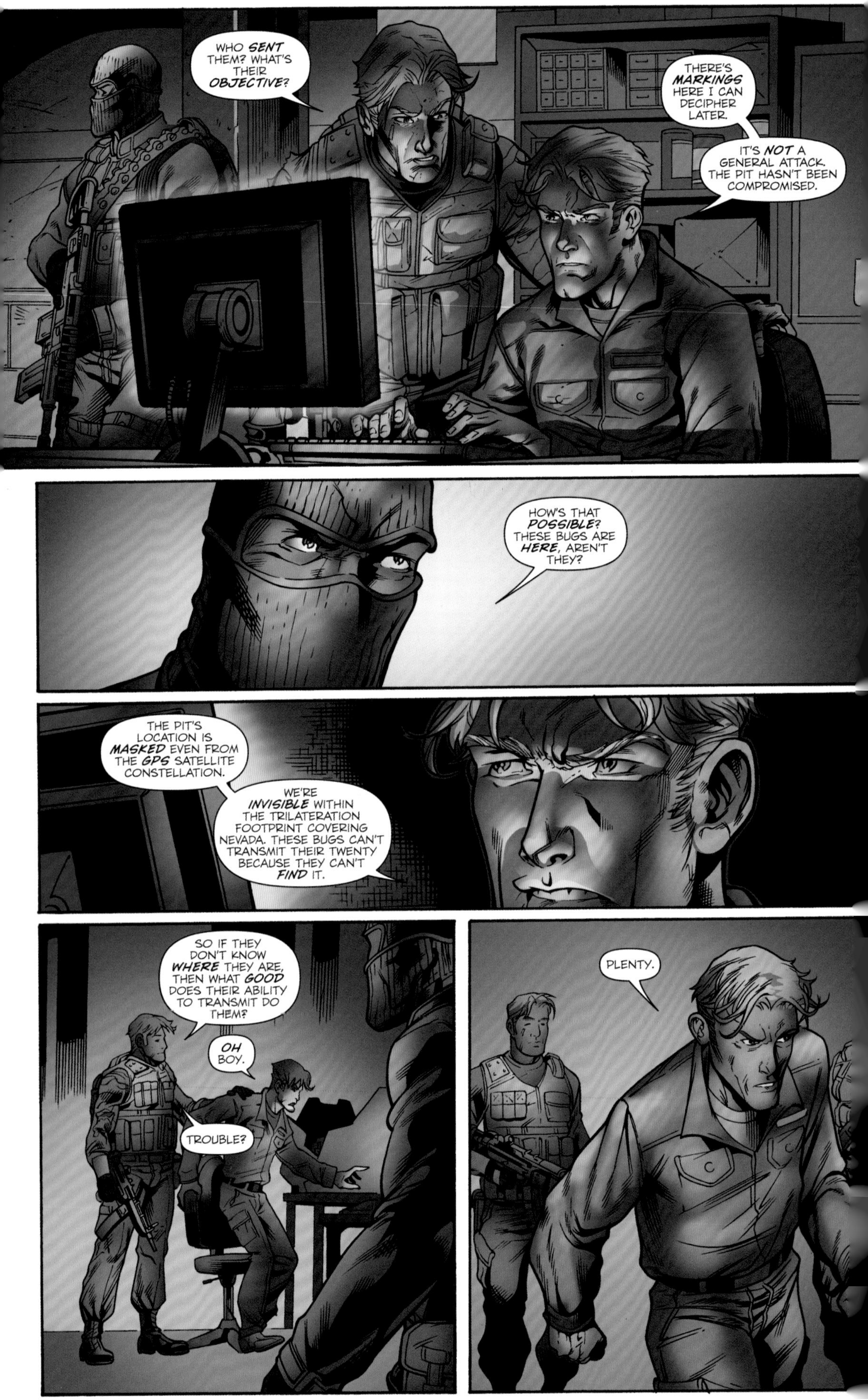
WHO SENT THEM? WHAT'S THEIR OBJECTIVE?
THERE'S MARKINGS HERE I CAN DECIPHER LATER.
IT'S NOT A GENERAL ATTACK. THE PIT HASN'T BEEN COMPROMISED.
HOW'S THAT POSSIBLE? THESE BUGS ARE HERE, AREN'T THEY?
THE PIT'S LOCATION IS MASKED EVEN FROM THE GPS SATELLITE CONSTELLATION.
WE'RE INVISIBLE WITHIN THE TRILATERATION FOOTPRINT COVERING NEVADA. THESE BUGS CAN'T TRANSMIT THEIR TWENTY BECAUSE THEY CAN'T FIND IT.
SO IF THEY DON'T KNOW WHERE THEY ARE, THEN WHAT GOOD DOES THEIR ABILITY TO TRANSMIT DO THEM?
OH BOY.
TROUBLE?
PLENTY.

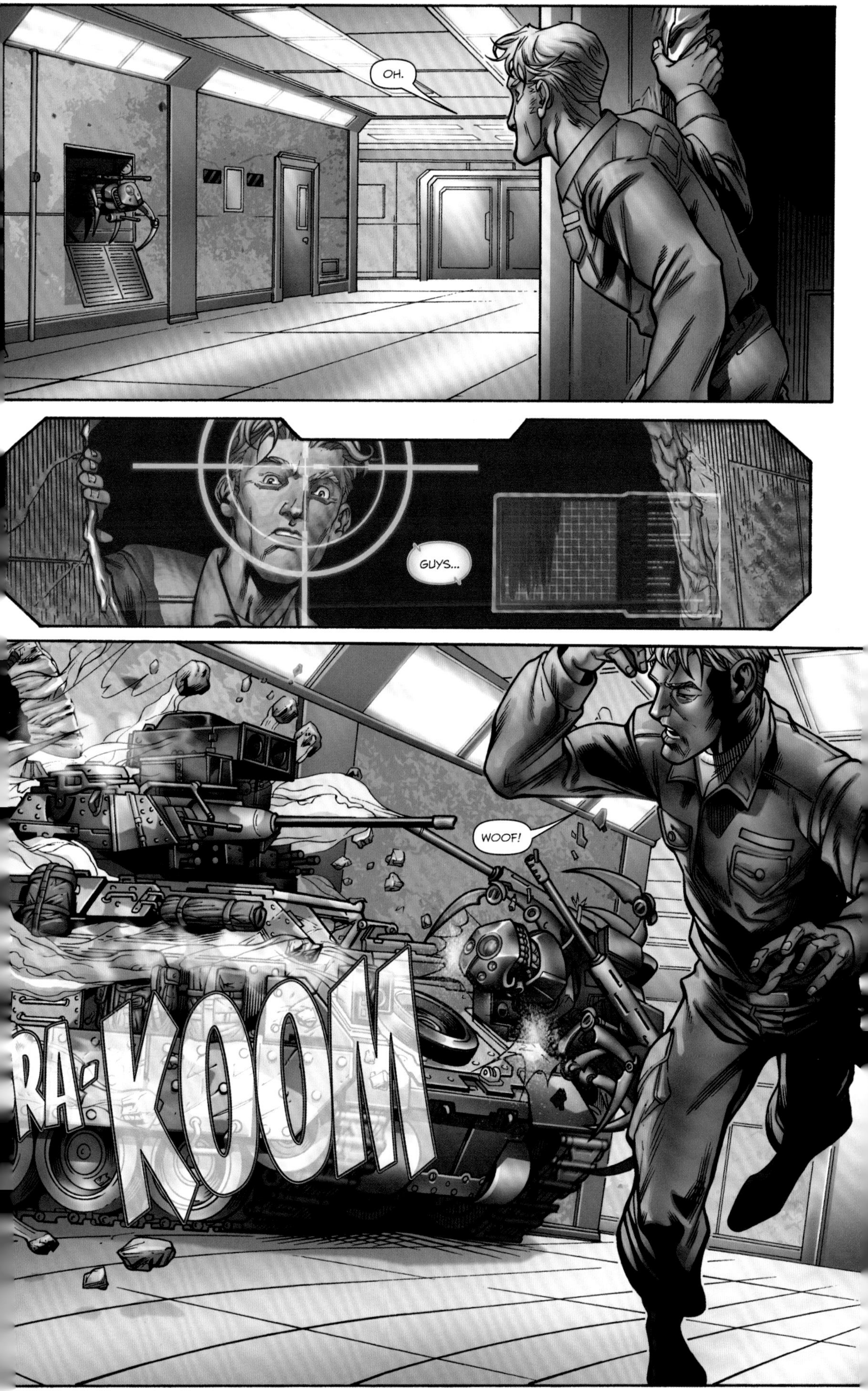
OH.
GUYS...
WOOF!
RA-KOOM

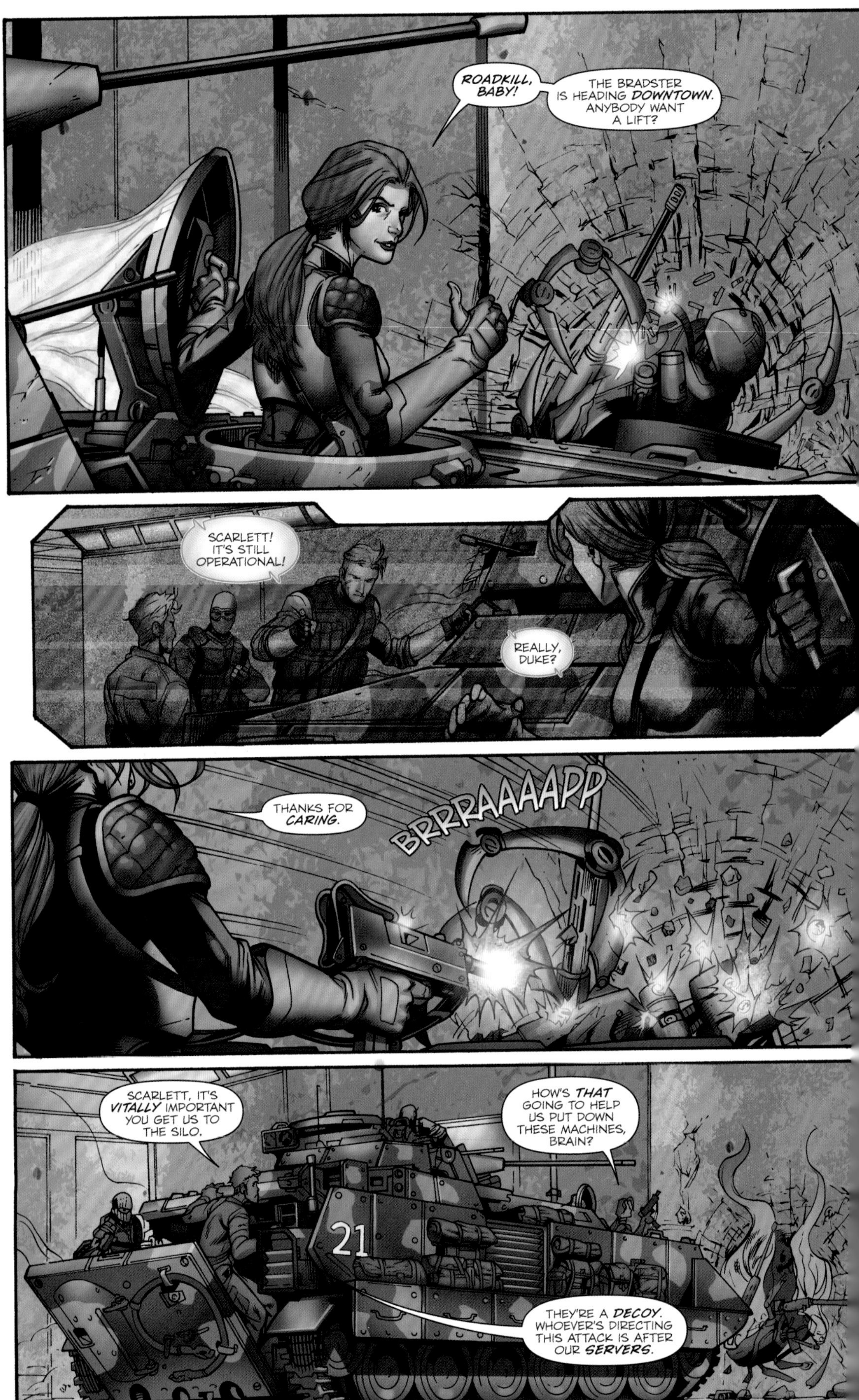
ROADKILL, BABY!
THE BRADSTER IS HEADING DOWNTOWN. ANYBODY WANT A LIFT?
SCARLETT! IT'S STILL OPERATIONAL!
REALLY, DUKE?
THANKS FOR CARING.
BRRRAAAAPP
SCARLETT, IT'S VITALLY IMPORTANT YOU GET US TO THE SILO.
HOW'S THAT GOING TO HELP US PUT DOWN THESE MACHINES, BRAIN?
THEY'RE A DECOY. WHOEVER'S DIRECTING THIS ATTACK IS AFTER OUR SERVERS.
21

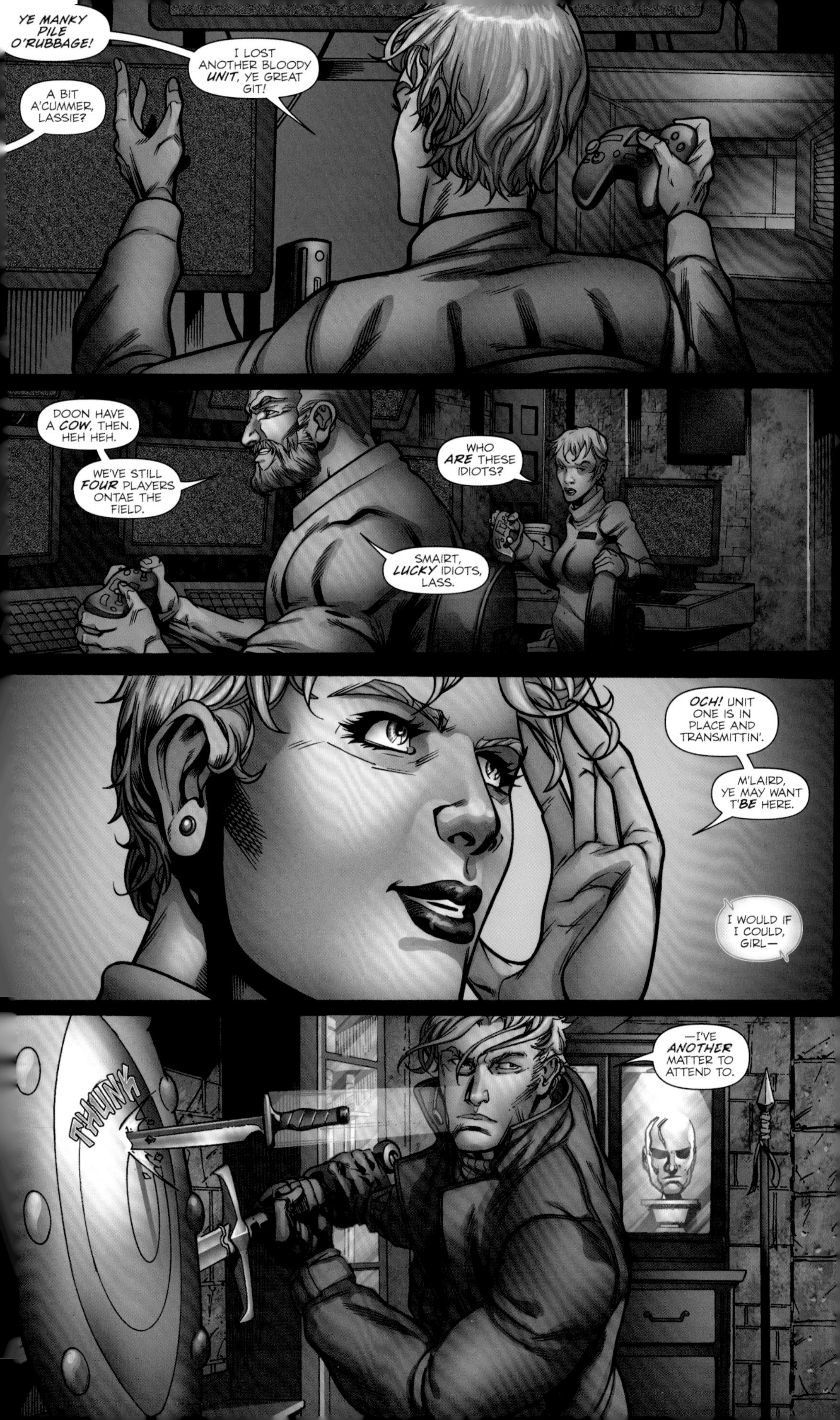
YE MANKY PILE O'RUBBAGE!
I LOST ANOTHER BLOODY UNIT, YE GREAT GIT!
A BIT A'CUMMER, LASSIE?
DOON HAVE A COW, THEN. HEH HEH.
WE'VE STILL FOUR PLAYERS ONTAE THE FIELD.
WHO ARE THESE IDIOTS?
SMAIRT, LUCKY IDIOTS, LASS.
OCH! UNIT ONE IS IN PLACE AND TRANSMITTIN'.
M'LAIRD, YE MAY WANT T'BE HERE.
I WOULD IF I COULD, GIRL—
—I'VE ANOTHER MATTER TO ATTEND TO.
THUNK

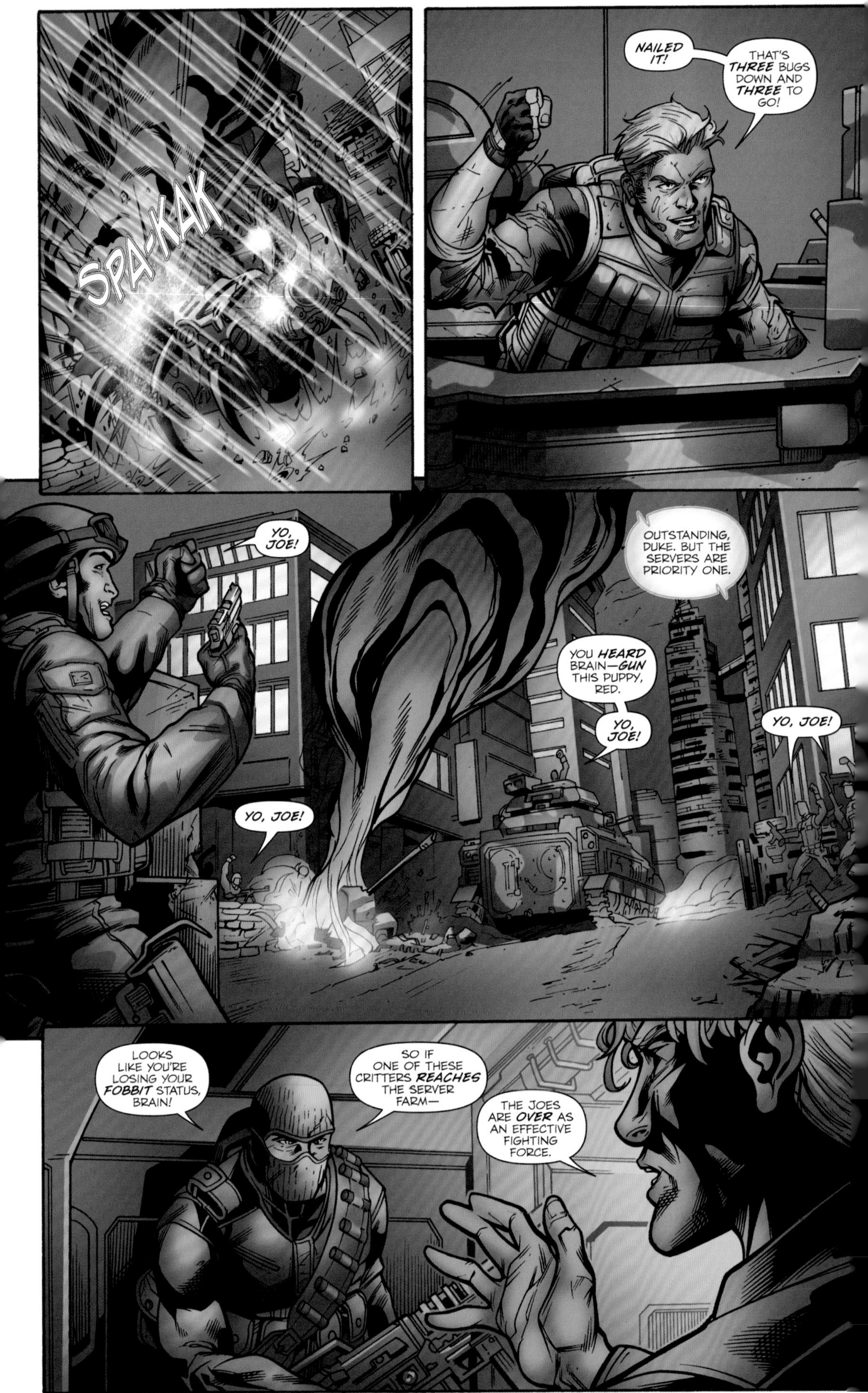
SPA-KAK
NAILED IT!
THAT'S THREE BUGS DOWN AND THREE TO GO!
YO, JOE!
OUTSTANDING, DUKE. BUT THE SERVERS ARE PRIORITY ONE.
YOU HEARD BRAIN—GUN THIS PUPPY, RED.
YO, JOE!
YO, JOE!
YO, JOE!
LOOKS LIKE YOU'RE LOSING YOUR FOBBIT STATUS, BRAIN!
SO IF ONE OF THESE CRITTERS REACHES THE SERVER FARM—
THE JOES ARE OVER AS AN EFFECTIVE FIGHTING FORCE.

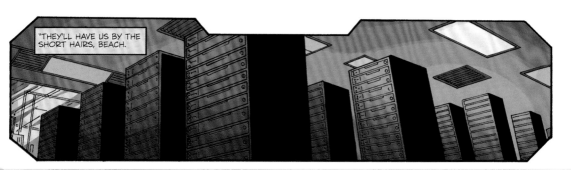

"THEY'LL HAVE US BY THE SHORT HAIRS, BEACH.

"THE SILO HOLDS ALL OUR PERSONNEL, STRATEGIC, CODE AND PROTOCOL FILES.

"IT'S A CLOSED SYSTEM. NOT ON ANY GRID OR NET."

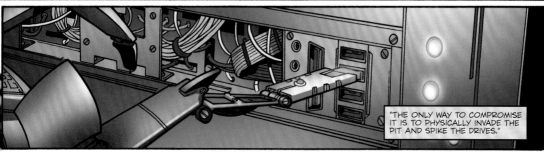

"THE ONLY WAY TO COMPROMISE IT IS TO PHYSICALLY INVADE THE PIT AND SPIKE THE DRIVES."

WE'RE *LINKED*, RORY. DE-ENCRYPTING... NOW.

LOVELY, LASS. LOOK FOR *ANYTHIN* PERTAININ' TO TELEPORTATION, PROBABILITY AMPLITUDE, OR THA' *MICHAELMAS* GEEZER.

ALL FILES TAGGED MICHAELMAS AN' RELATED CODENAME 'BRAINSTORM' NAKIT AS A NEWBAIRN.

DOWNLOAD *ALL* OF IT!

25%
67%
88%
88%
75%

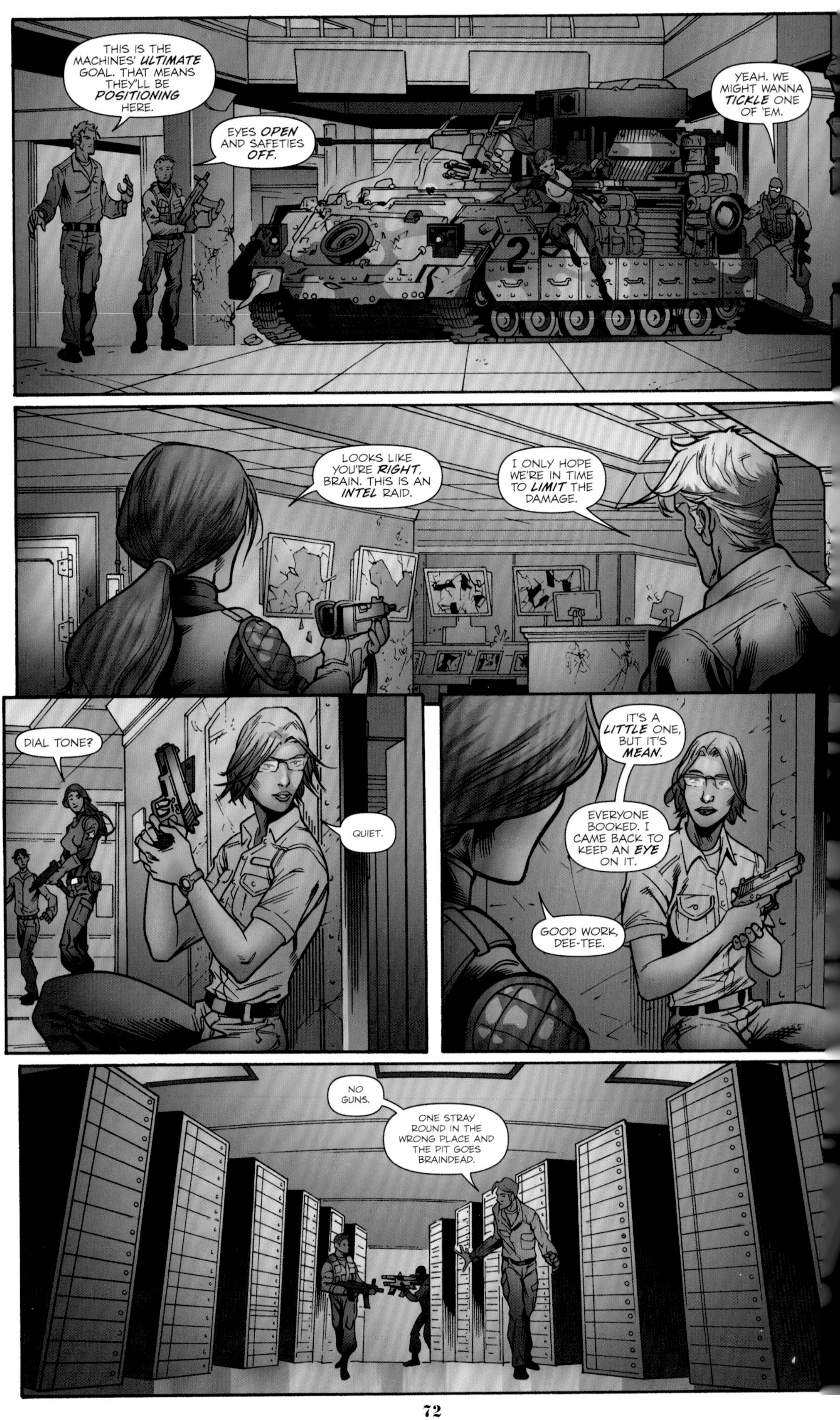
THIS IS THE MACHINES' ULTIMATE GOAL. THAT MEANS THEY'LL BE POSITIONING HERE.
EYES OPEN AND SAFETIES OFF.
YEAH. WE MIGHT WANNA TICKLE ONE OF 'EM.
LOOKS LIKE YOU'RE RIGHT, BRAIN. THIS IS AN INTEL RAID.
I ONLY HOPE WE'RE IN TIME TO LIMIT THE DAMAGE.
DIAL TONE?
QUIET.
IT'S A LITTLE ONE, BUT IT'S MEAN.
EVERYONE BOOKED. I CAME BACK TO KEEP AN EYE ON IT.
GOOD WORK, DEE-TEE.
NO GUNS.
ONE STRAY ROUND IN THE WRONG PLACE AND THE PIT GOES BRAINDEAD.

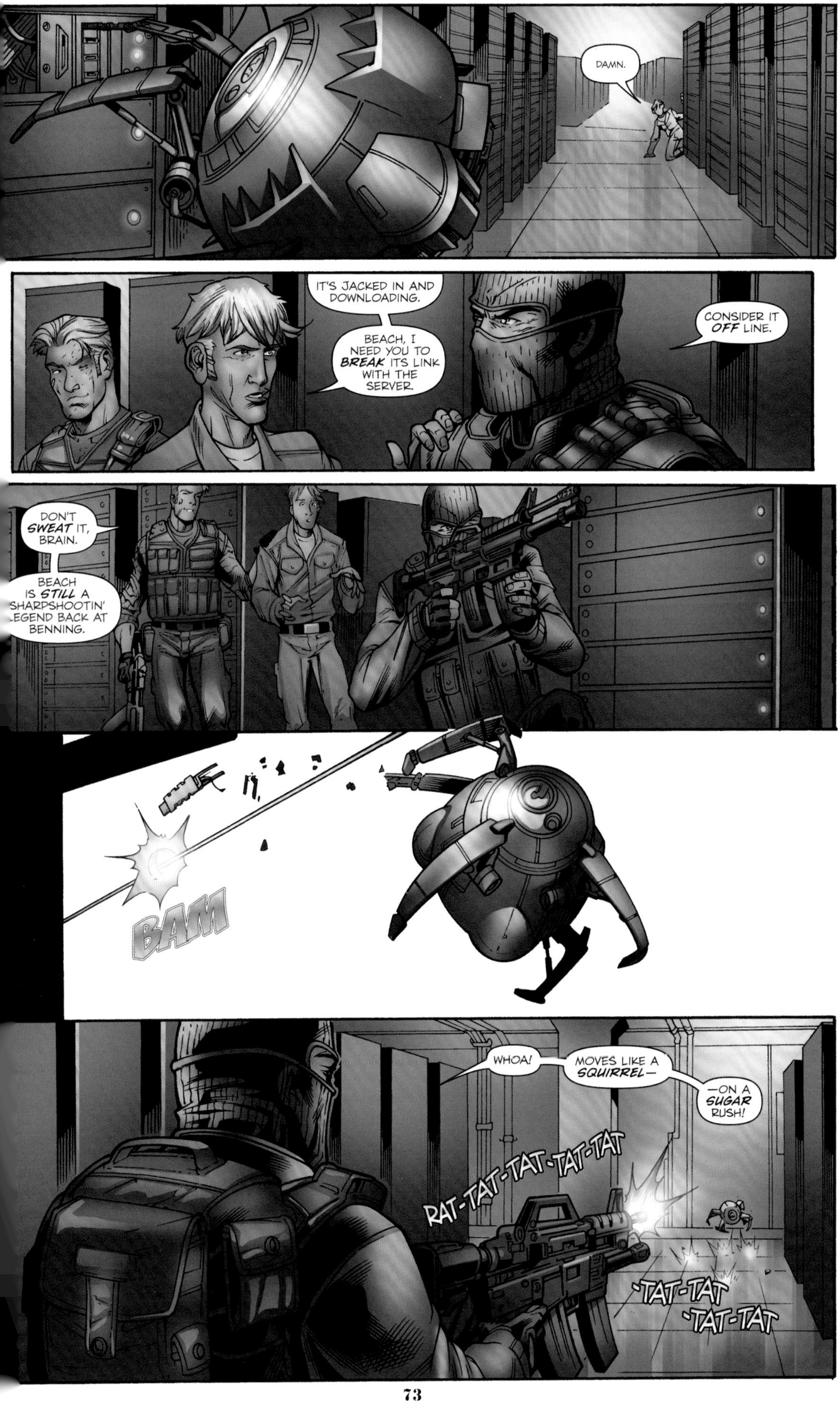
DAMN.
IT'S JACKED IN AND DOWNLOADING.
BEACH, I NEED YOU TO BREAK ITS LINK WITH THE SERVER.
CONSIDER IT OFF LINE.
DON'T SWEAT IT, BRAIN.
BEACH IS STILL A SHARPSHOOTIN' LEGEND BACK AT BENNING.
BAM
WHOA!
MOVES LIKE A SQUIRREL—
—ON A SUGAR RUSH!
RAT-TAT-TAT-TAT-TAT
-TAT-TAT
-TAT-TAT

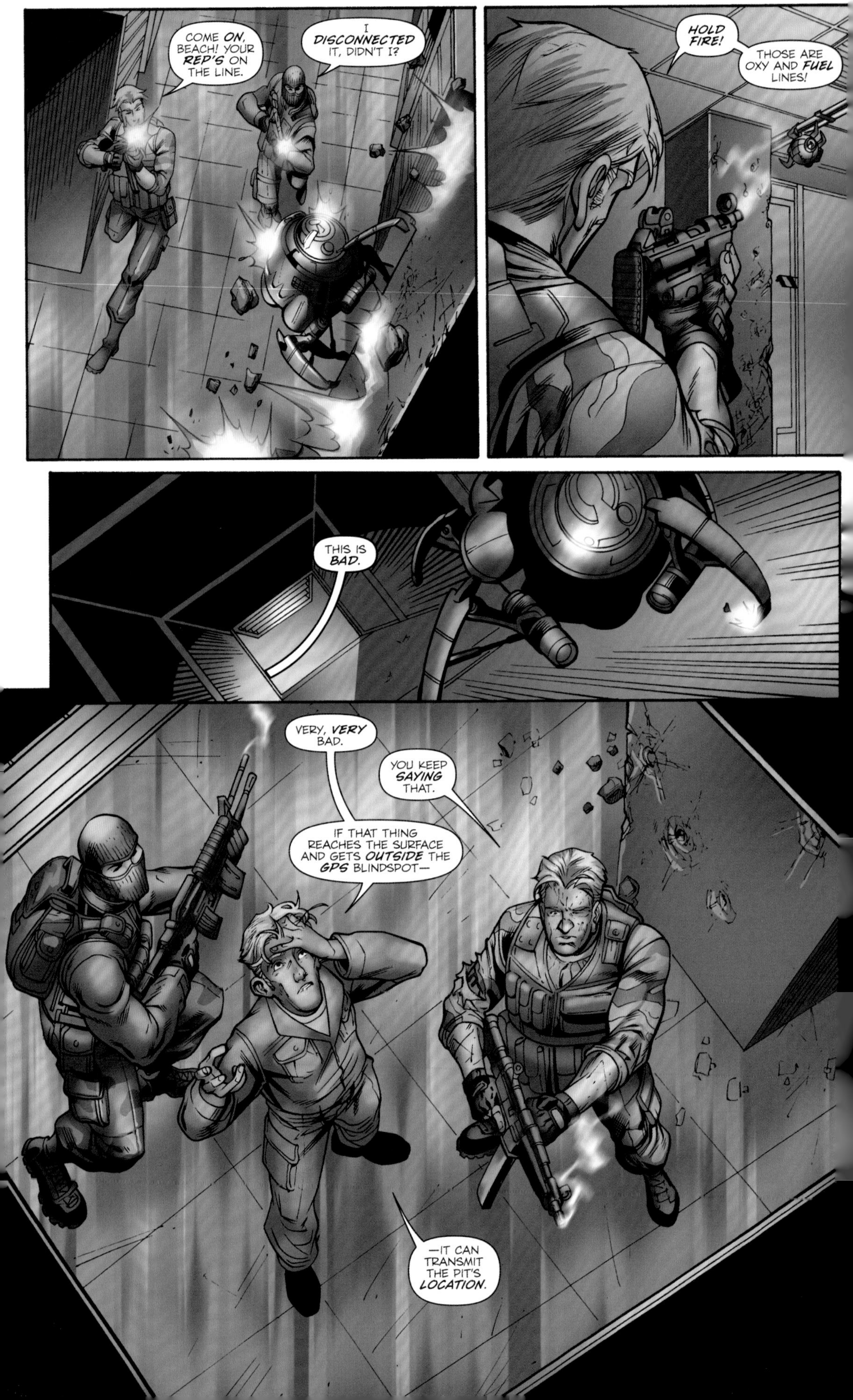
COME ON, BEACH! YOUR REP'S ON THE LINE.
I DISCONNECTED IT, DIDN'T I?
HOLD FIRE!
THOSE ARE OXY AND FUEL LINES!
THIS IS BAD.
VERY, VERY BAD.
YOU KEEP SAYING THAT.
IF THAT THING REACHES THE SURFACE AND GETS OUTSIDE THE GPS BLINDSPOT—
—IT CAN TRANSMIT THE PIT'S LOCATION.

CHAPTER 4

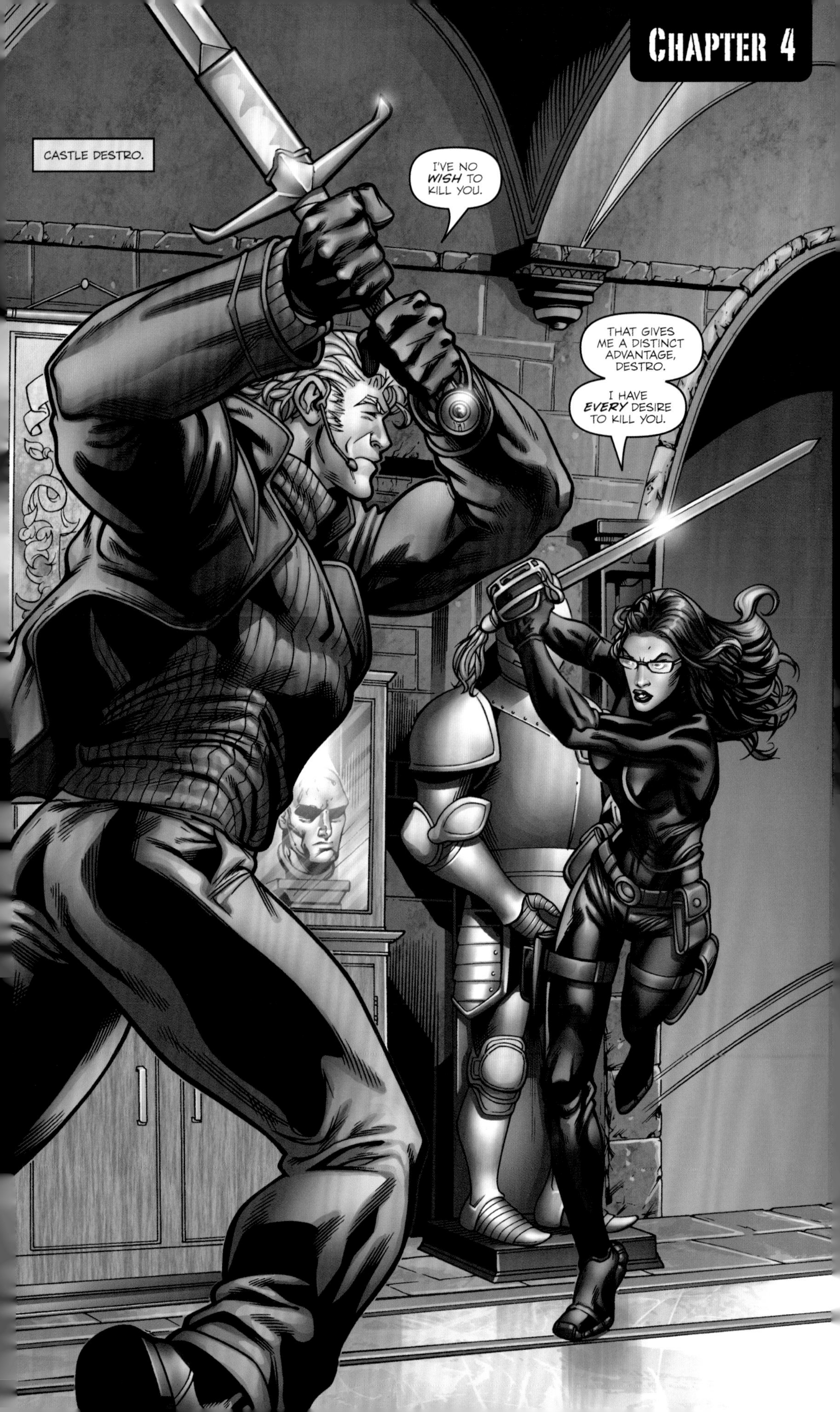
CASTLE DESTRO.
I'VE NO WISH TO KILL YOU.
THAT GIVES ME A DISTINCT ADVANTAGE, DESTRO.
I HAVE EVERY DESIRE TO KILL YOU.

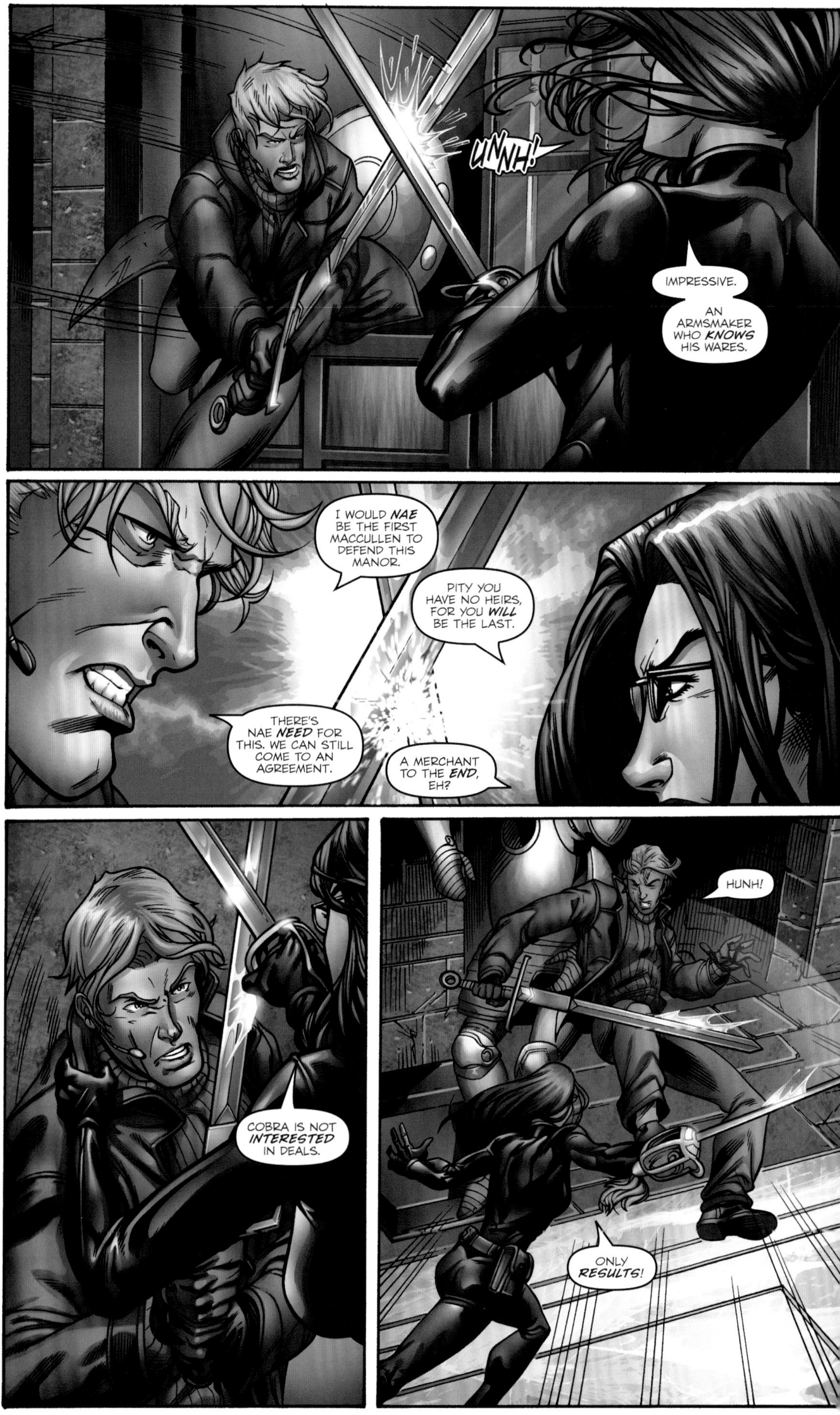
UNNH!
IMPRESSIVE.
AN ARMSMAKER WHO KNOWS HIS WARES.
I WOULD NAE BE THE FIRST MACCULLEN TO DEFEND THIS MANOR.
PITY YOU HAVE NO HEIRS, FOR YOU WILL BE THE LAST.
THERE'S NAE NEED FOR THIS. WE CAN STILL COME TO AN AGREEMENT.
A MERCHANT TO THE END, EH?
COBRA IS NOT INTERESTED IN DEALS.
HUNH!
ONLY RESULTS!

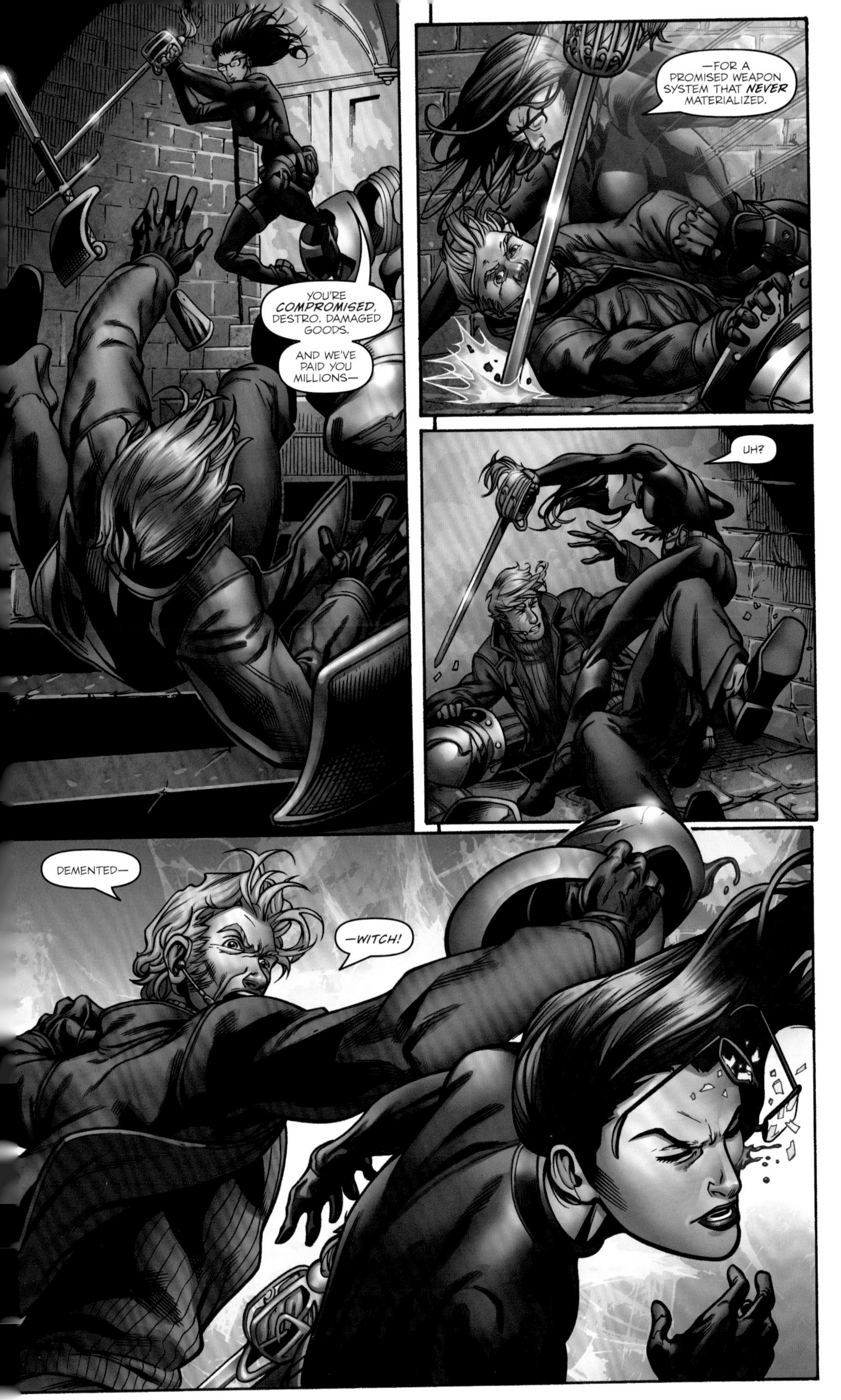
YOU'RE COMPROMISED, DESTRO. DAMAGED GOODS.
AND WE'VE PAID YOU MILLIONS—
—FOR A PROMISED WEAPON SYSTEM THAT NEVER MATERIALIZED.
UH?
DEMENTED—
—WITCH!

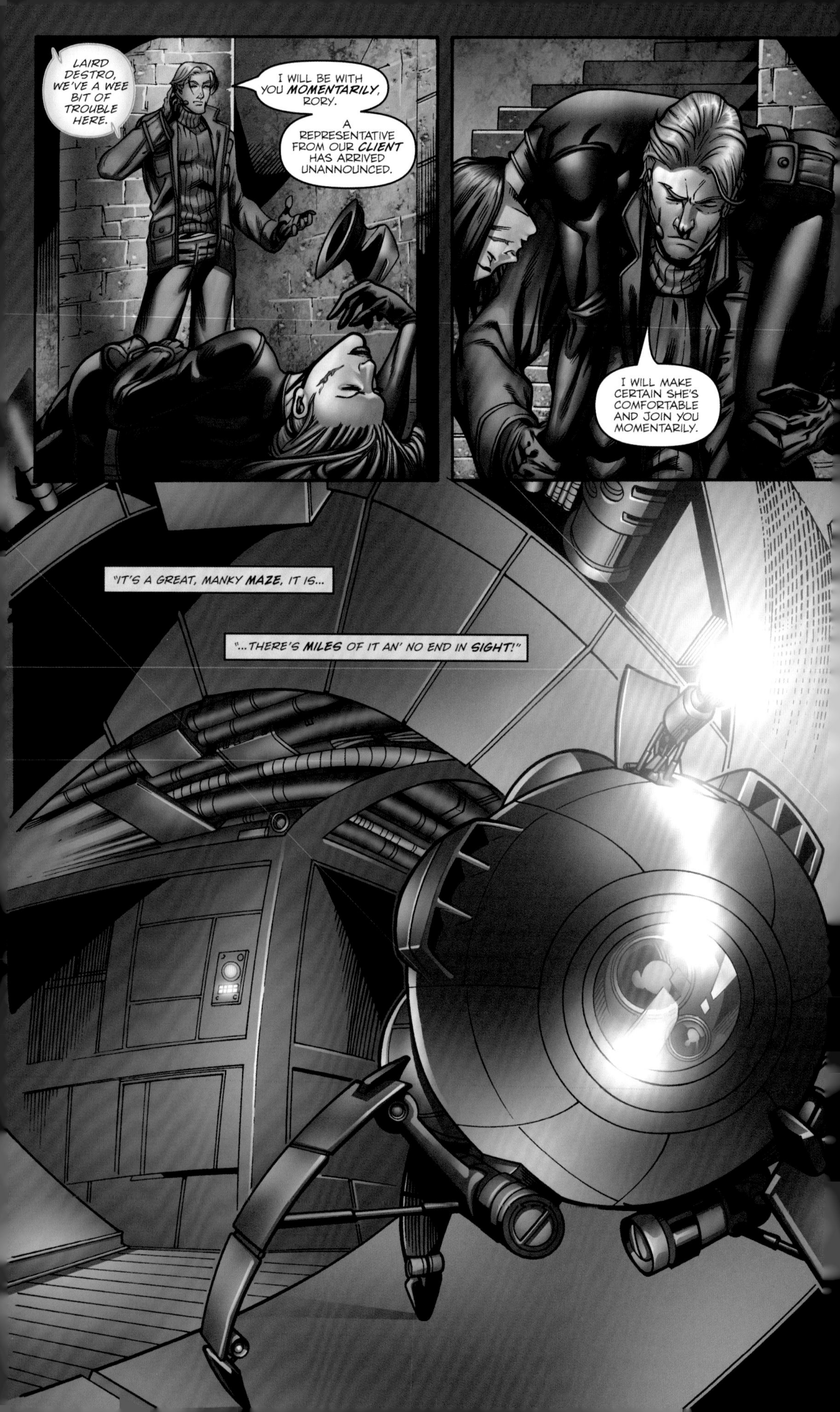
LAIRD DESTRO, WE'VE A WEE BIT OF TROUBLE HERE.
I WILL BE WITH YOU MOMENTARILY, RORY.
A REPRESENTATIVE FROM OUR CLIENT HAS ARRIVED UNANNOUNCED.
I WILL MAKE CERTAIN SHE'S COMFORTABLE AND JOIN YOU MOMENTARILY.
"IT'S A GREAT, MANKY MAZE, IT IS...
"...THERE'S MILES OF IT AN' NO END IN SIGHT!"

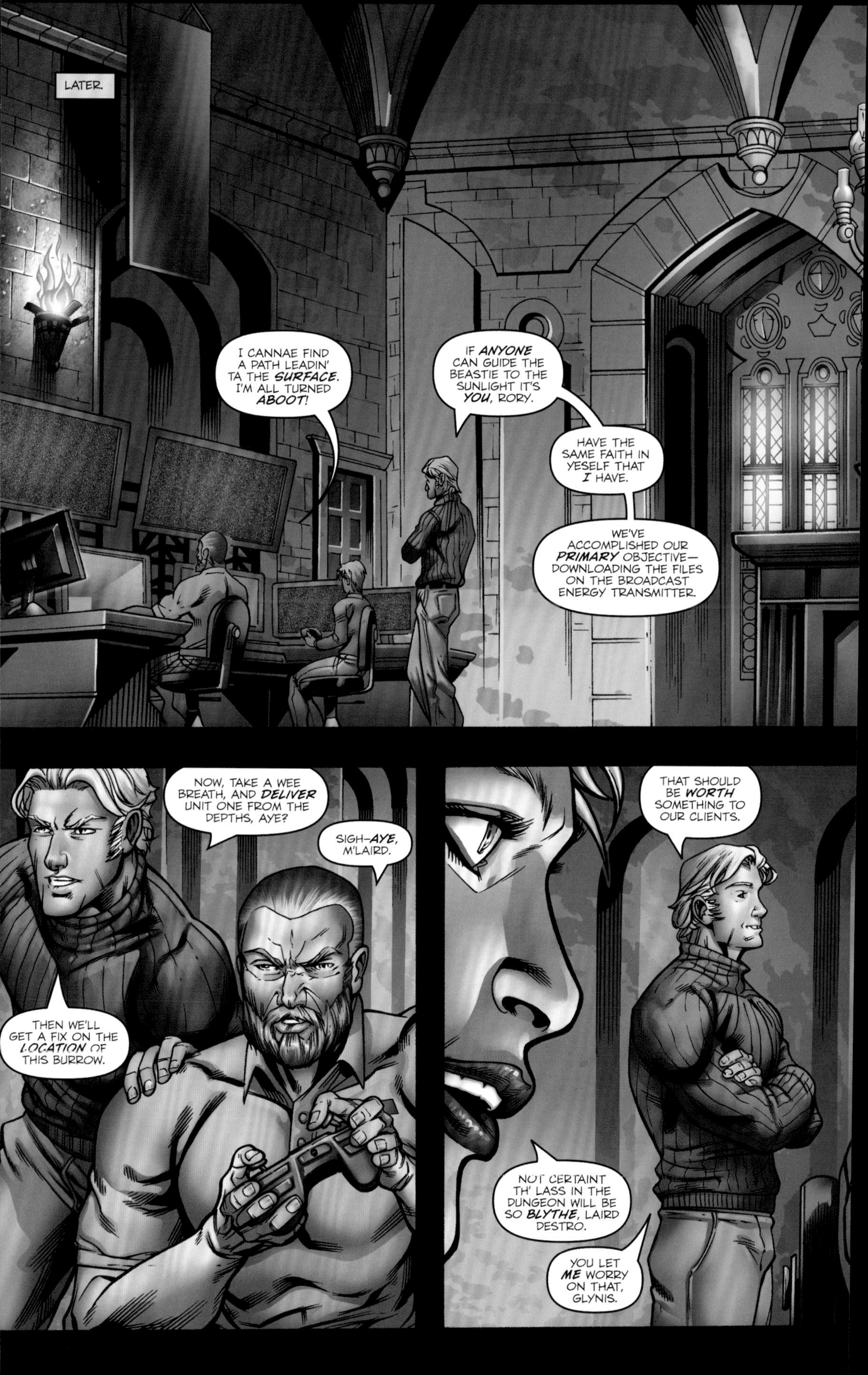
LATER.
I CANNAE FIND A PATH LEADIN' TA THE SURFACE. I'M ALL TURNED ABOOT!
IF ANYONE CAN GUIDE THE BEASTIE TO THE SUNLIGHT IT'S YOU, RORY.
HAVE THE SAME FAITH IN YESELF THAT I HAVE.
WE'VE ACCOMPLISHED OUR PRIMARY OBJECTIVE—DOWNLOADING THE FILES ON THE BROADCAST ENERGY TRANSMITTER.
NOW, TAKE A WEE BREATH, AND DELIVER UNIT ONE FROM THE DEPTHS, AYE?
SIGH—AYE, M'LAIRD.
THEN WE'LL GET A FIX ON THE LOCATION OF THIS BURROW.
THAT SHOULD BE WORTH SOMETHING TO OUR CLIENTS.
NOT CERTAINT TH' LASS IN THE DUNGEON WILL BE SO BLYTHE, LAIRD DESTRO.
YOU LET ME WORRY ON THAT, GLYNIS.

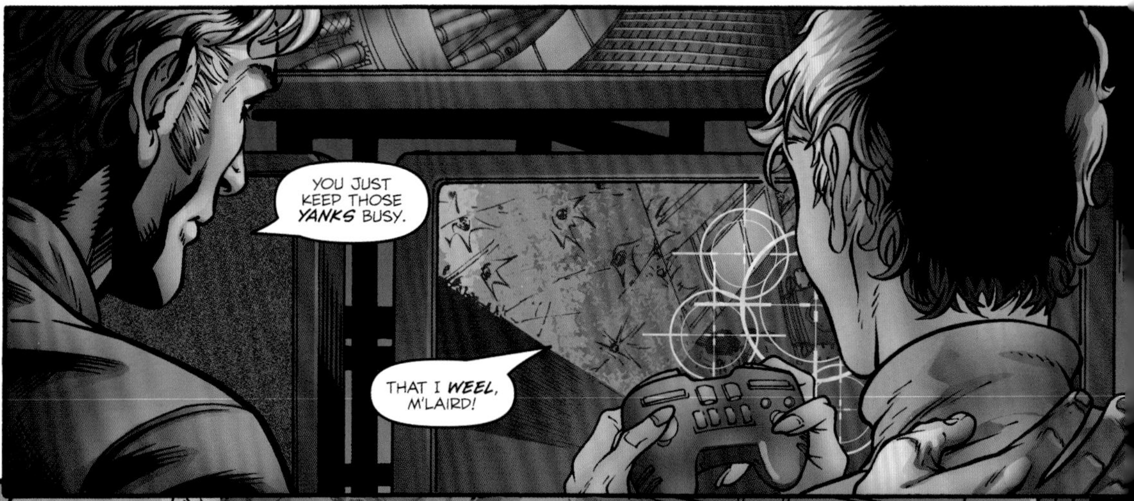
YOU JUST KEEP THOSE YANKS BUSY.
THAT I WEEL, M'LAIRD!

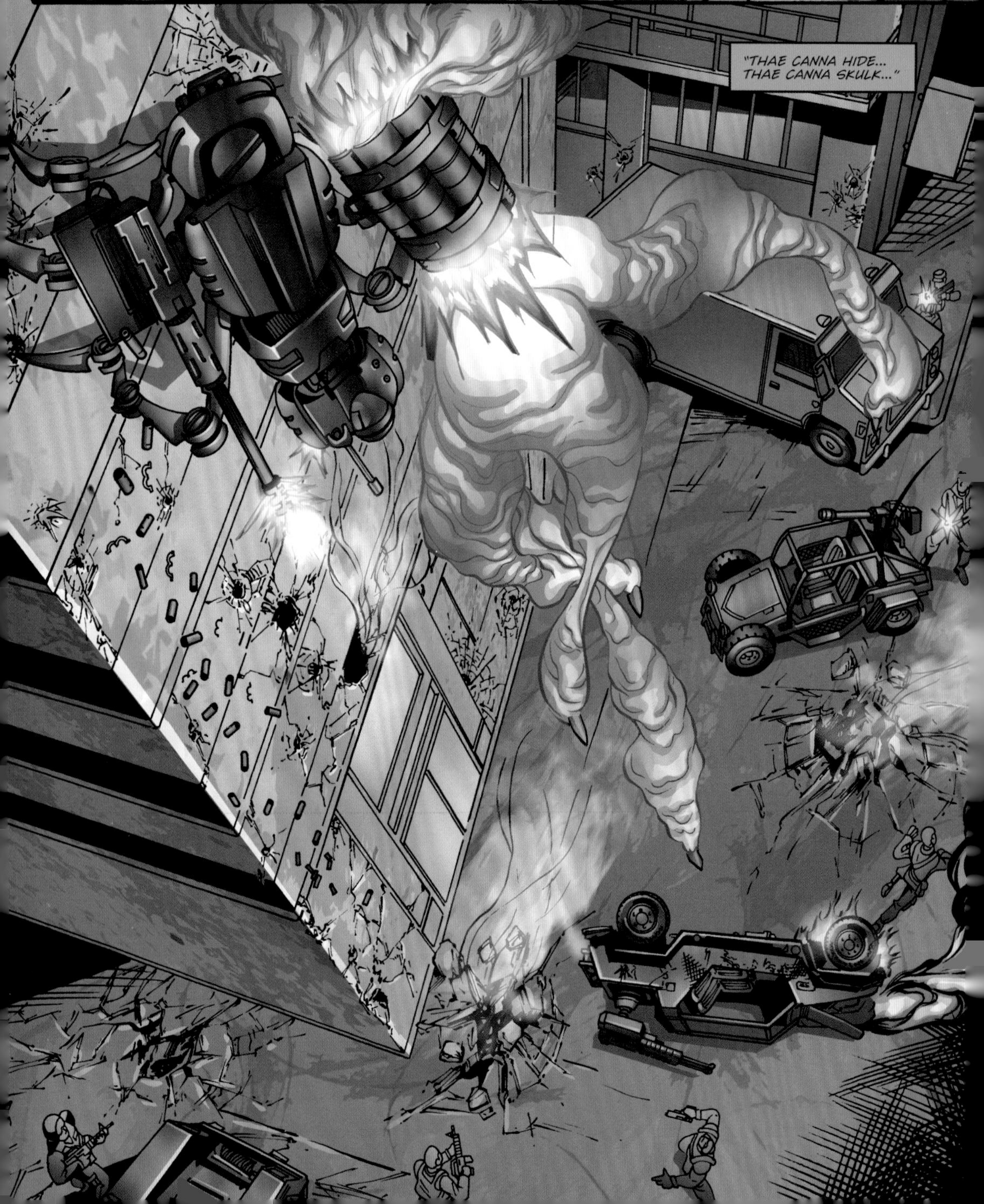
"THAE CANNA HIDE... THAE CANNA SKULK..."

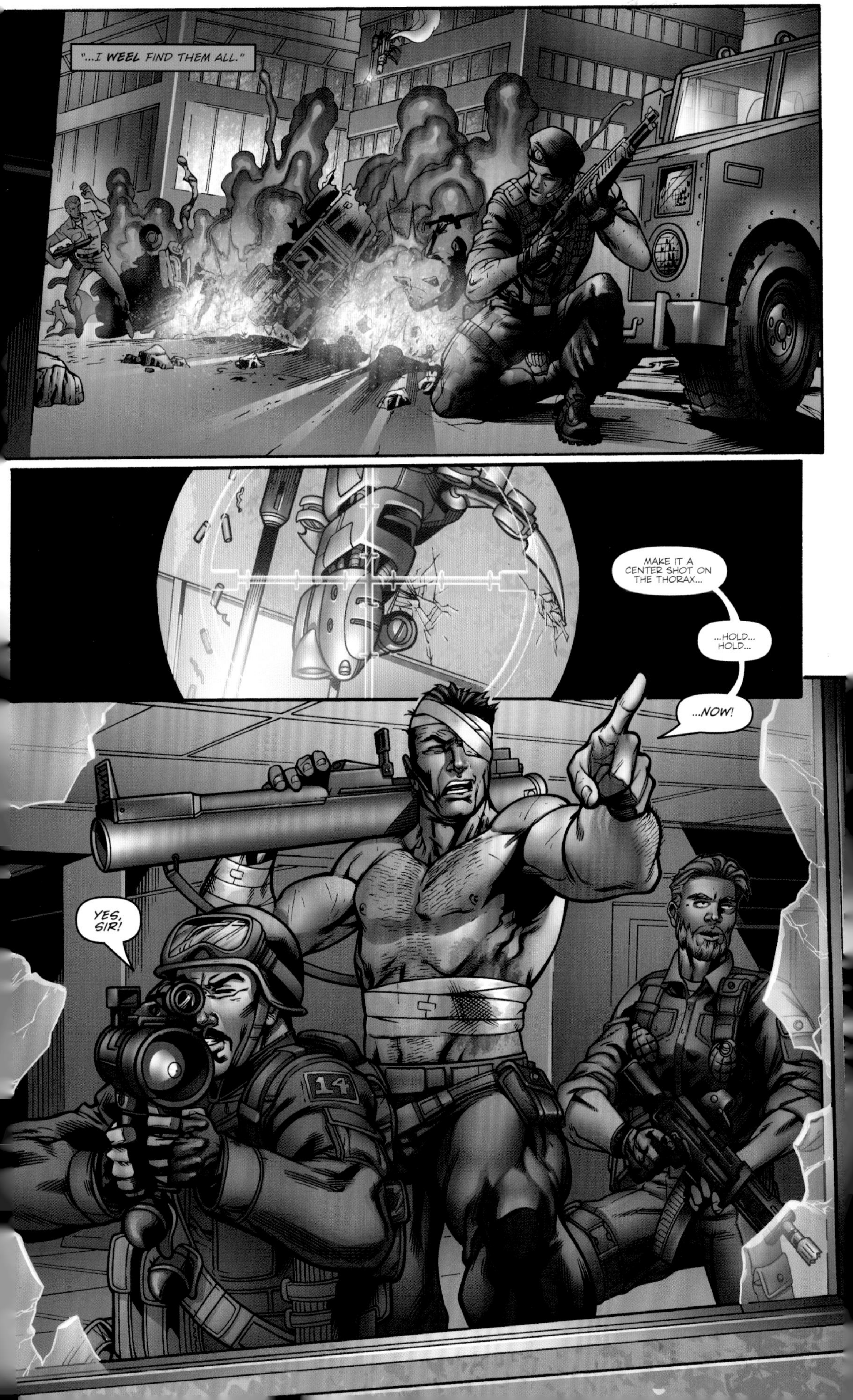
"...I WEEL FIND THEM ALL."
MAKE IT A CENTER SHOT ON THE THORAX...
...HOLD... HOLD...
...NOW!
YES, SIR!
14

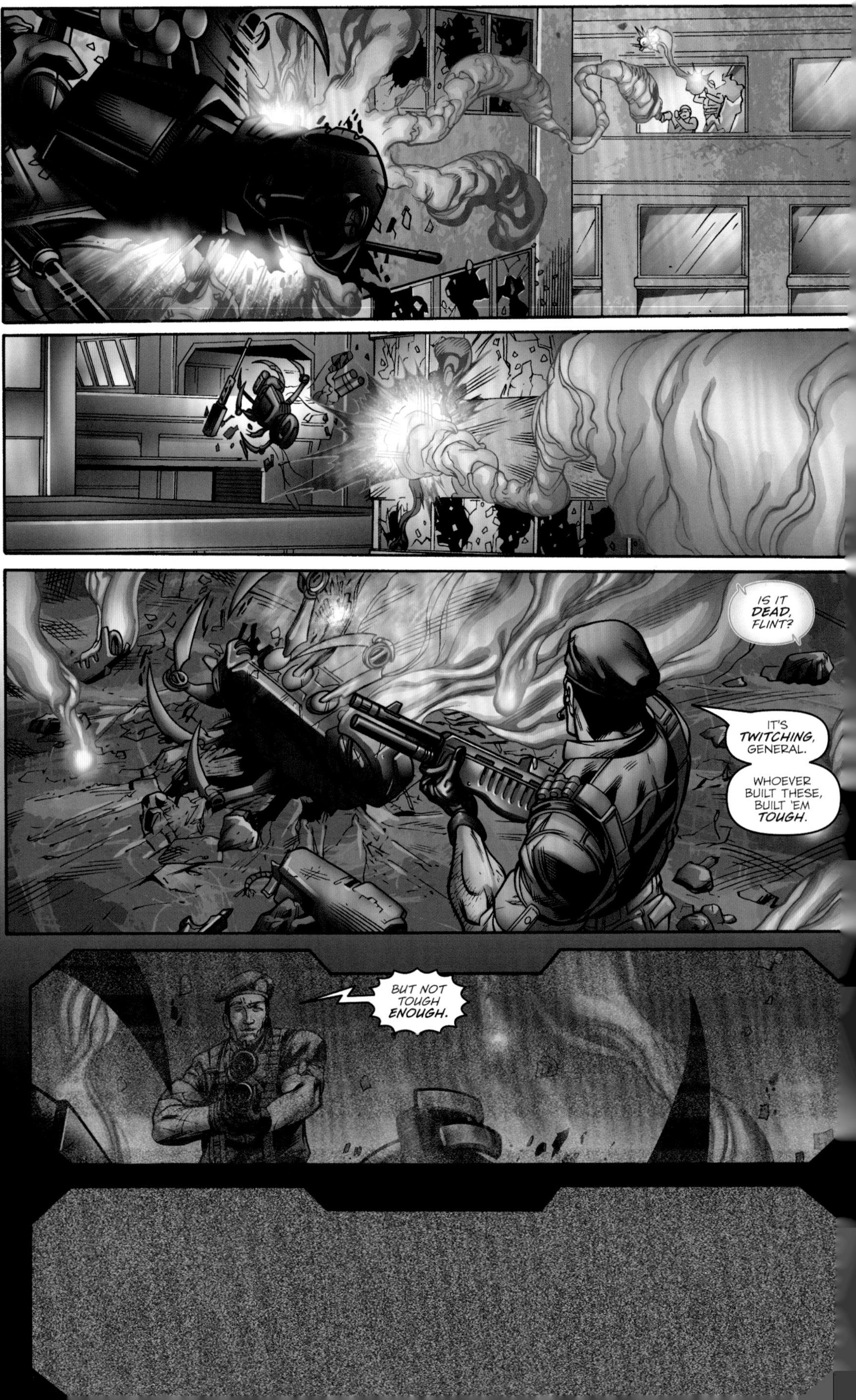

IS IT DEAD, FLINT?
IT'S TWITCHING, GENERAL.
WHOEVER BUILT THESE, BUILT 'EM TOUGH.
BUT NOT TOUGH ENOUGH.

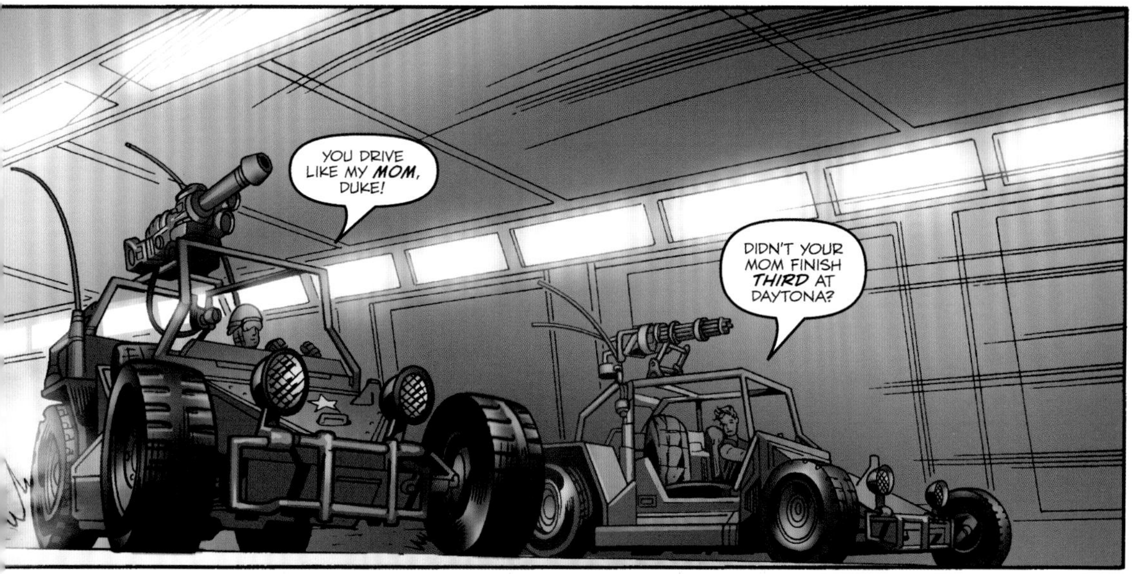
YOU DRIVE LIKE MY MOM, DUKE!
DIDN'T YOUR MOM FINISH THIRD AT DAYTONA?

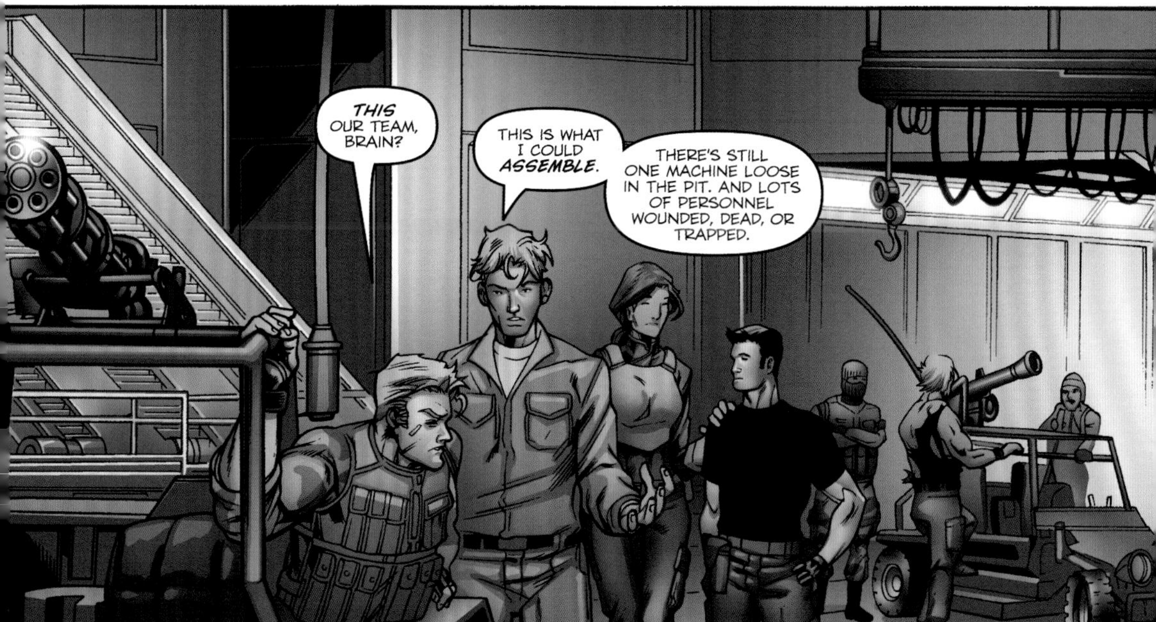
THIS OUR TEAM, BRAIN?
THIS IS WHAT I COULD ASSEMBLE.
THERE'S STILL ONE MACHINE LOOSE IN THE PIT. AND LOTS OF PERSONNEL WOUNDED, DEAD, OR TRAPPED.

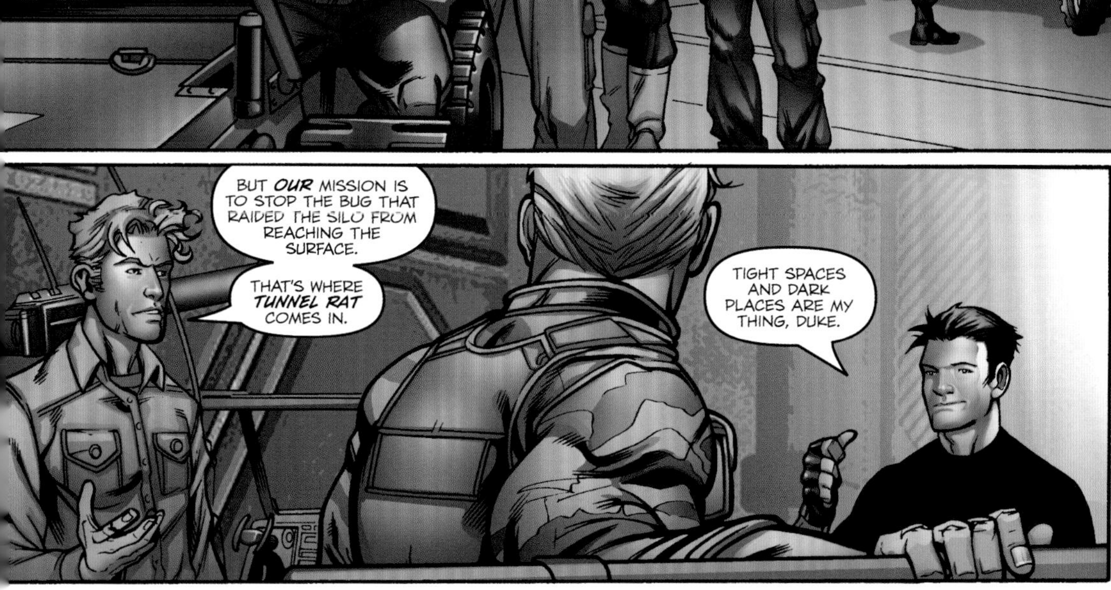
BUT OUR MISSION IS TO STOP THE BUG THAT RAIDED THE SILO FROM REACHING THE SURFACE.
THAT'S WHERE TUNNEL RAT COMES IN.
TIGHT SPACES AND DARK PLACES ARE MY THING, DUKE.

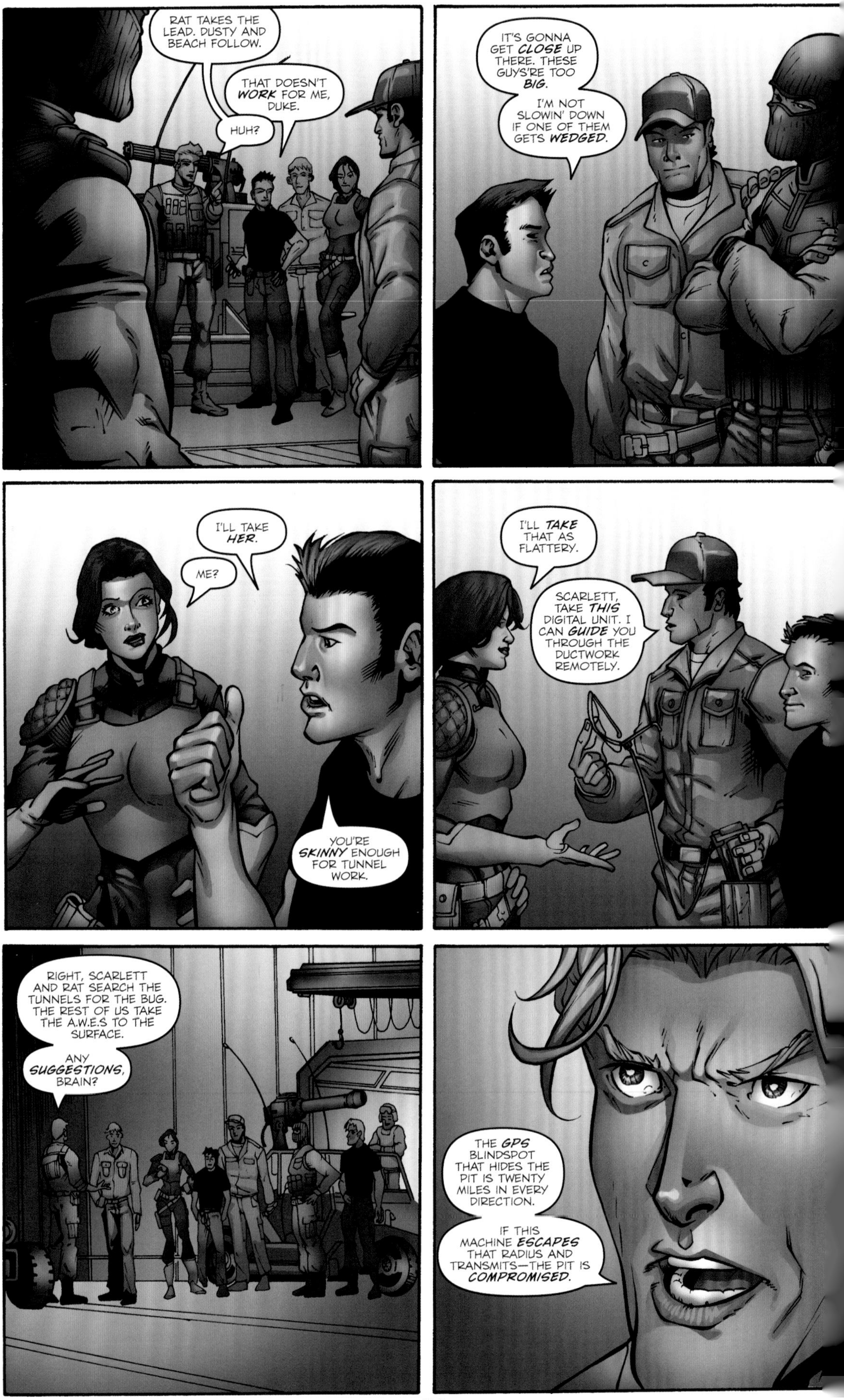

RAT TAKES THE LEAD. DUSTY AND BEACH FOLLOW.
THAT DOESN'T WORK FOR ME, DUKE.
HUH?
IT'S GONNA GET CLOSE UP THERE. THESE GUYS'RE TOO BIG.
I'M NOT SLOWIN' DOWN IF ONE OF THEM GETS WEDGED.
I'LL TAKE HER.
ME?
YOU'RE SKINNY ENOUGH FOR TUNNEL WORK.
I'LL TAKE THAT AS FLATTERY.
SCARLETT, TAKE THIS DIGITAL UNIT. I CAN GUIDE YOU THROUGH THE DUCTWORK REMOTELY.
RIGHT, SCARLETT AND RAT SEARCH THE TUNNELS FOR THE BUG. THE REST OF US TAKE THE A.W.E.S TO THE SURFACE.
ANY SUGGESTIONS, BRAIN?
THE GPS BLINDSPOT THAT HIDES THE PIT IS TWENTY MILES IN EVERY DIRECTION.
IF THIS MACHINE ESCAPES THAT RADIUS AND TRANSMITS—THE PIT IS COMPROMISED.

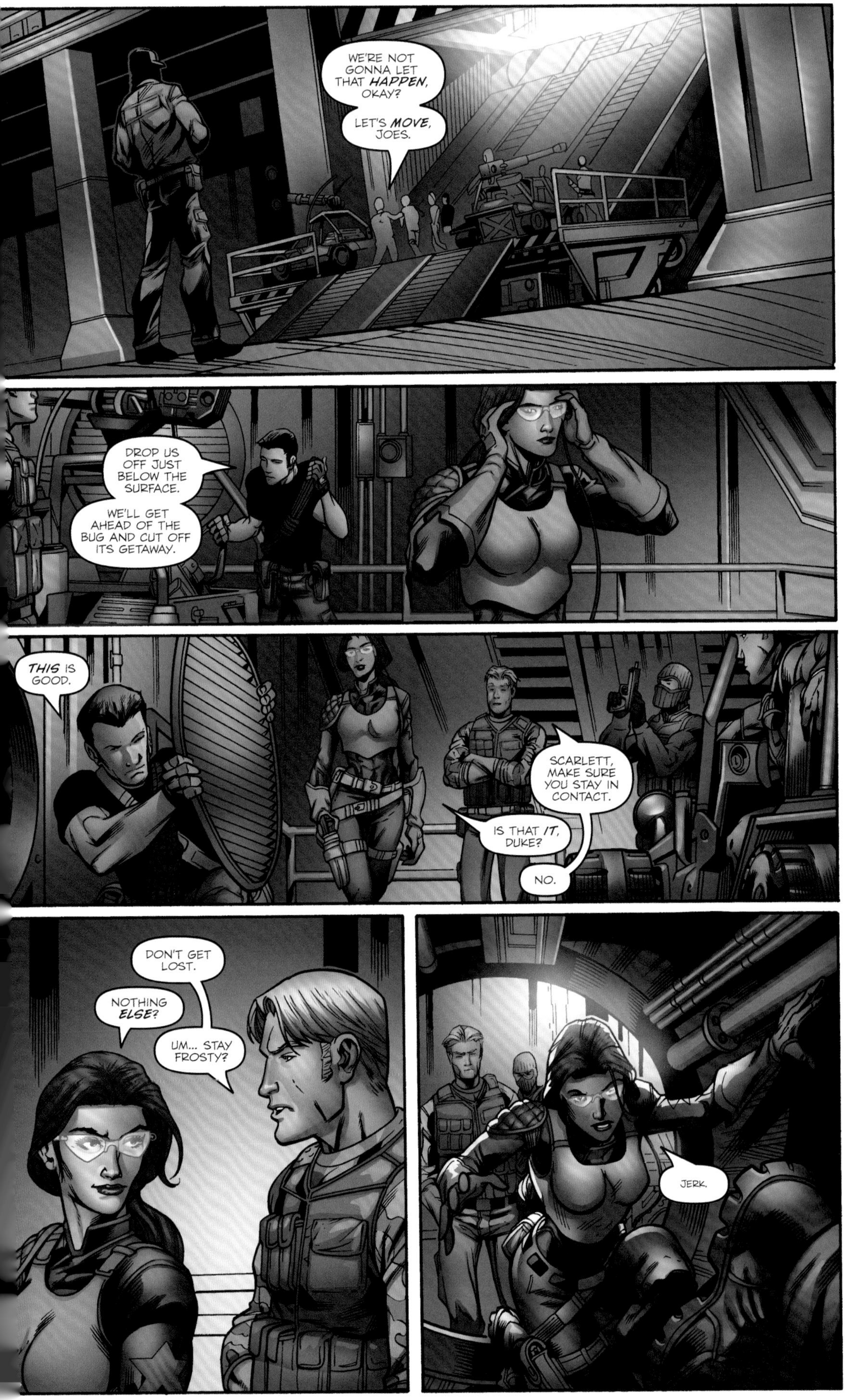
WE'RE NOT GONNA LET THAT HAPPEN, OKAY?
LET'S MOVE, JOES.
DROP US OFF JUST BELOW THE SURFACE.
WE'LL GET AHEAD OF THE BUG AND CUT OFF ITS GETAWAY.
THIS IS GOOD.
SCARLETT, MAKE SURE YOU STAY IN CONTACT.
IS THAT IT, DUKE?
NO.
DON'T GET LOST.
NOTHING ELSE?
UM... STAY FROSTY?
JERK.

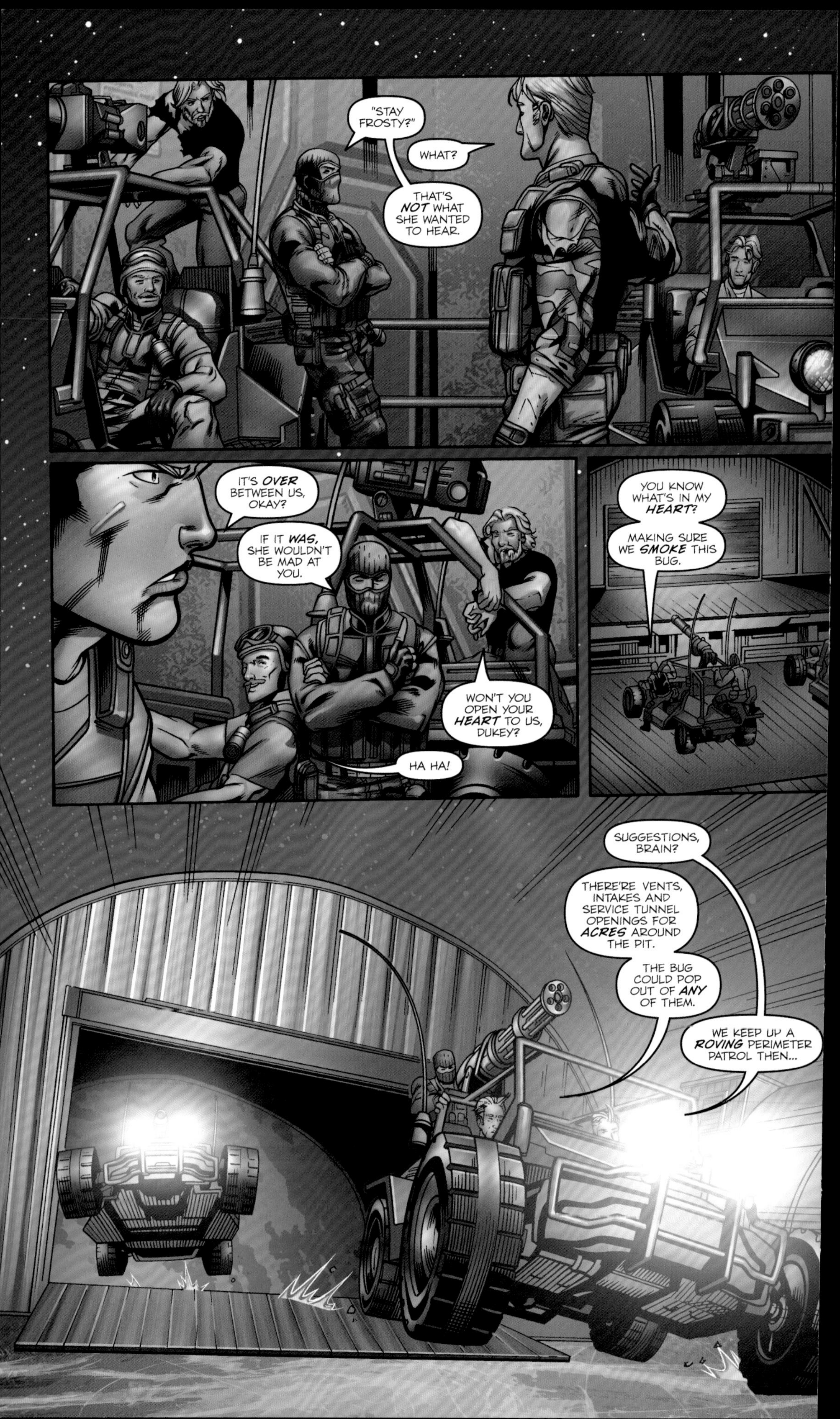

"STAY FROSTY?"
WHAT?
THAT'S *NOT* WHAT SHE WANTED TO HEAR.
IT'S *OVER* BETWEEN US, OKAY?
IF IT *WAS,* SHE WOULDN'T BE MAD AT YOU.
WON'T YOU OPEN YOUR *HEART* TO US, DUKEY?
HA HA!
YOU KNOW WHAT'S IN MY *HEART?*
MAKING SURE WE *SMOKE* THIS BUG.
SUGGESTIONS, BRAIN?
THERE'RE VENTS, INTAKES AND SERVICE TUNNEL OPENINGS FOR *ACRES* AROUND THE PIT.
THE BUG COULD POP OUT OF *ANY* OF THEM.
WE KEEP UP A *ROVING* PERIMETER PATROL THEN...

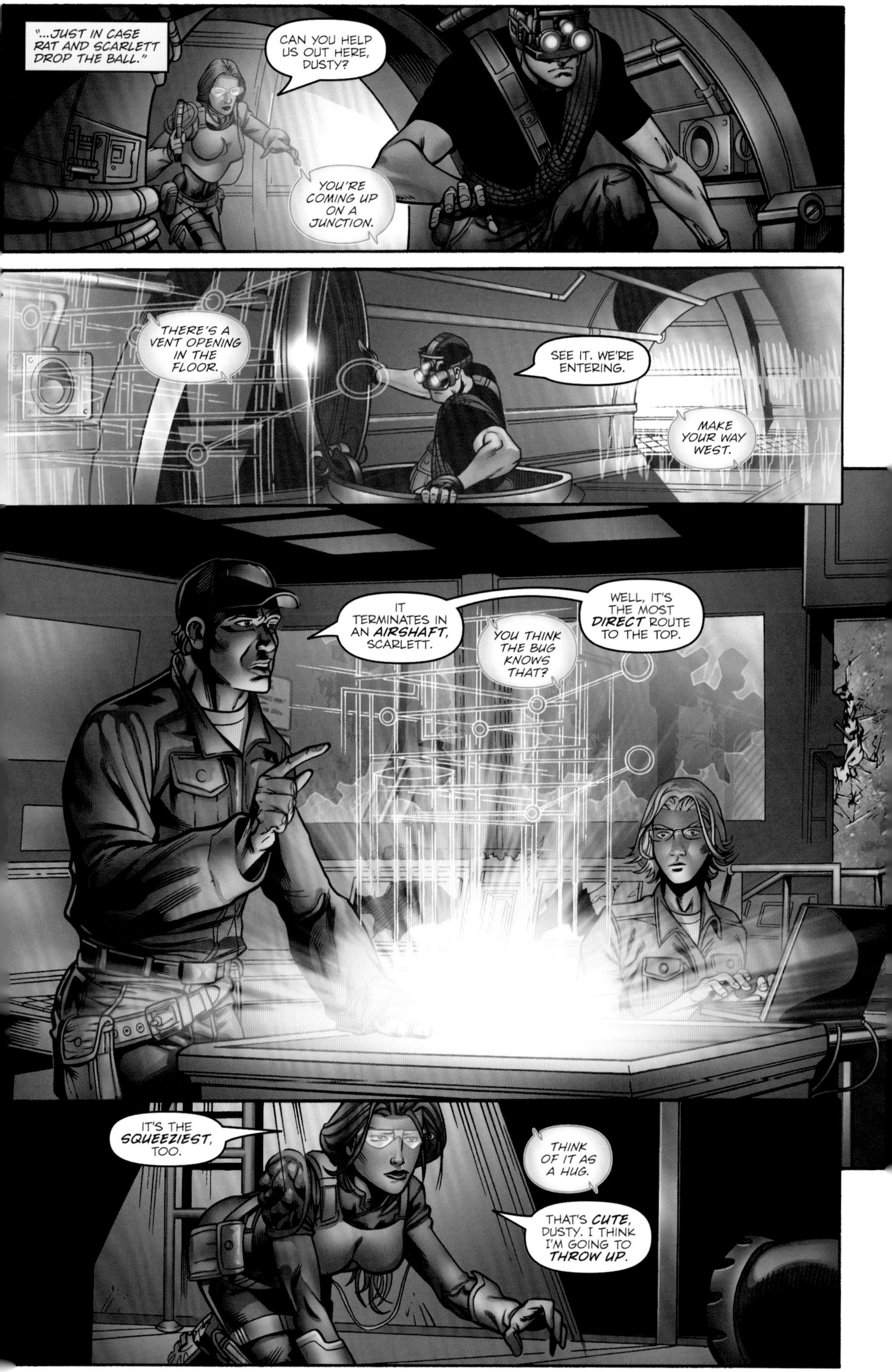
"...JUST IN CASE RAT AND SCARLETT DROP THE BALL."
CAN YOU HELP US OUT HERE, DUSTY?
YOU'RE COMING UP ON A JUNCTION.
THERE'S A VENT OPENING IN THE FLOOR.
SEE IT. WE'RE ENTERING.
MAKE YOUR WAY WEST.
IT TERMINATES IN AN AIRSHAFT, SCARLETT.
WELL, IT'S THE MOST DIRECT ROUTE TO THE TOP.
YOU THINK THE BUG KNOWS THAT?
IT'S THE SQUEEZIEST, TOO.
THINK OF IT AS A HUG.
THAT'S CUTE, DUSTY. I THINK I'M GOING TO THROW UP.

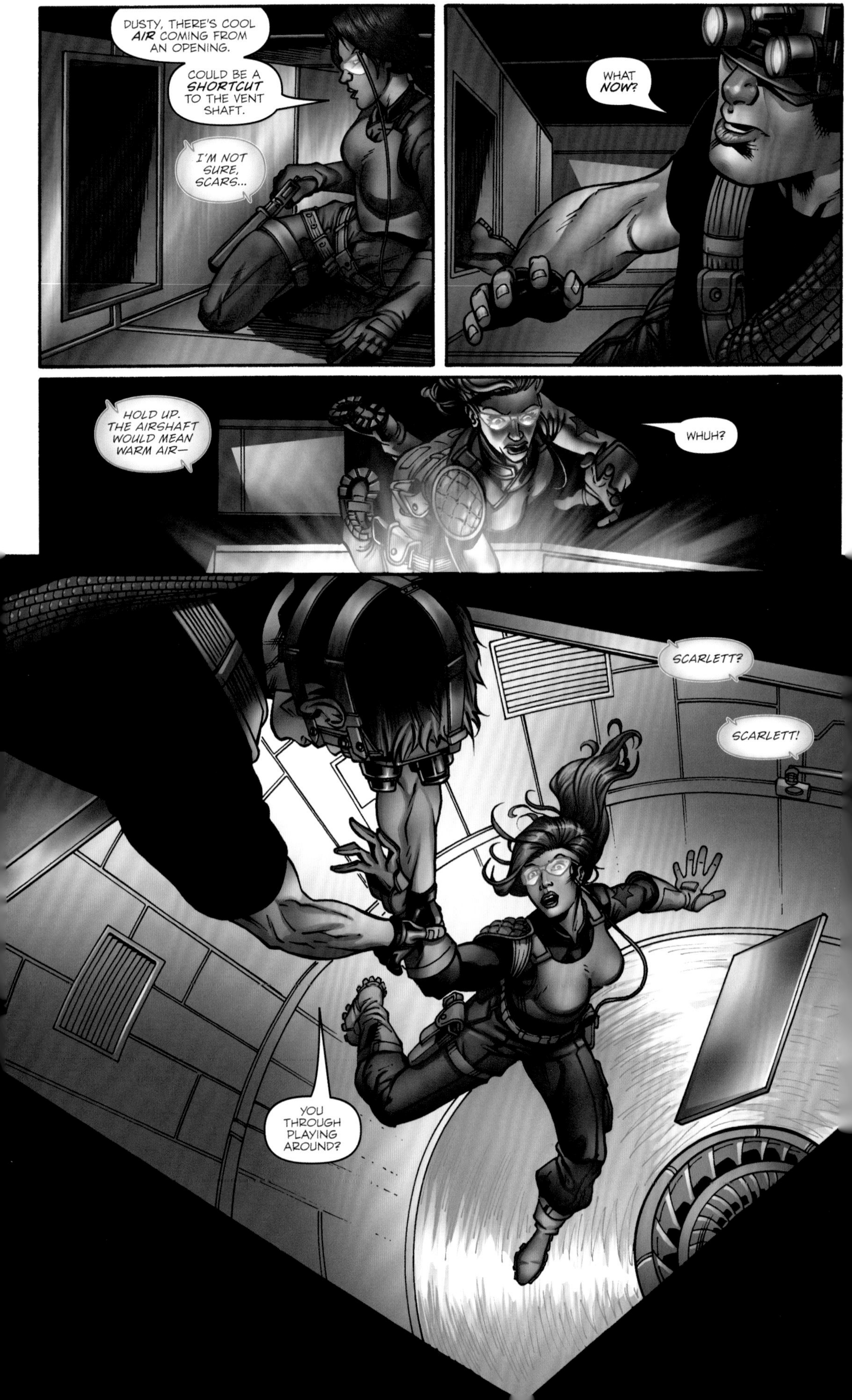
DUSTY, THERE'S COOL AIR COMING FROM AN OPENING.
COULD BE A SHORTCUT TO THE VENT SHAFT.
I'M NOT SURE, SCARS...
WHAT NOW?
HOLD UP. THE AIRSHAFT WOULD MEAN WARM AIR—
WHUH?
SCARLETT?
SCARLETT!
YOU THROUGH PLAYING AROUND?

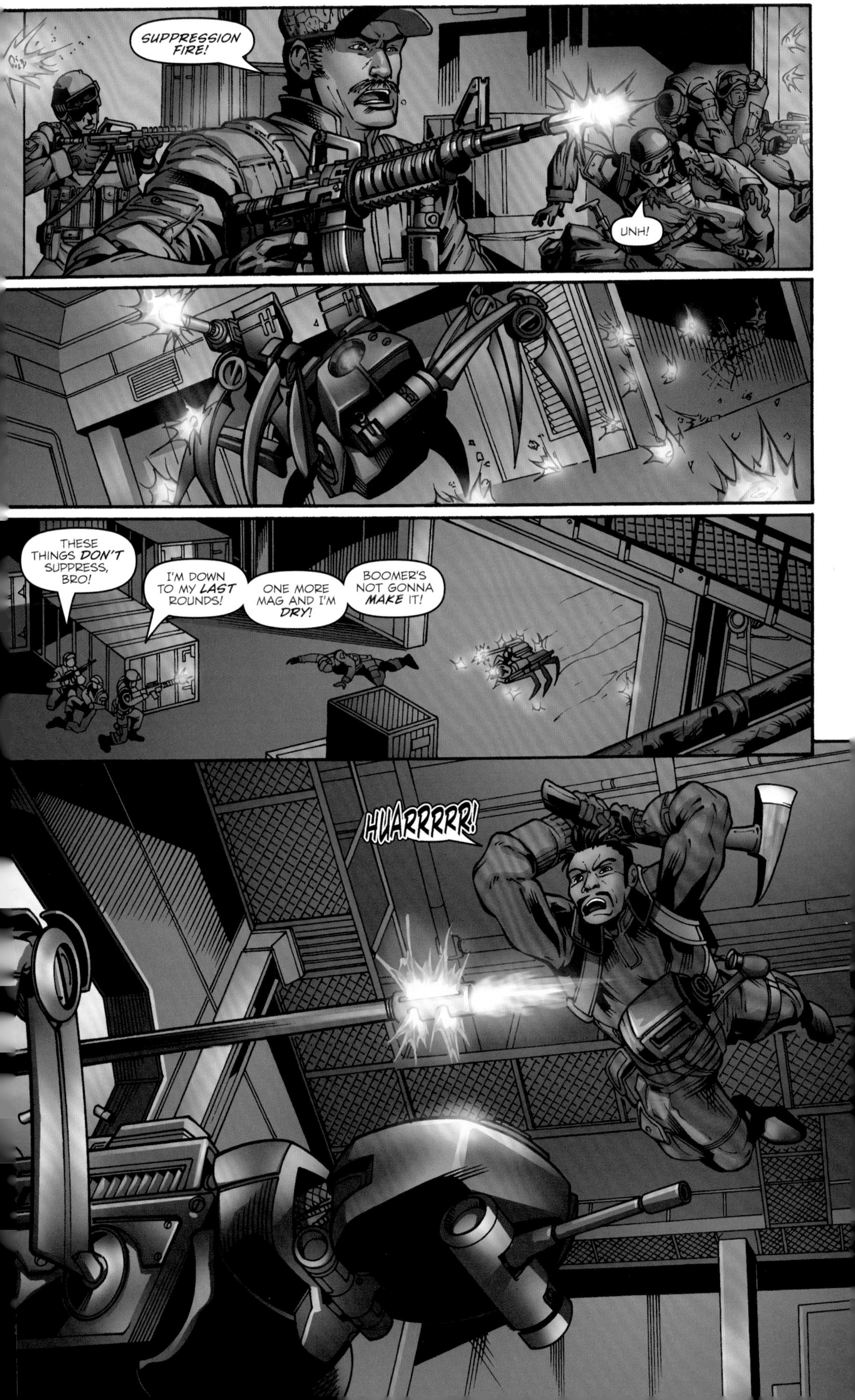
SUPPRESSION FIRE!
UNH!
THESE THINGS DON'T SUPPRESS, BRO!
I'M DOWN TO MY LAST ROUNDS!
ONE MORE MAG AND I'M DRY!
BOOMER'S NOT GONNA MAKE IT!
HUARRRRR!

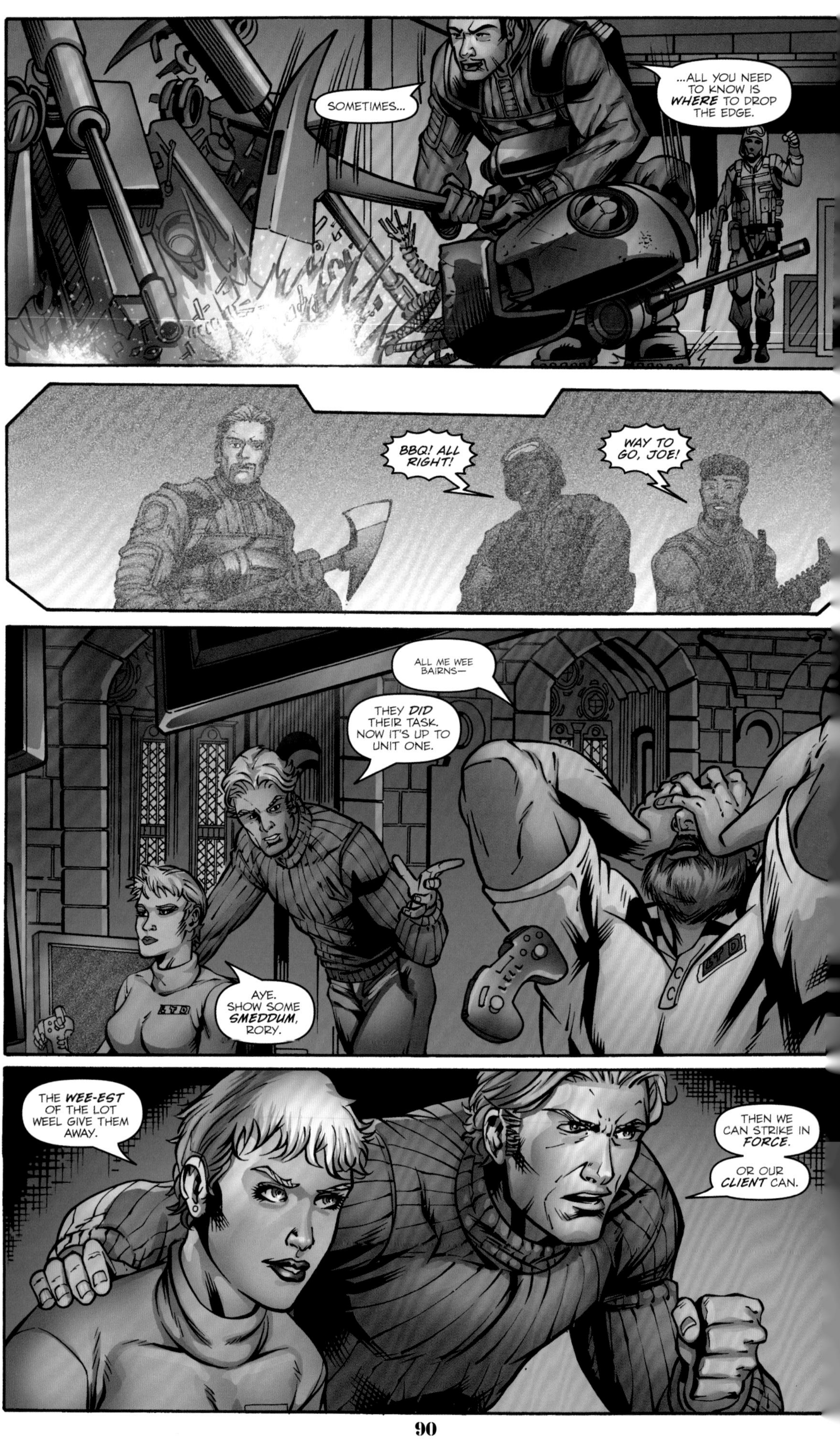
SOMETIMES...
...ALL YOU NEED TO KNOW IS WHERE TO DROP THE EDGE.
BBQ! ALL RIGHT!
WAY TO GO, JOE!
ALL ME WEE BAIRNS—
THEY DID THEIR TASK. NOW IT'S UP TO UNIT ONE.
AYE. SHOW SOME SMEDDUM, RORY.
THE WEE-EST OF THE LOT WEEL GIVE THEM AWAY.
THEN WE CAN STRIKE IN FORCE.
OR OUR CLIENT CAN.

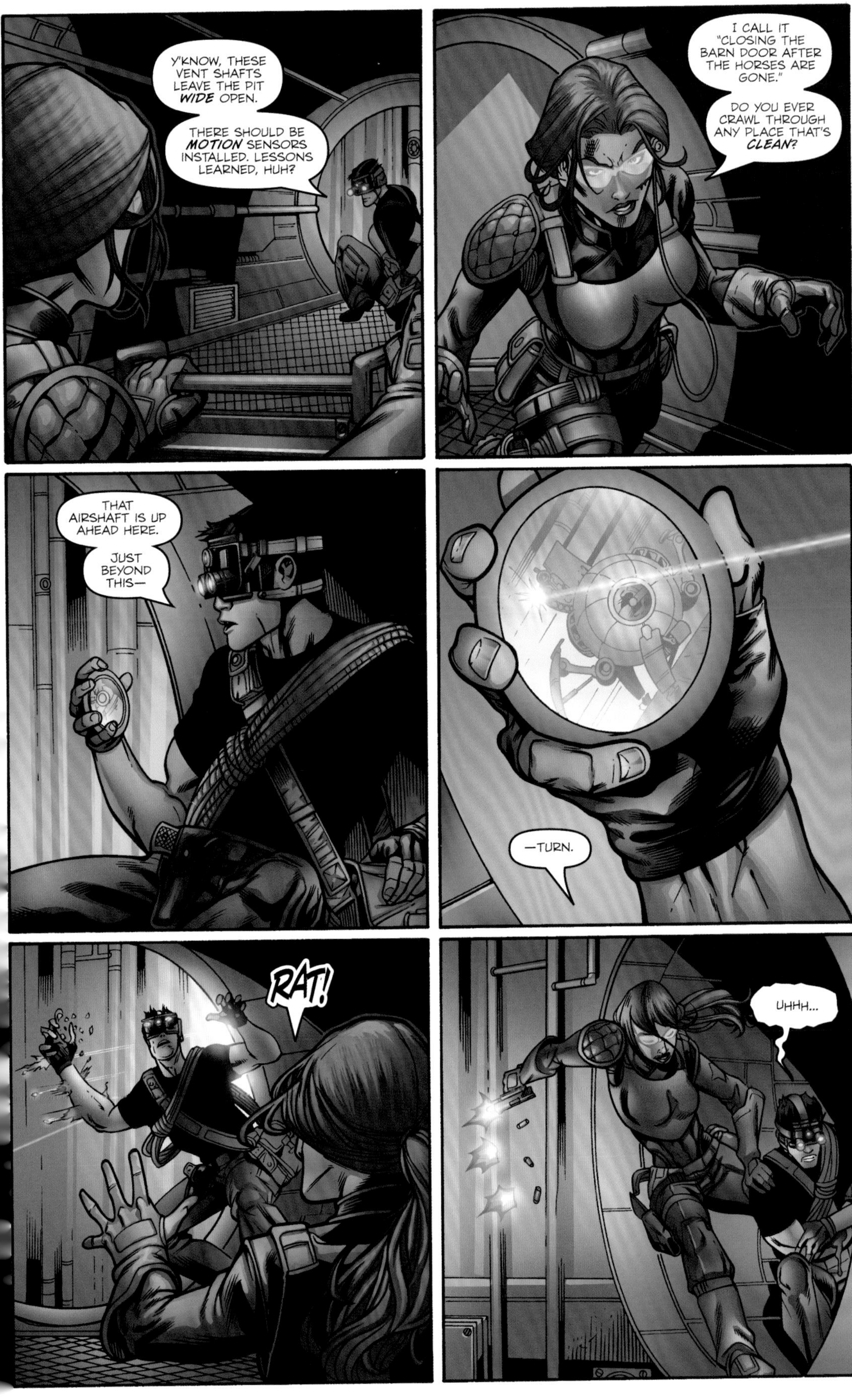
Y'KNOW, THESE VENT SHAFTS LEAVE THE PIT WIDE OPEN.
THERE SHOULD BE MOTION SENSORS INSTALLED. LESSONS LEARNED, HUH?
I CALL IT "CLOSING THE BARN DOOR AFTER THE HORSES ARE GONE."
DO YOU EVER CRAWL THROUGH ANY PLACE THAT'S CLEAN?
THAT AIRSHAFT IS UP AHEAD HERE.
JUST BEYOND THIS—
—TURN.
RAT!
UHHH...

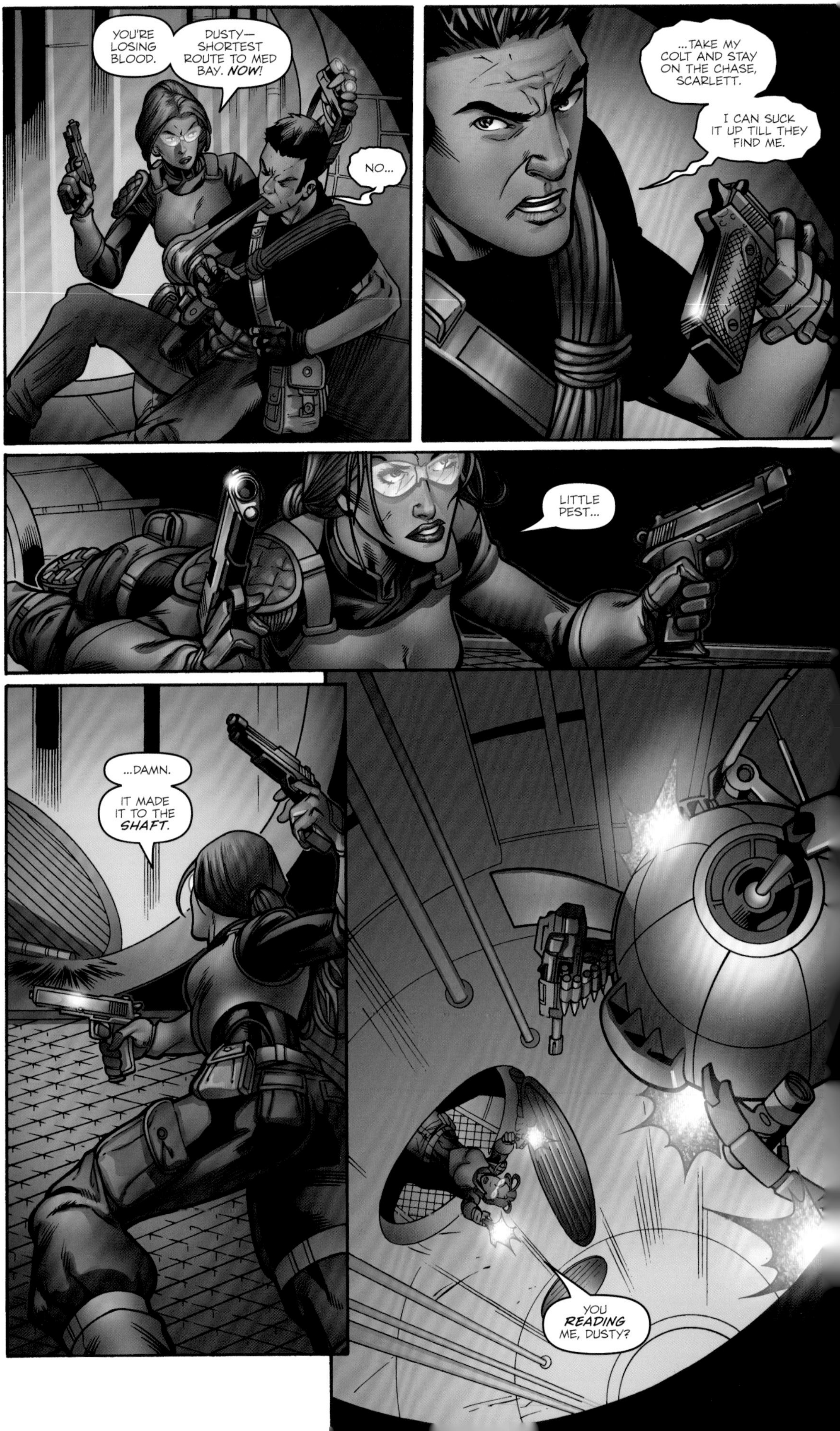
YOU'RE LOSING BLOOD.
DUSTY— SHORTEST ROUTE TO MED BAY. NOW!
NO...
...TAKE MY COLT AND STAY ON THE CHASE, SCARLETT.
I CAN SUCK IT UP TILL THEY FIND ME.
LITTLE PEST...
...DAMN.
IT MADE IT TO THE SHAFT.
YOU READING ME, DUSTY?

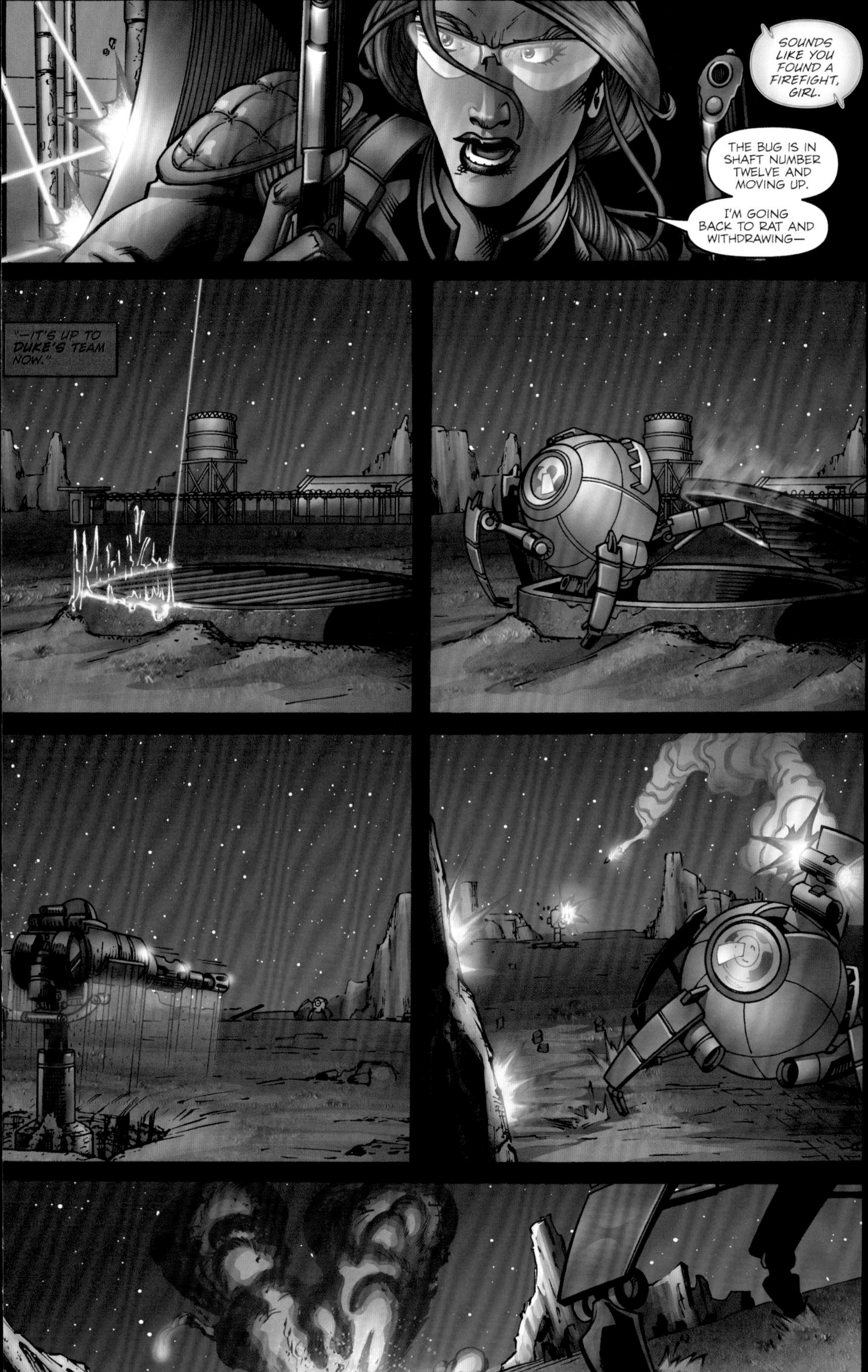
SOUNDS LIKE YOU FOUND A FIREFIGHT, GIRL.
THE BUG IS IN SHAFT NUMBER TWELVE AND MOVING UP.
I'M GOING BACK TO RAT AND WITHDRAWING—
"—IT'S UP TO DUKE'S TEAM NOW."

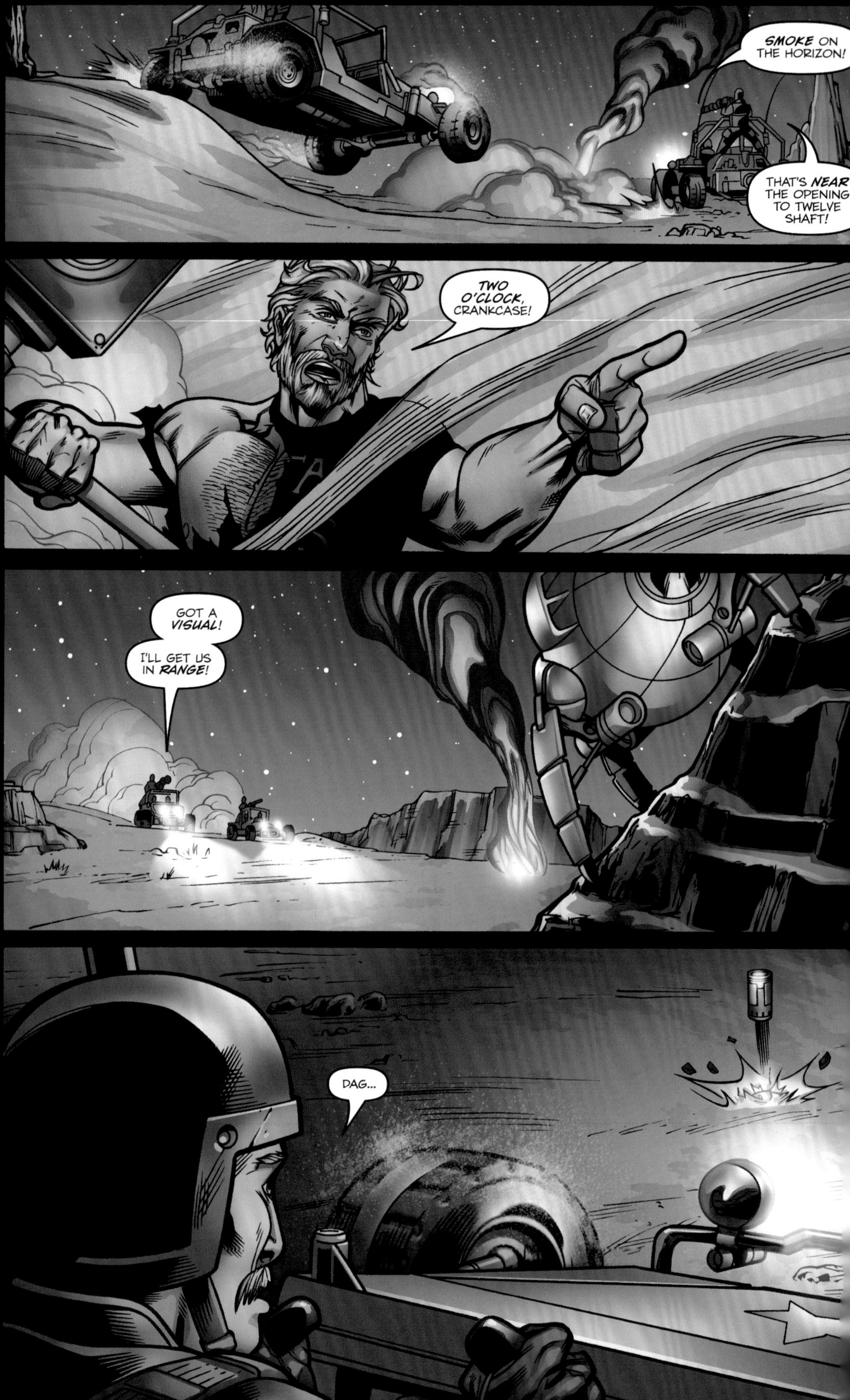
SMOKE ON THE HORIZON!
THAT'S NEAR THE OPENING TO TWELVE SHAFT!
TWO O'CLOCK, CRANKCASE!
GOT A VISUAL!
I'LL GET US IN RANGE!
DAG...

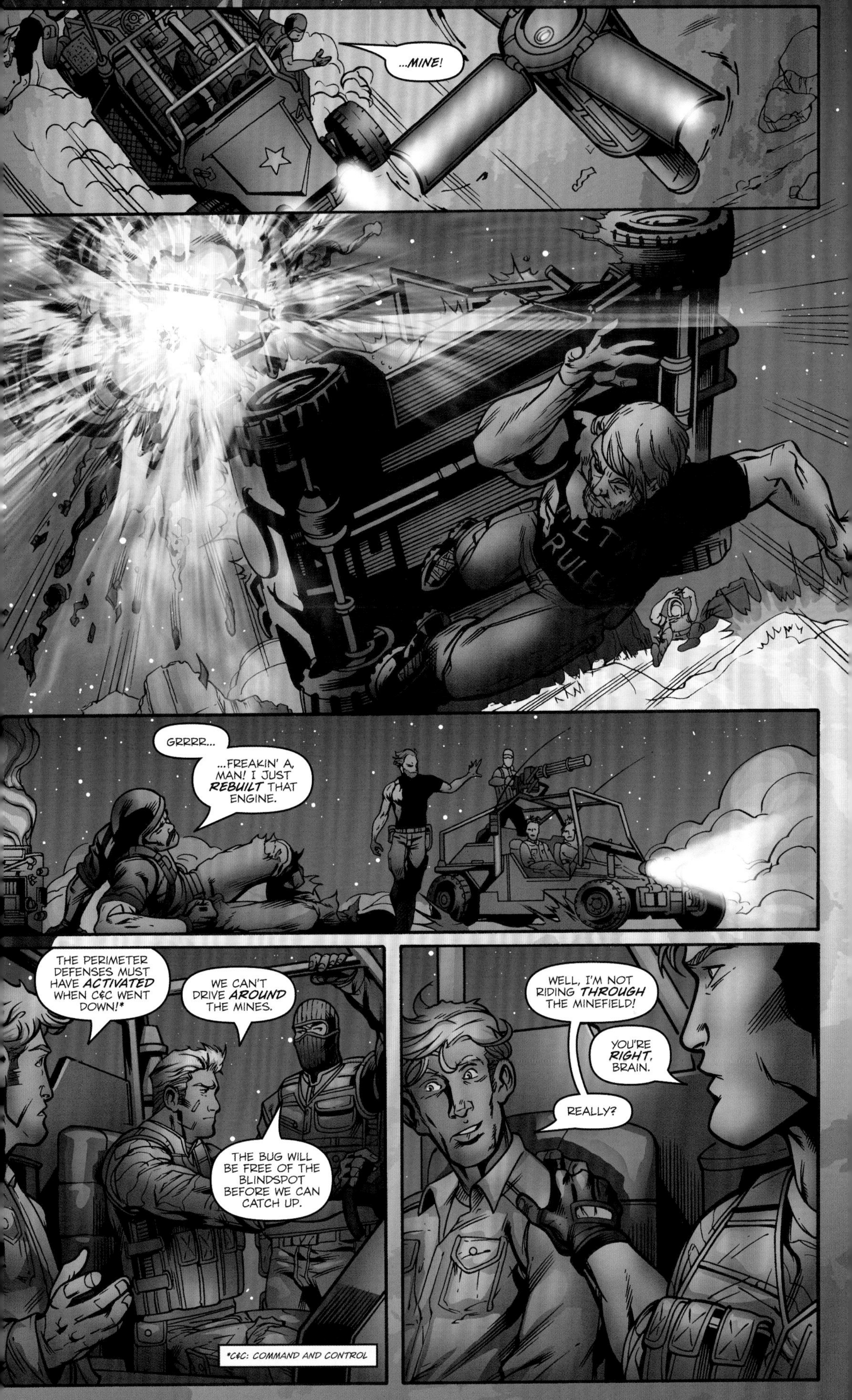
...MINE!
GRRRR...
...FREAKIN' A, MAN! I JUST REBUILT THAT ENGINE.
THE PERIMETER DEFENSES MUST HAVE ACTIVATED WHEN C&C WENT DOWN!*
WE CAN'T DRIVE AROUND THE MINES.
THE BUG WILL BE FREE OF THE BLINDSPOT BEFORE WE CAN CATCH UP.
*C&C: COMMAND AND CONTROL
WELL, I'M NOT RIDING THROUGH THE MINEFIELD!
YOU'RE RIGHT, BRAIN.
REALLY?

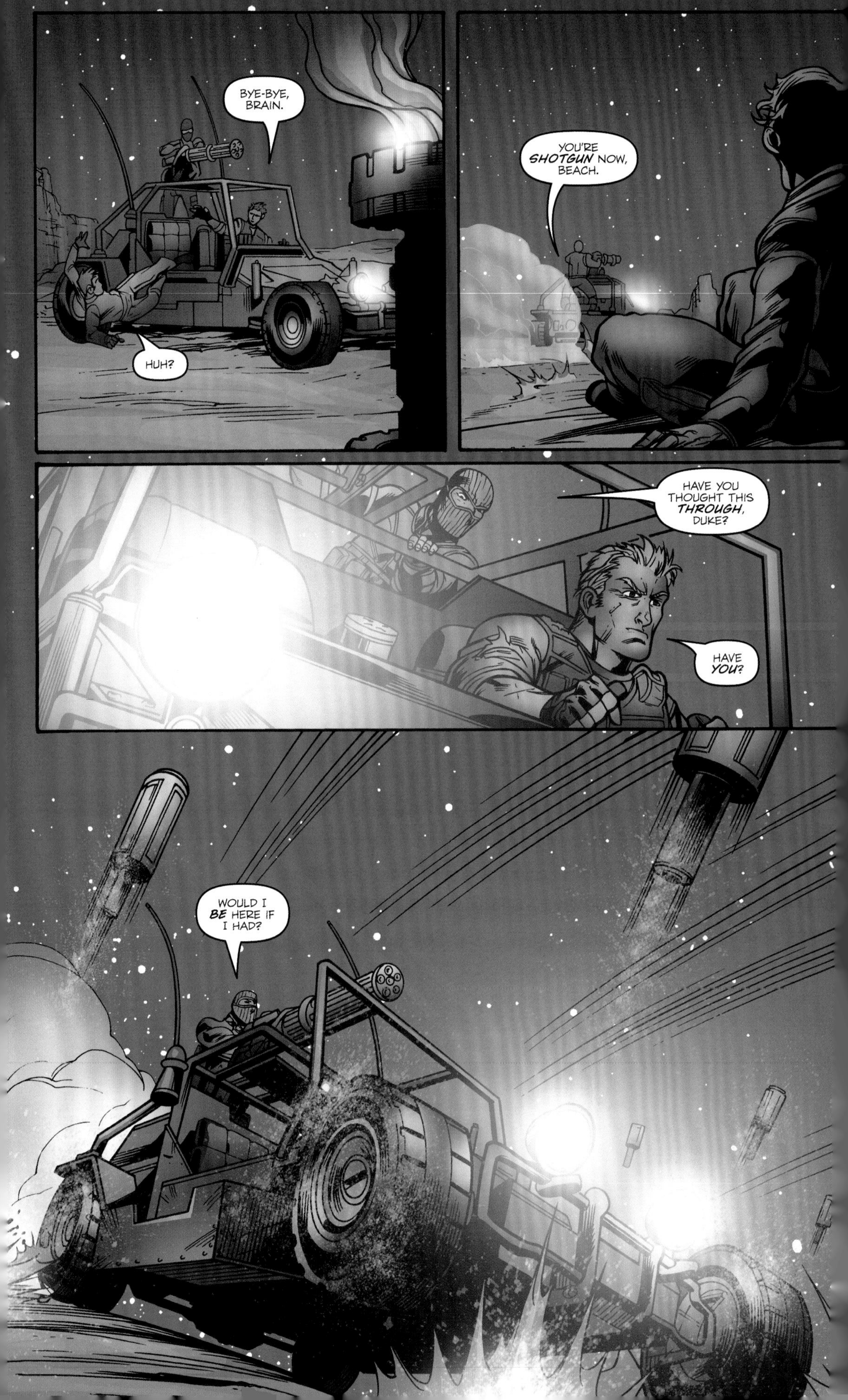
BYE-BYE, BRAIN.
HUH?
YOU'RE **SHOTGUN** NOW, BEACH.
HAVE YOU THOUGHT THIS **THROUGH**, DUKE?
HAVE **YOU**?
WOULD I **BE** HERE IF I HAD?

CHAPTER 5

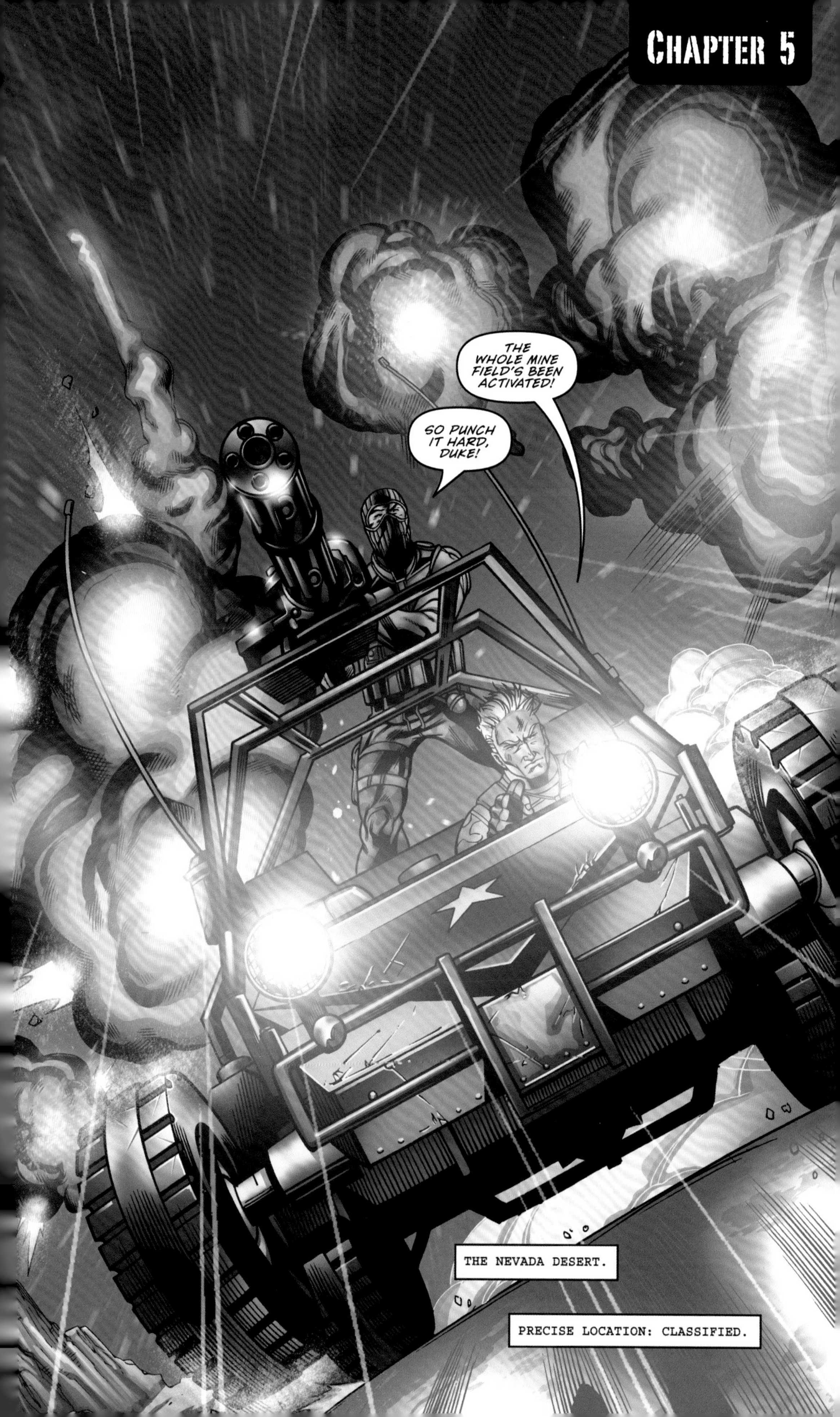
THE WHOLE MINE FIELD'S BEEN ACTIVATED!
SO PUNCH IT HARD, DUKE!
THE NEVADA DESERT.
PRECISE LOCATION: CLASSIFIED.

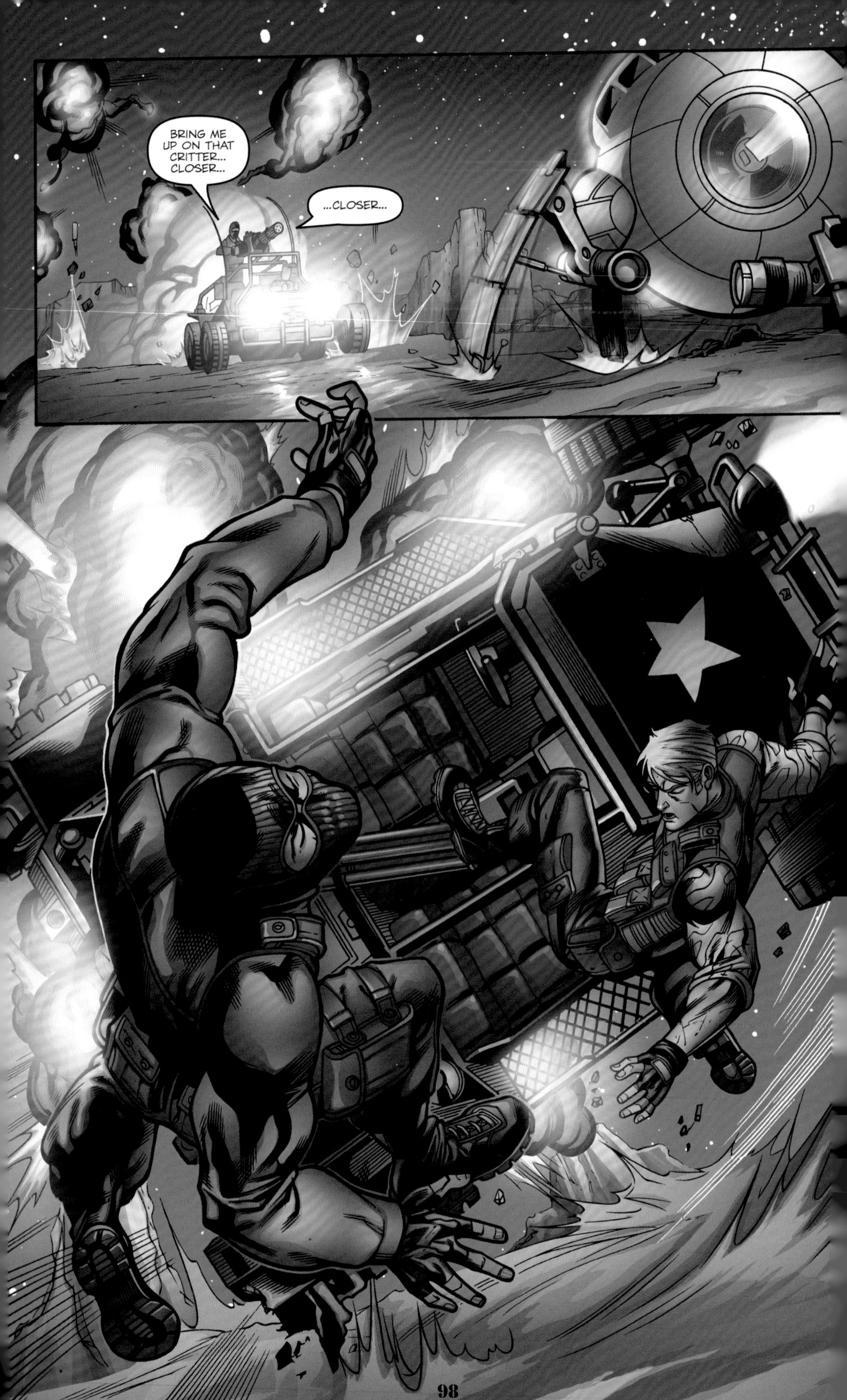
BRING ME UP ON THAT CRITTER... CLOSER...
...CLOSER...

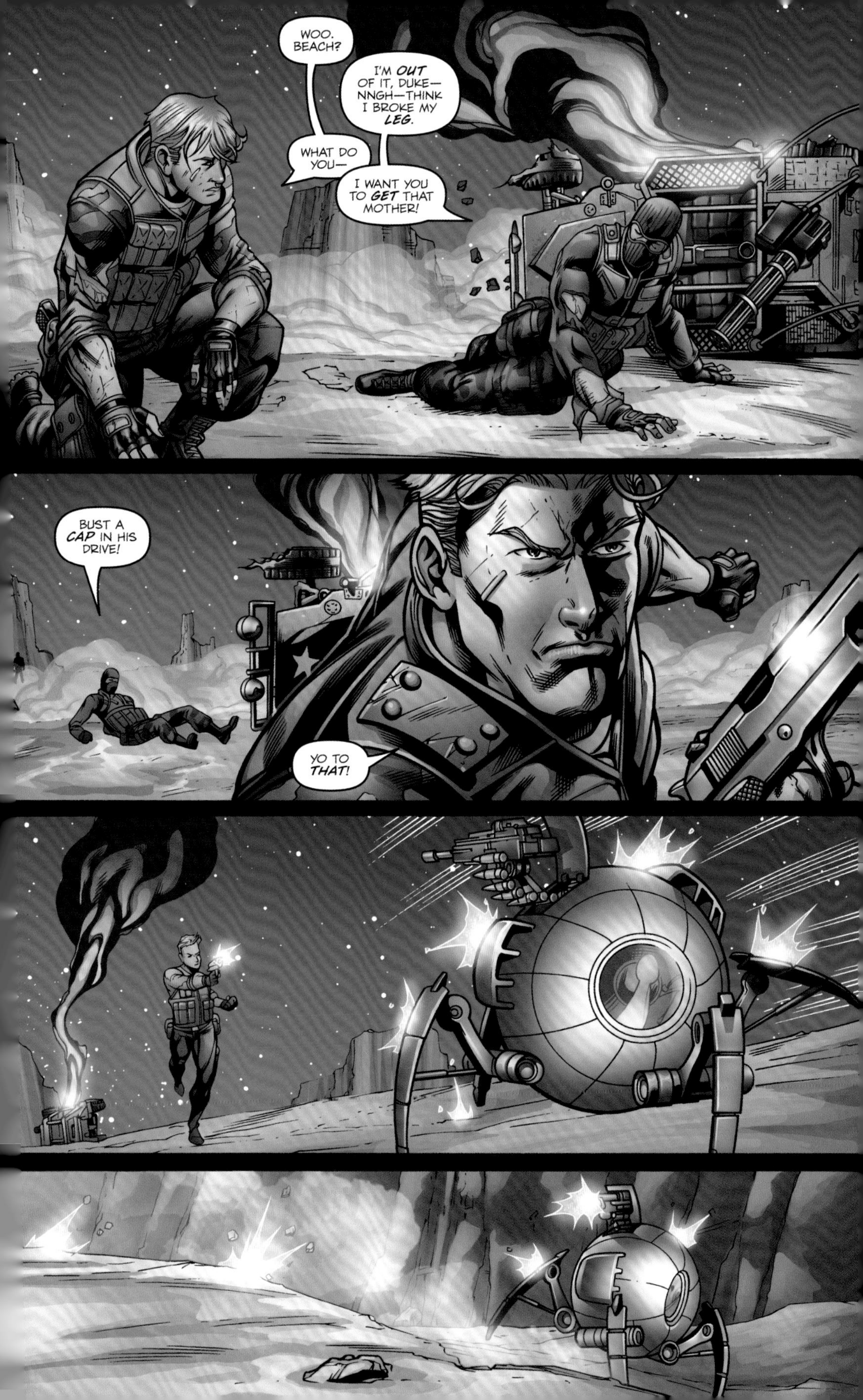
WOO. BEACH?
WHAT DO YOU—
I'M OUT OF IT, DUKE—NNGH—THINK I BROKE MY LEG.
I WANT YOU TO GET THAT MOTHER!
BUST A CAP IN HIS DRIVE!
YO TO THAT!

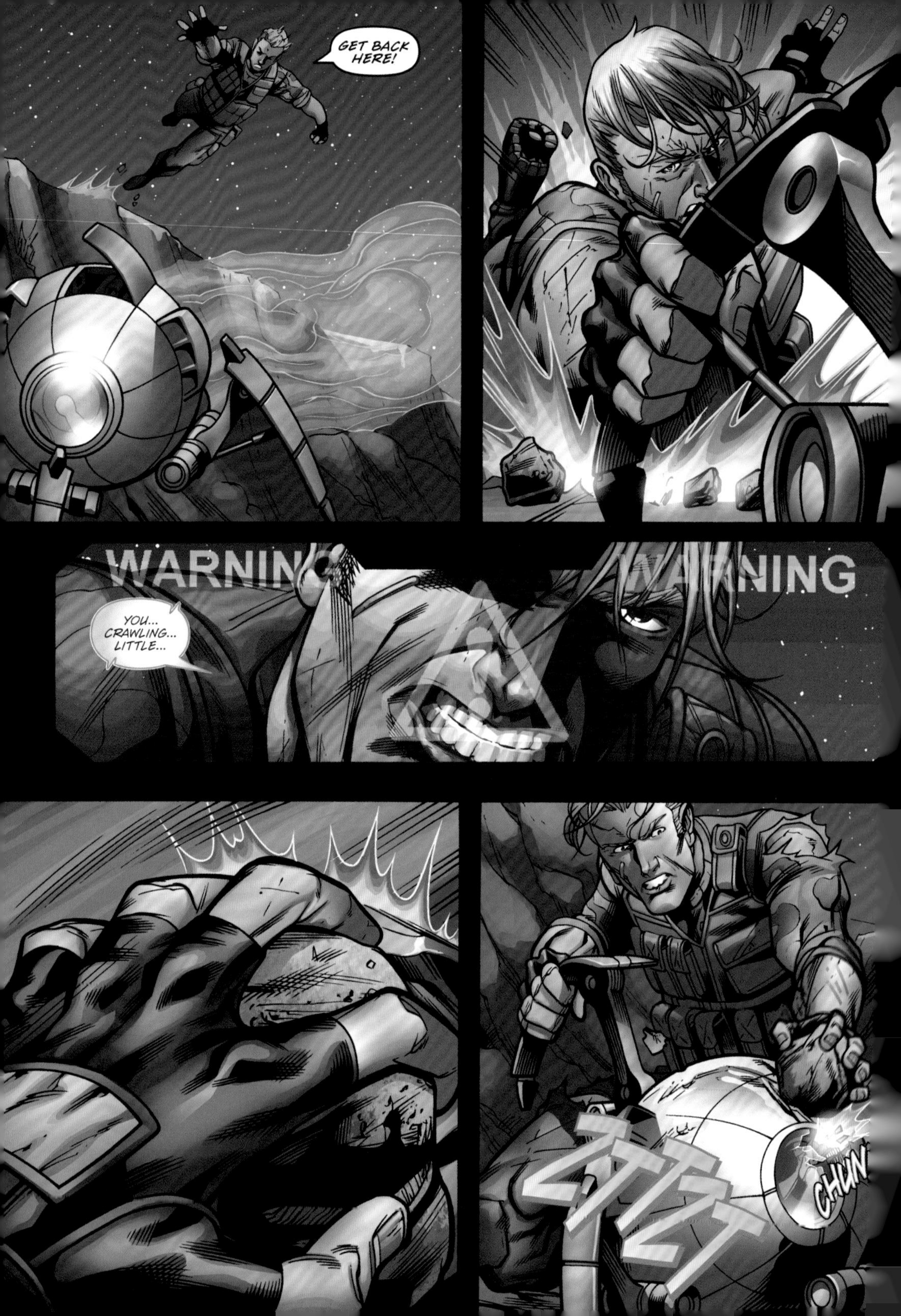
GET BACK HERE!
WARNING
WARNING
YOU... CRAWLING... LITTLE...
CHUN

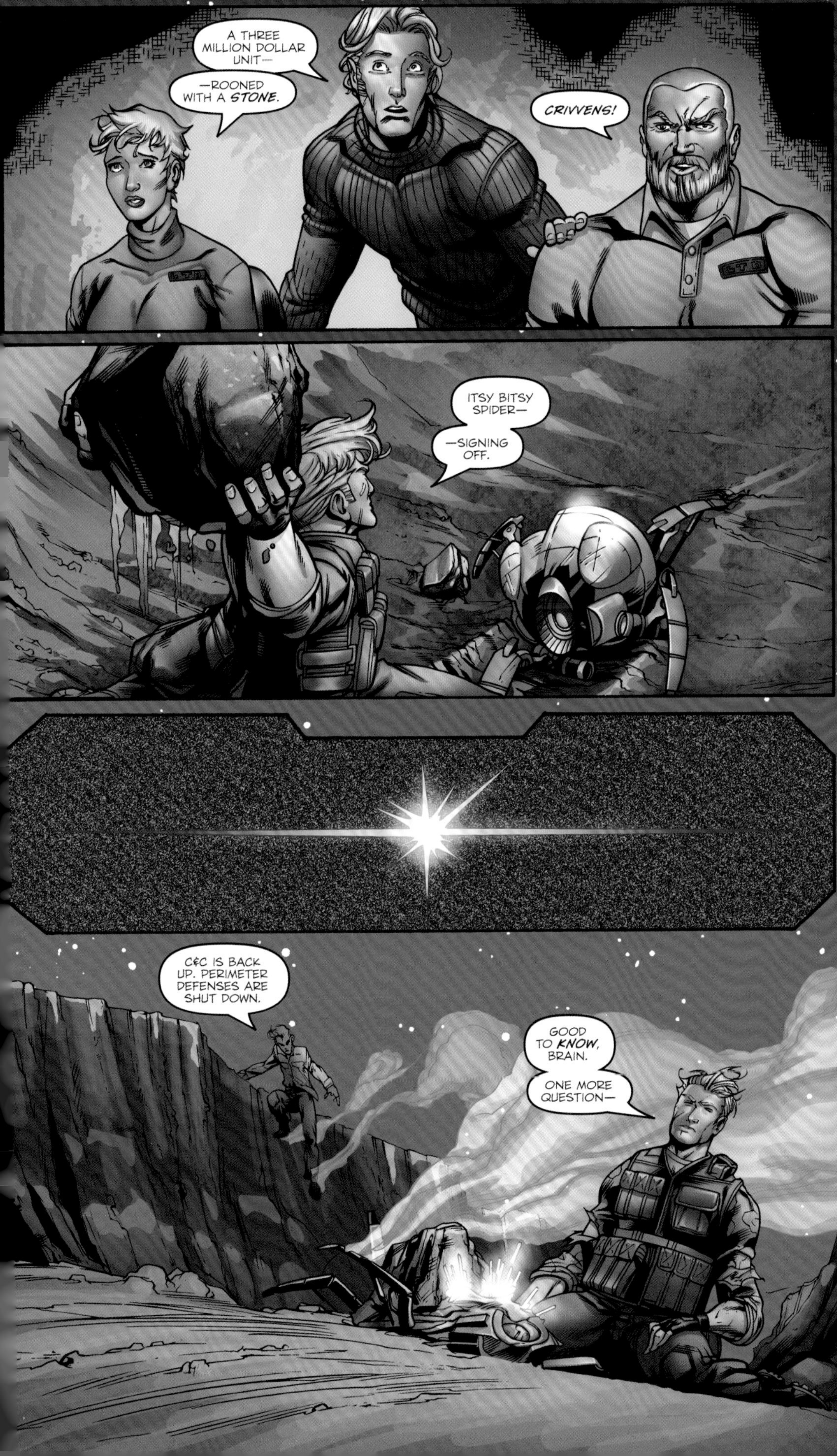
A THREE MILLION DOLLAR UNIT—
—ROONED WITH A STONE.
CRIVVENS!
ITSY BITSY SPIDER—
—SIGNING OFF.
C&C IS BACK UP. PERIMETER DEFENSES ARE SHUT DOWN.
GOOD TO KNOW, BRAIN.
ONE MORE QUESTION—

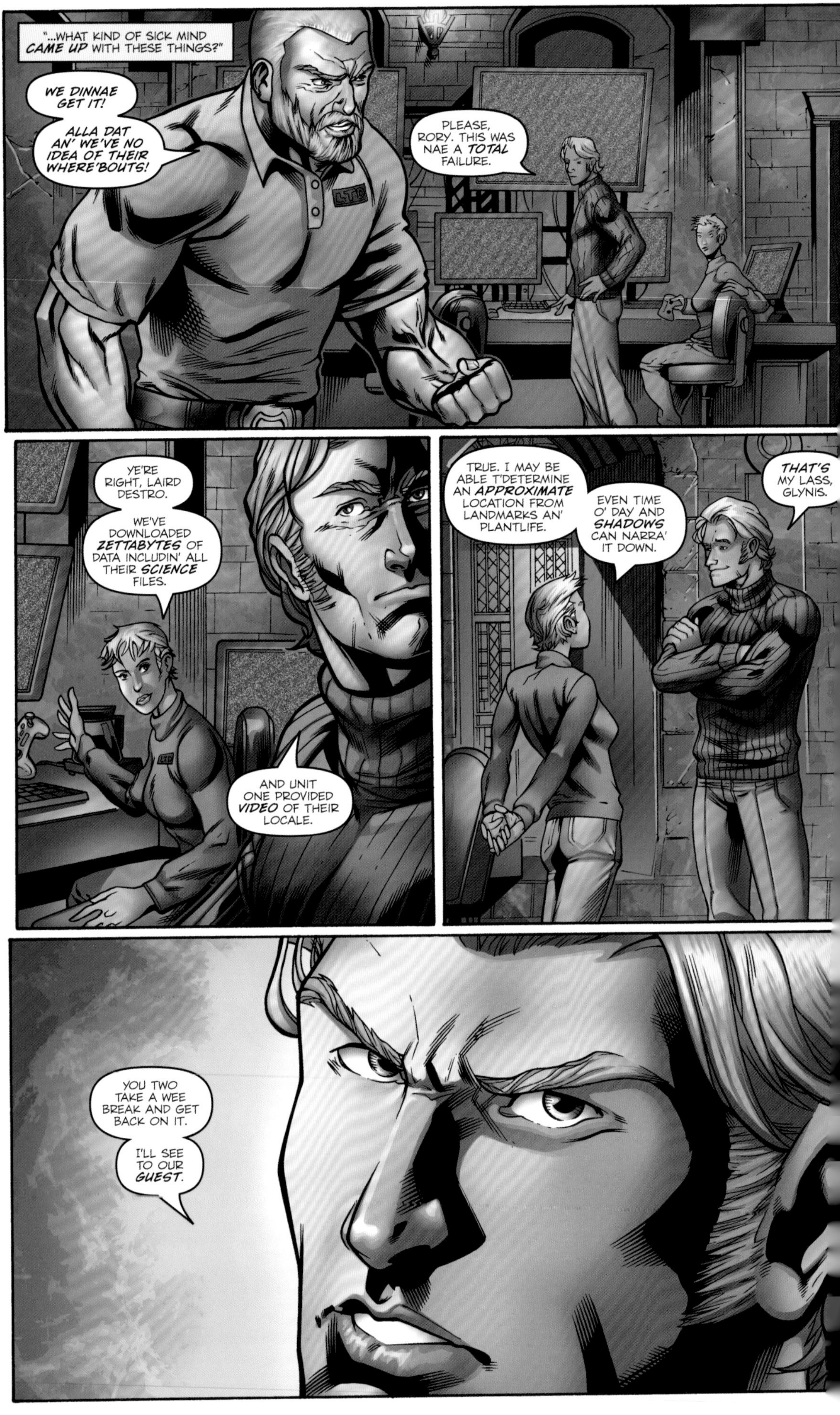
"...WHAT KIND OF SICK MIND CAME UP WITH THESE THINGS?"
WE DINNAE GET IT!
ALLA DAT AN' WE'VE NO IDEA OF THEIR WHERE'BOUTS!
PLEASE, RORY. THIS WAS NAE A TOTAL FAILURE.
YE'RE RIGHT, LAIRD DESTRO.
WE'VE DOWNLOADED ZETTABYTES OF DATA INCLUDIN' ALL THEIR SCIENCE FILES.
AND UNIT ONE PROVIDED VIDEO OF THEIR LOCALE.
TRUE. I MAY BE ABLE T'DETERMINE AN APPROXIMATE LOCATION FROM LANDMARKS AN' PLANTLIFE.
EVEN TIME O' DAY AND SHADOWS CAN NARRA' IT DOWN.
THAT'S MY LASS, GLYNIS.
YOU TWO TAKE A WEE BREAK AND GET BACK ON IT.
I'LL SEE TO OUR GUEST.

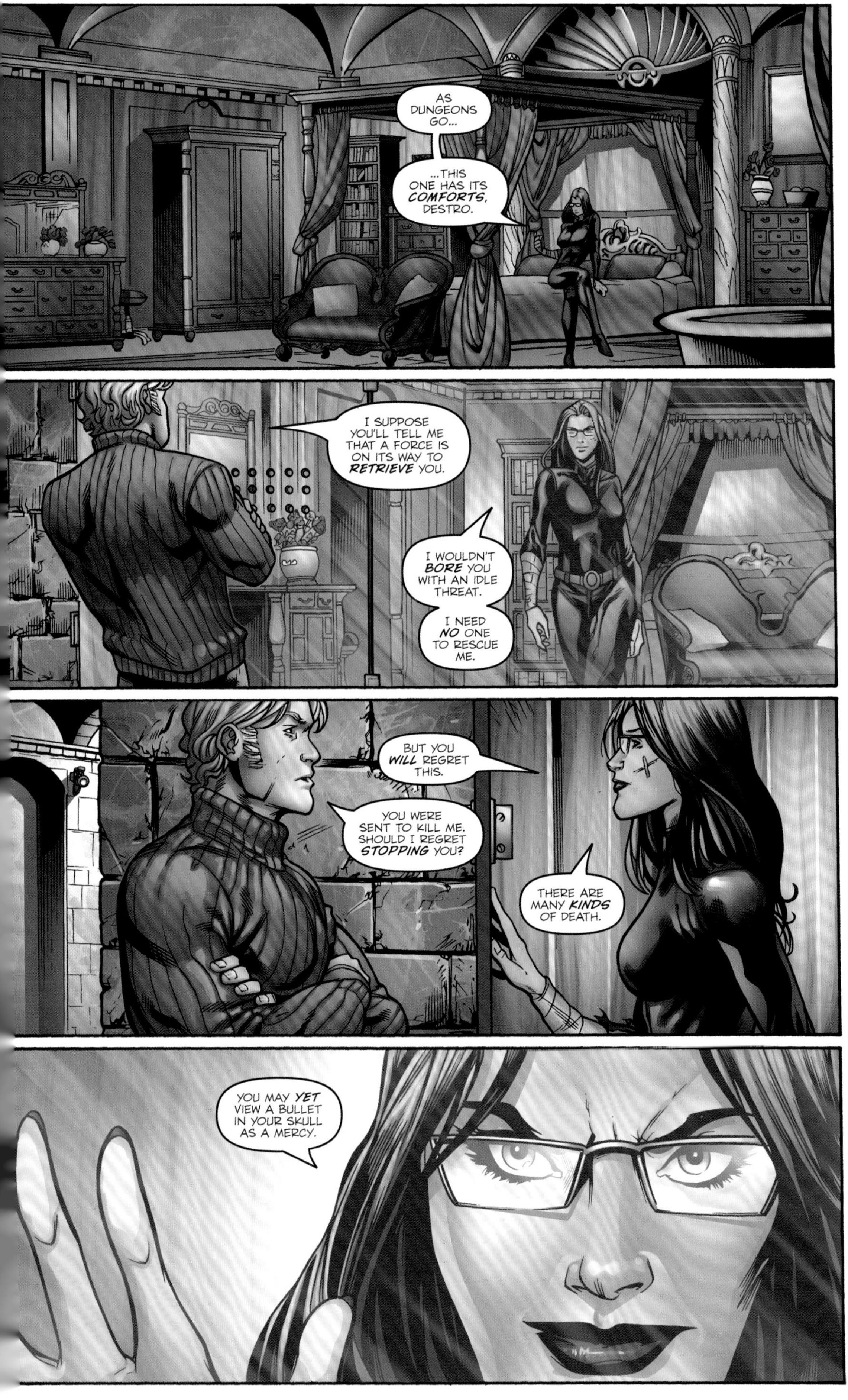

AS DUNGEONS GO...
...THIS ONE HAS ITS COMFORTS, DESTRO.
I SUPPOSE YOU'LL TELL ME THAT A FORCE IS ON ITS WAY TO RETRIEVE YOU.
I WOULDN'T BORE YOU WITH AN IDLE THREAT.
I NEED NO ONE TO RESCUE ME.
BUT YOU WILL REGRET THIS.
YOU WERE SENT TO KILL ME. SHOULD I REGRET STOPPING YOU?
THERE ARE MANY KINDS OF DEATH.
YOU MAY YET VIEW A BULLET IN YOUR SKULL AS A MERCY.

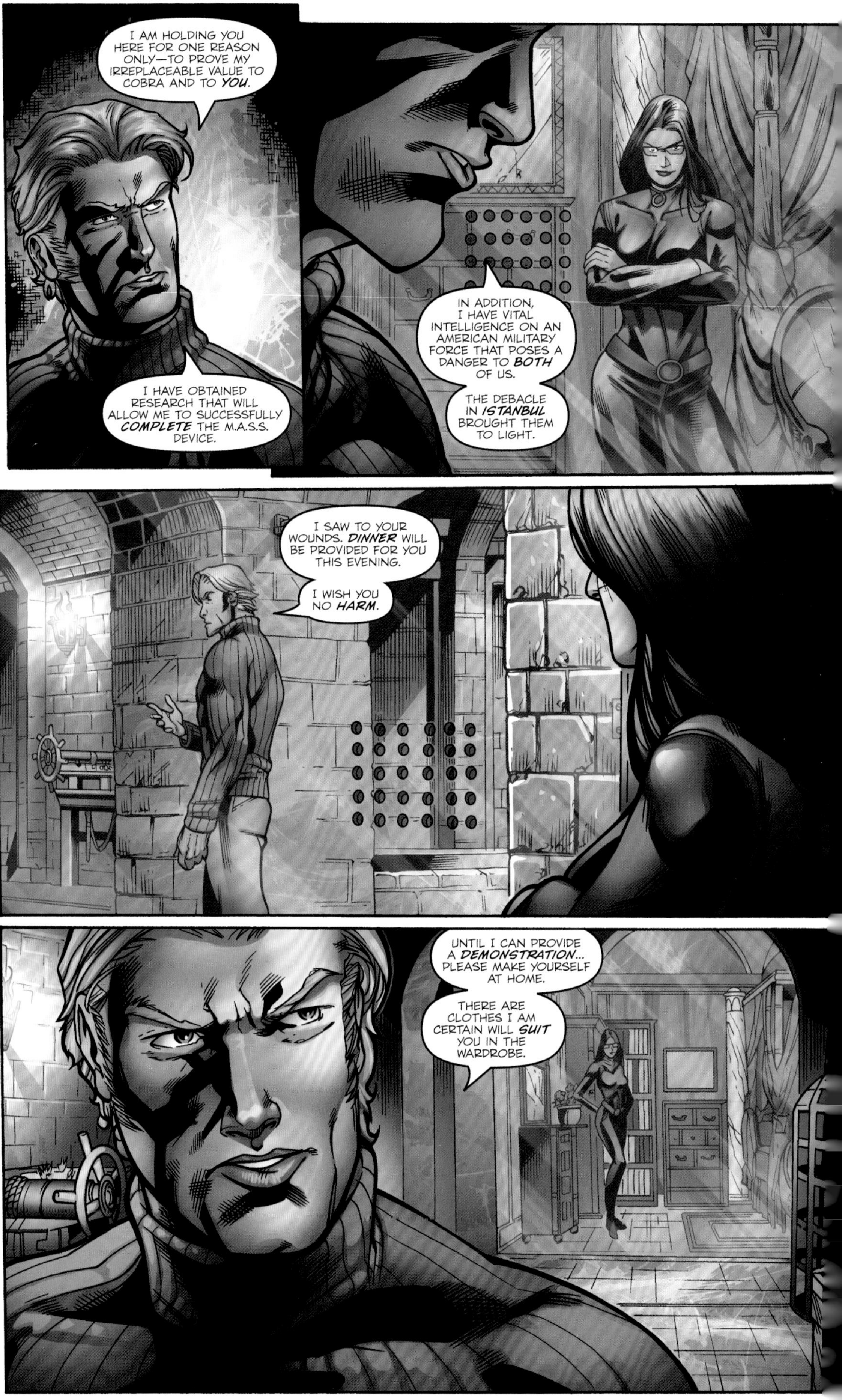
I AM HOLDING YOU HERE FOR ONE REASON ONLY—TO PROVE MY IRREPLACEABLE VALUE TO COBRA AND TO *YOU*.
I HAVE OBTAINED RESEARCH THAT WILL ALLOW ME TO SUCCESSFULLY *COMPLETE* THE M.A.S.S. DEVICE.
IN ADDITION, I HAVE VITAL INTELLIGENCE ON AN AMERICAN MILITARY FORCE THAT POSES A DANGER TO *BOTH* OF US.
THE DEBACLE IN *ISTANBUL* BROUGHT THEM TO LIGHT.
I SAW TO YOUR WOUNDS. *DINNER* WILL BE PROVIDED FOR YOU THIS EVENING.
I WISH YOU NO *HARM*.
UNTIL I CAN PROVIDE A *DEMONSTRATION*... PLEASE MAKE YOURSELF AT HOME.
THERE ARE CLOTHES I AM CERTAIN WILL *SUIT* YOU IN THE WARDROBE.

THE PIT.

THIS IS AN *INFORMAL* DE-BRIEF, PEOPLE.

YOU ALL HAVE WORK TO DO SO MAKE THIS SHORT AND SWEET, DUKE.

NO CRITICAL STRUCTURAL DAMAGE TO THE PIT. COMMUNICATIONS ARE BACK UP.

WE'VE SUFFERED CASUALTIES, GENERAL HAWK. TWELVE DEAD AND FIFTY WOUNDED.

INCLUDING *YOURSELF*, SIR. ARE YOU CERTAIN YOU'RE *UP* TO THIS, GENERAL?

I GOT A LITTLE *SINGED*, SCARLETT. BUT MY *PRIDE* TOOK A BEATING.

WHAT DO WE KNOW ABOUT THOSE DAMNED *BUGS* THAT INVADED THE PIT?

WE JUST *WAKE UP* AND FIND THEM CRAWLING IN EVERY CORNER?

WE HAVE A FEW LEADS TO GO ON, SIR.

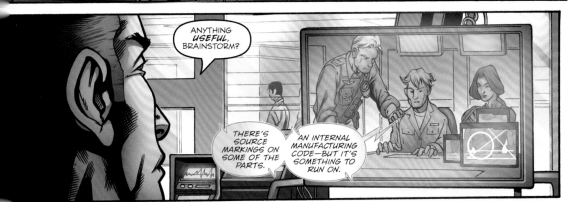

ANYTHING *USEFUL*, BRAINSTORM?

THERE'S SOURCE MARKINGS ON SOME OF THE PARTS.

AN INTERNAL MANUFACTURING CODE—BUT IT'S SOMETHING TO RUN ON.

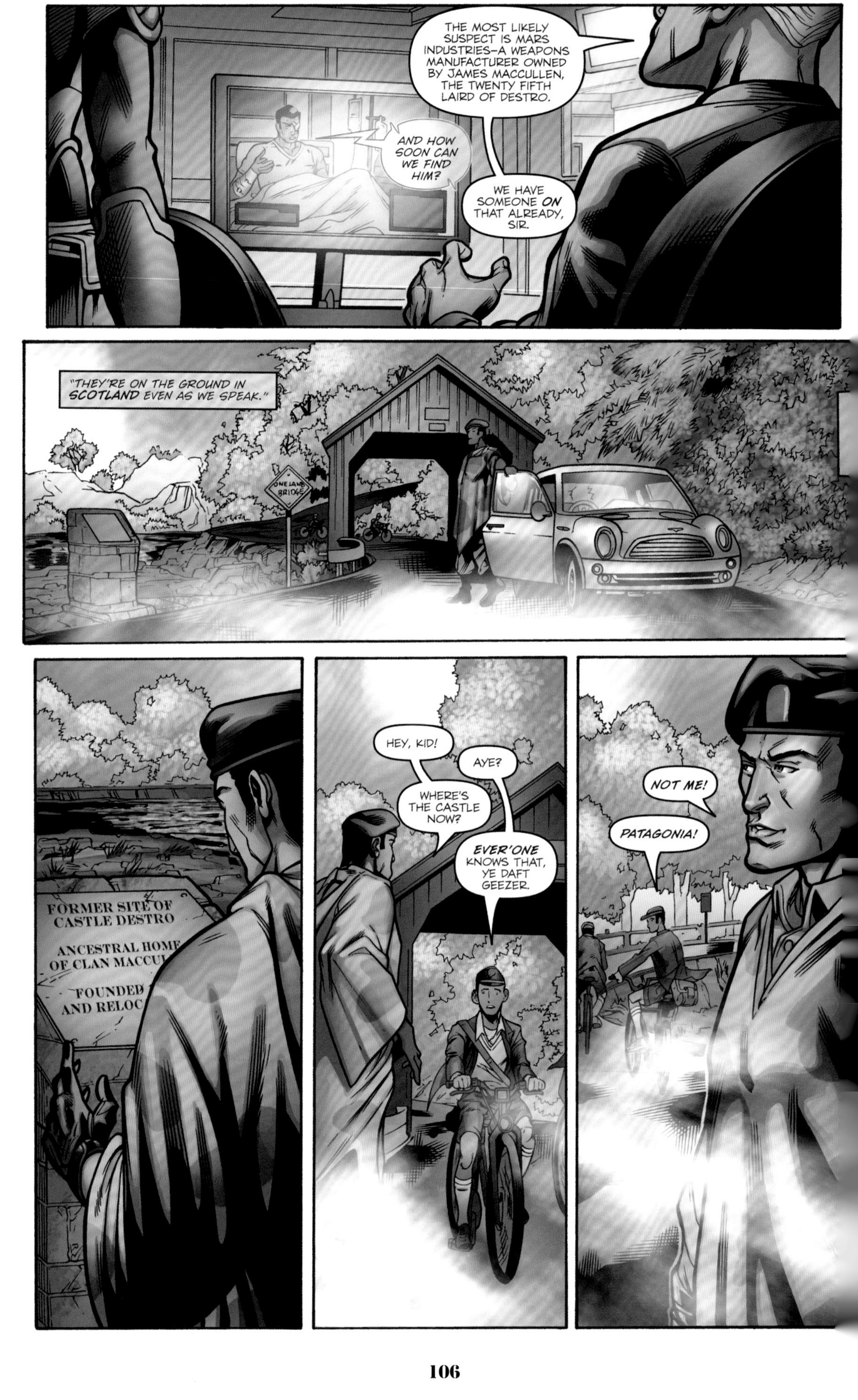
THE MOST LIKELY SUSPECT IS MARS INDUSTRIES—A WEAPONS MANUFACTURER OWNED BY JAMES MACCULLEN, THE TWENTY FIFTH LAIRD OF DESTRO.
AND HOW SOON CAN WE FIND HIM?
WE HAVE SOMEONE ON THAT ALREADY, SIR.
"THEY'RE ON THE GROUND IN SCOTLAND EVEN AS WE SPEAK."
ONE LANE BRIDGE
FORMER SITE OF CASTLE DESTRO
ANCESTRAL HOME OF CLAN MACCU
FOUNDED
AND RELOC
HEY, KID!
AYE?
WHERE'S THE CASTLE NOW?
EVER'ONE KNOWS THAT, YE DAFT GEEZER.
NOT ME!
PATAGONIA!

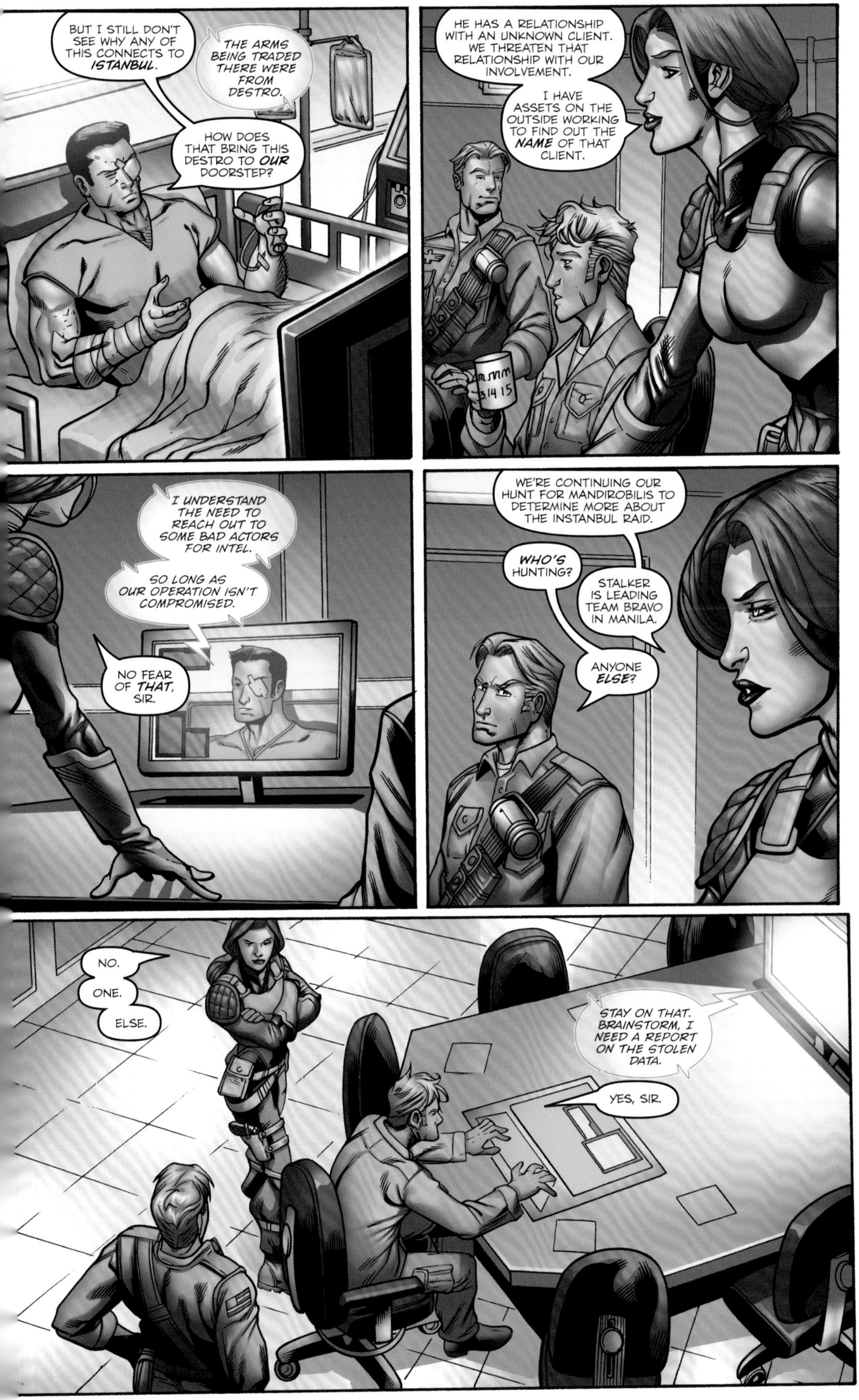
BUT I STILL DON'T SEE WHY ANY OF THIS CONNECTS TO ISTANBUL.
THE ARMS BEING TRADED THERE WERE FROM DESTRO.
HOW DOES THAT BRING THIS DESTRO TO OUR DOORSTEP?
HE HAS A RELATIONSHIP WITH AN UNKNOWN CLIENT. WE THREATEN THAT RELATIONSHIP WITH OUR INVOLVEMENT.
I HAVE ASSETS ON THE OUTSIDE WORKING TO FIND OUT THE NAME OF THAT CLIENT.
I UNDERSTAND THE NEED TO REACH OUT TO SOME BAD ACTORS FOR INTEL.
SO LONG AS OUR OPERATION ISN'T COMPROMISED.
NO FEAR OF THAT, SIR.
WE'RE CONTINUING OUR HUNT FOR MANDIROBILIS TO DETERMINE MORE ABOUT THE INSTANBUL RAID.
WHO'S HUNTING?
STALKER IS LEADING TEAM BRAVO IN MANILA.
ANYONE ELSE?
NO.
ONE.
ELSE.
STAY ON THAT. BRAINSTORM, I NEED A REPORT ON THE STOLEN DATA.
YES, SIR.

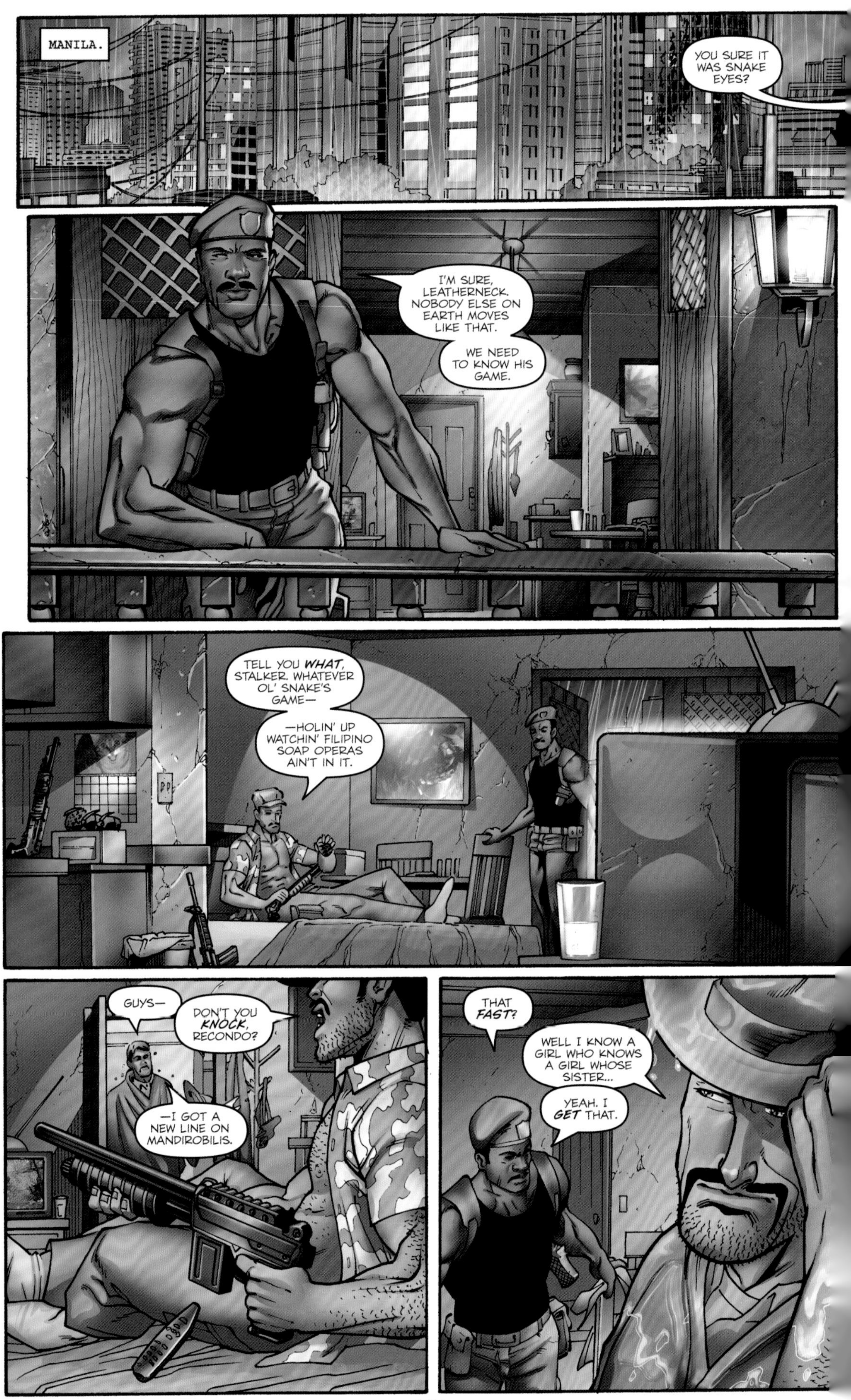
MANILA.
YOU SURE IT WAS SNAKE EYES?
I'M SURE, LEATHERNECK. NOBODY ELSE ON EARTH MOVES LIKE THAT.
WE NEED TO KNOW HIS GAME.
TELL YOU WHAT, STALKER. WHATEVER OL' SNAKE'S GAME—
—HOLIN' UP WATCHIN' FILIPINO SOAP OPERAS AIN'T IN IT.
GUYS—
DON'T YOU KNOCK, RECONDO?
—I GOT A NEW LINE ON MANDIROBILIS.
THAT FAST?
WELL I KNOW A GIRL WHO KNOWS A GIRL WHOSE SISTER...
YEAH. I GET THAT.

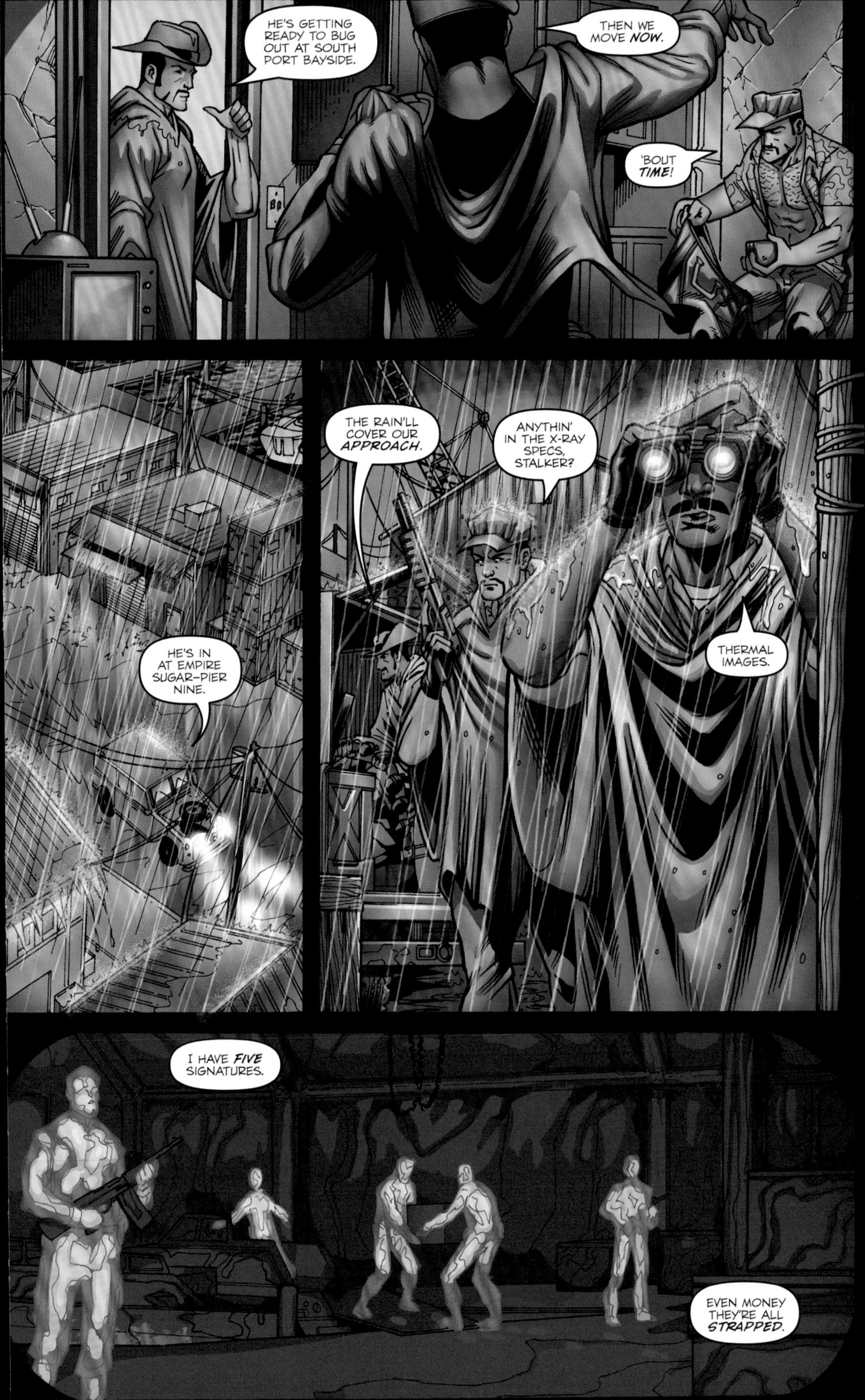
HE'S GETTING READY TO BUG OUT AT SOUTH PORT BAYSIDE.
THEN WE MOVE *NOW*.
'BOUT *TIME!*
HE'S IN AT EMPIRE SUGAR-PIER NINE.
THE RAIN'LL COVER OUR *APPROACH*.
ANYTHIN' IN THE X-RAY SPECS, STALKER?
THERMAL IMAGES.
I HAVE *FIVE* SIGNATURES.
EVEN MONEY THEY'RE ALL *STRAPPED*.

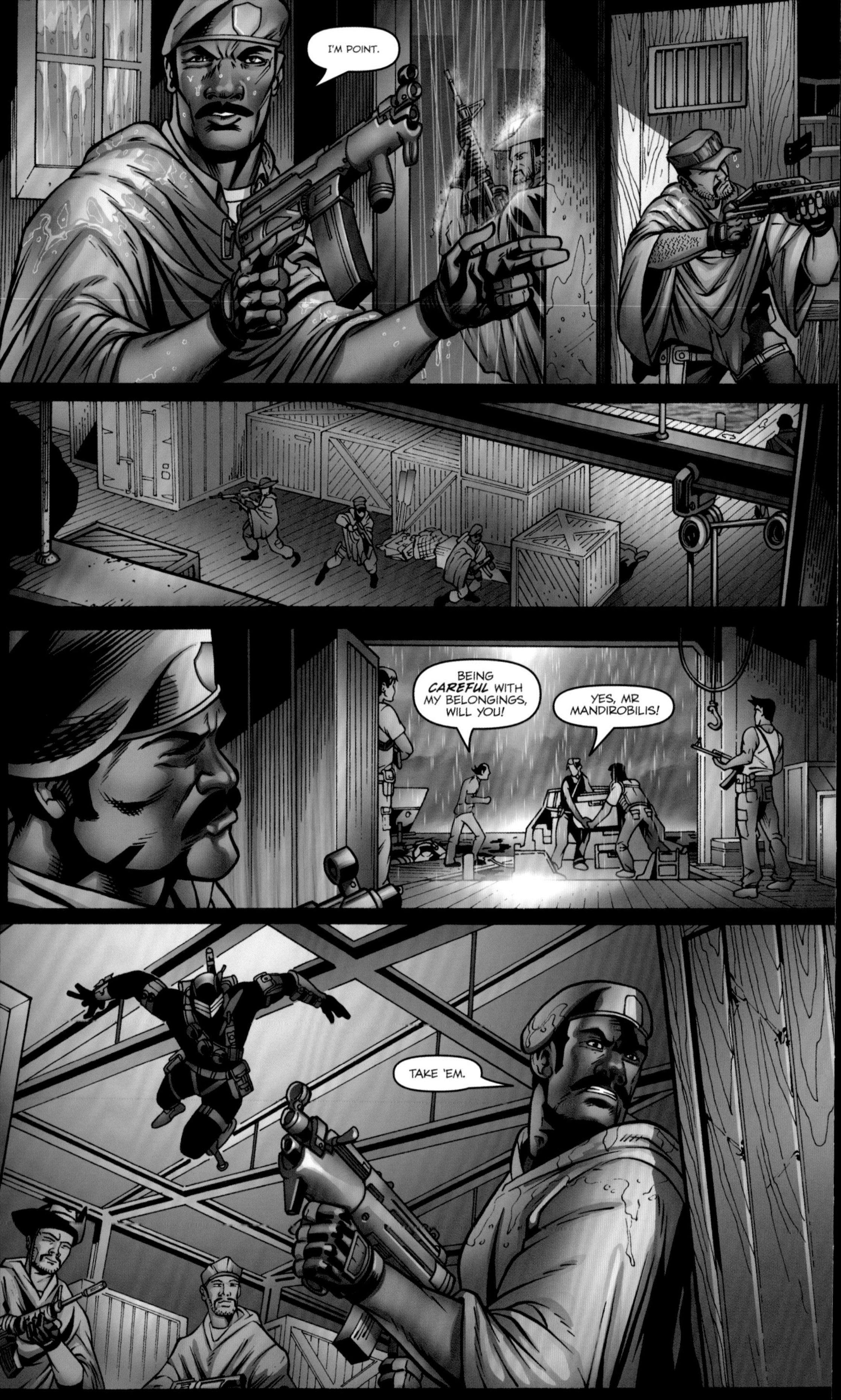
I'M POINT.
BEING CAREFUL WITH MY BELONGINGS, WILL YOU!
YES, MR MANDIROBILIS!
TAKE 'EM.

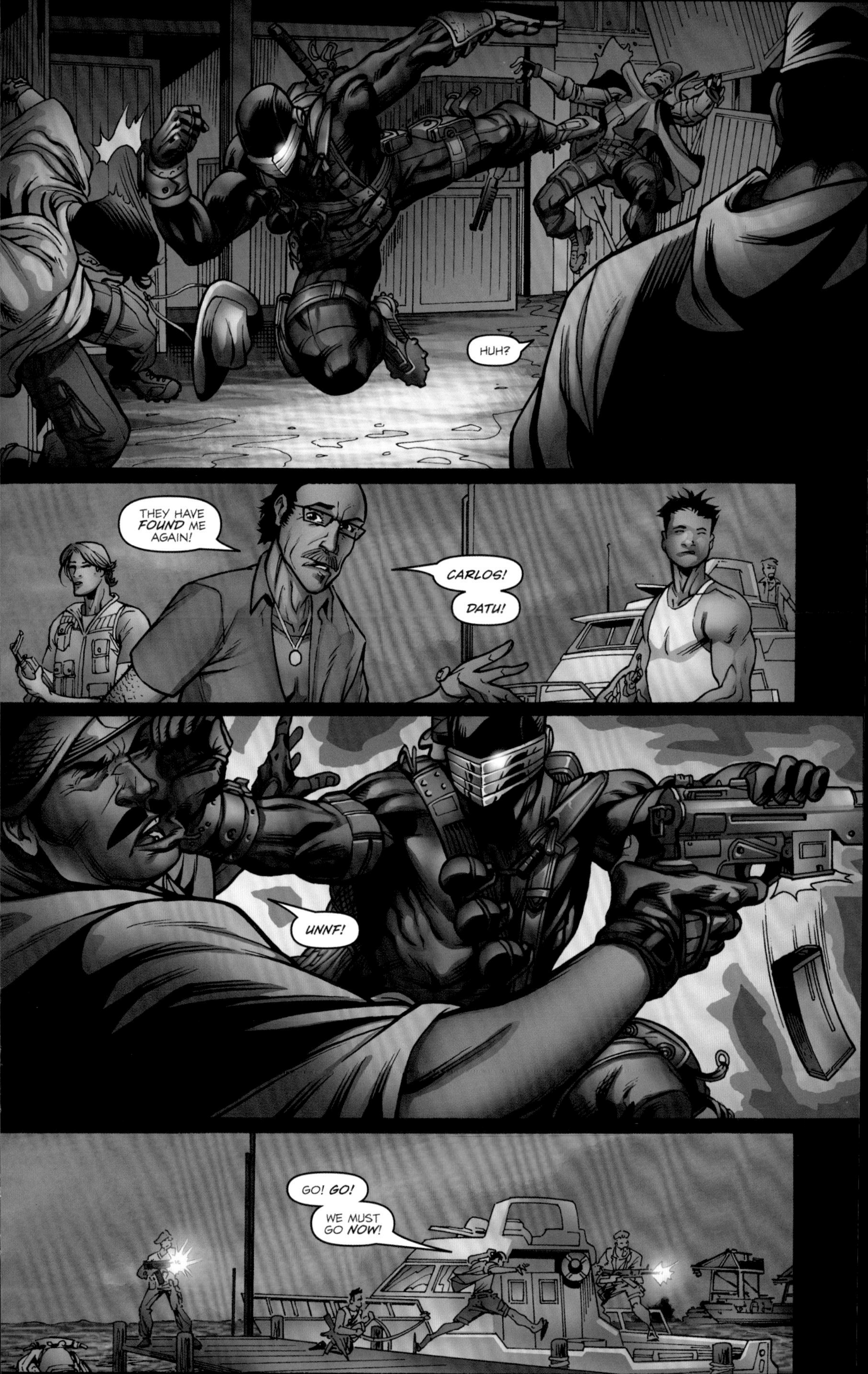
HUH?
THEY HAVE FOUND ME AGAIN!
CARLOS!
DATU!
UNNF!
GO! GO!
WE MUST GO NOW!

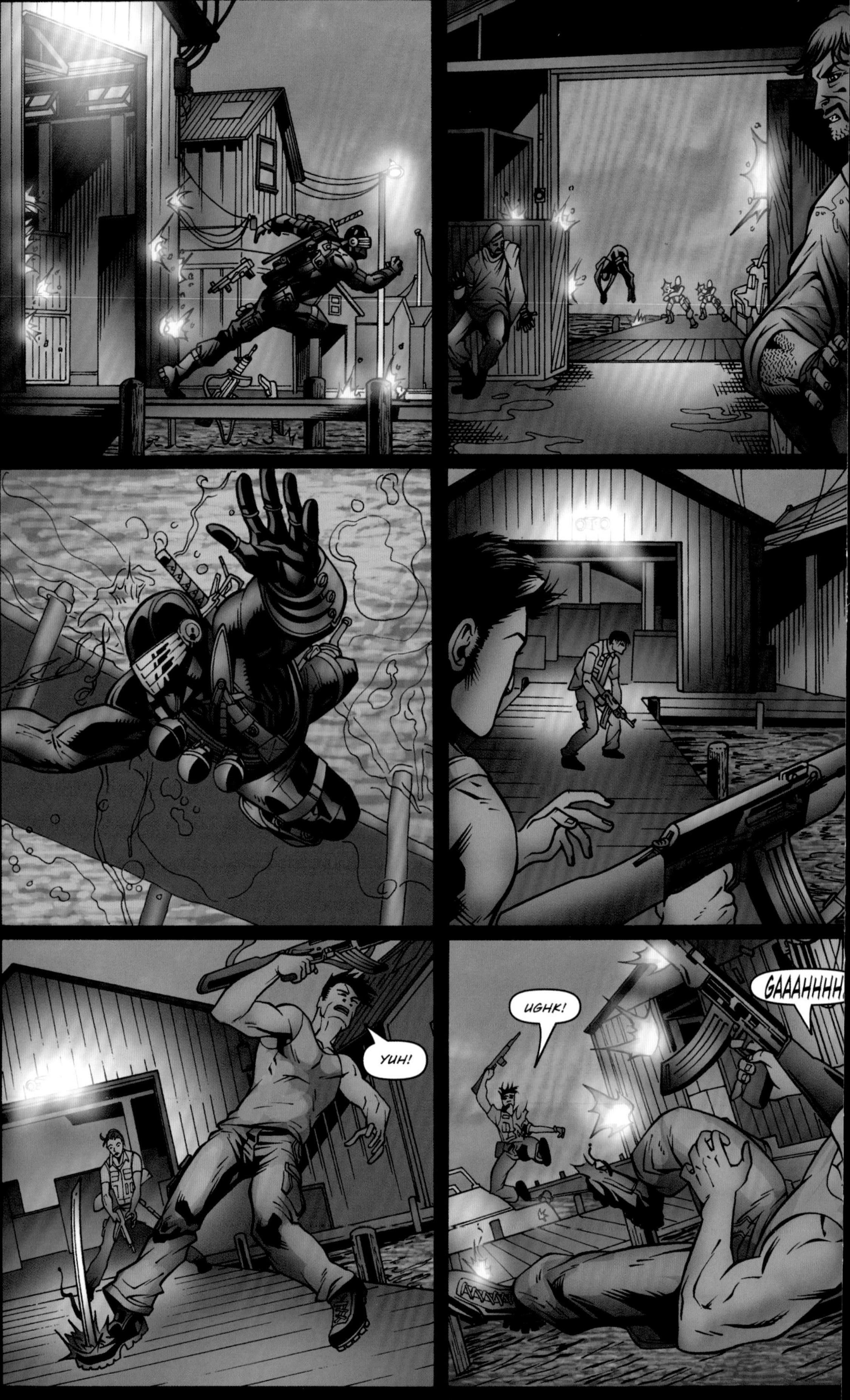
YUH!
UGHK!
GAAAHHHH

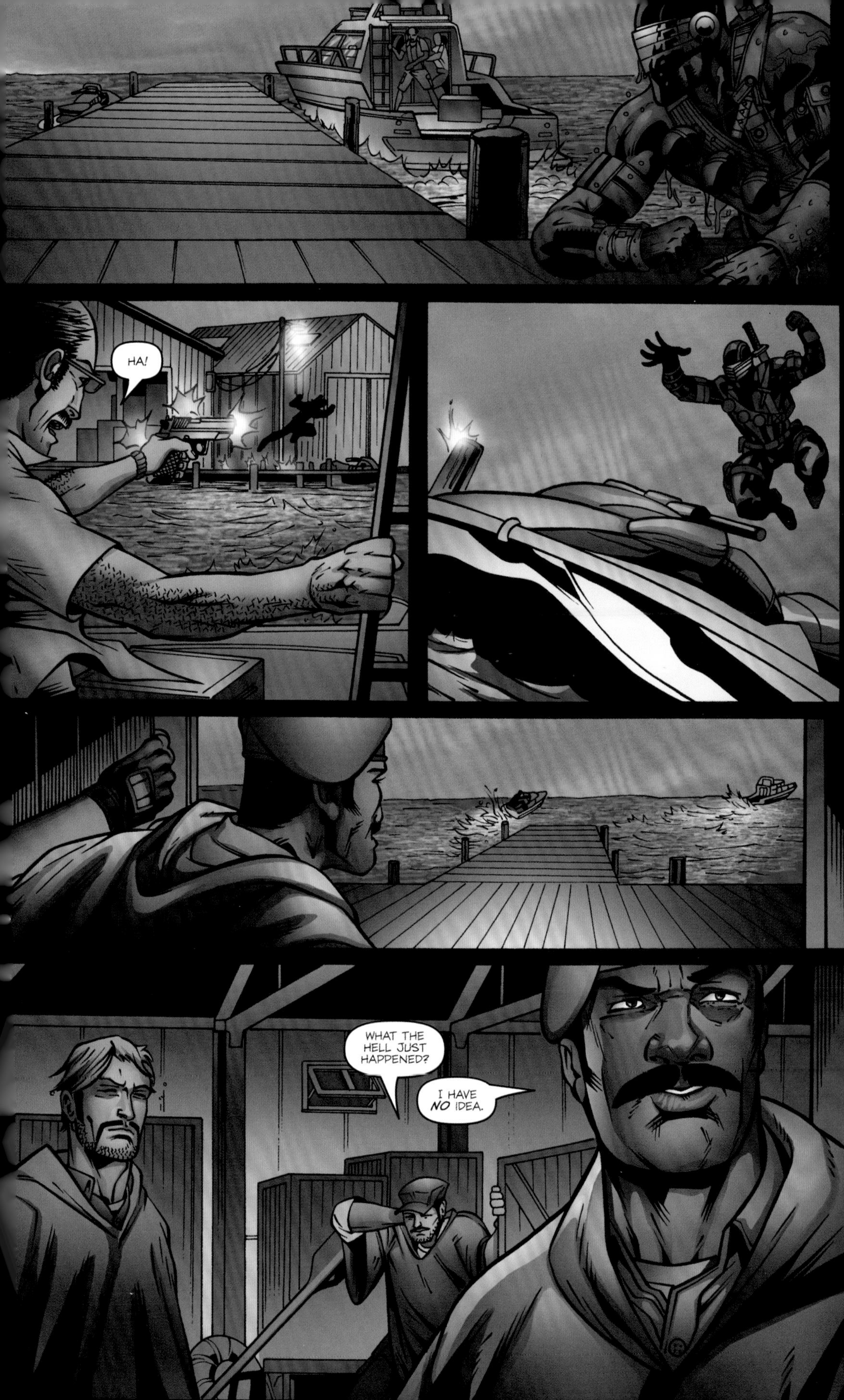
HA!
WHAT THE HELL JUST HAPPENED?
I HAVE NO IDEA.

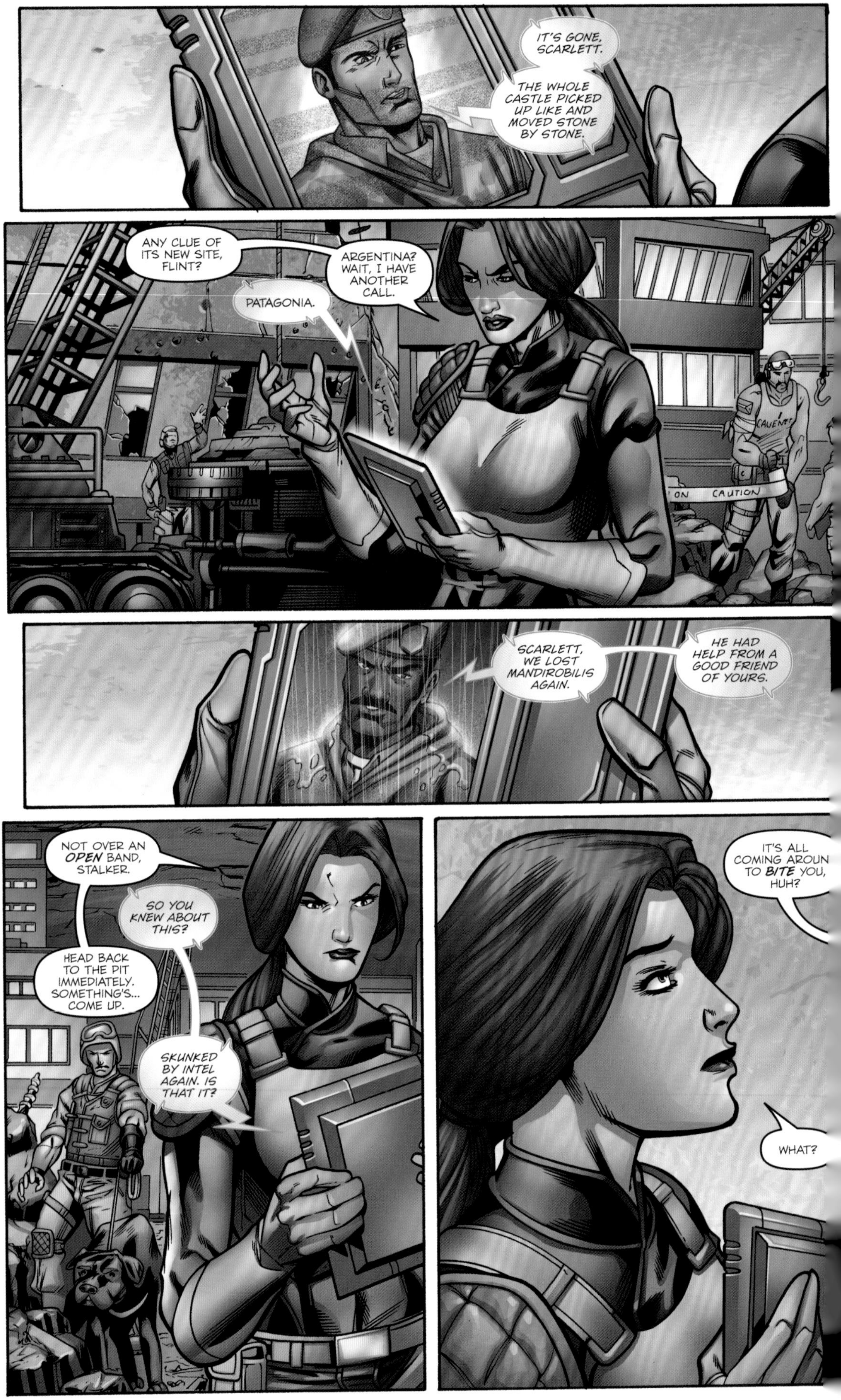
IT'S GONE, SCARLETT.
THE WHOLE CASTLE PICKED UP LIKE AND MOVED STONE BY STONE.
ANY CLUE OF ITS NEW SITE, FLINT?
PATAGONIA.
ARGENTINA? WAIT, I HAVE ANOTHER CALL.
CAUTION
SCARLETT, WE LOST MANDIROBILIS AGAIN.
HE HAD HELP FROM A GOOD FRIEND OF YOURS.
NOT OVER AN OPEN BAND, STALKER.
HEAD BACK TO THE PIT IMMEDIATELY. SOMETHING'S... COME UP.
SO YOU KNEW ABOUT THIS?
SKUNKED BY INTEL AGAIN. IS THAT IT?
IT'S ALL COMING AROUN TO BITE YOU, HUH?
WHAT?

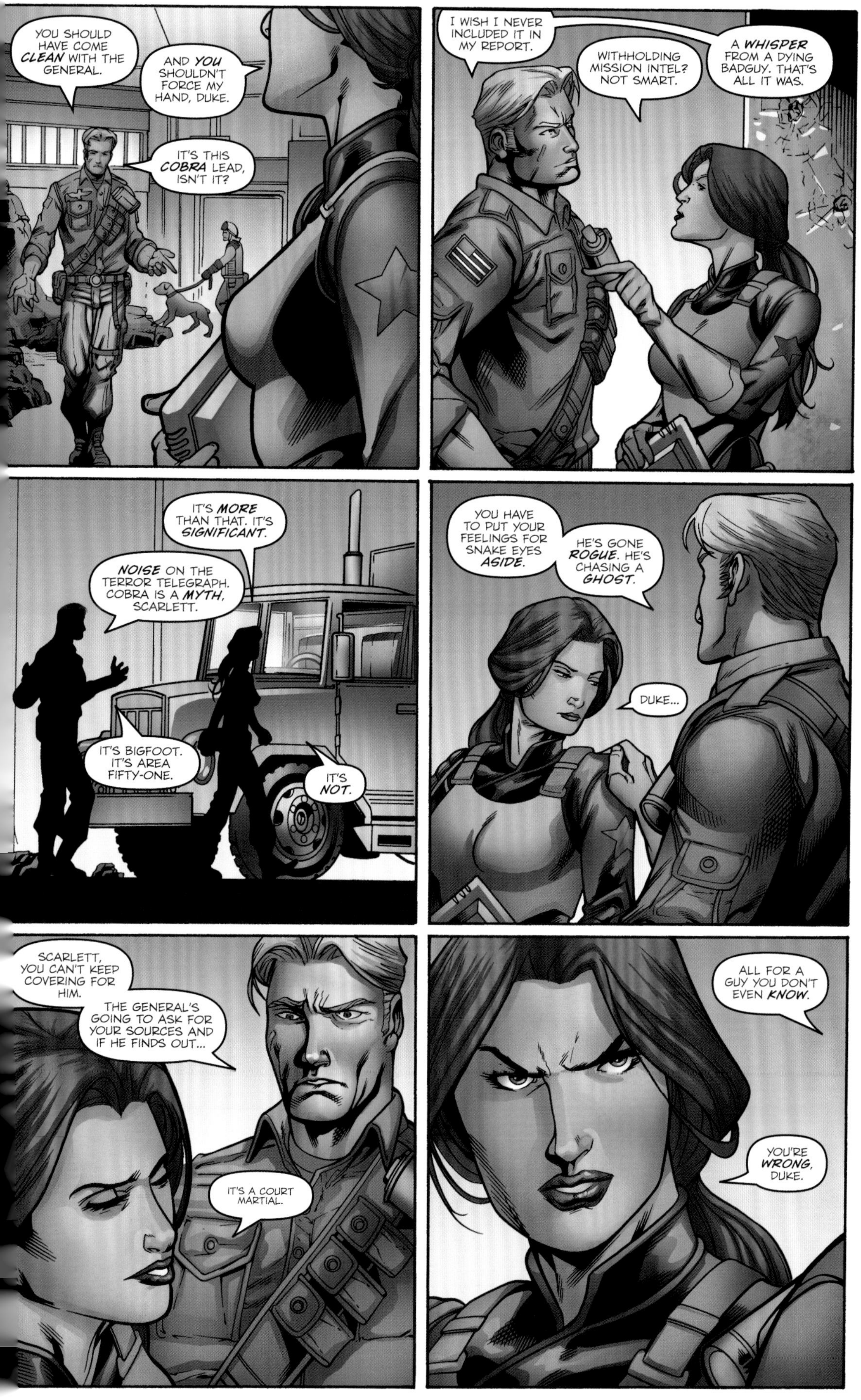
YOU SHOULD HAVE COME CLEAN WITH THE GENERAL.
AND YOU SHOULDN'T FORCE MY HAND, DUKE.
IT'S THIS COBRA LEAD, ISN'T IT?
I WISH I NEVER INCLUDED IT IN MY REPORT.
WITHHOLDING MISSION INTEL? NOT SMART.
A WHISPER FROM A DYING BADGUY. THAT'S ALL IT WAS.
IT'S MORE THAN THAT. IT'S SIGNIFICANT.
NOISE ON THE TERROR TELEGRAPH. COBRA IS A MYTH, SCARLETT.
IT'S BIGFOOT. IT'S AREA FIFTY-ONE.
IT'S NOT.
YOU HAVE TO PUT YOUR FEELINGS FOR SNAKE EYES ASIDE.
HE'S GONE ROGUE. HE'S CHASING A GHOST.
DUKE...
SCARLETT, YOU CAN'T KEEP COVERING FOR HIM.
THE GENERAL'S GOING TO ASK FOR YOUR SOURCES AND IF HE FINDS OUT...
IT'S A COURT MARTIAL.
ALL FOR A GUY YOU DON'T EVEN KNOW.
YOU'RE WRONG, DUKE.

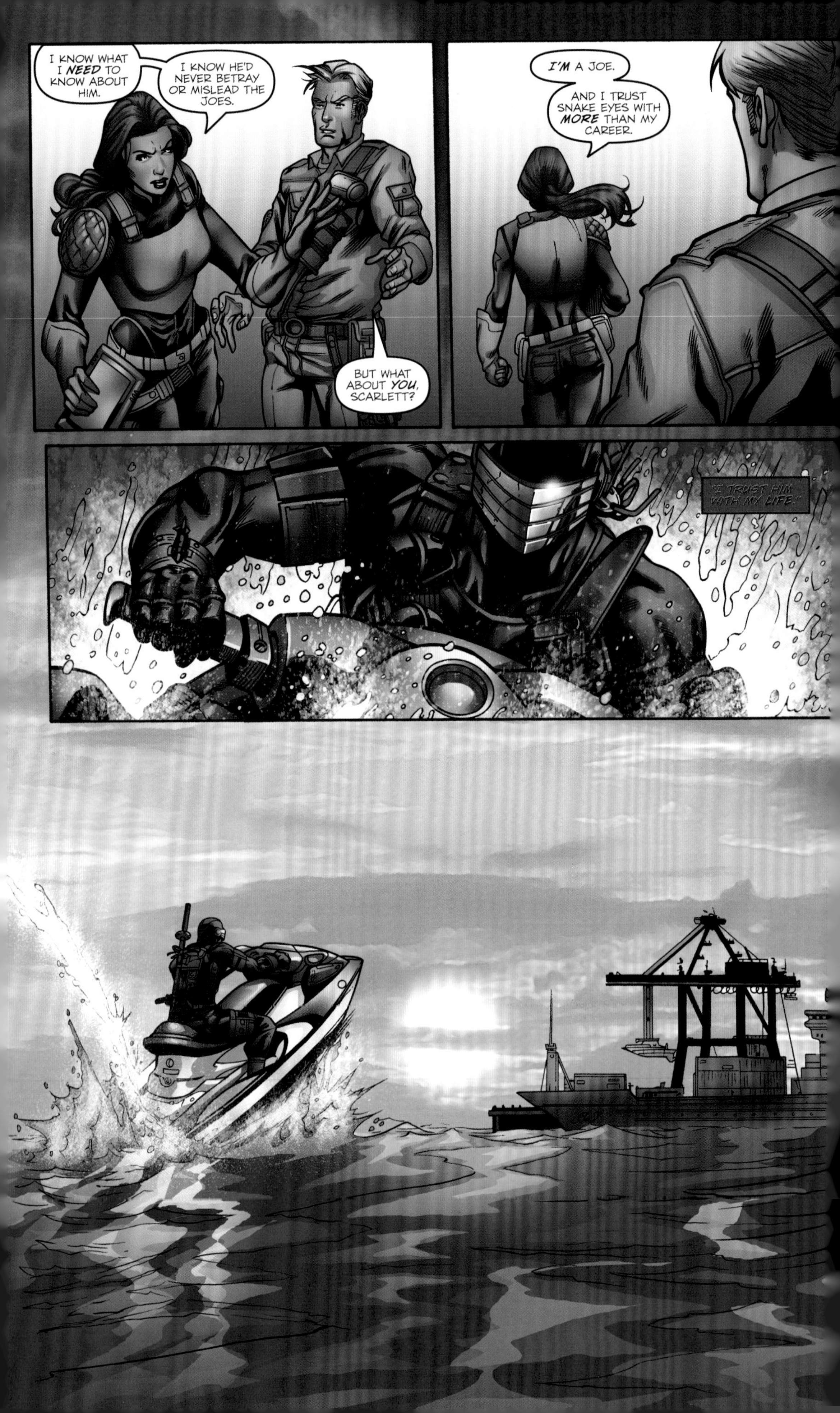
I KNOW WHAT I **NEED** TO KNOW ABOUT HIM.
I KNOW HE'D NEVER BETRAY OR MISLEAD THE JOES.
BUT WHAT ABOUT ***YOU***, SCARLETT?
I'M A JOE.
AND I TRUST SNAKE EYES WITH ***MORE*** THAN MY CAREER.
"I TRUST HIM WITH MY ***LIFE***."

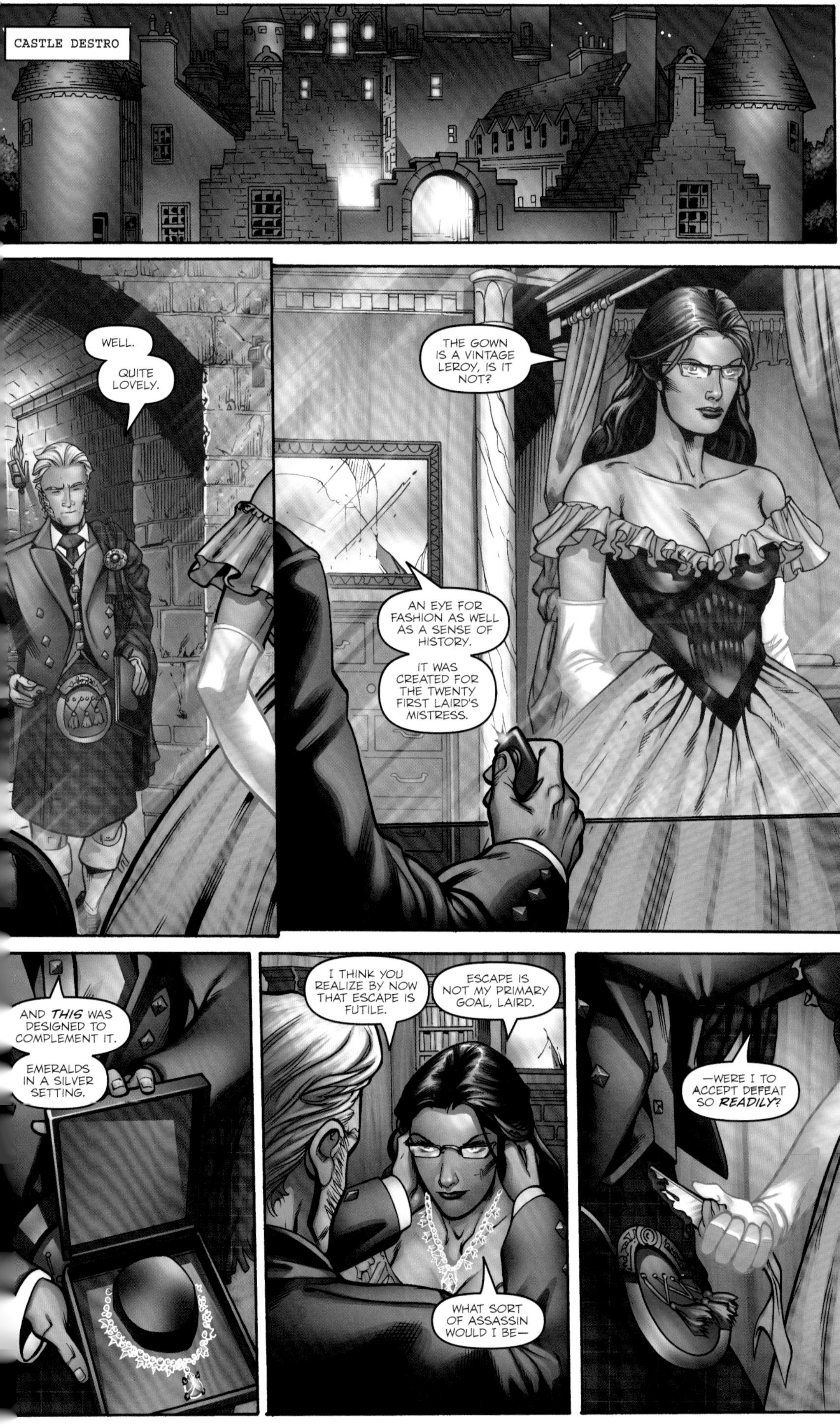
CASTLE DESTRO
WELL.
QUITE LOVELY.
THE GOWN IS A VINTAGE LEROY, IS IT NOT?
AN EYE FOR FASHION AS WELL AS A SENSE OF HISTORY.
IT WAS CREATED FOR THE TWENTY FIRST LAIRD'S MISTRESS.
AND *THIS* WAS DESIGNED TO COMPLEMENT IT.
EMERALDS IN A SILVER SETTING.
I THINK YOU REALIZE BY NOW THAT ESCAPE IS FUTILE.
ESCAPE IS NOT MY PRIMARY GOAL, LAIRD.
WHAT SORT OF ASSASSIN WOULD I BE—
—WERE I TO ACCEPT DEFEAT SO *READILY*?

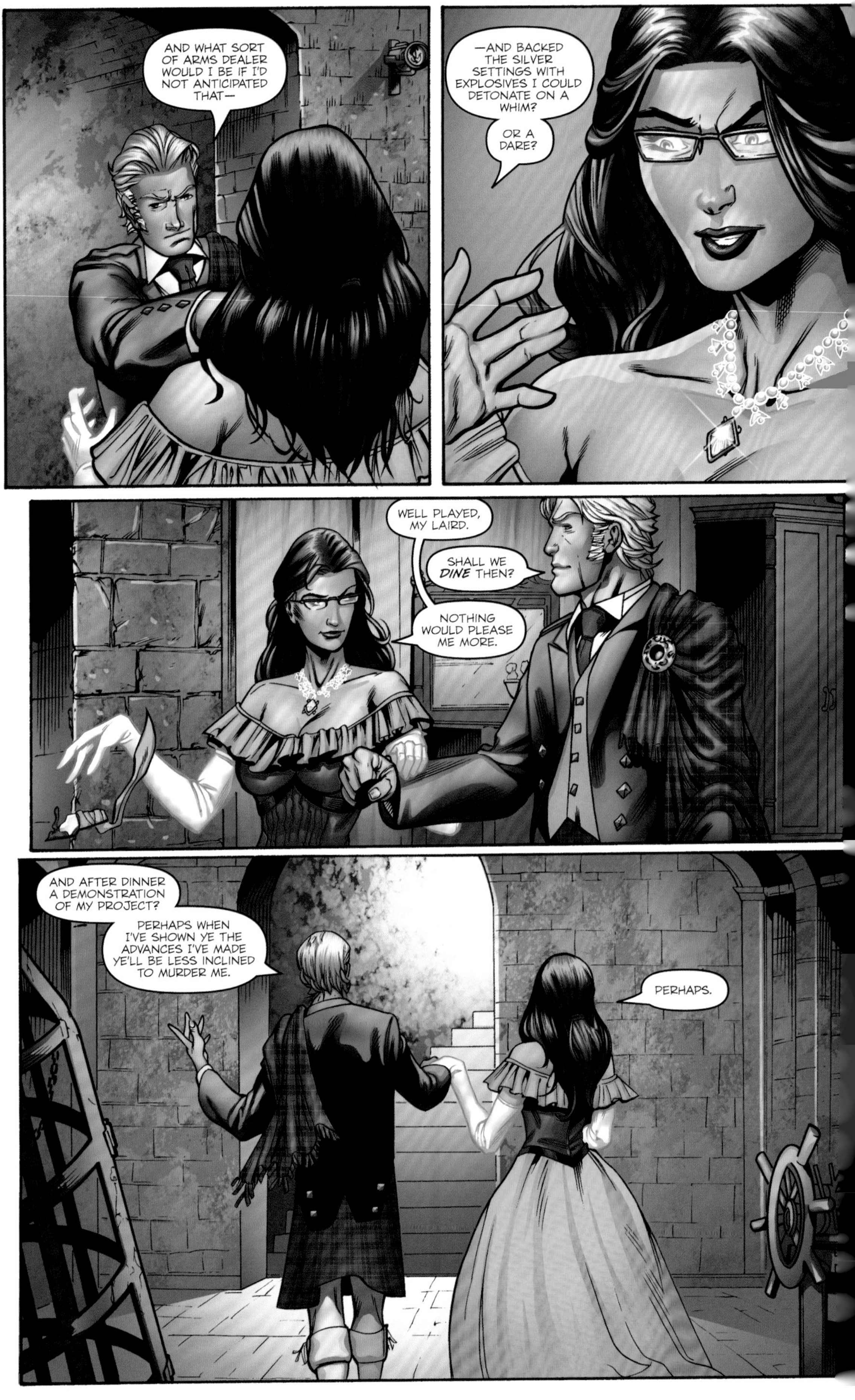
AND WHAT SORT OF ARMS DEALER WOULD I BE IF I'D NOT ANTICIPATED THAT—
—AND BACKED THE SILVER SETTINGS WITH EXPLOSIVES I COULD DETONATE ON A WHIM?
OR A DARE?
WELL PLAYED, MY LAIRD.
SHALL WE DINE THEN?
NOTHING WOULD PLEASE ME MORE.
AND AFTER DINNER A DEMONSTRATION OF MY PROJECT?
PERHAPS WHEN I'VE SHOWN YE THE ADVANCES I'VE MADE YE'LL BE LESS INCLINED TO MURDER ME.
PERHAPS.

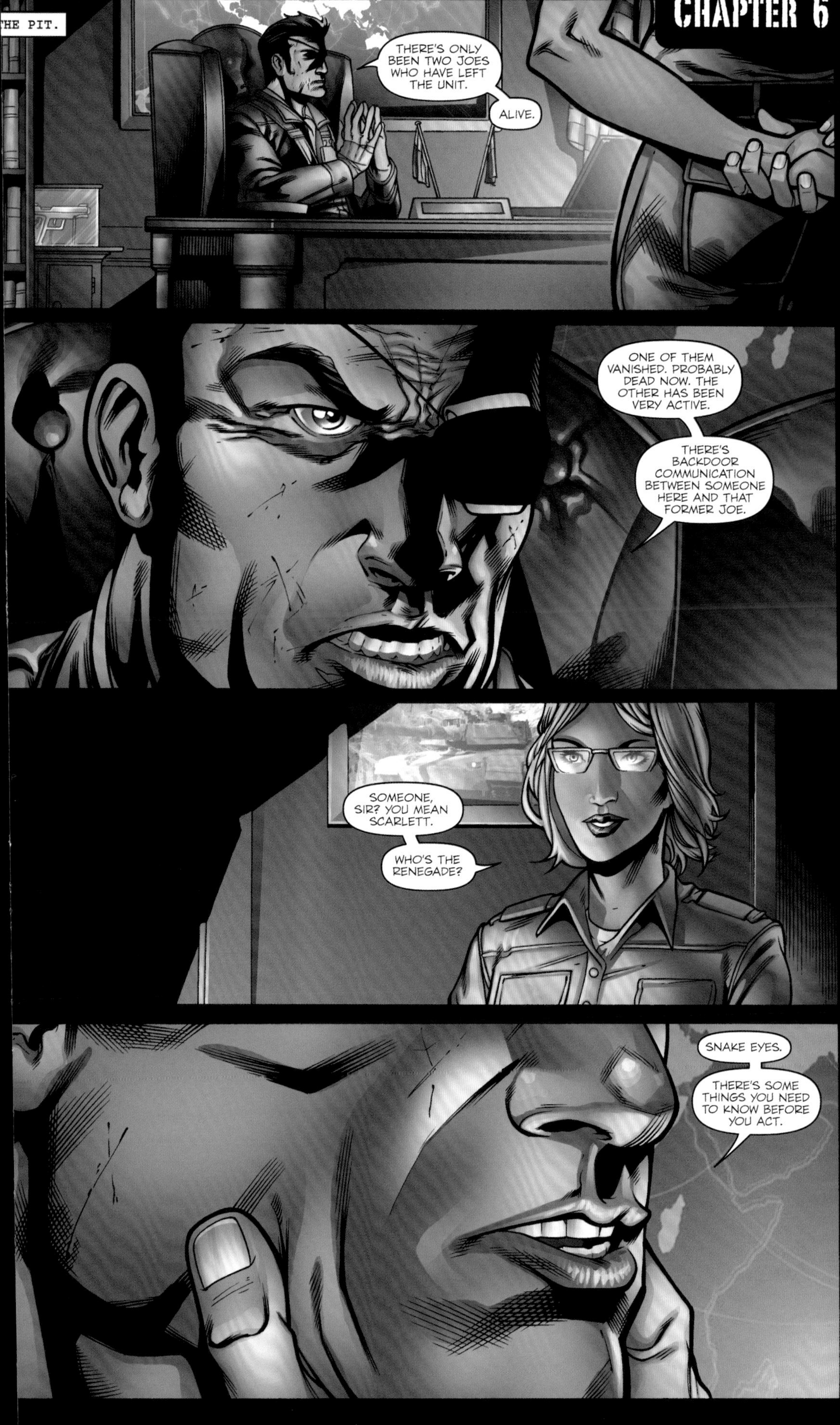
THE PIT.
CHAPTER 6
THERE'S ONLY BEEN TWO JOES WHO HAVE LEFT THE UNIT.
ALIVE.
ONE OF THEM VANISHED. PROBABLY DEAD NOW. THE OTHER HAS BEEN VERY ACTIVE.
THERE'S BACKDOOR COMMUNICATION BETWEEN SOMEONE HERE AND THAT FORMER JOE.
SOMEONE, SIR? YOU MEAN SCARLETT.
WHO'S THE RENEGADE?
SNAKE EYES.
THERE'S SOME THINGS YOU NEED TO KNOW BEFORE YOU ACT.

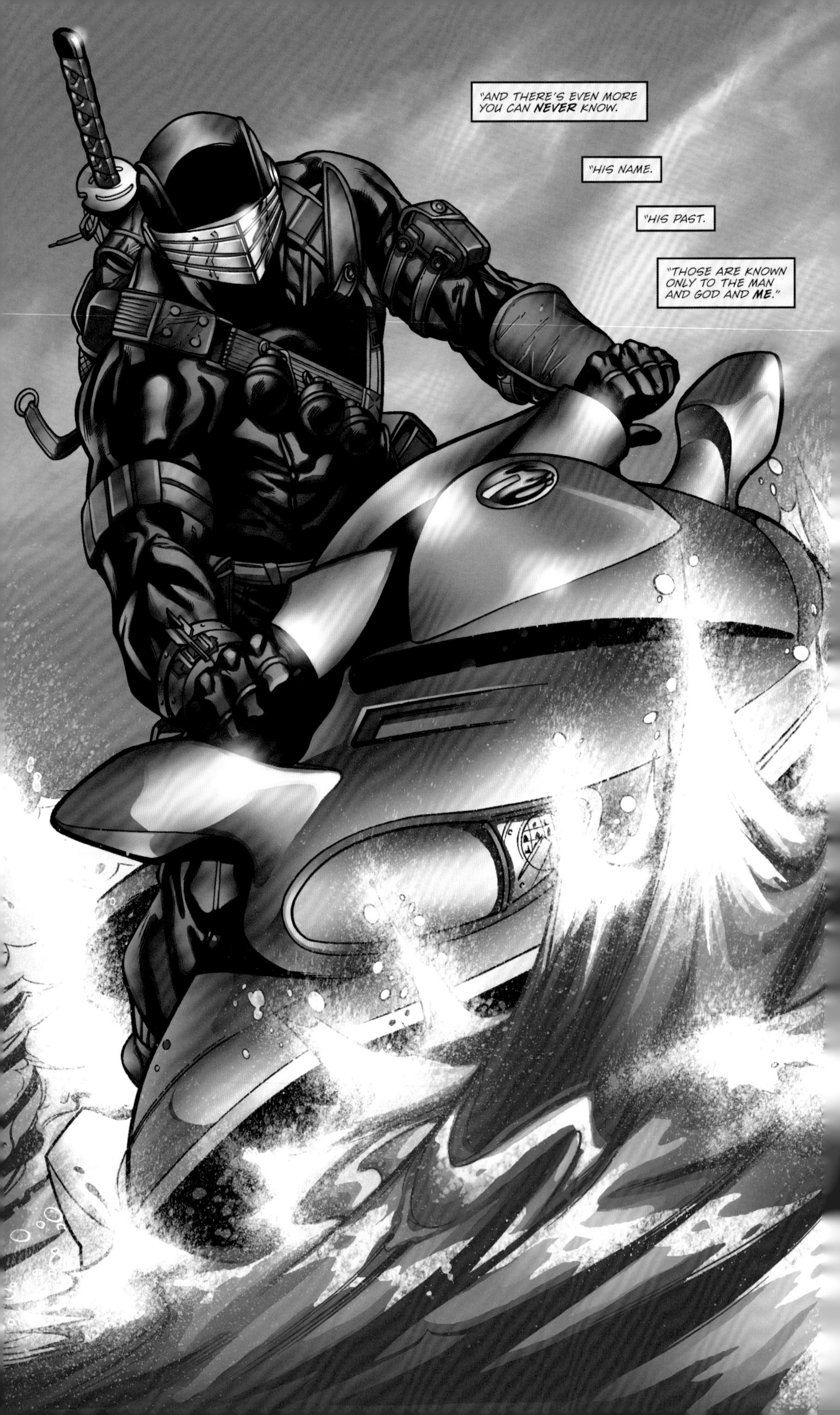
"AND THERE'S EVEN MORE YOU CAN NEVER KNOW.
"HIS NAME.
"HIS PAST.
"THOSE ARE KNOWN ONLY TO THE MAN AND GOD AND ME."

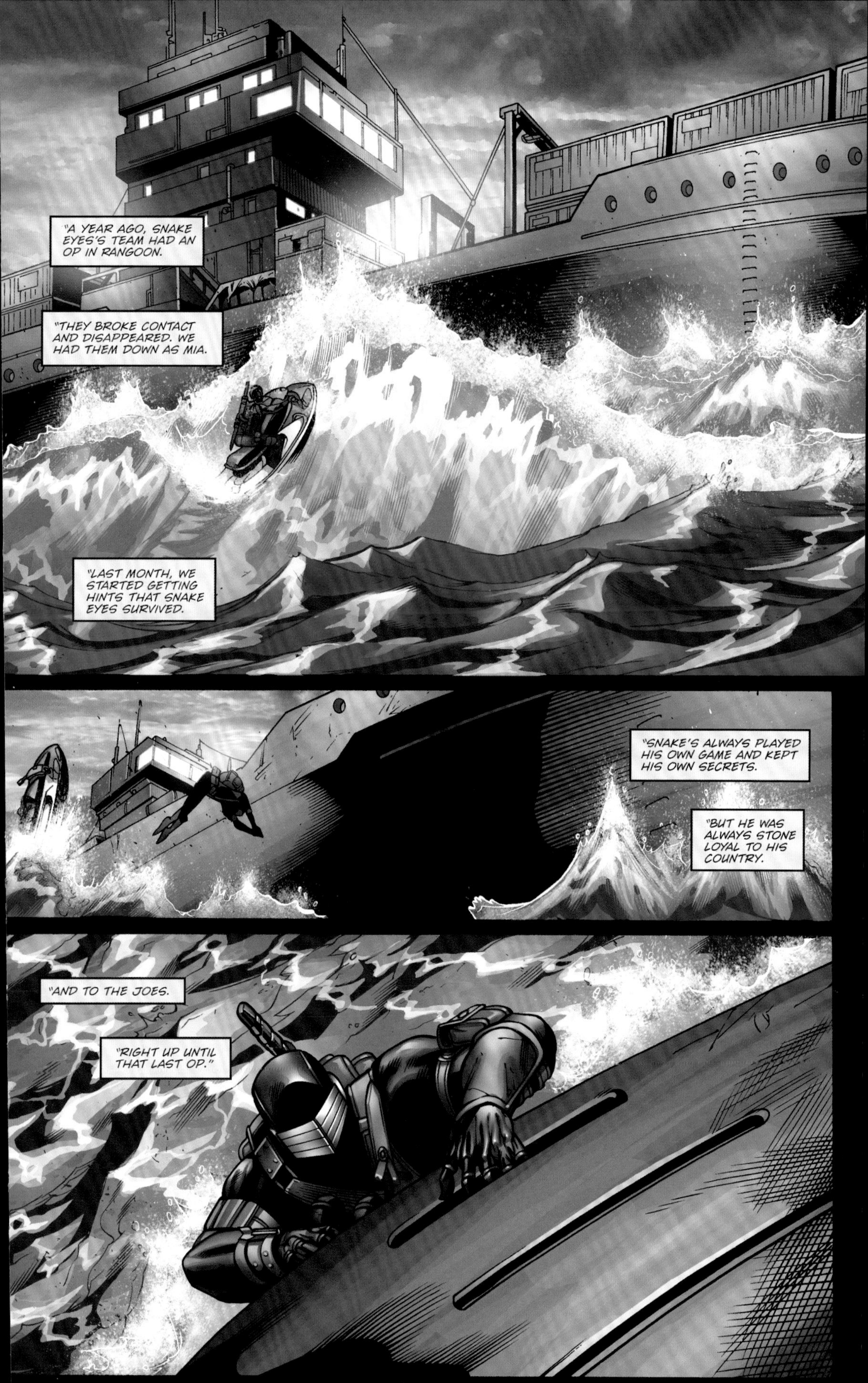
"A YEAR AGO, SNAKE EYES'S TEAM HAD AN OP IN RANGOON.
"THEY BROKE CONTACT AND DISAPPEARED. WE HAD THEM DOWN AS MIA.
"LAST MONTH, WE STARTED GETTING HINTS THAT SNAKE EYES SURVIVED.
"SNAKE'S ALWAYS PLAYED HIS OWN GAME AND KEPT HIS OWN SECRETS.
"BUT HE WAS ALWAYS STONE LOYAL TO HIS COUNTRY.
"AND TO THE JOES.
"RIGHT UP UNTIL THAT LAST OP."

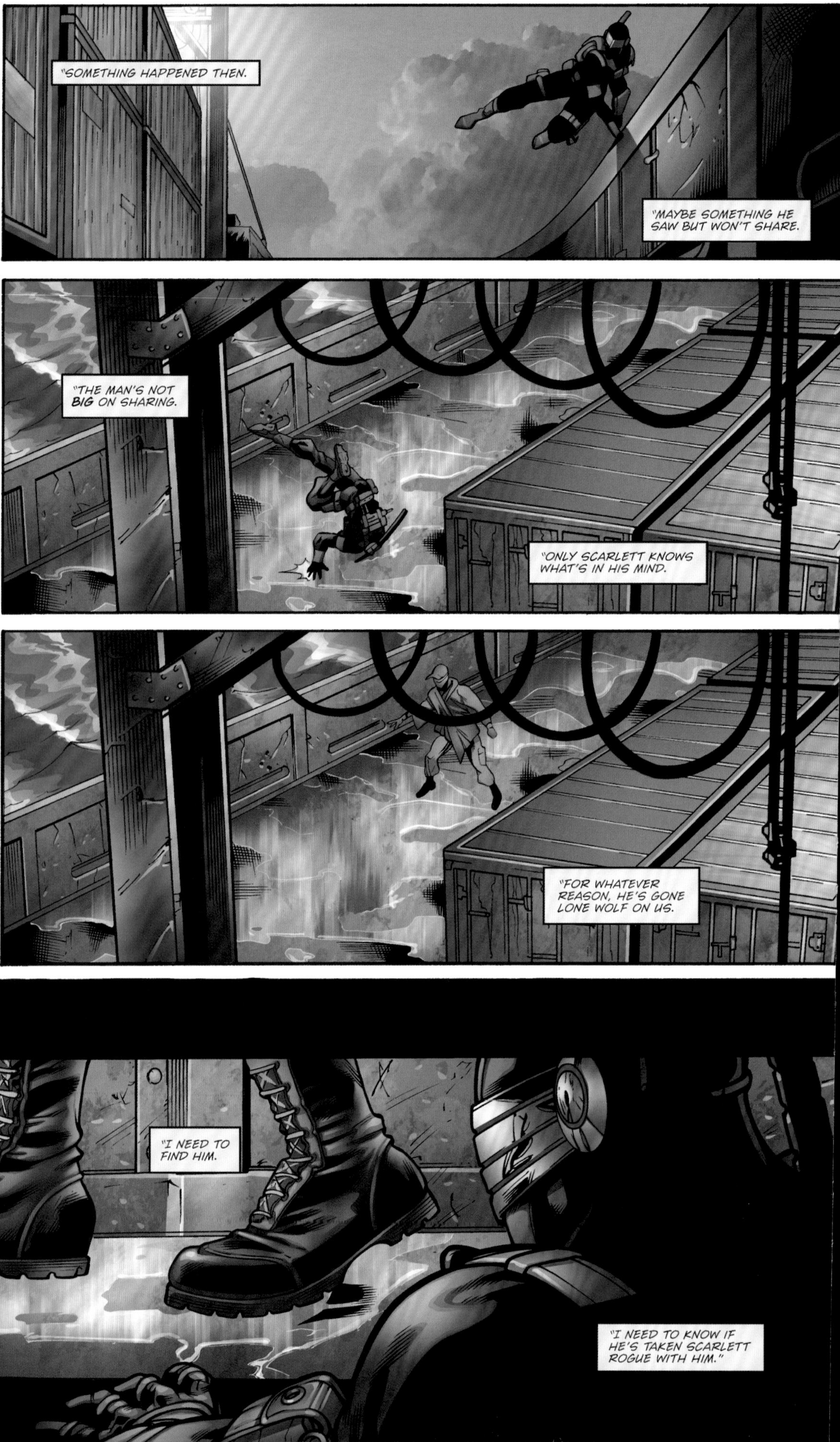
"SOMETHING HAPPENED THEN.
"MAYBE SOMETHING HE SAW BUT WON'T SHARE.
"THE MAN'S NOT BIG ON SHARING.
"ONLY SCARLETT KNOWS WHAT'S IN HIS MIND.
"FOR WHATEVER REASON, HE'S GONE LONE WOLF ON US.
"I NEED TO FIND HIM.
"I NEED TO KNOW IF HE'S TAKEN SCARLETT ROGUE WITH HIM."

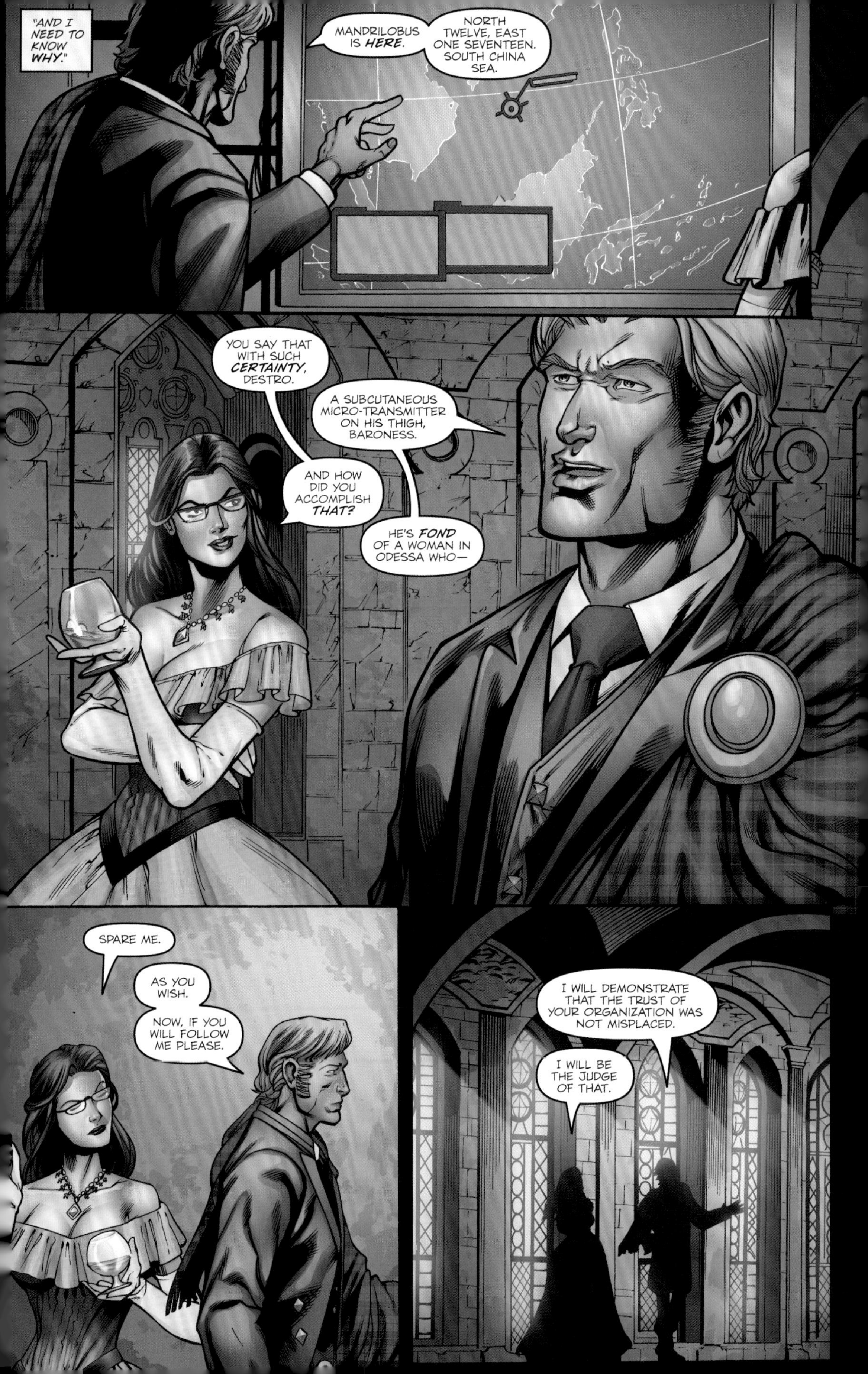
"AND I NEED TO KNOW WHY."
MANDRILOBUS IS HERE.
NORTH TWELVE, EAST ONE SEVENTEEN. SOUTH CHINA SEA.
YOU SAY THAT WITH SUCH CERTAINTY, DESTRO.
A SUBCUTANEOUS MICRO-TRANSMITTER ON HIS THIGH, BARONESS.
AND HOW DID YOU ACCOMPLISH THAT?
HE'S FOND OF A WOMAN IN ODESSA WHO—
SPARE ME.
AS YOU WISH.
NOW, IF YOU WILL FOLLOW ME PLEASE.
I WILL DEMONSTRATE THAT THE TRUST OF YOUR ORGANIZATION WAS NOT MISPLACED.
I WILL BE THE JUDGE OF THAT.

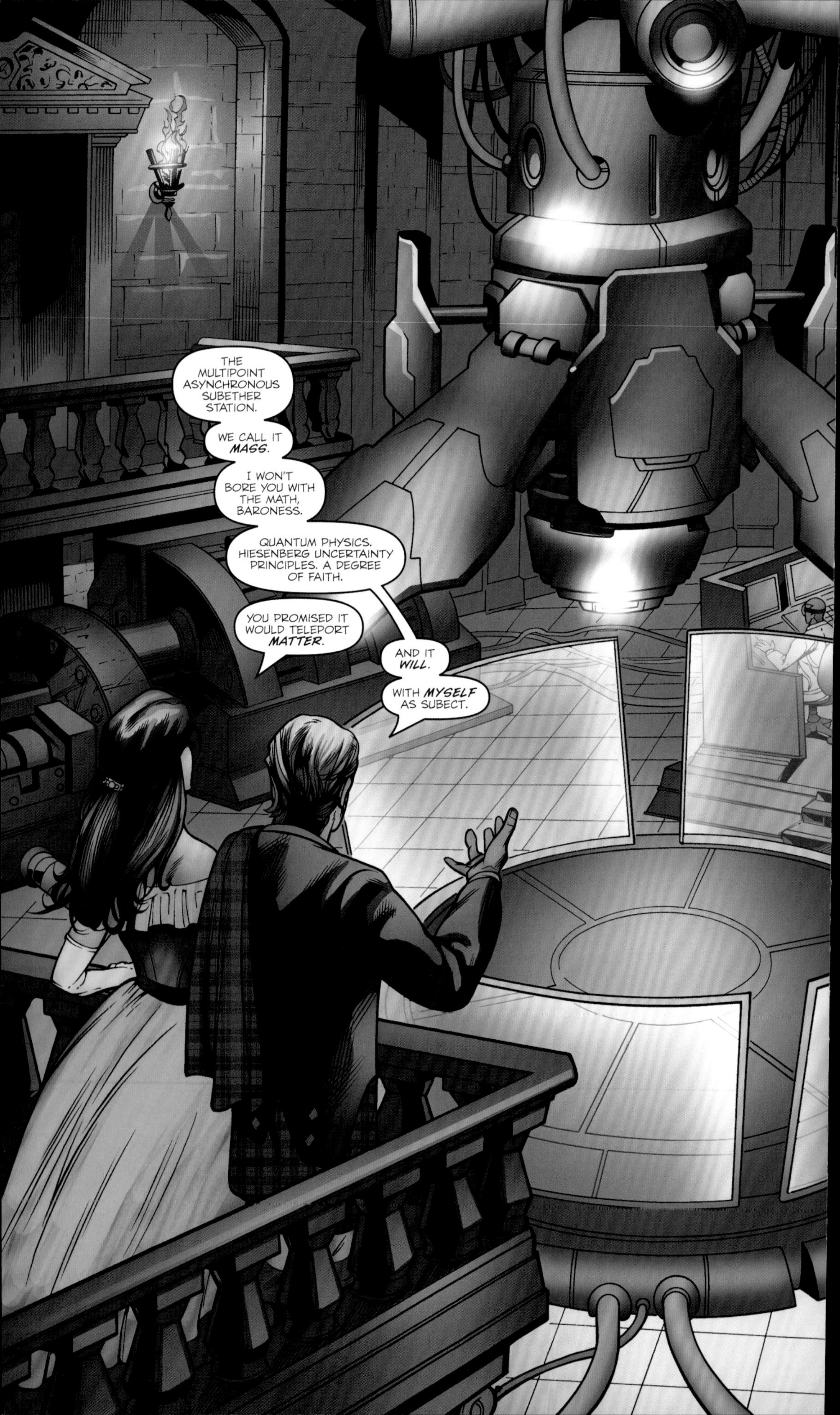
THE MULTIPOINT ASYNCHRONOUS SUBETHER STATION.
WE CALL IT MASS.
I WON'T BORE YOU WITH THE MATH, BARONESS.
QUANTUM PHYSICS. HIESENBERG UNCERTAINTY PRINCIPLES. A DEGREE OF FAITH.
YOU PROMISED IT WOULD TELEPORT MATTER.
AND IT WILL.
WITH MYSELF AS SUBECT.

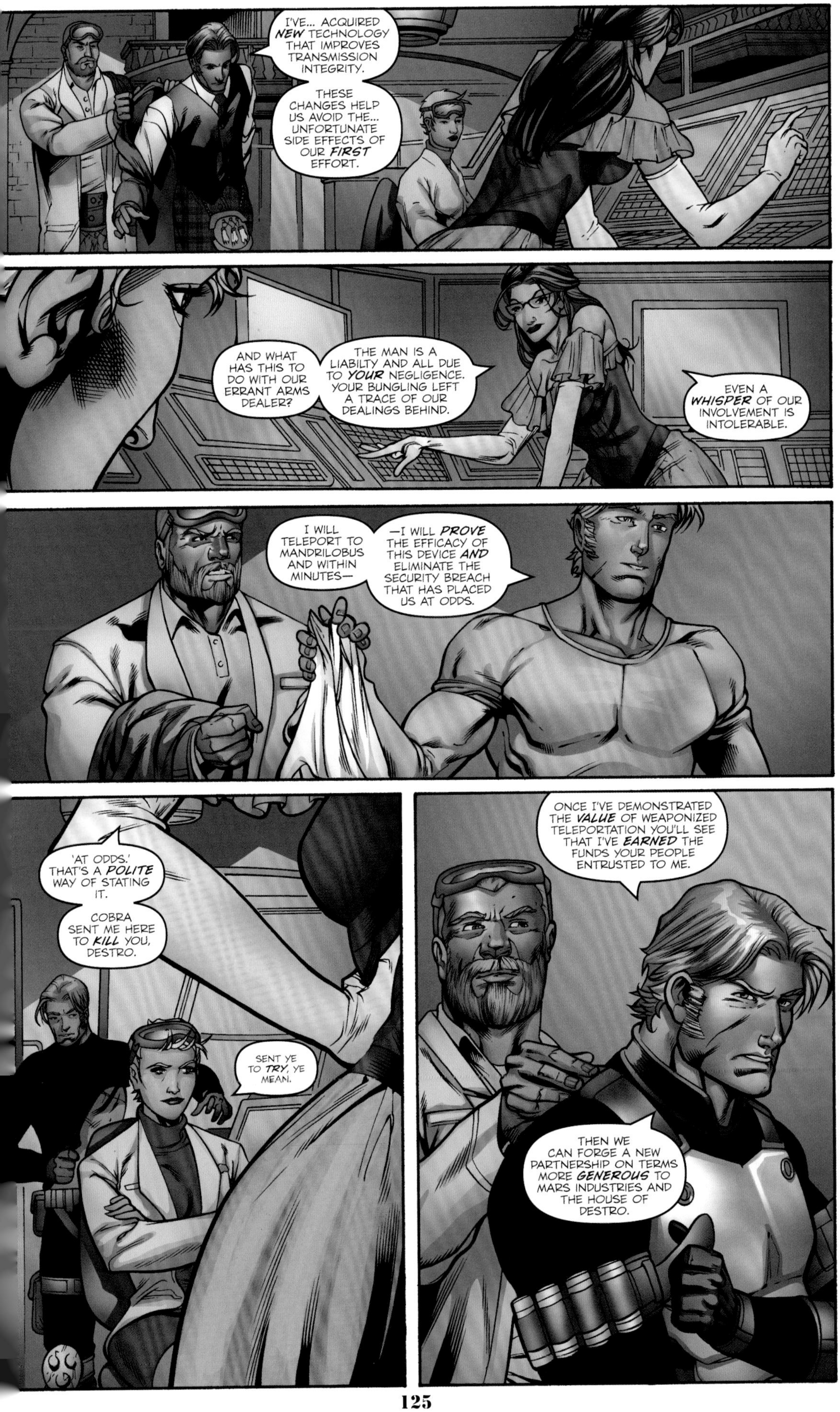
I'VE... ACQUIRED NEW TECHNOLOGY THAT IMPROVES TRANSMISSION INTEGRITY.
THESE CHANGES HELP US AVOID THE... UNFORTUNATE SIDE EFFECTS OF OUR FIRST EFFORT.
AND WHAT HAS THIS TO DO WITH OUR ERRANT ARMS DEALER?
THE MAN IS A LIABILTY AND ALL DUE TO YOUR NEGLIGENCE. YOUR BUNGLING LEFT A TRACE OF OUR DEALINGS BEHIND.
EVEN A WHISPER OF OUR INVOLVEMENT IS INTOLERABLE.
I WILL TELEPORT TO MANDRILOBUS AND WITHIN MINUTES—
—I WILL PROVE THE EFFICACY OF THIS DEVICE AND ELIMINATE THE SECURITY BREACH THAT HAS PLACED US AT ODDS.
'AT ODDS.' THAT'S A POLITE WAY OF STATING IT.
COBRA SENT ME HERE TO KILL YOU, DESTRO.
SENT YE TO TRY, YE MEAN.
ONCE I'VE DEMONSTRATED THE VALUE OF WEAPONIZED TELEPORTATION YOU'LL SEE THAT I'VE EARNED THE FUNDS YOUR PEOPLE ENTRUSTED TO ME.
THEN WE CAN FORGE A NEW PARTNERSHIP ON TERMS MORE GENEROUS TO MARS INDUSTRIES AND THE HOUSE OF DESTRO.

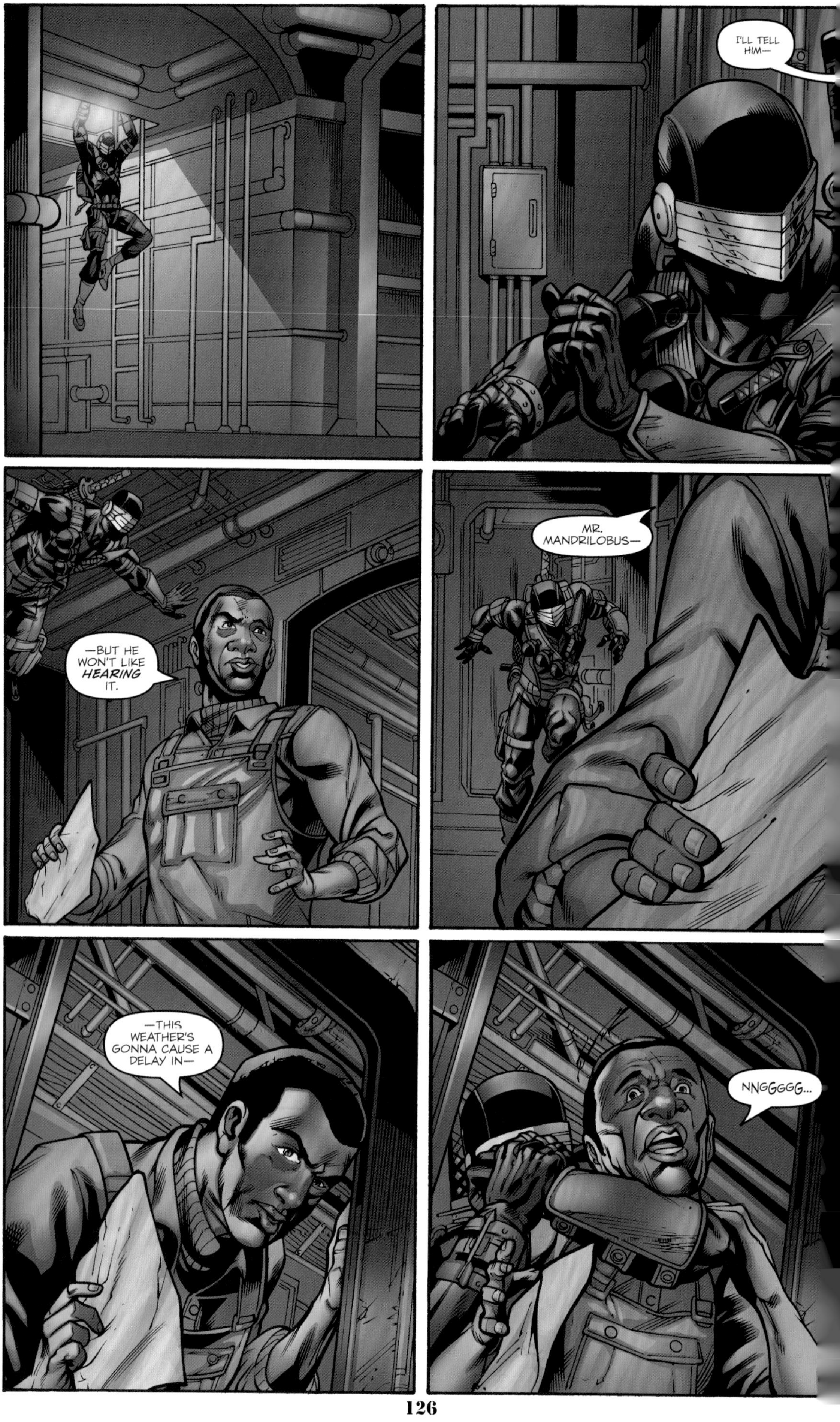
I'LL TELL HIM—
—BUT HE WON'T LIKE *HEARING* IT.
MR. MANDRILOBUS—
—THIS WEATHER'S GONNA CAUSE A DELAY IN—
NNGGGGG...

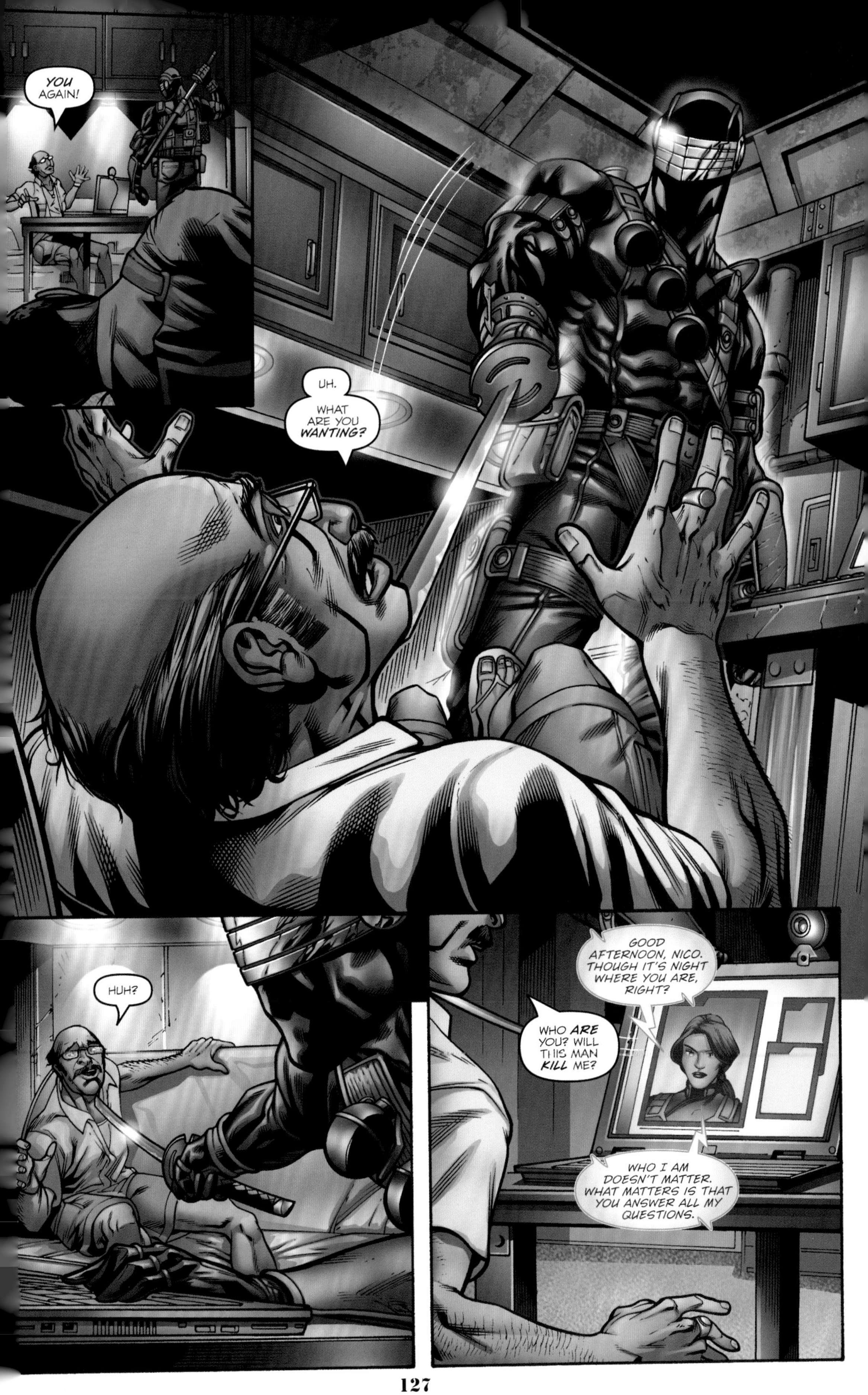
YOU AGAIN!
UH.
WHAT ARE YOU WANTING?
HUH?
GOOD AFTERNOON, NICO. THOUGH IT'S NIGHT WHERE YOU ARE, RIGHT?
WHO ARE YOU? WILL THIS MAN KILL ME?
WHO I AM DOESN'T MATTER. WHAT MATTERS IS THAT YOU ANSWER ALL MY QUESTIONS.

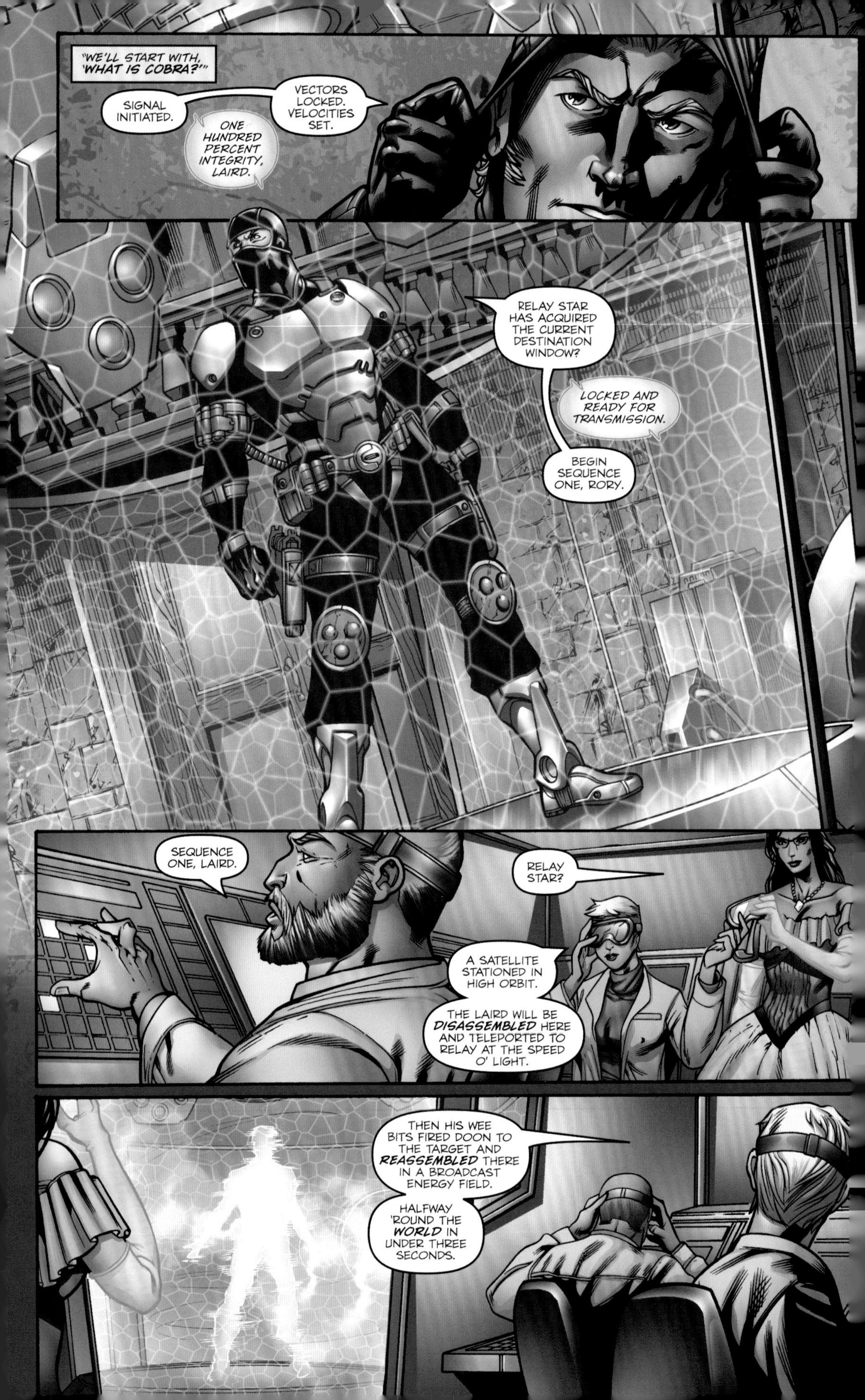
"WE'LL START WITH, '**WHAT IS COBRA?**'"
SIGNAL INITIATED.
VECTORS LOCKED. VELOCITIES SET.
ONE HUNDRED PERCENT INTEGRITY, LAIRD.
RELAY STAR HAS ACQUIRED THE CURRENT DESTINATION WINDOW?
LOCKED AND READY FOR TRANSMISSION.
BEGIN SEQUENCE ONE, RORY.
SEQUENCE ONE, LAIRD.
RELAY STAR?
A SATELLITE STATIONED IN HIGH ORBIT.
THE LAIRD WILL BE **DISASSEMBLED** HERE AND TELEPORTED TO RELAY AT THE SPEED O' LIGHT.
THEN HIS WEE BITS FIRED DOON TO THE TARGET AND **REASSEMBLED** THERE IN A BROADCAST ENERGY FIELD.
HALFWAY 'ROUND THE **WORLD** IN UNDER THREE SECONDS.

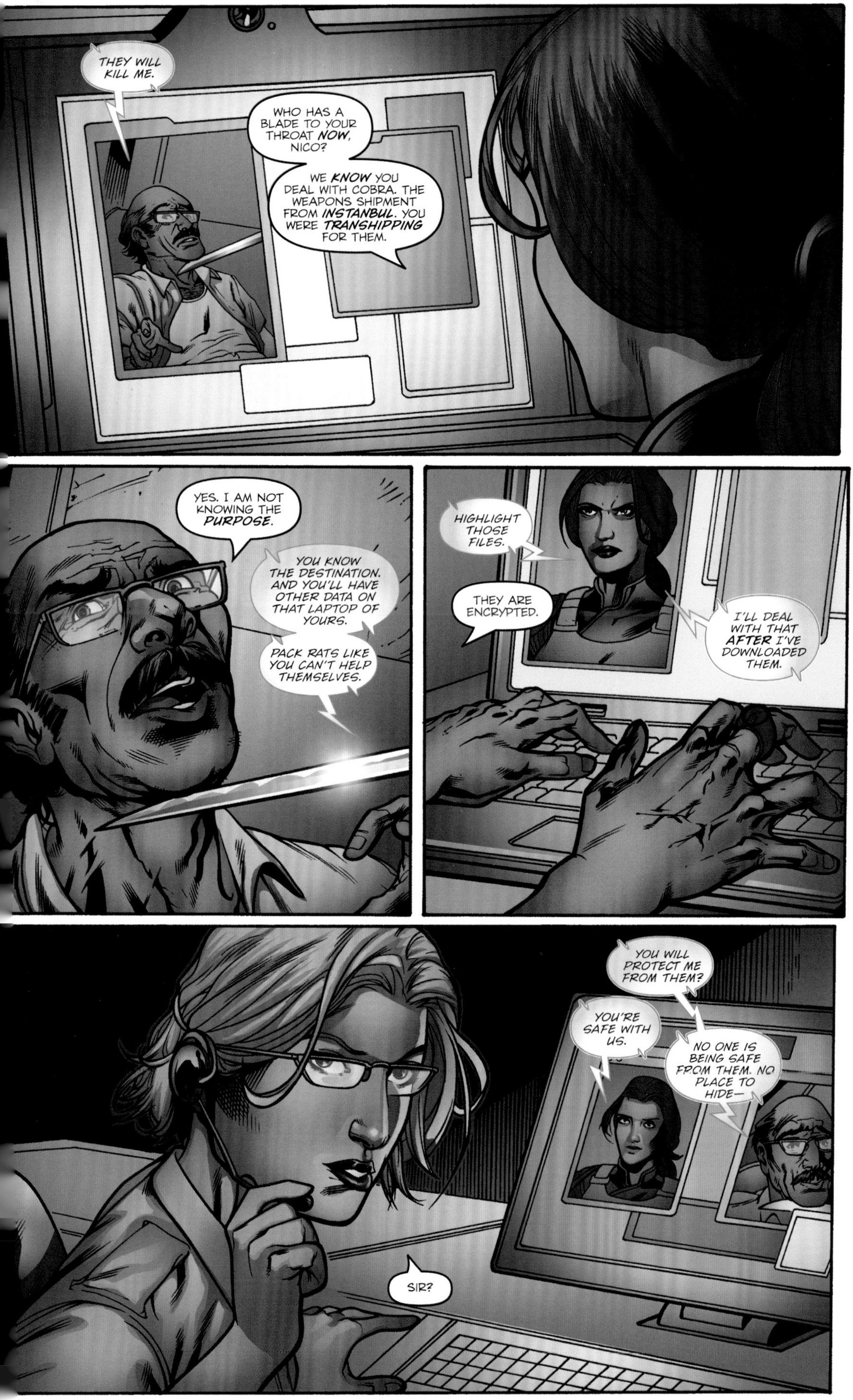
THEY WILL KILL ME.
WHO HAS A BLADE TO YOUR THROAT NOW, NICO?
WE KNOW YOU DEAL WITH COBRA. THE WEAPONS SHIPMENT FROM INSTANBUL. YOU WERE TRANSHIPPING FOR THEM.
YES. I AM NOT KNOWING THE PURPOSE.
YOU KNOW THE DESTINATION. AND YOU'LL HAVE OTHER DATA ON THAT LAPTOP OF YOURS.
PACK RATS LIKE YOU CAN'T HELP THEMSELVES.
HIGHLIGHT THOSE FILES.
THEY ARE ENCRYPTED.
I'LL DEAL WITH THAT AFTER I'VE DOWNLOADED THEM.
YOU WILL PROTECT ME FROM THEM?
YOU'RE SAFE WITH US.
NO ONE IS BEING SAFE FROM THEM. NO PLACE TO HIDE—
SIR?

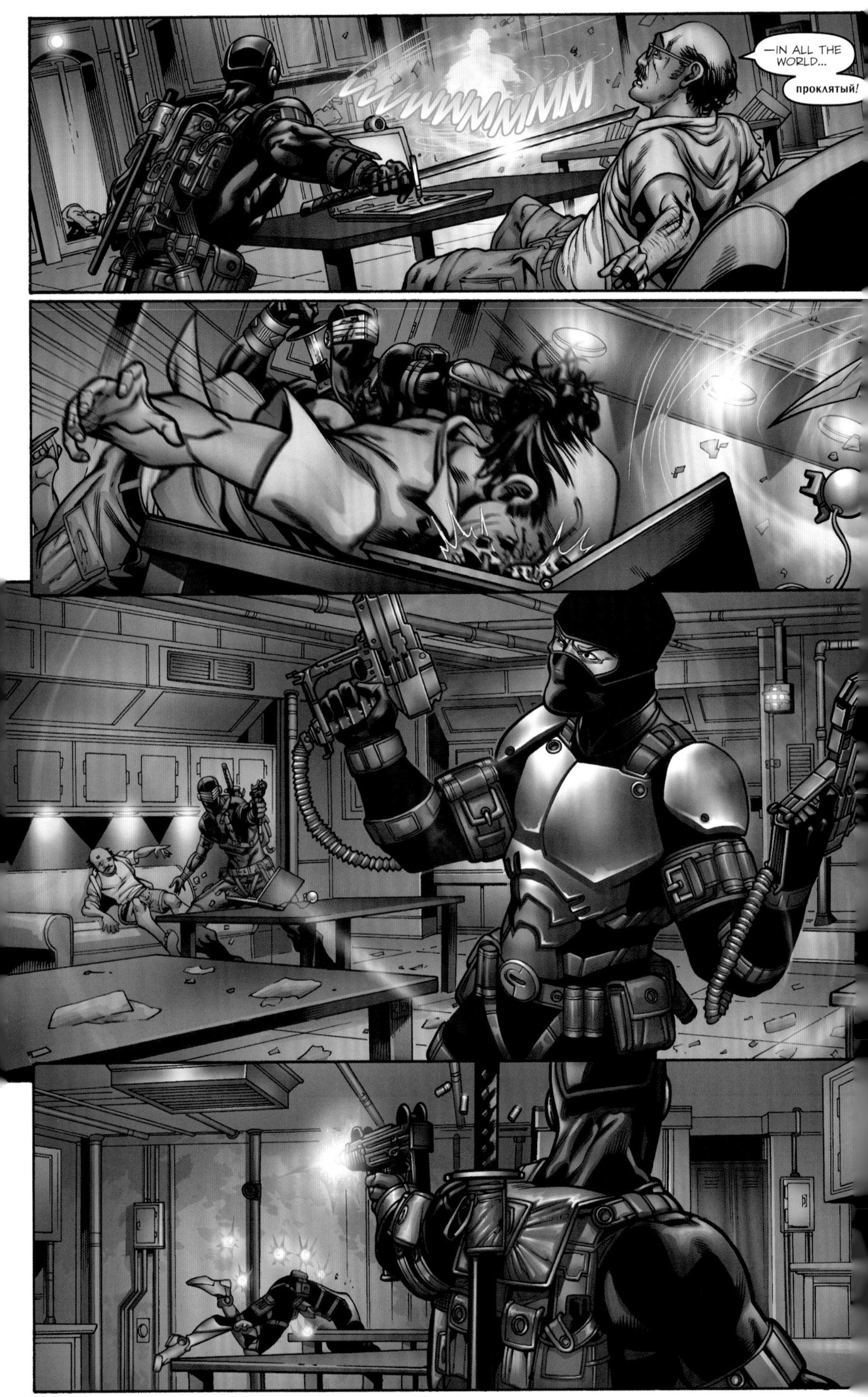
—IN ALL THE WORLD...
проклятый!
WWWWMMMMM

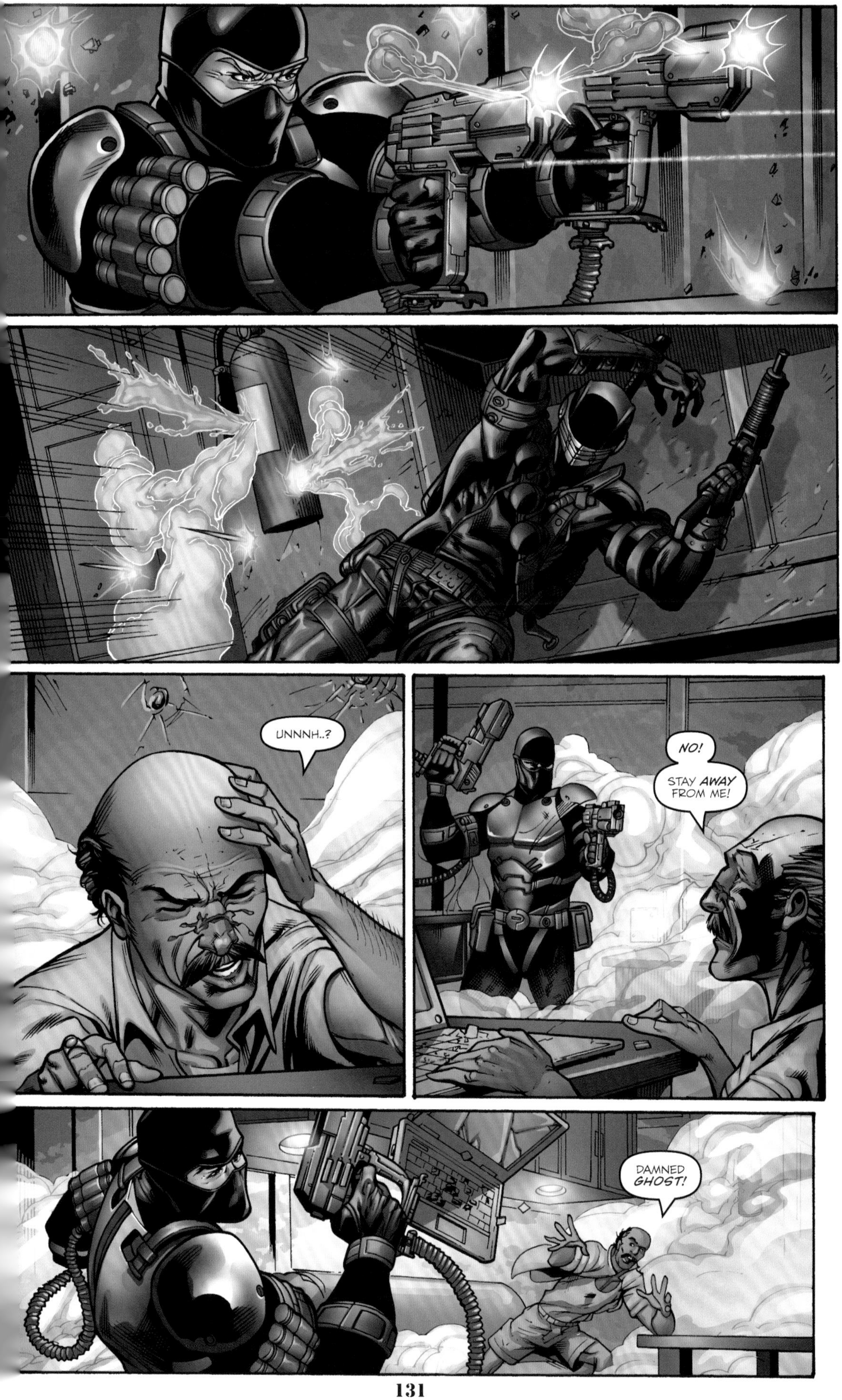
UNNNH..?
NO!
STAY AWAY FROM ME!
DAMNED GHOST!

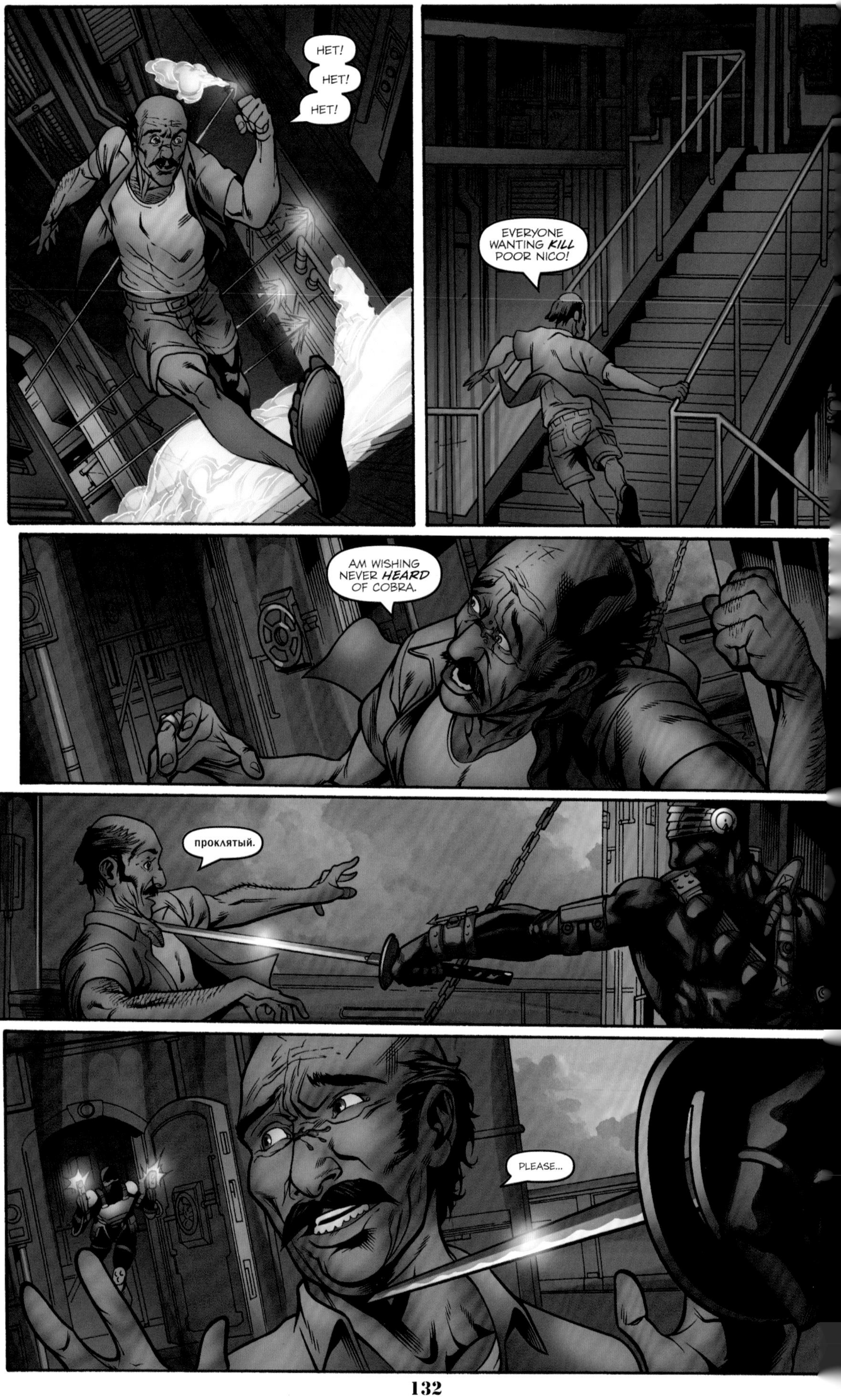
HET!
HET!
HET!
EVERYONE WANTING KILL POOR NICO!
AM WISHING NEVER HEARD OF COBRA.
проклятый.
PLEASE...

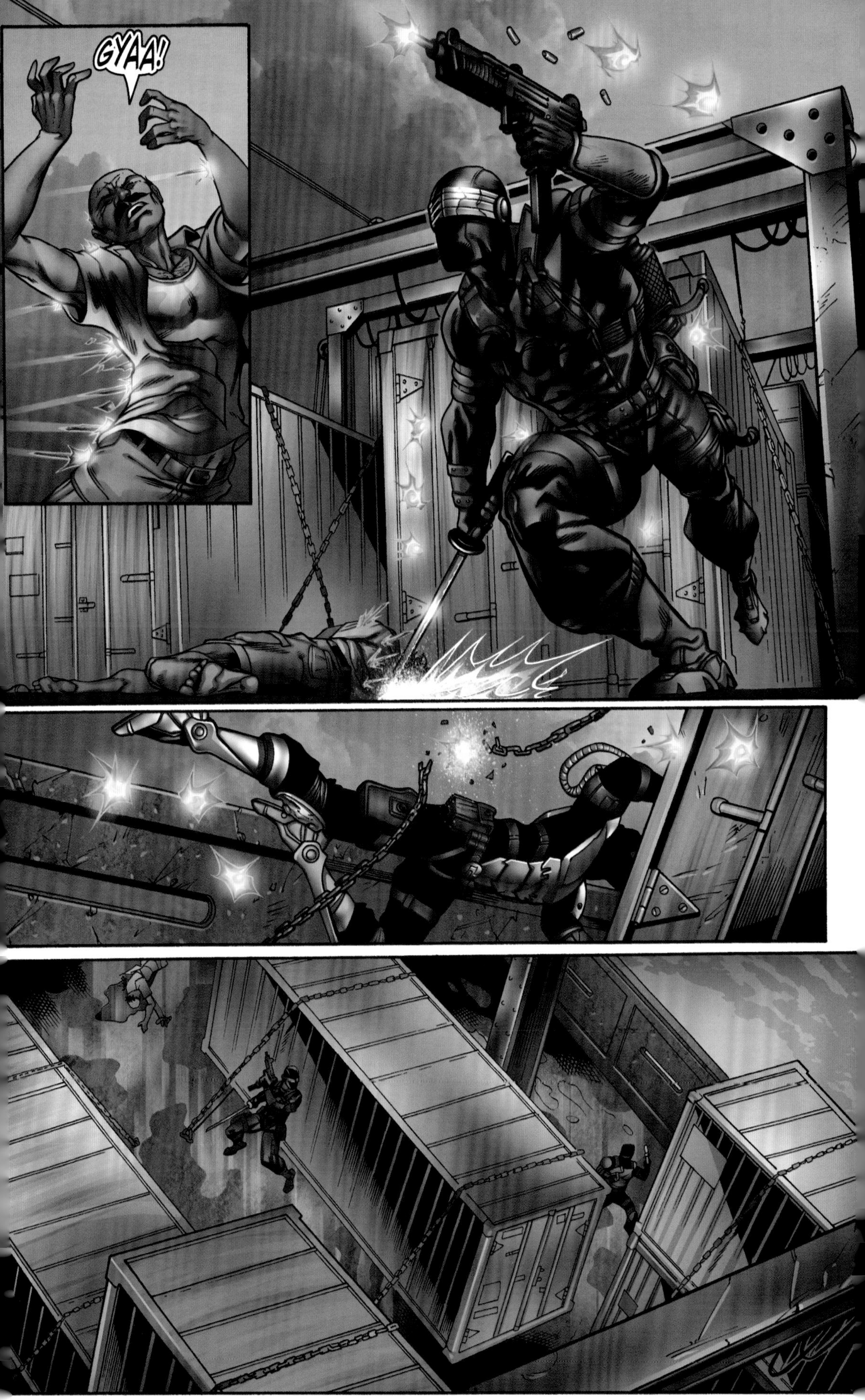
GYAA!

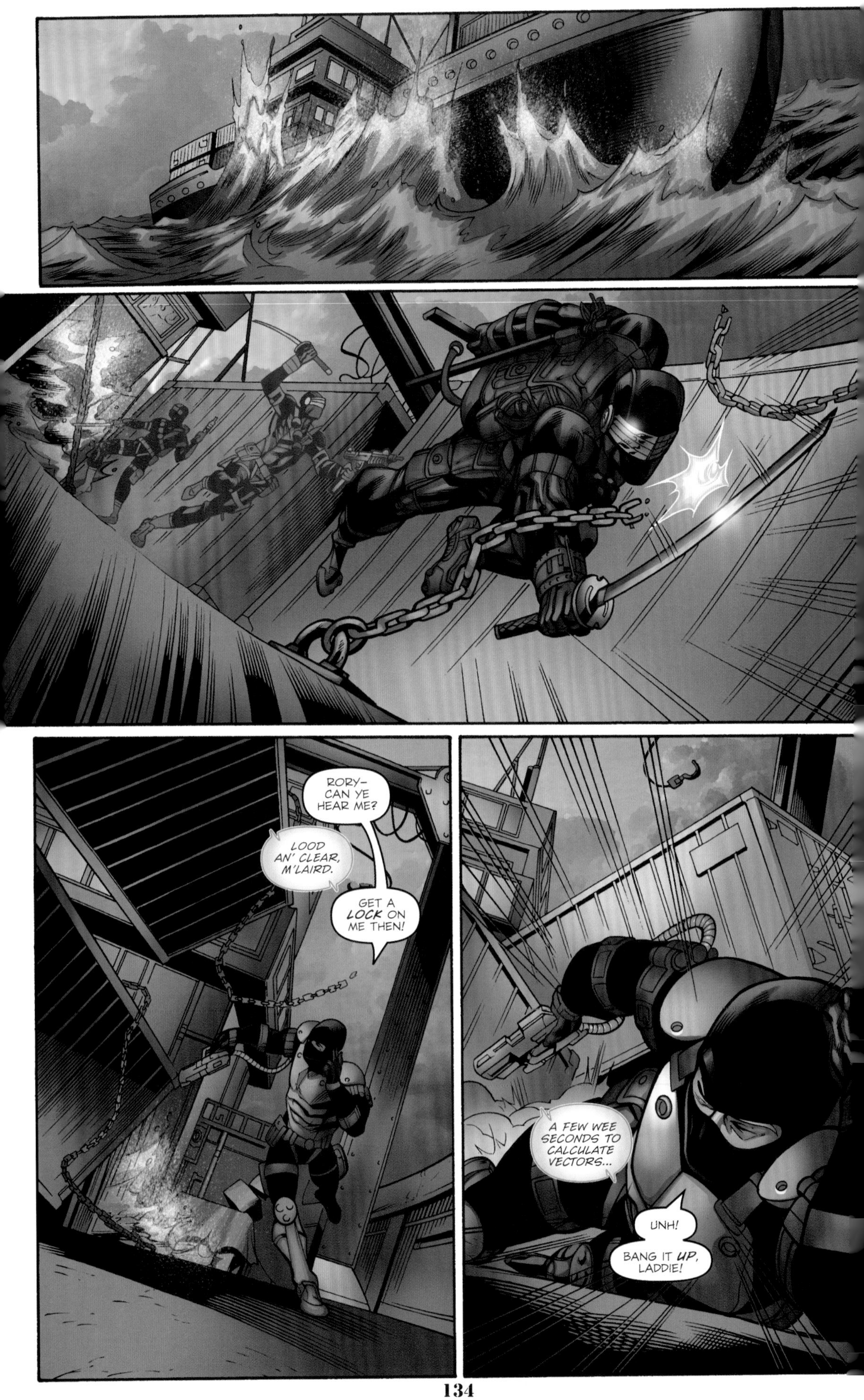
RORY– CAN YE HEAR ME?
LOOD AN' CLEAR, M'LAIRD.
GET A LOCK ON ME THEN!
A FEW WEE SECONDS TO CALCULATE VECTORS...
UNH!
BANG IT UP, LADDIE!

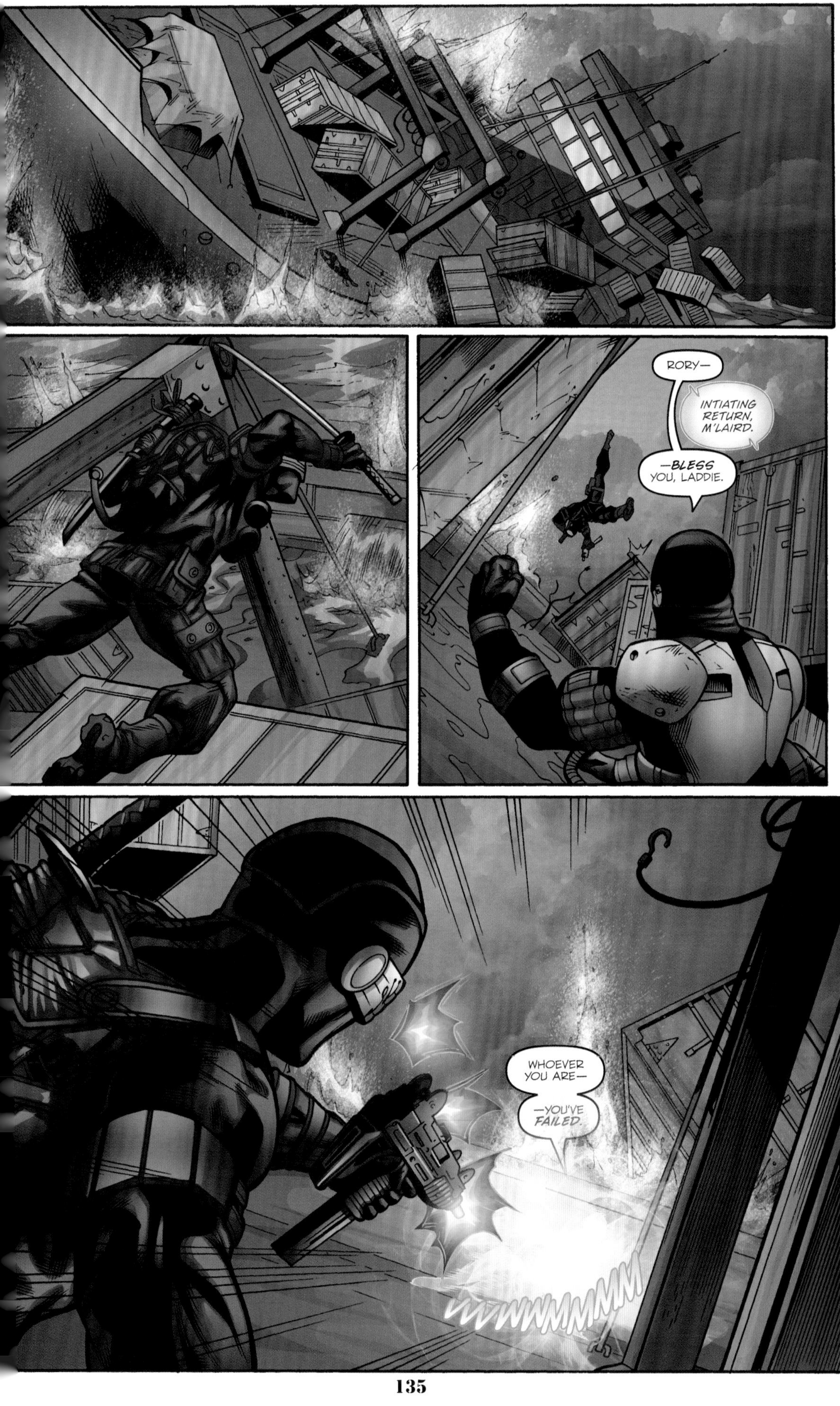

RORY—
INTIATING RETURN, M'LAIRD.
—BLESS YOU, LADDIE.
WHOEVER YOU ARE—
—YOU'VE FAILED.
VVVVWWMMMMM

DROP THE WEAPONS.

MOVE AND YOU DIE.

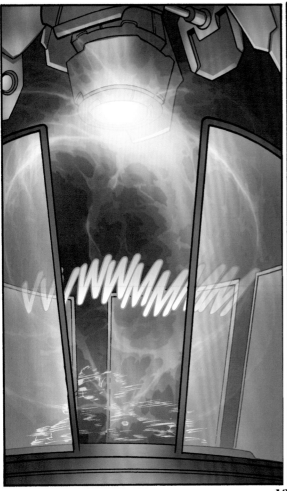

UHHHH...

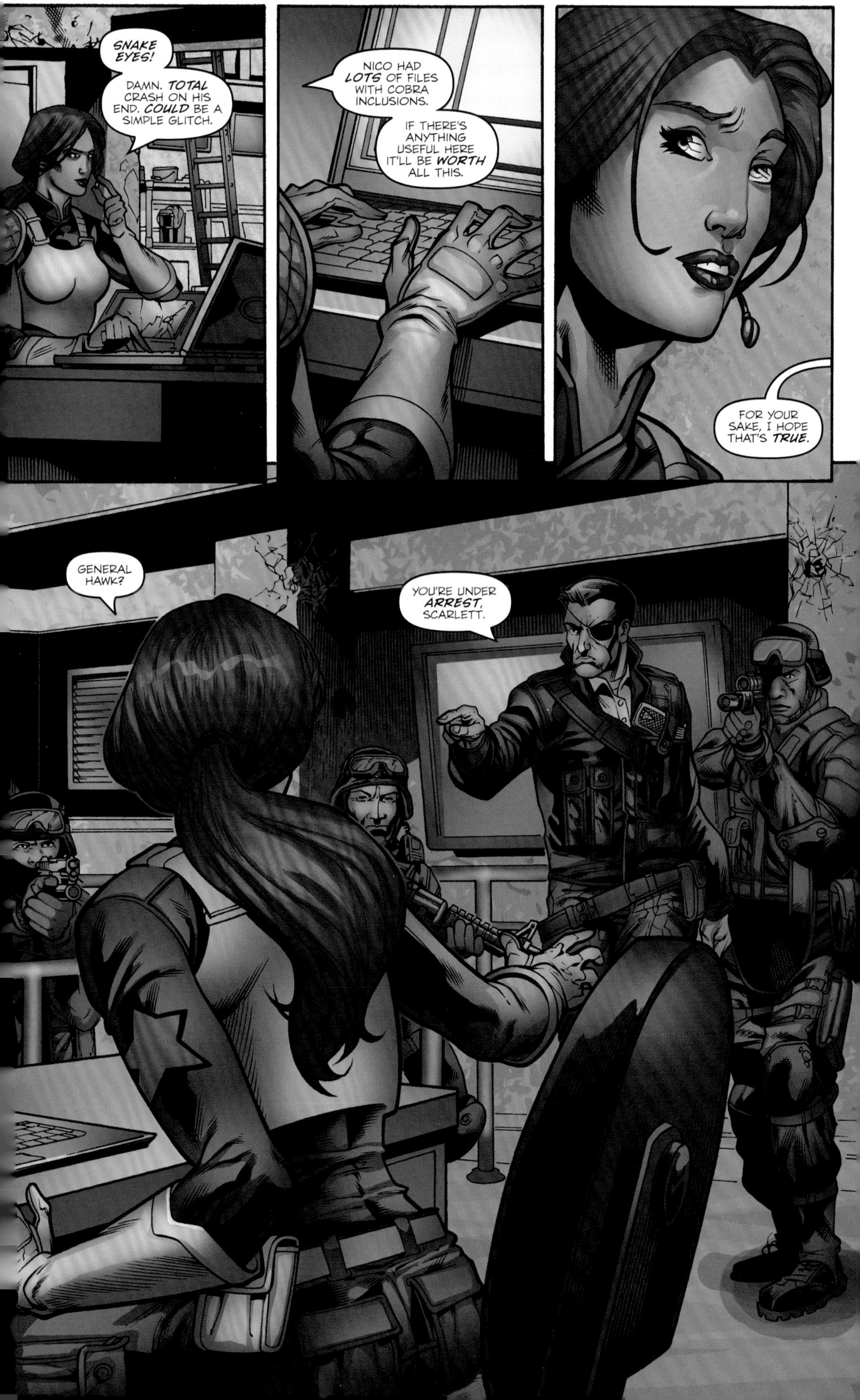
SNAKE EYES!
DAMN. TOTAL CRASH ON HIS END. COULD BE A SIMPLE GLITCH.
NICO HAD LOTS OF FILES WITH COBRA INCLUSIONS.
IF THERE'S ANYTHING USEFUL HERE IT'LL BE WORTH ALL THIS.
FOR YOUR SAKE, I HOPE THAT'S TRUE.
GENERAL HAWK?
YOU'RE UNDER ARREST, SCARLETT.

ALMICHTIE GOD...

MOLECULAR BOND... LOSING CHARGE...

...CONTAINMENT FIELD... NOW...

WHAT'S HAPPENING TO DESTRO?

GLYNIS! HE'S SAUNTIN' AWA BEFORE ME EYES!

HIS STRUCTURAL INTEGRITY IS *FAILING* AT THE MOLECULAR LEVEL. A BLOODY *BREAKDOON* IN THE HIGGS MECHANISM.

"WE KEN IT'S WHAT WENT WRONG WITH OOR FIRST EFFORT.

"POOR SOD *EVAPORATED* AFORE WE COULD CALL 'IM BACK, HE DID.

"WE COULDNA KEEP THE *SIGNAL* CONSTANT.

"NEVER MADE IT *HOME* TO CASTLE DESTRO FOR FULL RE-INTEGRATION.

"THE LAIRD'LL SHARE HIS FATE WIOOT *RESTORE* HIS HETEROTIC FIELD, YE KE

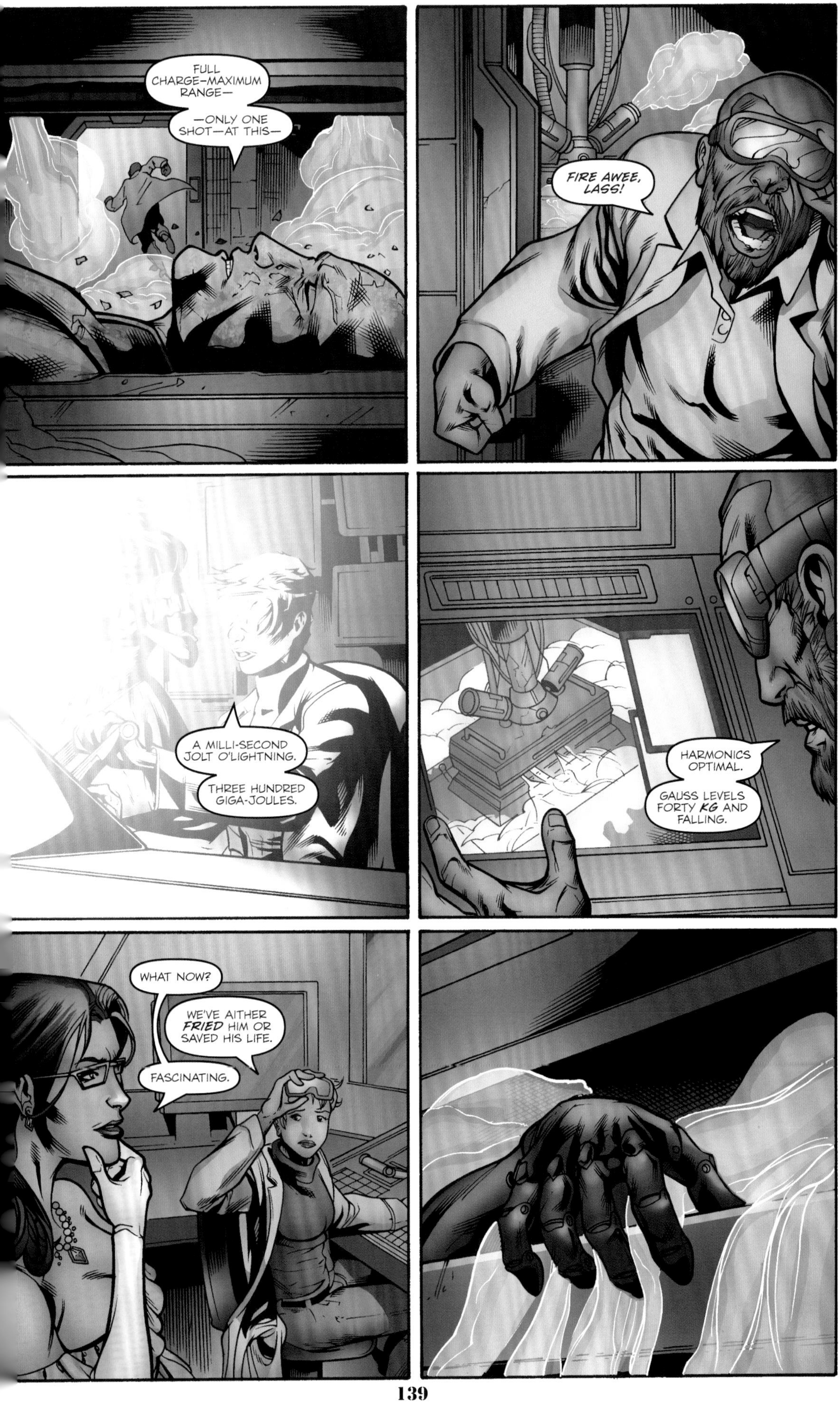
FULL CHARGE—MAXIMUM RANGE—
—ONLY ONE SHOT—AT THIS—
FIRE AWEE, LASS!
A MILLI-SECOND JOLT O'LIGHTNING.
THREE HUNDRED GIGA-JOULES.
HARMONICS OPTIMAL.
GAUSS LEVELS FORTY KG AND FALLING.
WHAT NOW?
WE'VE AITHER FRIED HIM OR SAVED HIS LIFE.
FASCINATING.

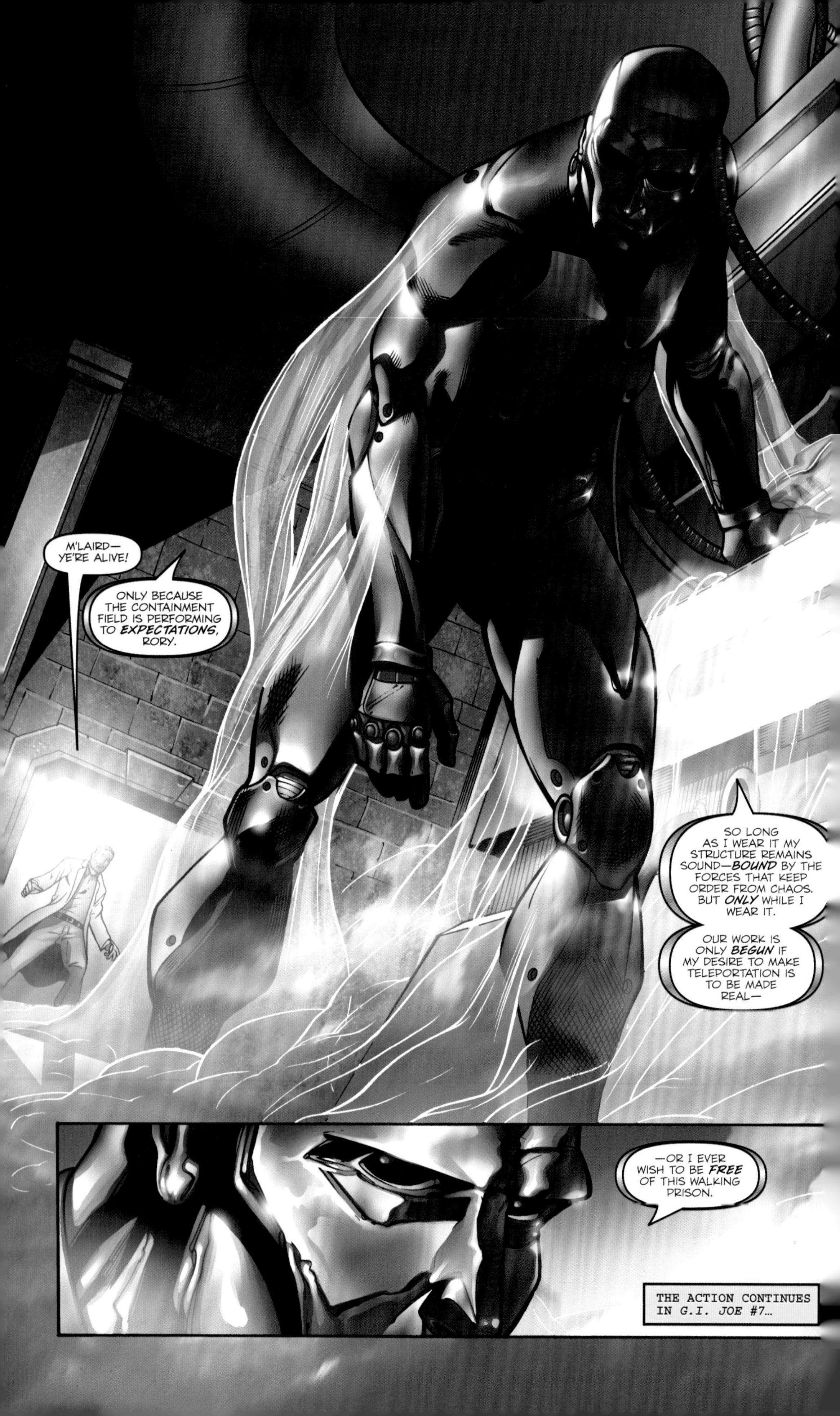
M'LAIRD— YE'RE ALIVE!
ONLY BECAUSE THE CONTAINMENT FIELD IS PERFORMING TO *EXPECTATIONS*, RORY.
SO LONG AS I WEAR IT MY STRUCTURE REMAINS SOUND—*BOUND* BY THE FORCES THAT KEEP ORDER FROM CHAOS. BUT *ONLY* WHILE I WEAR IT.
OUR WORK IS ONLY *BEGUN* IF MY DESIRE TO MAKE TELEPORTATION IS TO BE MADE REAL—
—OR I EVER WISH TO BE *FREE* OF THIS WALKING PRISON.
THE ACTION CONTINUES IN *G.I. JOE #7*...

ART BY ROBERT ATKINS & CHRIS SOTOMAYER

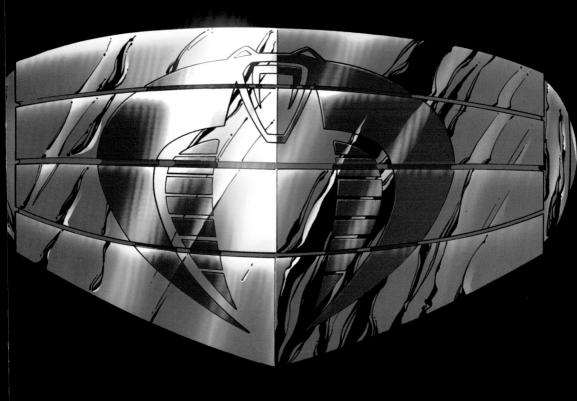

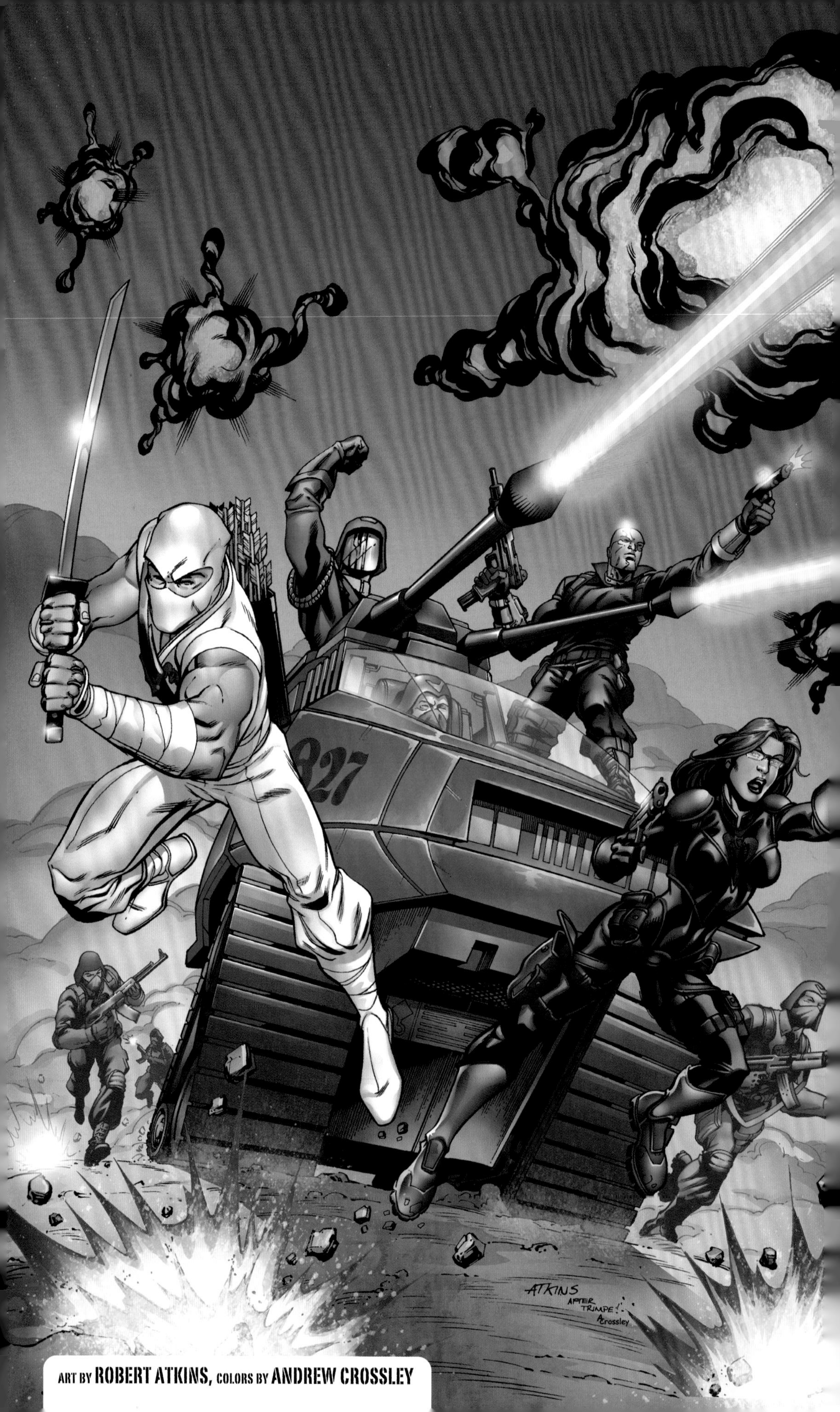
327
ATKINS
AFTER TRIMPE!
ACrossley

ART BY ROBERT ATKINS, COLORS BY ANDREW CROSSLEY

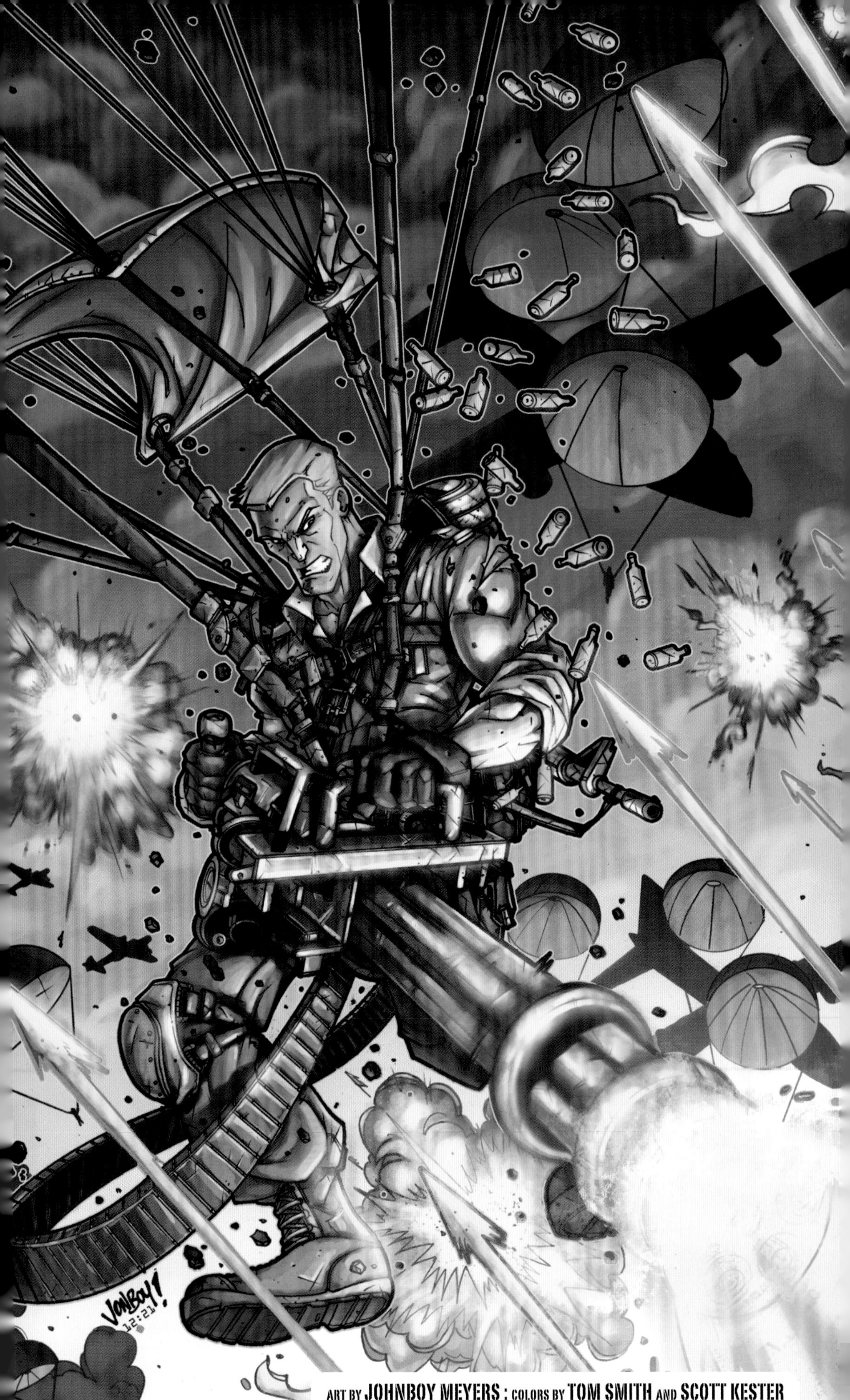
JONBOY!
12:21

ART BY JOHNBOY MEYERS : COLORS BY TOM SMITH AND SCOTT KESTER

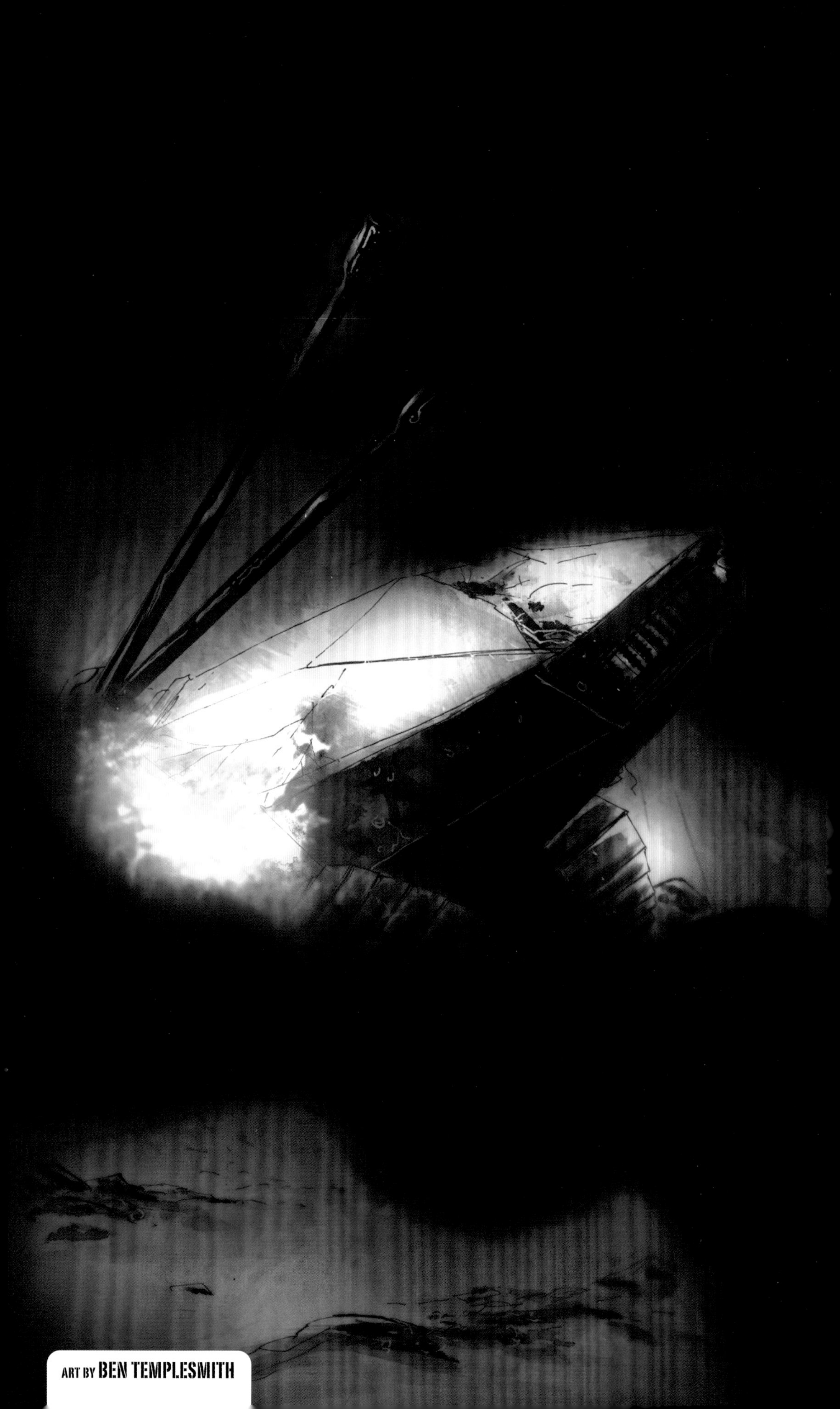

ART BY BEN TEMPLESMITH

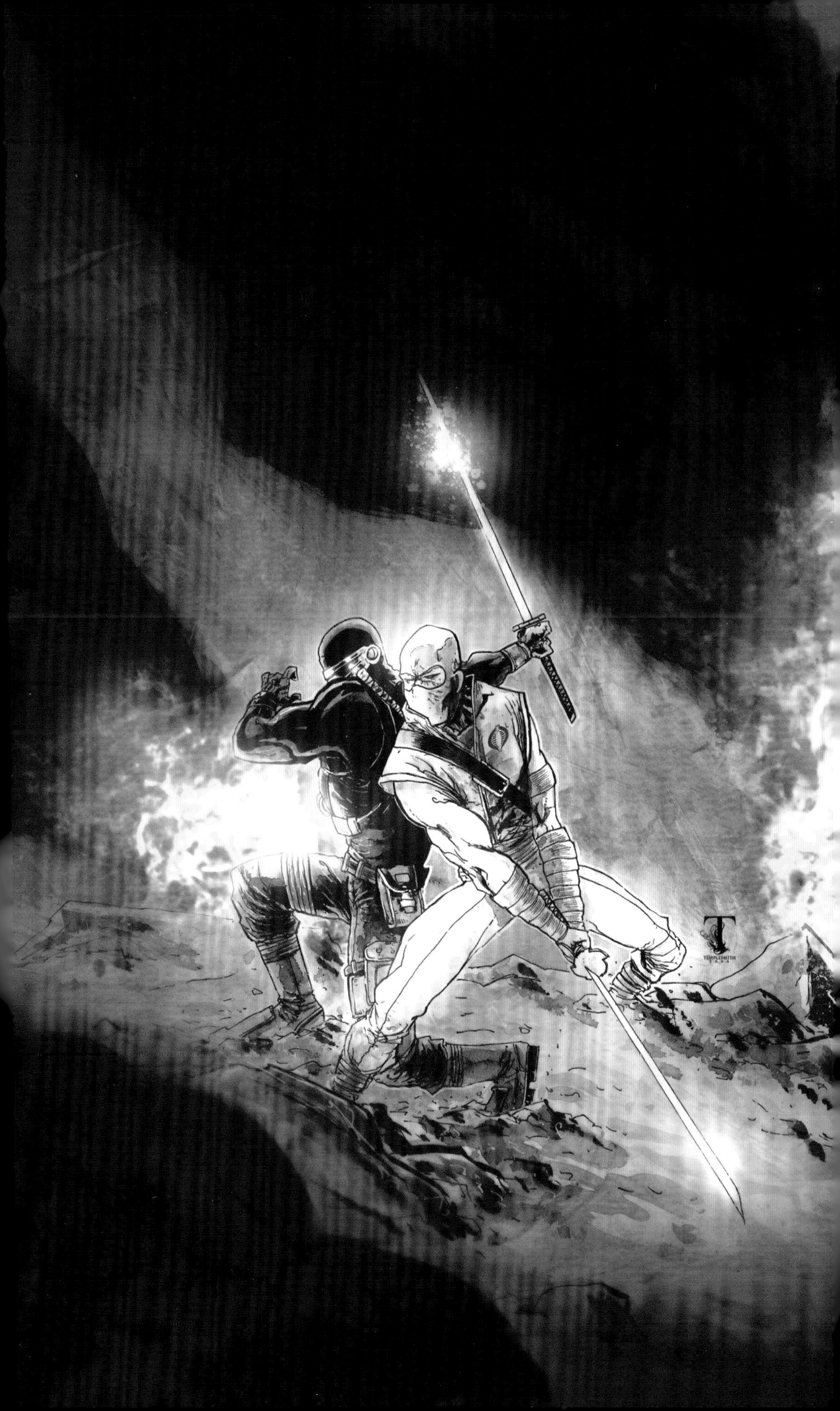
TEMPLESMITH

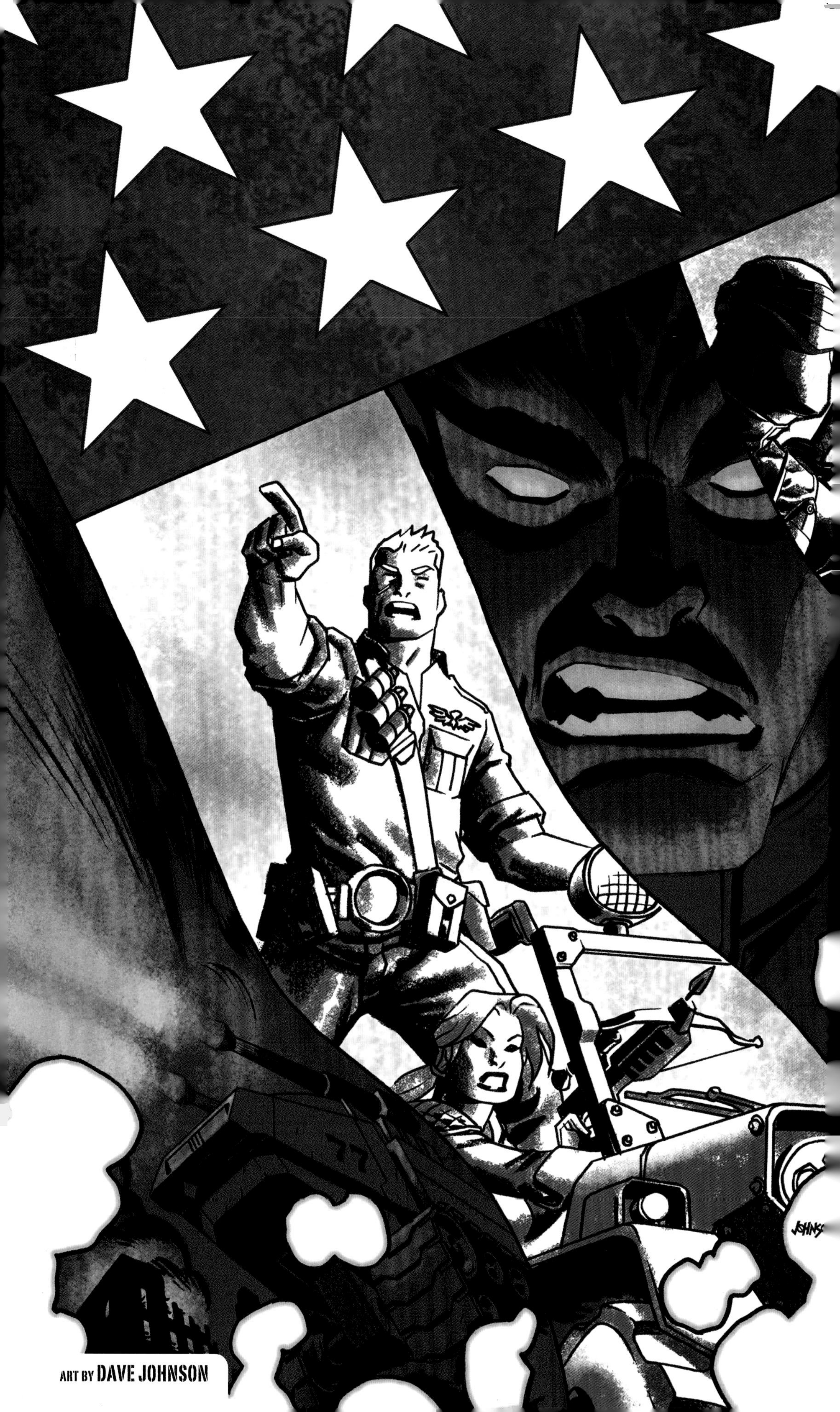

ART BY DAVE JOHNSON

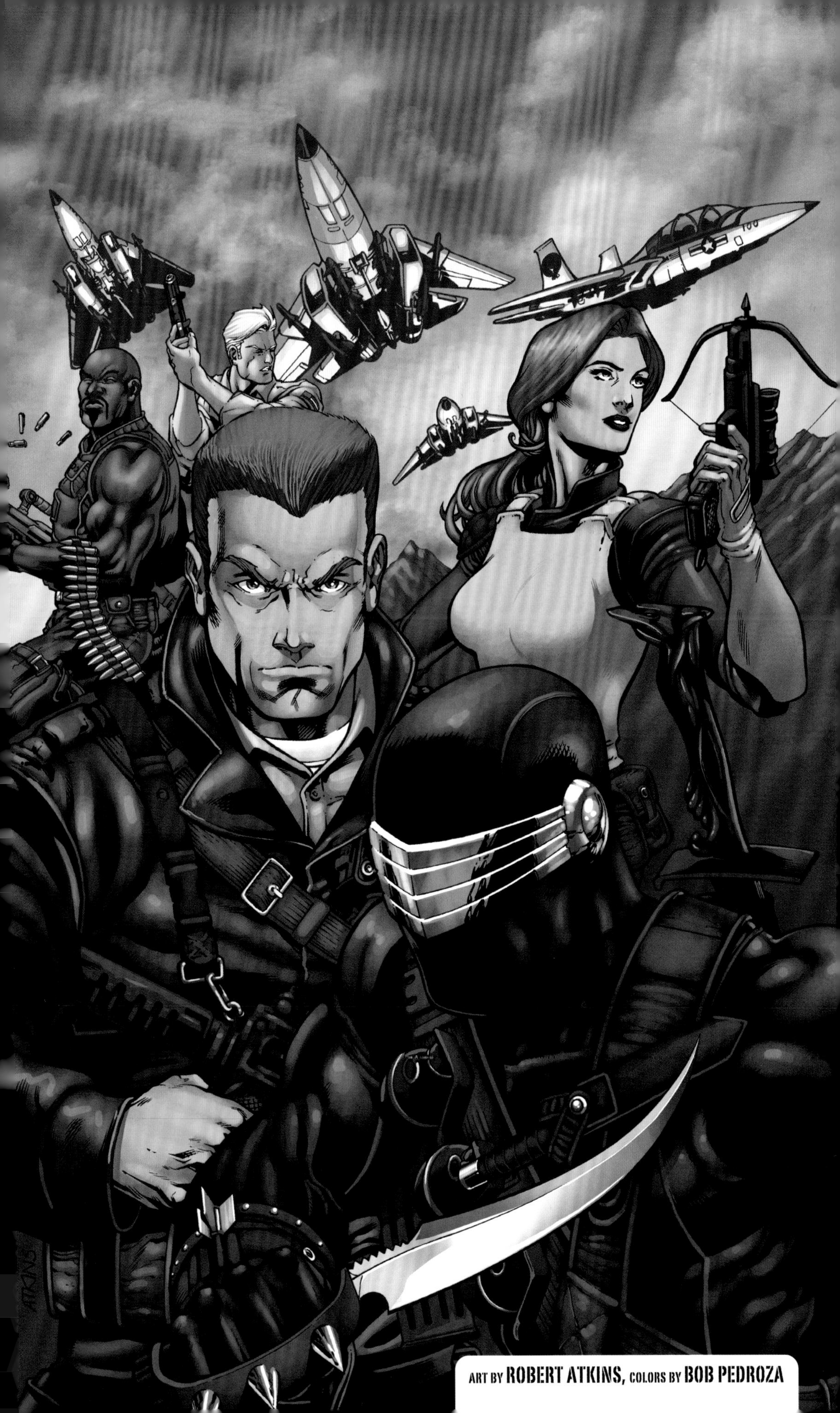

ART BY **ROBERT ATKINS**, COLORS BY **BOB PEDROZA**

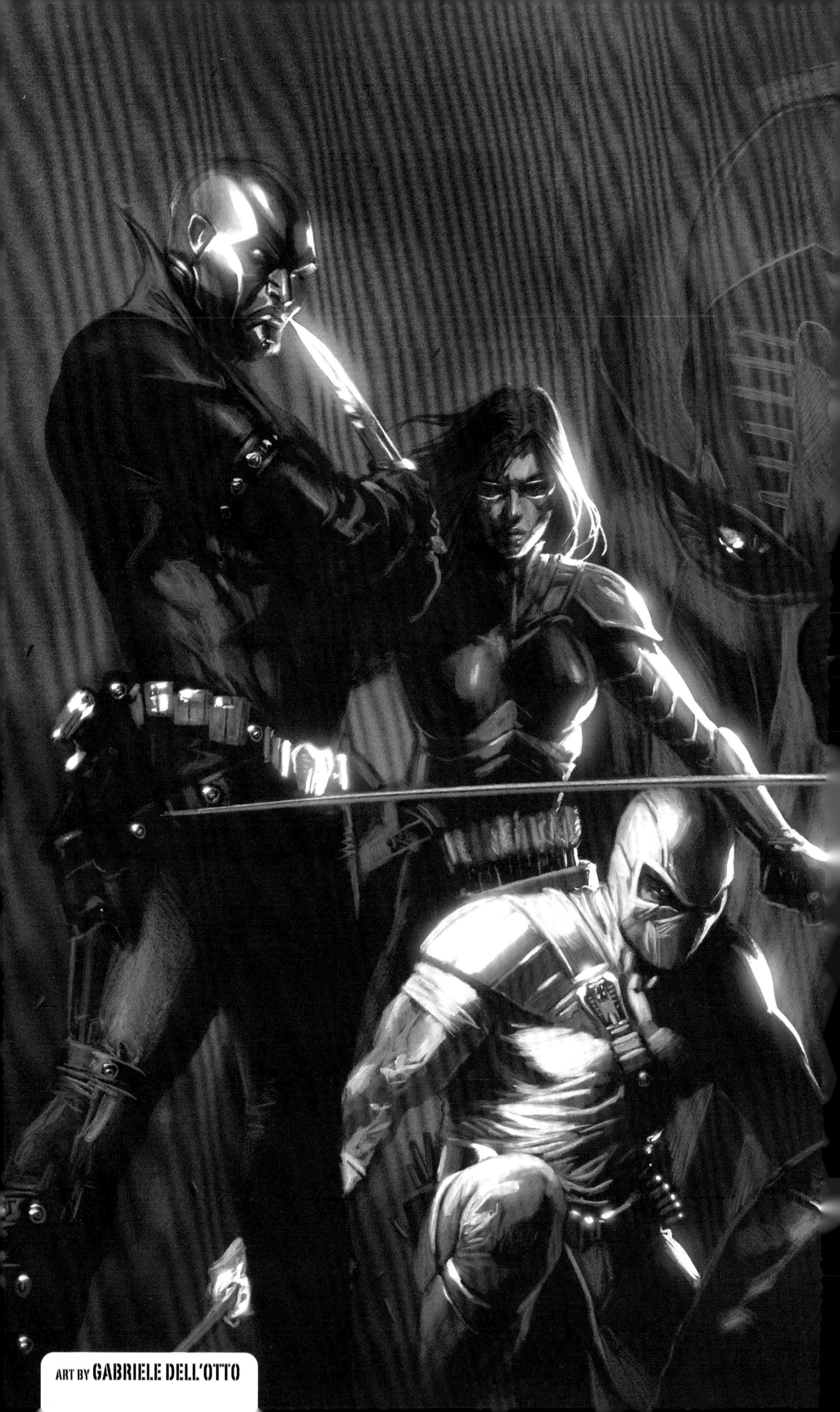

ART BY GABRIELE DELL'OTTO

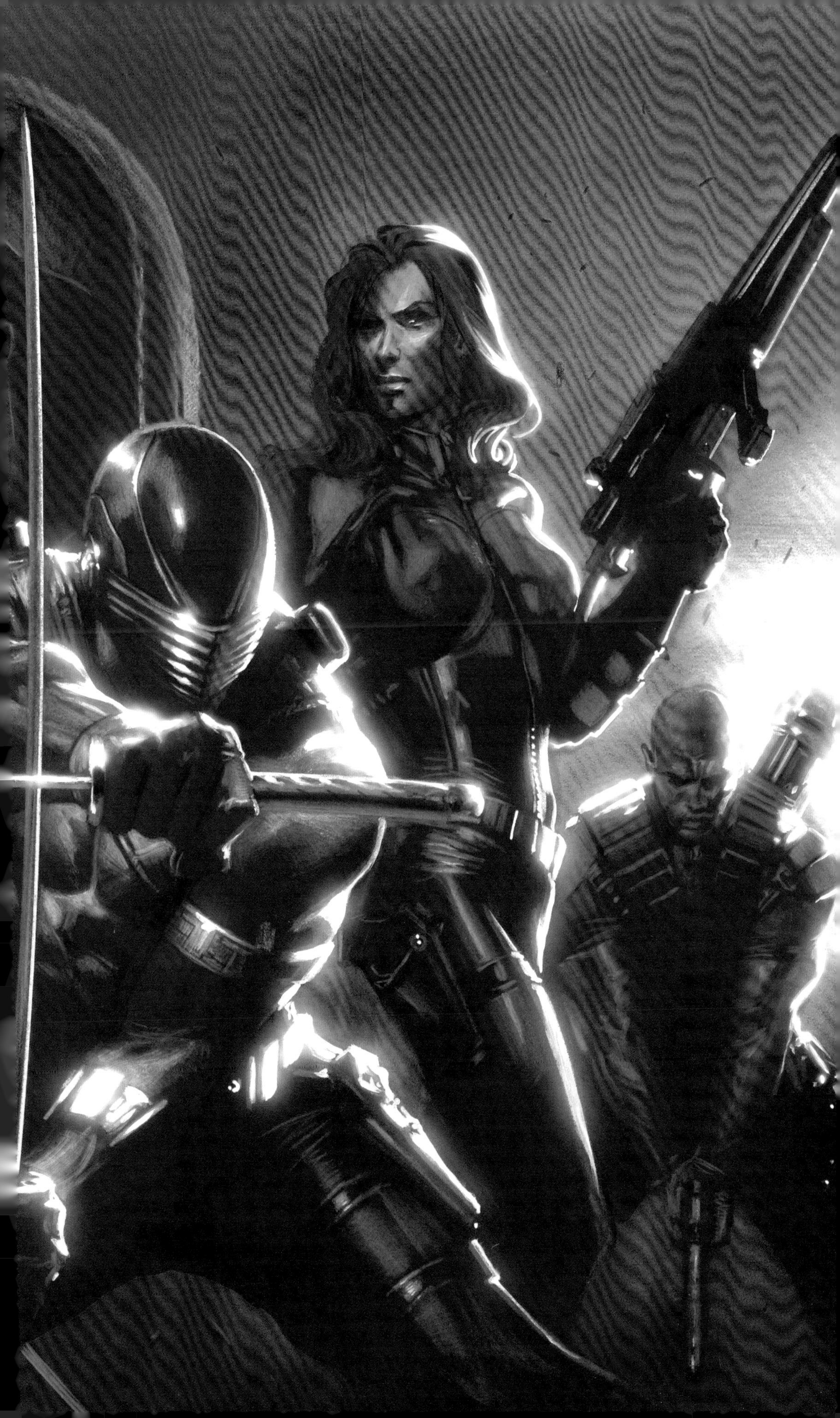

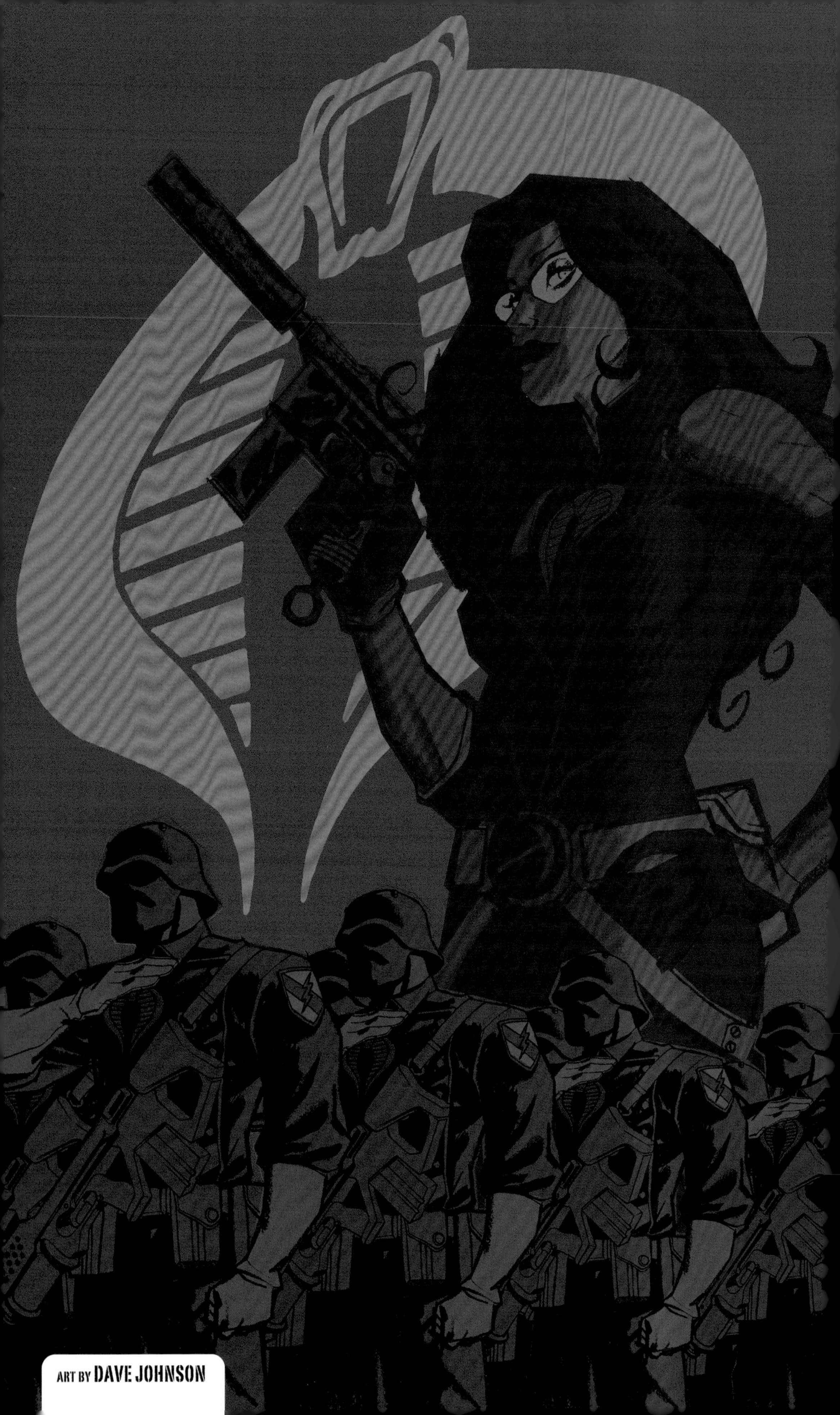

ART BY DAVE JOHNSON

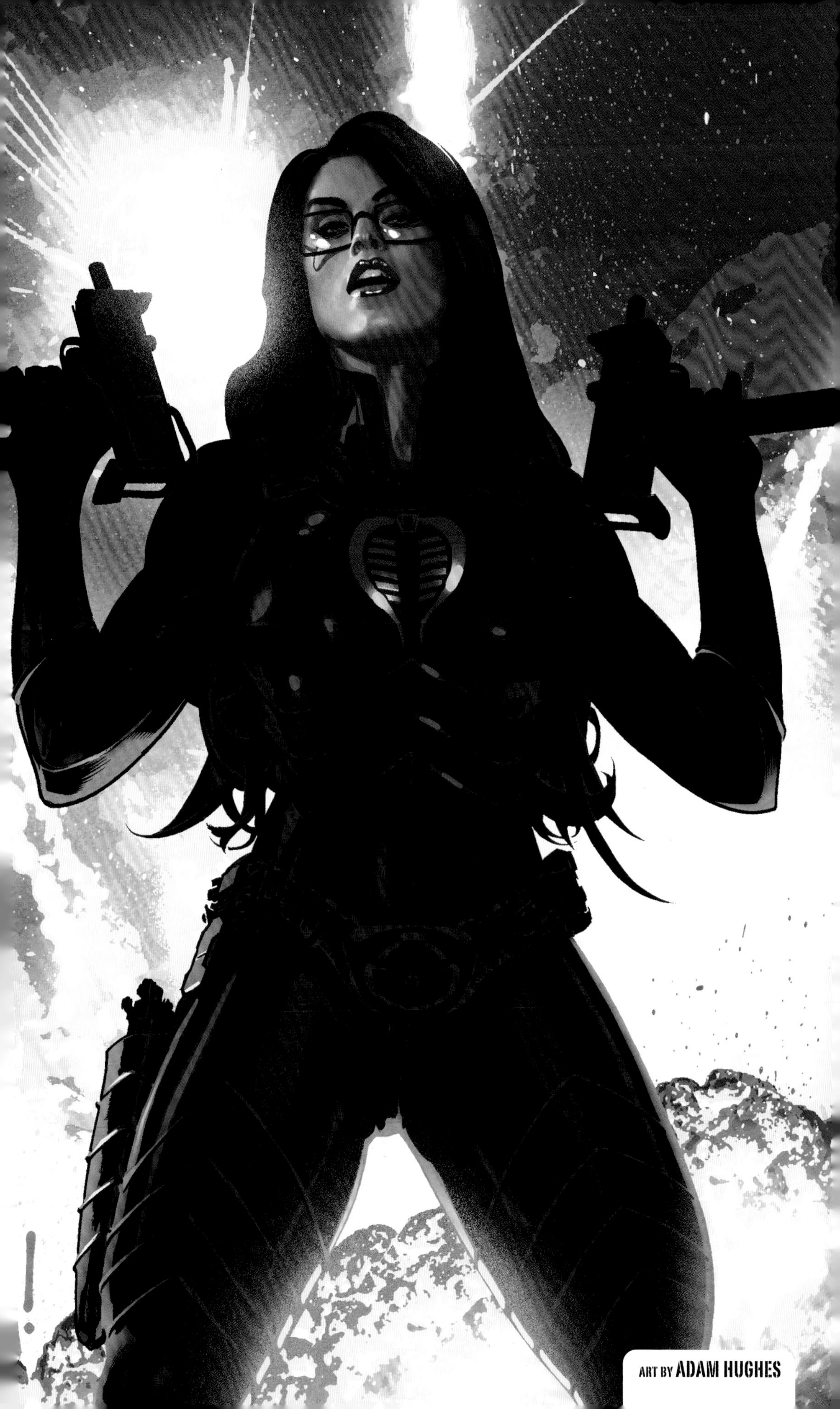

ART BY ADAM HUGHES

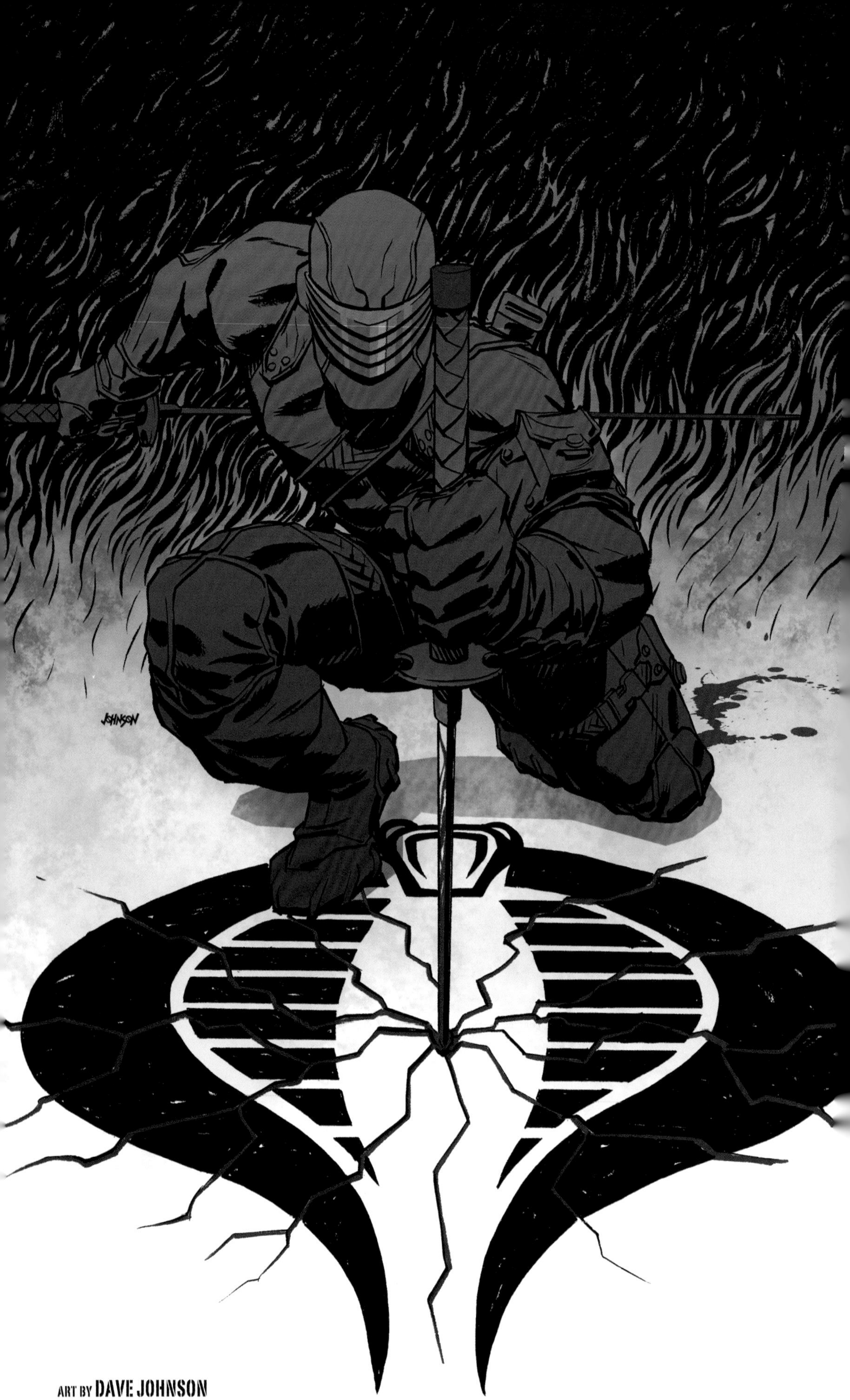
JOHNSON

ART BY DAVE JOHNSON

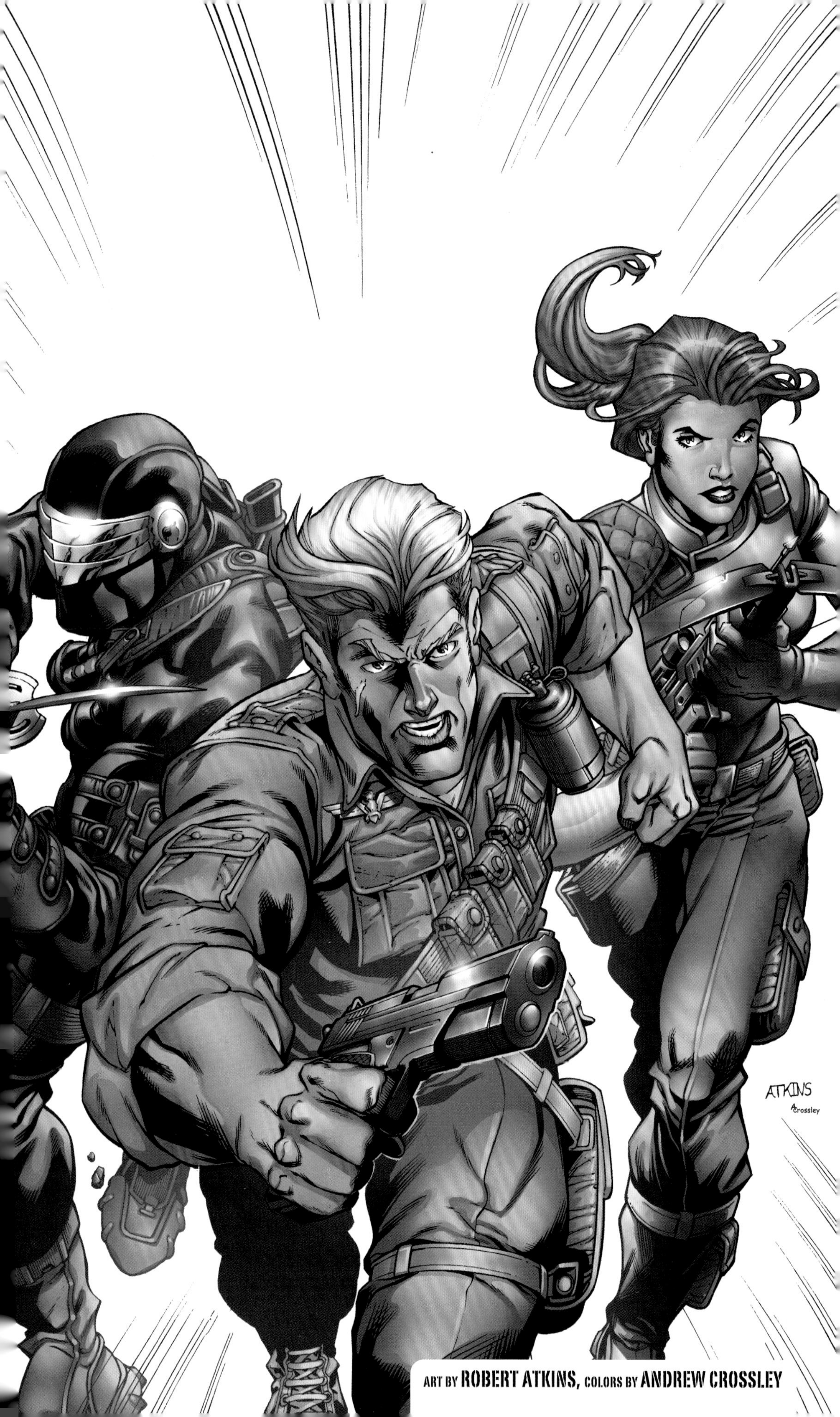
ATKINS
A. Crossley

ART BY ROBERT ATKINS, COLORS BY ANDREW CROSSLEY

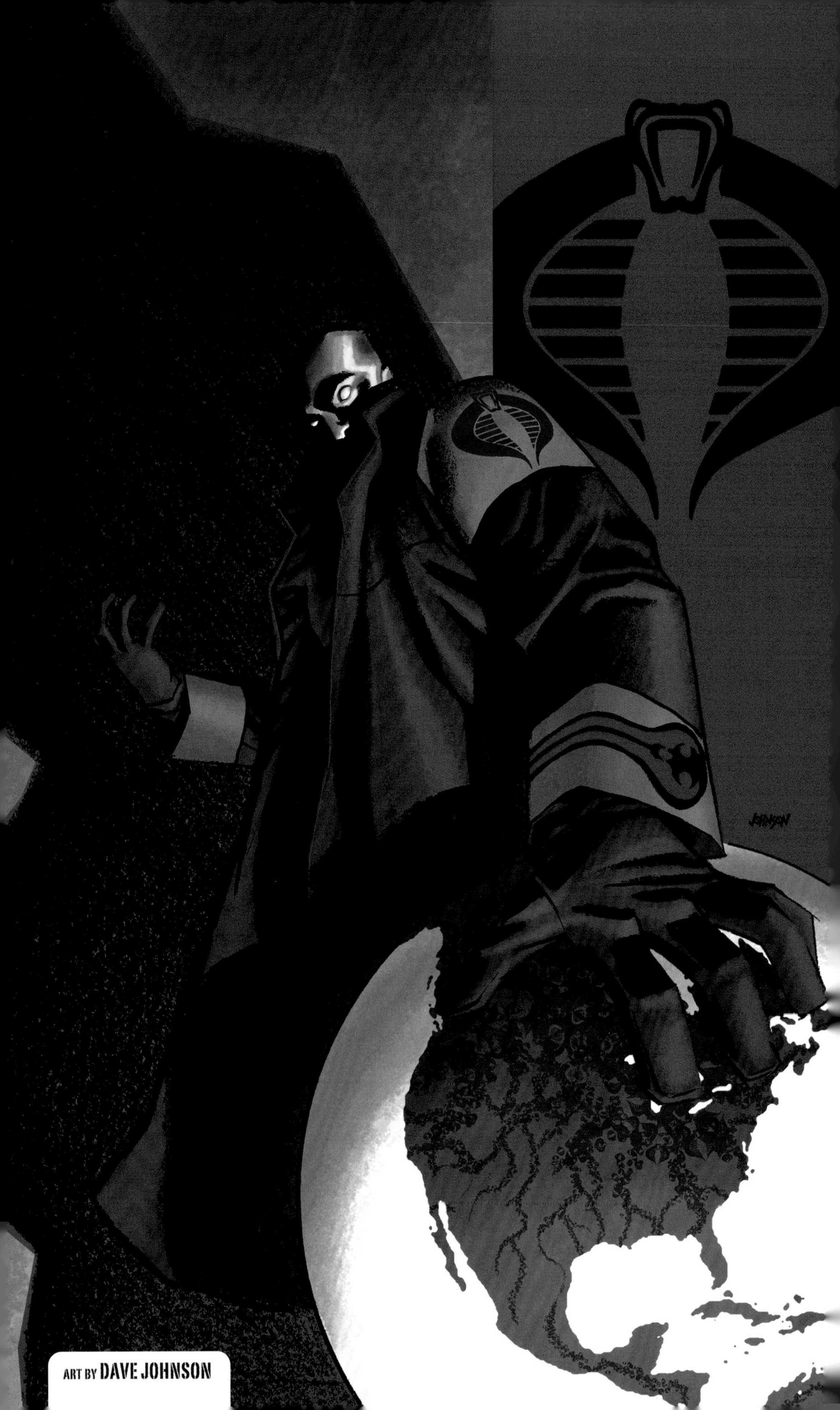
JOHNSON

ART BY DAVE JOHNSON

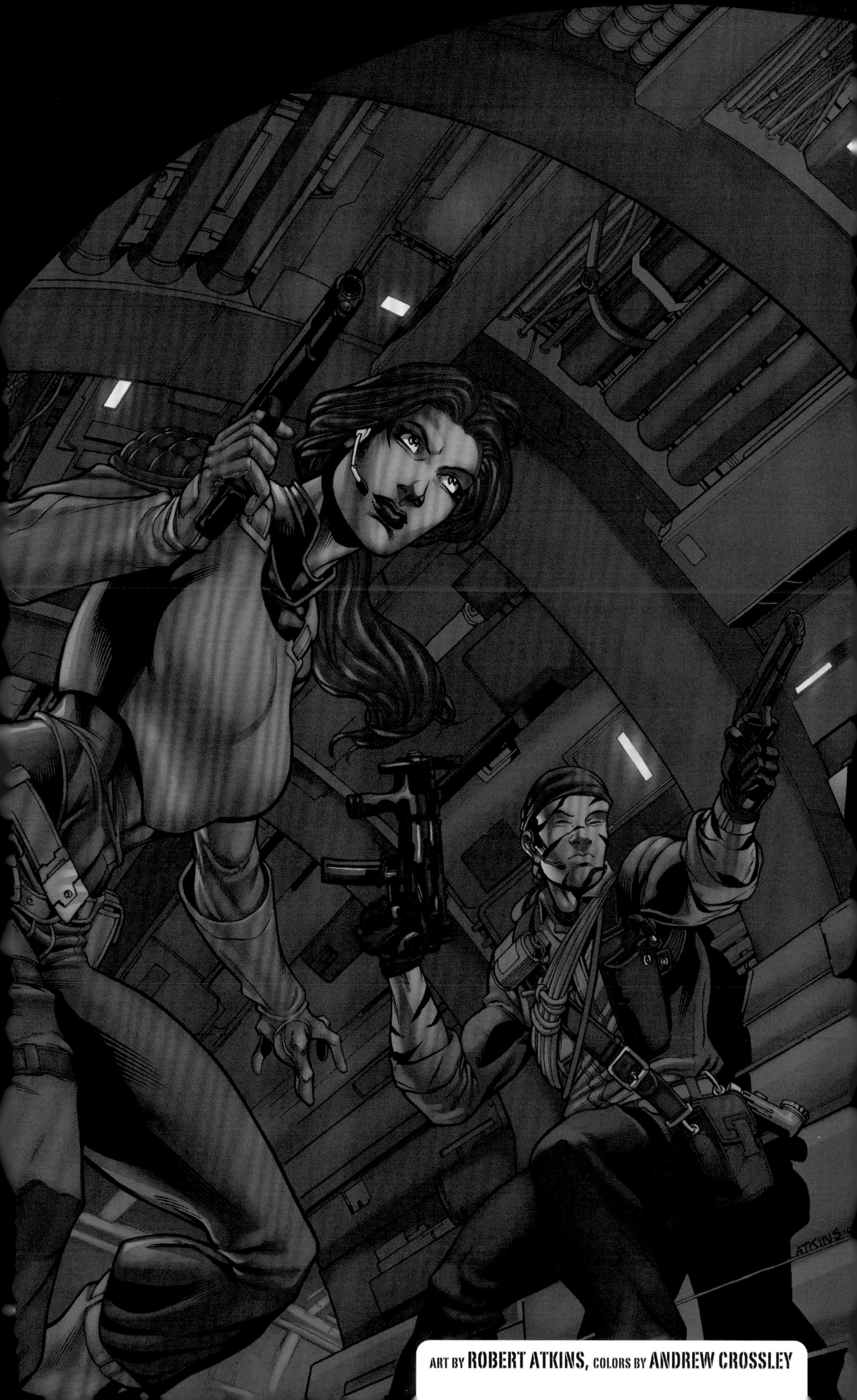
ATKINS

ART BY **ROBERT ATKINS**, COLORS BY **ANDREW CROSSLEY**

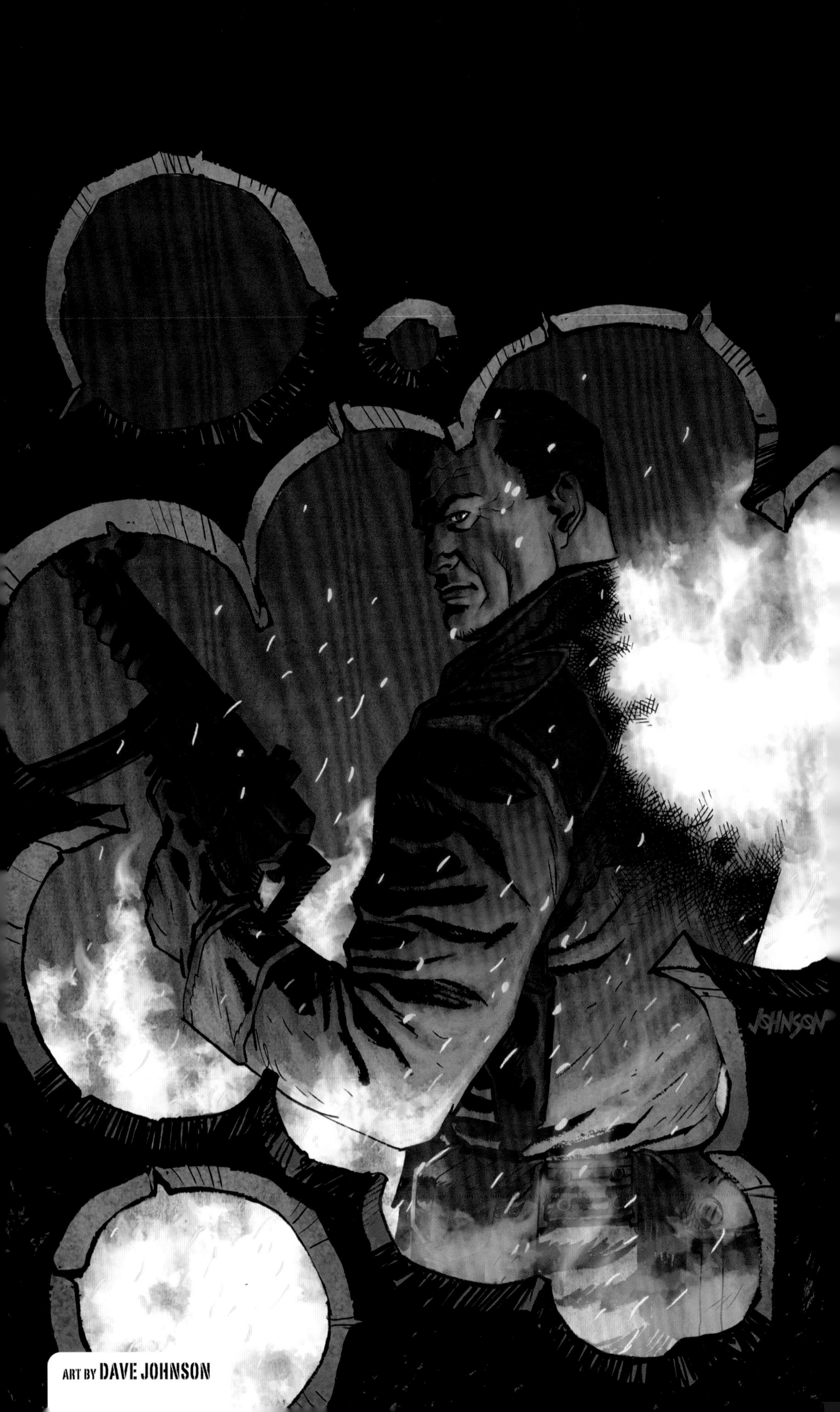
JOHNSON

ART BY DAVE JOHNSON

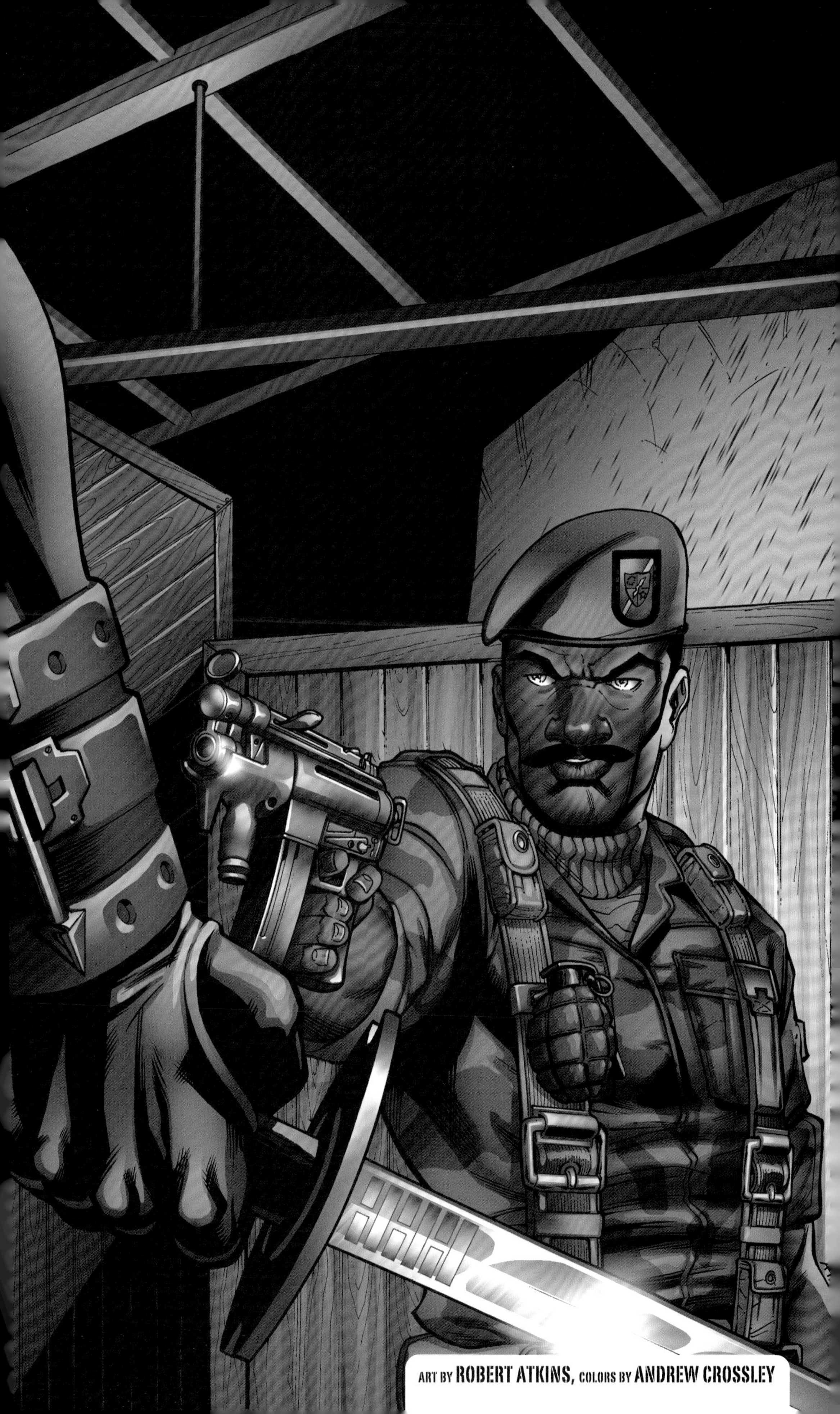

ART BY ROBERT ATKINS, COLORS BY ANDREW CROSSLEY

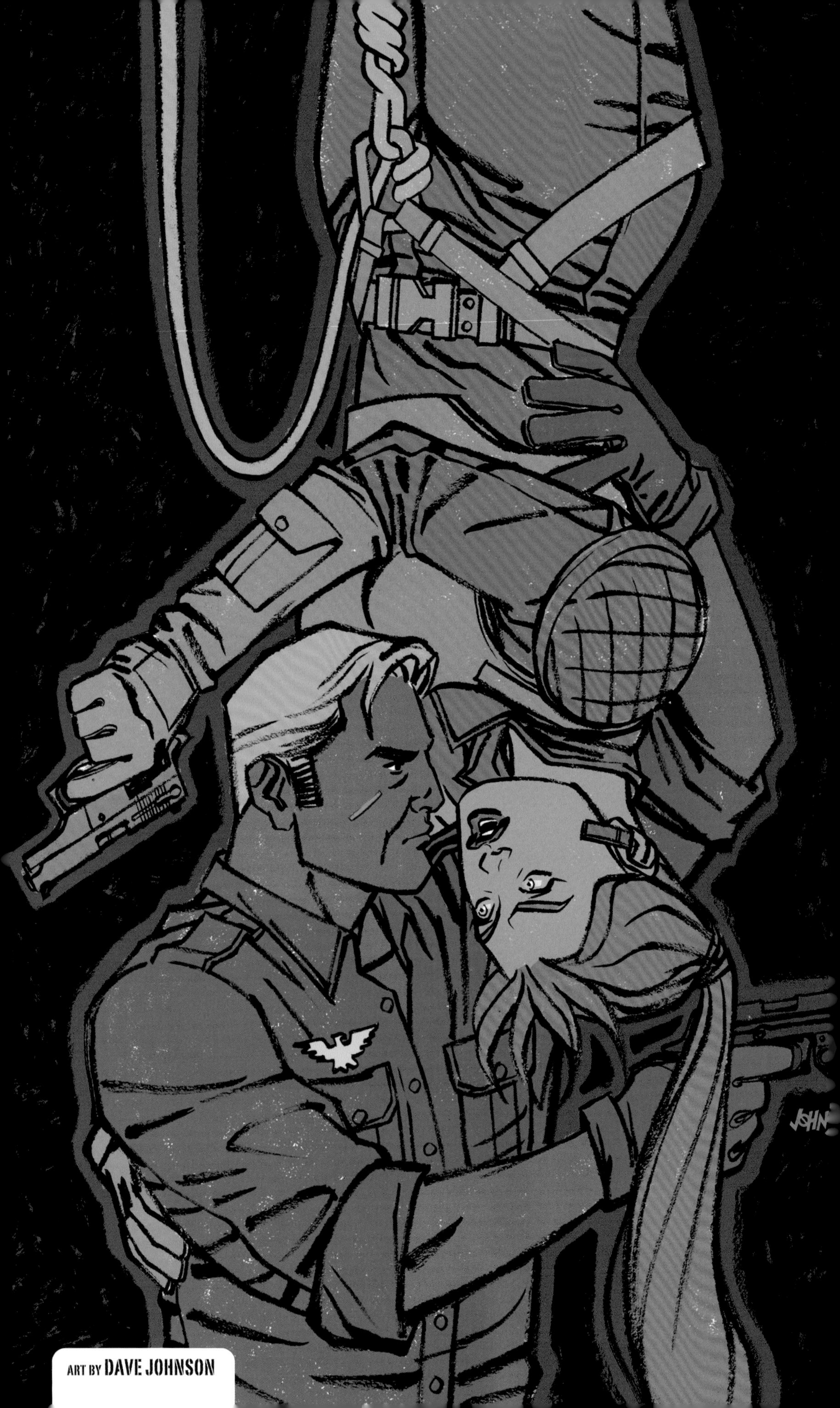
JOHN

ART BY DAVE JOHNSON

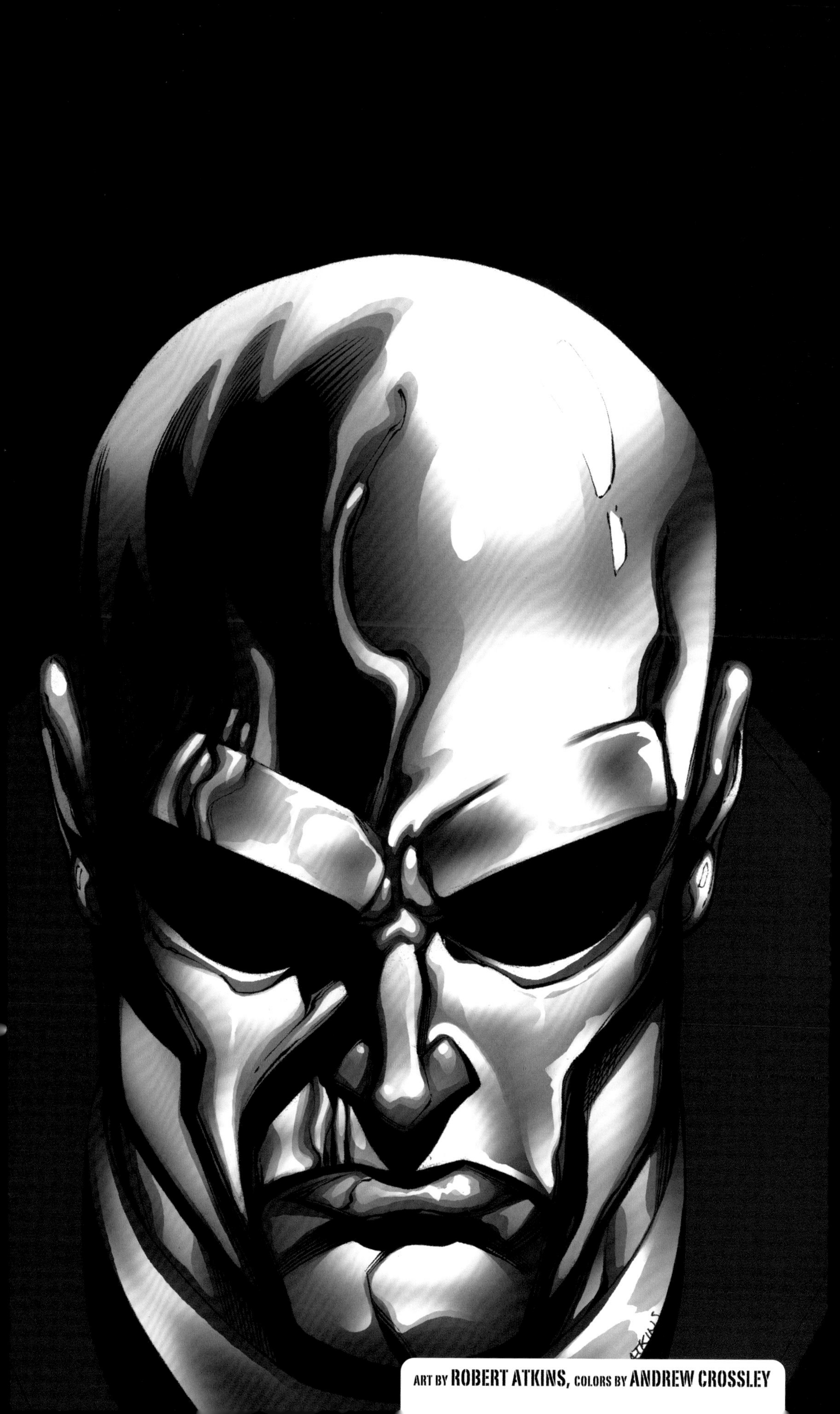

ART BY ROBERT ATKINS, COLORS BY ANDREW CROSSLEY

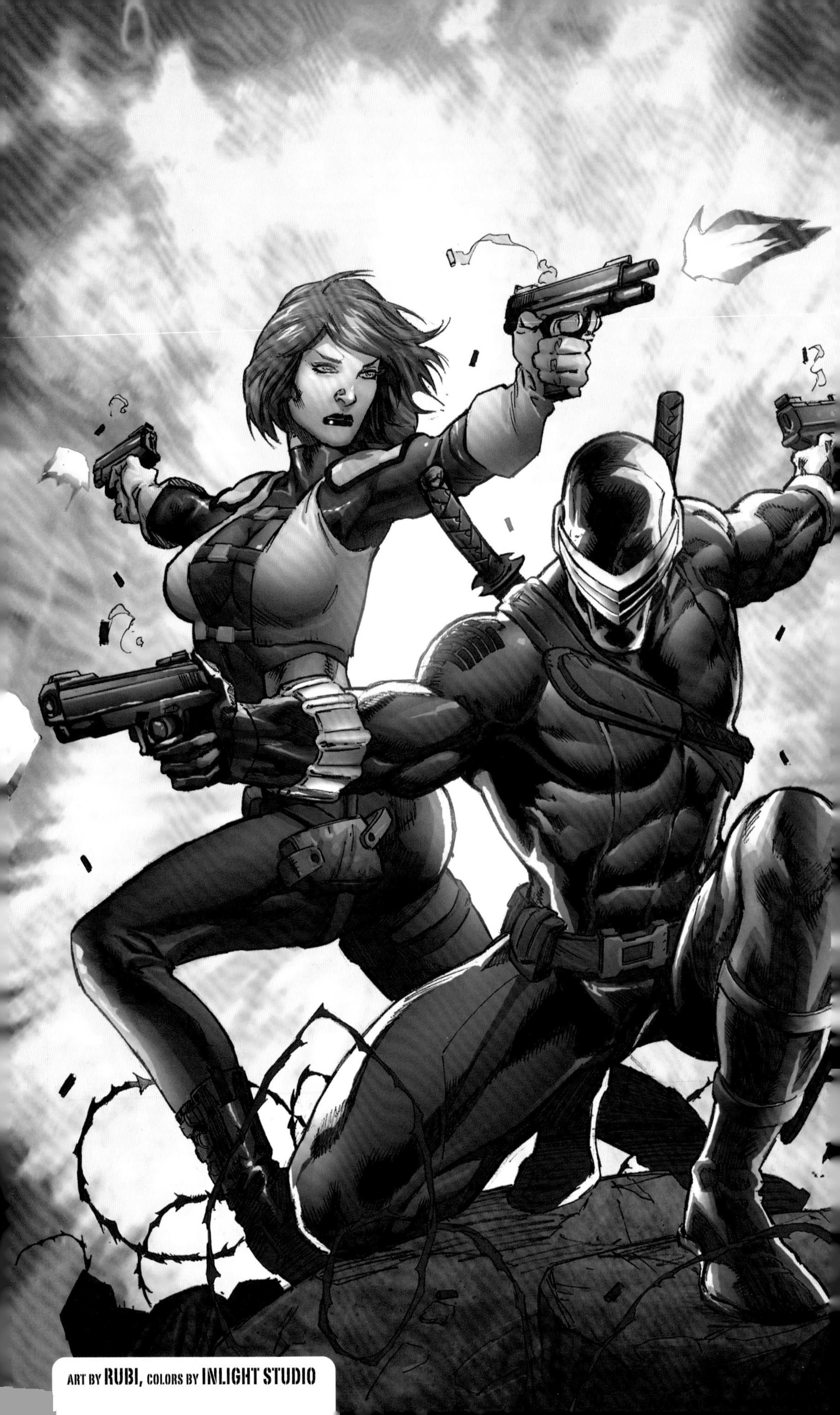

ART BY RUBI, COLORS BY INLIGHT STUDIO

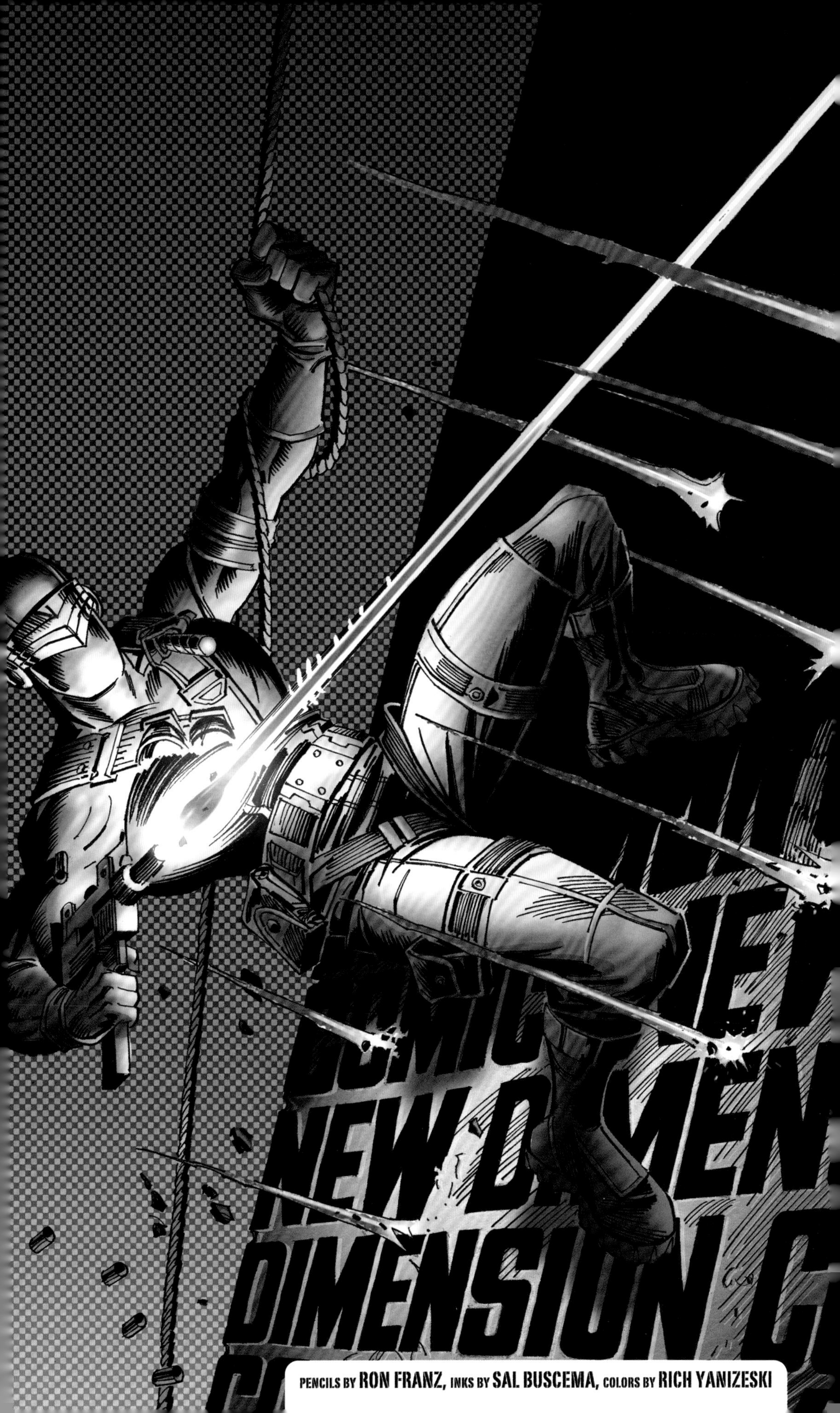
DIMENSION

PENCILS BY RON FRANZ, INKS BY SAL BUSCEMA, COLORS BY RICH YANIZESKI

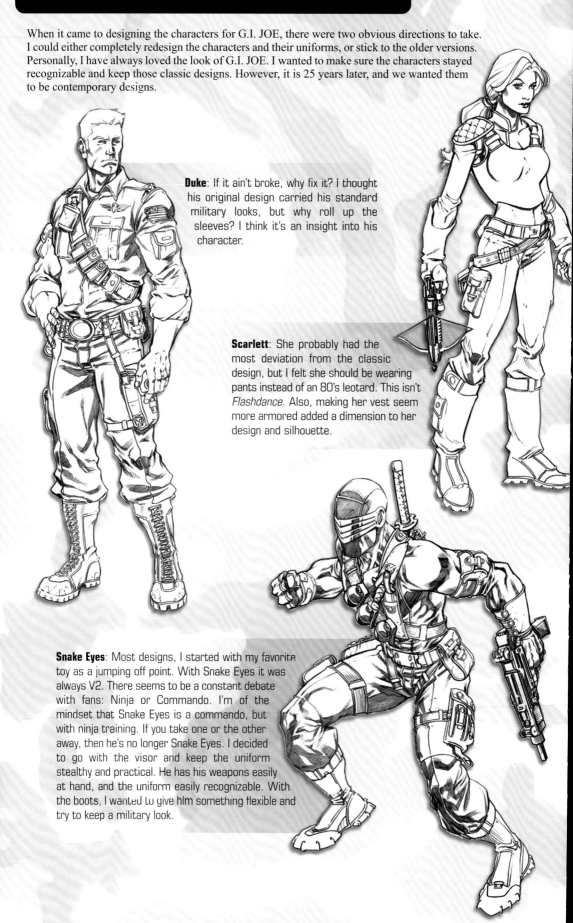

Character Designs by Robert Atkins

When it came to designing the characters for G.I. JOE, there were two obvious directions to take. I could either completely redesign the characters and their uniforms, or stick to the older versions. Personally, I have always loved the look of G.I. JOE. I wanted to make sure the characters stayed recognizable and keep those classic designs. However, it is 25 years later, and we wanted them to be contemporary designs.

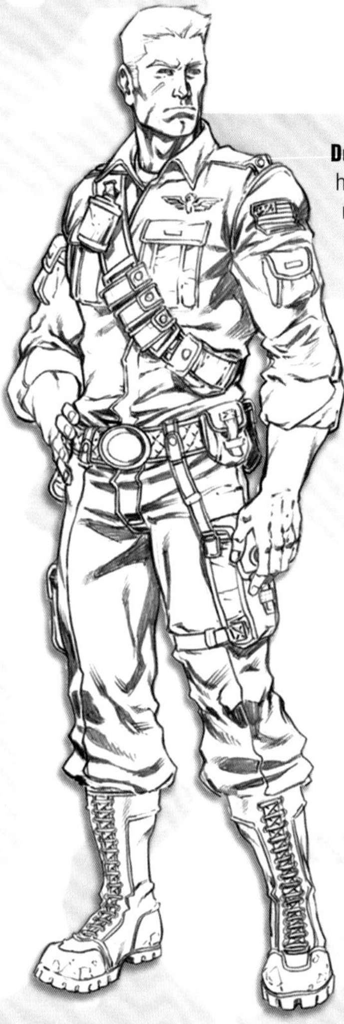

Duke: If it ain't broke, why fix it? I thought his original design carried his standard military looks, but why roll up the sleeves? I think it's an insight into his character.

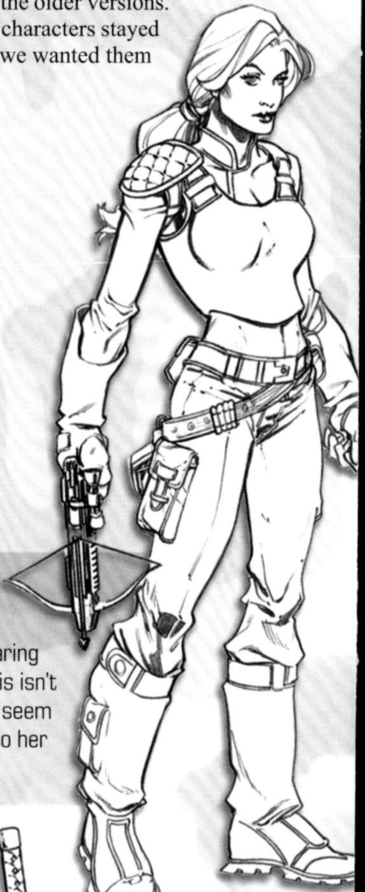

Scarlett: She probably had the most deviation from the classic design, but I felt she should be wearing pants instead of an 80's leotard. This isn't *Flashdance*. Also, making her vest seem more armored added a dimension to her design and silhouette.

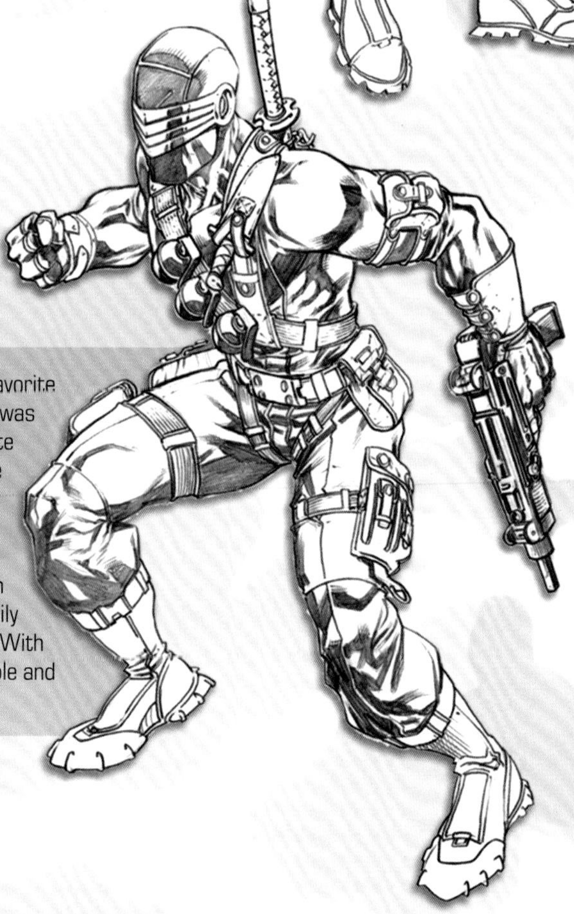

Snake Eyes: Most designs, I started with my favorite toy as a jumping off point. With Snake Eyes it was always V2. There seems to be a constant debate with fans: Ninja or Commando. I'm of the mindset that Snake Eyes is a commando, but with ninja training. If you take one or the other away, then he's no longer Snake Eyes. I decided to go with the visor and keep the uniform stealthy and practical. He has his weapons easily at hand, and the uniform easily recognizable. With the boots, I wanted to give him something flexible and try to keep a military look.

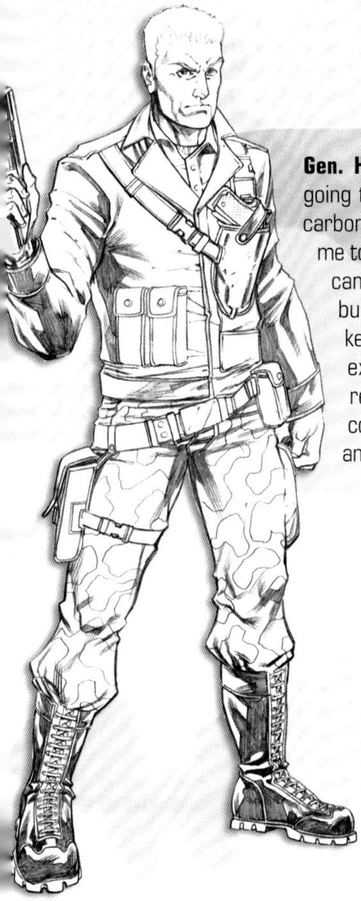

Gen. Hawk: I'm pretty sure we're always going to hear that Duke and Gen. Hawk are carbon copies of each other and that bugs me to no end. For as casual as Duke's attire can look, I wanted Gen. Hawk to be all business. I streamlined the jacket and kept it high-buttoned again as an expression of character. Again, fairly regular military attire, but wanted to convey a guy who runs a tight command and demands respect.

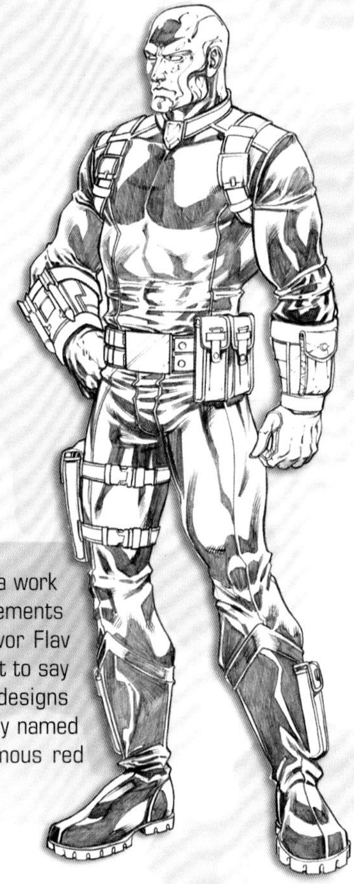

Destro: I ain't gonna lie....this is a work in progress. I wanted to keep elements from his old design, but the Flavor Flav medallion had to go. But that's not to say certain elements from the old designs can't work. In fact, I know this guy named Andy who is all about the enormous red collar. We'll see what happens.

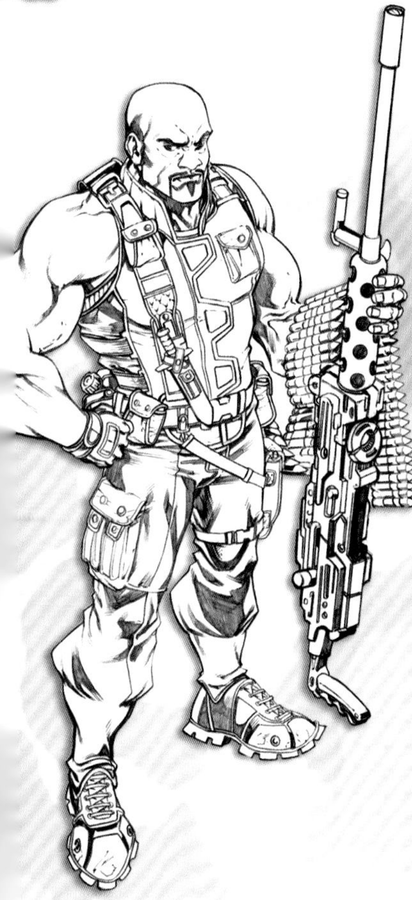

Heavy Duty: So here we have Heavy Duty, and I have always enjoyed his V2 uniform. It stuck out and kept his design unique, but not outlandish. His ability to treat a .50 Cal HMG like it was a .22 from my Cub Scout days blew my mind! Still, I figure he'd work up a sweat lugging that gun around, so I made sure to give him a breathable armored vest, canteen, and close quarter weapons for good measure.

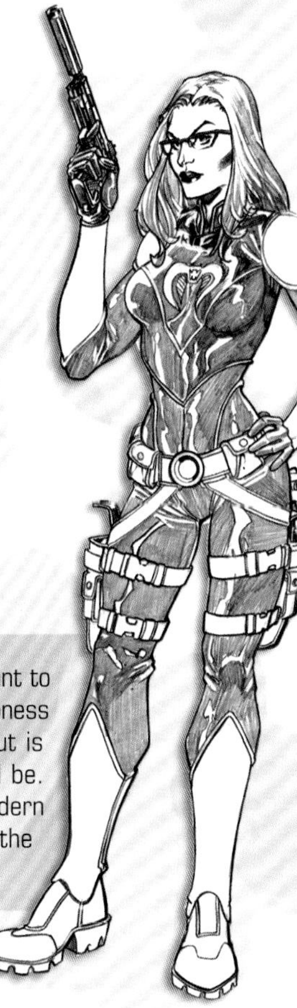

Baroness: High heels are out. We want to bring to the Cobra organization a Baroness that is confident and aristocratic, but is willing and able to scrap when need be. Again, I wanted to make more modern changes like the glasses, but keep the design recognizable.

G.I. JOE INTERVIEWS

IDW: So here we are, years after G.I. JOE launched in the '80s. We've got both new blood here and some of you who have a history with the JOE characters, too. So, how does it feel to be involved on the ground floor for the first time in 20 years?

Chuck Dixon: It's a great franchise and none of us would be here without Larry. In fact, I probably wouldn't be in comics if it weren't for Larry's early encouragement when I was trying to break in. I loved his run in the '80s and really look forward to being on the team with him. It keeps us honest and keeps us all on track knowing he's here.

Larry Hama: Not much different. Still batting completely in the dark…

Mike Costa: It's a real honor for me. Surreal, actually. I feel bad for Chris though. When he was a kid they were still pulling carved blocks of wood on wheels with a frayed string or something.

Christos Gage: Was Costa even born 20 years ago?

IDW: Quickly, how did each of you get involved in this historic launch?

LH: I got the call from IDW as soon as they got the license. This was in direct contrast to Marvel, where I was literally the last person asked.

CD: Well, I've had a long relationship with IDW and I know which end of a gun the bullets come out of. I guess that was enough of an edge.

CG: Andy Schmidt and I have history from his days at Marvel, so he called and asked if I was interested.

MC: Chris called me to do all the hard work. We sang a karaoke duet down in San Diego and I guess he figured we made a pretty good team.

IDW: What is your personal history with JOE, the toys, cartoon, or comic?

CG: I remember buying Marvel's Treasury-sized compilation of the first few issues in a toy store in the '80s…that Herb Trimpe cover was magic!

CD: I had a Joe (a Marine) the first year they launched back in '64.

IDW: Is there a difference in your approach if you were a fan versus if, like Larry, you were involved in the original creation?

LH: I'm starting all over again, so it's all completely new for me as well. I'm coming at it from the viewpoint that that the characters are sort of like the ones we know, but the world they inhabit is completely realistic.

CD: It's always been Larry's show. What I know about Joe I learned from him. Larry brought an edge to his stories not usually associated with comics based on toy lines.

MC: Yeah, the difference is respectful terror. Larry is the king and I cower in his shadow.

IDW: How do you feel as a part of a team of creators? Are you finding that you're riffing off of the stuff that each other is doing? Are you working independently?

CD: Andy's keeping us well informed of what we're all up to. Because of the way IDW is approaching this, I need to build from what Larry's laying down and Mike and Christos need to follow the overall progression of what I'm doing. I'm setting up a lot of Joe protocol as well as re-establishing things like The Pit. Mike and Christos are also throwing lots of cool stuff into the mix that I can play with. There's a lot of back forth and this is only the beginning.

MC: Look, I'm working with Larry Hama, the man who shaped these characters; Chuck Dixon, who defined military-action in modern comics for me with "Team 7" all those years ago; and Chris Gage, who among other things is a golden-throated singer. That is a murderer's row of talent.

IDW: If all three series are G.I. JOE comics, then how can they possibly be different enough to merit their own book? In other words, what makes your JOE book different and important in comparison to the other two?

CD: I guess mine is the all-purpose Joe book. It has the full cast in an über-epic telling about their first encounters with Cobra. I'm not exploring the deeper stuff that the other guys are getting into.

MC: Well, obviously our book is about Cobra, so we're getting an in-depth look at the opposite side of the coin Think of it like "Wicked." Without the singing.

LH: I'm trying to reimagine Snake Eyes from a Cormac McCarthy POV.

DW: I hear Cobra is being treated a bit differently this time around. Why the new approach?

CD: It's the perfect approach for new readers. They're in at the ground floor even more than the readers in the '80s. Playing Cobra out in more of a Keyser Söze approach adds a lot to their mystique. New readers can discover the characters for the first time in their own way and old fans can get those goosebumps of kind of knowing what (and who) is coming next. Larry set Cobra's coolness factor at ten. Now we're just pushing the dial to eleven.

CG: The threats to the world have changed since the Cold War era, when Cobra was first conceived, and we want to make sure they're still every bit as relevant and deadly as they were back then… while staying true to what we know and fear about them.

MC: …So things like the Cobra-La might not fit into that approach. Luckily, things like hard-core military action and soul-shattering moral choices do.

DW: With the changes to Cobra in play, can we expect other twists and turns?

LH: Durn tootin'.

CD: The challenge is to meet longtime fans' expectations and then exceed them without violating the core of what Larry's laid down. What we start with is solid stuff. There's a reason this comic kicked ass in the '80s and outsold everything else. So no one wants to mess with that. But it's an opportunity to go back and re-visit the material and amp it up and nuance it in a way that wasn't possible then. Personally, what I've seen of what Larry's doing in his book is the perfect demonstration of what makes this re-launch so exciting. He's exploring the world of Joe from a whole new perspective.

DW: How about any new characters?

LH: I had to come up with somebody to out-bad Cobra Commander and Destro. He's shaping up pretty nicely.

CD: I have some supporting characters. I'm adding to the cast. But mostly I'm dealing with the guys and gals already established. But I'm creating a few newbies for story purposes.

IDW: Are there any characters that we know and love that will NOT be around?

> *"Yeah, the difference is respectful terror. Larry is the king and I cower in his shadow."*

CD: At first we're revealing these guys at a more deliberate pace.

MC: Everybody has their favorites, and I can't speak for Larry and Chuck, but I got the line-up I wanted for our book.

LH: It's a pretty safe bet that Raptor won't be around.

IDW: Rumor has it that Chuckles has his own book. What idiot let that happen?

MC: Dude, have you seen the animated *G.I. Joe: The Movie* from 1987? He picks up a missile and throws it at a tank! But seriously… he was the only man for this job. You'll see.

IDW: Thanks, Larry, Chuck, Mike, and Chris for answering a few questions for us. Any parting words?

LH: Buying multiple copies of my books is always a good idea in case you inadvertently get some of those automatically self-destructing ones…

MC: Yo, Joe!

CD: Just that I'm having a lot of fun. I really hope that translates through the work.

CG: I can't resist, either… Yo, Joe!

FIELD REPORT: OPERATION G.I. JOE

ATTENDEES: DIXON, HAMA, COSTA, GAGE, ATKINS, FEISTER, FUSO,
JOHNSON, DELL'OTTO, DiVITO, CHAYKIN
MEETING TRANSCRIPT: MAINFRAME
CLASSIFICATION CODE: CRSD-01-MKRI-00004
CLEARANCE AUTHORIZATION: CLASSIFIED - RED

DATE: 25 AUGUST 2008
LOCATION: CLASSIFIED.

MISSION PARAMETERS: TOTAL ANNIHILATION OF EXPECTATIONS

MISSION CONTROL STATEMENT:
Gentlemen, you've been assembled as the ultimate fighting force
to take on G.I. Joe. What this means is that you have to be the
best of the best in your field of expertise. There is no room
for error.

Readers will be taken by force. Dynamic storytelling and stunning
artwork will win the day. Your skills must be honed to their
finest. All previous and prior commitments are hereby suspended.
Your goal--your only goal--is to achieve total domination of the
G.I. Joe fan's imagination.

Many of your targets were once held captive, salivating for every
30 days to pass, but have since escaped. You will recapture them.
And you won't let go.

In addition, you have new targets. They are new to the field of
battle. Be wary, these targets are elusive but you WILL win
them over.

Your weapons are your wits and your training. No gimmicks. Tell
your stories and tell them well.

Failure is not an option.

Yo, Joe!

END TRANSCRIPT.